GENDER/BODY/KNOWLEDGE

15−

GENDER/BODY/KNOWLEDGE

Feminist Reconstructions
of Being and Knowing

Edited by
ALISON M. JAGGAR
and
SUSAN R. BORDO

RUTGERS UNIVERSITY PRESS
New Brunswick and London

Muriel Dimen's essay, "Power, Sexuality, and Intimacy," first appeared, in a slightly different form, in her book *Surviving Sexual Contradictions* (New York: Macmillan, 1986), copyright © 1986 by Muriel Dimen. Alison M. Jaggar's essay, "Love and Knowledge: Emotion in Feminist Epistemology," copyright © 1989 by *Inquiry: An Interdisciplinary Journal of Philosophy*.

Library of Congress Cataloging-in Publication Data
Gender/body/knowledge.

  Bibliography: p.
  Includes index.
  1. Body, Human. 2. Sex role. 3. Knowledge, Theory of.
4. Feminism. I. Jaggar, Alison M. II. Bordo, Susan
BD450.G4455 1989   110   88-18370
ISBN 0-8135-1378-2
ISBN 0-8135-1379-0 (pbk.)

British Cataloging-in-Publication information available

Second paperback printing, 1990

Contents

GENDER/BODY/KNOWLEDGE

INTRODUCTION

The authors of the papers collected in this volume were all participants in one, or occasionally both, of the seminars conducted in 1985 by Alison Jaggar, a philosopher, first holder of the Blanche, Edith, and Irving Laurie New Jersey Chair in Women's Studies at Douglass College of Rutgers University. The topics of the two seminars were, respectively, "Feminist Reconstructions of the Self and Society" and "Feminist Ways of Knowing." Susan Bordo, also a philosopher, was a Visiting Scholar at Douglass College during the first seminar and a regular participant in the second. In addition to philosophy, participants in the seminars represented a variety of disciplines: sociology, political science, biochemistry, psychology, history, literature, and theology. Some seminar participants were academics: others had no academic affiliation. The group included a playwright and actress, a therapist, an educational tester, and two homemakers. In addition, most people were or had been active in feminist politics or other political movements.

Forerunners of almost all the pieces published here were presented in one of the seminars and have been enriched by seminar discussion. Because of the seminar participants' heterogeneity, our weekly meetings were lively and diverse. At the same time, the thematic focus of the seminars, coupled with the regular interchange between seminar members, generated increasing continuity and coherence in presentations and discussions. As the seminars progressed through the year, certain themes and issues continually emerged. The editors identified what they viewed as the most central themes and asked the contributors to rework their papers focusing more directly on them. The result is a collection that works on several levels.

Many of the essays open with a survey of the traditions challenged by feminists within particular disciplines, thus enabling this volume to serve as a guide to some central disciplinary paradigms as well as feminist reconstructions of them. In addition to traversing several disciplines, the collection also crosses a spectrum of the various theoretical and ideological commitments around which contemporary feminists have situated themselves. No one intellectual or political orthodoxy forms an invisible spine for this volume. Instead, the book includes many different perspectives— "Marxist-feminist," "liberal feminist," "cultural feminist," and various "postmodern feminisms"—although the quotation marks indicate the editors' discomfort with these labels, even as we acknowledge their preliminary usefulness. The essays do not explicitly address each other, but all approach recurrent themes in different ways; they can often be juxtaposed in implicit argument with each other. Thus, the volume not only maps new territory that feminists are staking out within their disciplines, but also introduces some of the most important debates, divisions, and commonalities that have emerged within the last decade of western feminism.

Underlying the disciplinary, methodological, and ideological diversity of the essays is a fundamental thematic unity. This unity, discernible beneath the interplay of several minor themes, consists of an emerging feminist challenge to conceptions of knowledge and reality that have dominated the western intellectual tradition at least since the seventeenth century.

The seventeenth century in Europe was a period of economic change and social unrest. It was marked by the continuing development of mercantile capitalism, the increasing dominance of town over country and the establishment of protestantism over large areas of Europe. Not coincidentally, the seventeenth century was also a period of intellectual revolution. Ideals that had been fermenting for two hundred years finally matured into compelling new models of physical and social reality. Just as prevailing views of the cosmos were metamorphosed in a series of scientific revolutions so accepted understandings of human nature and society were transformed through the development of secular epistemologies and political theories.

Revolutionary as these new understandings were in many respects, they did not break entirely with the earlier western tradition. Instead, they can in some respects be seen as rearticulating themes that had been prominent in Greek and medieval thought. Nevertheless, the new understandings did constitute a distinctively modern formulation of these themes and reworked them into a tacit framework that has shaped most western philosophy and science until the twentieth century.

The decisive formulation of this framework was achieved in the seventeenth century by René Descartes. His successors made various modifications of the Cartesian framework but generally accepted a number of Descartes's most crucial epistemological assumptions, including:

1. Reality has an objective structure or nature unaffected by or independent of either human understandings of or perspectives on it. Philosophers sometimes refer to this assumption as "metaphysical realism."

2. The structure or nature of reality in principle is accessible to human understanding or knowledge. When considered with the first point, this assumption sometimes is called "objectivism."

3. Humans approach the task of gaining knowledge of the world as solitary individuals, rather than as socially constituted members of historically changing groups. This assumption may be called "epistemological individualism."

4. The principal human faculty for attaining knowledge of reality is reason (rationalism), sometimes working in conjunction with the senses (empiricism). This assumption has been called the rationalist bias.

5. The faculties of reason and sensation are potentially the same for all human beings, regardless of their culture or class, race or sex (universalism). Differences in the situations of human beings, rather than being recognized as providing alternative perspectives on reality, are seen as conquerable impediments to a neutral, "objective" view of things.

Given these assumptions, the Cartesian tradition takes the task of epistemology to identify a method by which individual investigators may best utilize their faculties to gain knowledge of the objective structure of reality—what Descartes called the identification of "the method for rightly conducting the reason."

6. The recommended methods typically endeavor to show how systematic knowledge may be inferred validly from certain or indubitable premises. The assumption that genuine or reliable knowledge is built from simple components that are thought of as epistemologically certain or indubitable is known by philosophers as foundationalism.

The foregoing epistemological assumptions typically are accompanied by characteristically dualist ontologies that sharply separate the universal from the particular, culture from nature, mind from body, and reason from emotion. These epistemological and ontological assumptions fit together to constitute a firm and familiar framework for understanding nature, human nature, and human knowledge. Descartes's critical quest for certainty, order, and clarity was carried on by western thinkers, although not without dissent and challenge, until it reached its culmination in the positivism and neo-positivism of Anglo-American analytic philosophy.

3

In the past hundred years, however, the challenges have strengthened and multiplied: individual voices have become choruses of dissent. Marxism, for example, has challenged methodological individualism and sometimes objectivism, emphasizing how our beliefs about reality arise out of particular forms of social organization, and urging a more historical understanding of the production of knowledge. American naturalists such as James and Dewey mounted radical attacks, as Nietzsche had earlier, on both rationalism and universalism, protesting against the Cartesian ideal of reason as a "pure" realm, capable of being freed (given the right method) from the contaminating influences of emotion, instinct, will, sentiment, and value. More recently, foundationalism has been under attack from deconstructionism and other "poststructuralist" perspectives and even from within the Anglo-American analytic tradition itself (for example, Rorty 1979).

Contemporary feminist epistemology shares the growing sense that the Cartesian framework is fundamentally inadequate, an obsolete and self-deluded world view badly in need of reconstruction and revisioning. In its rejection of this framework, feminism borrows from the insights of other traditions, including Marxist historicism, psychoanalytic theory, literary theory, and sociology of knowledge. However, the claim that the Cartesian framework, in addition to other biases, is not gender neutral distinguishes contemporary feminism from these other approaches. The contributors to this volume argue this claim in various ways.

The first section of the volume focuses on the body, which has emerged as a recurrent theme in recent feminist writing. The body, notoriously and ubiquitously associated with the female, regularly has been cast, from Plato to Descartes to modern positivism, as the chief enemy of objectivity. Contemporary feminists, in response, have begun to explore alternatives to traditional, mind-centered approaches to knowledge, revisioning the body's role in intellectual insight and insisting on the centrality of the body in the reproduction and transformation of culture.

But what *is* the body? Within our dominant traditions, the very concept of body has been formed in opposition to that of the mind. It is defined as the arena of the biologically given, the material, the immanent. It also has been conceptualized, since the seventeenth century, as that which marks the boundaries between the "inner" self and the "external" world. In the essays printed here, there emerge not *one* body but *many* bodies, some of them offering themselves in sharp distinction to such historical notions: the body as locus of social praxis, as cultural text, as social construction, as the tablet on which new visions of an "écriture féminine" are inscribed, as the marker of union rather than disjunction between the human and "natural" world.

4

The first two essays explore the body as a cultural medium, whose changing forms and meanings reflect historical conflict and change and on which the politics of gender are inscribed with special clarity. Susan Bordo's essay, an example of the emerging feminist interest in the work of Michel Foucault, is an exploration of the role of the body, as both a cultural text and a site of practical social control, in the reproduction of femininity. Through a detailed cultural reading of hysteria, agoraphobia, and anorexia nervosa, she argues for the necessity of reconstructing feminist discourse about the body to account more adequately for the "insidious and often paradoxical pathways of modern social control."

Muriel Dimen's essay turns to sexuality, another area in which the life of the body mirrors and serves male-dominated culture. Dimen focuses on the social construction of alienated sexuality and its consequences for the female sense of self, our experience of desire, and our attitudes toward the flesh. Dimen's essay, which alternates dazzlingly between literary, philosophical, and anecdotal style, is a "reconstruction," too, of the traditional divisions that have insisted on maintaining the separateness and purity of the discursive forms. The very "body" of her text is a critique of the Cartesian ordering of reality into separate, "clear and distinct" components.

The next two essays explore feminist attempts to "revision" the female body so as to reflect the *subjectivity* of women, rather than the objectifying male gaze. Arleen Dallery's essay on écriture féminine is a counterpoint to Dimen's essay on alienated sexuality. In it, she explores recent French feminism's "rewriting" of the body and its emphasis on the potentially "radical alterity" of women's sexuality and pleasure as a source of new, nonphallocratic metaphors. She considers, in particular, the political implications of this intellectual movement and the various charges that have been raised against it (largely by American feminists), arguing that most of those charges have been based on a deep misunderstanding of the theoretics of the body implied in French feminism. At the conclusion, she raises some provocative and probing questions about American feminists' attraction to androgyny and what it suggests about their own cultural fear of difference.

Eileen O'Neill's essay offers a new reconceptualization of pornography and obscenity, in which context assumes prime importance in the interpretation of imagery. In establishing her claim, she catalogs central themes in the work of various women artists, as they endeavor to "re-vision Eros" and the female body around female subjectivity rather than the male spectator. Her essay is not only a wonderful introduction to the revolutionary work being done by contemporary feminist artists, but it also provides a breath of fresh theoretical air for those who feel trapped by the prevailing terms of the pornography debate.

The last two essays in Part I are bold reconstructions of long-standing associations between women, body, materiality, and nature; both focus on some pernicious dualisms that have rent our culture. Donna Wilshire's piece functions on two levels: it argues for the importance of myth, metaphor, and archetype as sources of knowledge long excluded from our dominant traditions; it explores the particular image of the mythic Virgin Mother Goddess as embodying a world view, unlike our own, "that was female-centered in its epistemology and its concept of what is divine." Wilshire here discovers, in a historical image of woman, something not dissimilar from the écriture féminine described by Dallery: a nonphallocentric patterning of reality. Her experience and perspective as a performing artist are evident in the drama and vitality of her piece.

Ynestra King's essay, much more explicitly than others in this section, commits itself to "healing the wound" of dualism, in particular the nature/culture opposition around which are clustered so many attitudes and practices of modernity. Arguing that none of the traditional feminisms have incorporated adequately an ecological perspective, King offers the theory and practice of "eco-feminism." Reclaiming the old metaphor of earth as organism, King extends the concept of body to include not only our own bodies but also the body of the earth—each of which we have tried equally hard to tame. Theoretically highly sophisticated yet committed to the primacy of praxis, King's approach is not easily categorized within existing feminist schools of thought. Her piece forces a reevaluation, not only of our culture's attitudes toward the earth but also of the alignments, priorities, and orthodoxies within contemporary feminism.

From Part I, there emerges the conception of the knowing subject as a historically particular individual who is social, embodied, interested, emotional, and rational and whose body, interests, emotions, and reason are fundamentally constituted by her particular historical context. This conception of the knowing subject is shared by much contemporary critical thought, but it is developed in distinctively feminist ways by our authors. In Part II of this volume, the contributors draw on this conception to offer critiques of dominant epistemological and ethical traditions and point to alternative ways of knowing.

The first three papers in this part directly challenge the rationalist bias of western epistemology. Alison Jaggar dissents from prevailing conceptualizations of emotion, which oppose emotion both to intellect and perception and in so doing, she claims, impoverish and distort our understandings of all these faculties. Sketching an enriched conception of emotion, she argues that emotion is an indispensable even if unrecognized part of all knowledge, in science as well as in daily life, and indicates some ways in which feminists may draw on the epistemological resource of women's distinctive emotional experience.

Joan Tronto focuses on a particular emotion, caring, that has been high-lighted in recent feminist theory. She undertakes a painstaking evaluation of the hopes expressed by some feminists that an "ethics of care" may supplement or even supplant conventional "masculine" approaches to ethics. Tronto finds that reflection on women's practice of caring exposes significant inadequacies in existing moral theory but that the caring practices of contemporary women are presently insufficient to constitute the basis of a new feminist ethics. She diagnoses the source of this inadequacy in the fact that women's caring has evolved within structures of male dominance and concludes that a feminist appropriation of care is possible only in the context of a fundamental restructuring of our social and political institutions. Jaggar and Tronto both deny the possibility of stirring a little feeling into existing forms of scientific and moral theorizing and point instead to the need for a radical revisioning of the prevailing opposition between emotion and thought.

While Tronto demonstrates the incompleteness of traditional ethical theory from a feminist perspective, Lynne Arnault deconstructs the thought of one leading exponent of the classical tradition to reveal that such theory is inadequate even on its own terms. Arnault argues that, even in order to meet its own criteria for moral discourse, classical moral theory must take a "trip to left field" by incorporating some central insights of feminist ethics. Along the way to left field, Arnault exposes fundamental conceptual and ethical problems involved in the liberal conception of the self and so provides further development of the themes prominent among authors represented in Part I of this volume.

Sondra Farganis and Ruth Berman both cover broad territory in their discussions of the social, physical, and biological sciences. Farganis undertakes a survey of the characteristic features of feminist conceptions of social science, explaining how feminist epistemology both draws on and goes beyond other contemporary antipositivist approaches. Her paper provides a comprehensive introduction to contemporary feminist philosophy of social science.

Ruth Berman has written one of the most ambitious papers in the volume, offering a feminist perspective on western science so rich and wide-ranging that it defies brief summary. Berman argues that the modern scientific bias against women, many aspects of which have been identified by feminist critics, is endemic given science's basic conception of itself and its method. She traces the origins of this conception back to the dualistic philosophies of classical Greece and through the seventeenth-century machine model of nature that, she argues, is another version of dualism. She shows how both ancient and modern forms of dualism reflect and justify exploitative social relations, especially, though not exclusively, the exploitation of women.

Berman believes western science is so fundamentally oppressive that it is impervious to gradual reform. The elimination of scientific bias against women and other dominated groups requires that science must be transformed completely by replacing the machine model with a dialectical materialist approach, an approach possible, however, only in the context of a more egalitarian society than presently exists. Berman concludes that women, whose exploitation is fundamental to maintaining the status quo, must take the lead in the simultaneous transformation of society and science.

The last essay in this part is Uma Narayan's critical reflection on the project of feminist epistemology from the perspective of a nonwestern feminist. Narayan endorses the general enterprise of feminist epistemology, but she demonstrates how western feminists often have interpreted this undertaking in a way that is ethnocentric, especially in making generalizations about supposedly masculine and feminine ways of knowing that do not hold outside a western context. Narayan vividly evokes the dilemmas and conflicts faced by nonwestern feminists when they seek to appropriate the epistemological insights of western feminism.

The second part of the volume consists primarily in theoretical reflection on the nature of knowledge, especially moral and scientific thinking. In Part III five authors explore the practical applicability of the earlier, metalevel, discussions. Rhoda Linton describes the method she has developed for helping groups clarify their thinking and their politics, a method that utilizes a computer to provide a conceptual framework in which participants can identify areas of agreement and disagreement. Linton explains her reasons for viewing this method as feminist and then recounts, with a frankness that those who were present at her seminar will find both painful and hilarious, the difficulties she encountered when demonstrating to the group how the method could be used in conceptualizing feminism. Linton speculates on possible reasons for the limited success of this demonstration and concludes with some reflections on the potential of her method for assisting feminist activists.

Donna Perry's essay is a historical and thematic survey of the social origins, emerging intellectual stages, and current debates within feminist literary criticism in the United States. Read in conjunction with Arleen Dallery's essay, a picture emerges, not only of the distinctive characters of French and Anglo-American feminist criticism but also of recurrent philosophical and methodological questions shared with other feminist projects represented in this volume. In particular, Perry's focus on the feminist critique of "objective" criticism and her revisioning of the value of the subjective, interested response have clear counterpoints to many other essays in this volume.

Amy Ling's essay on Chinamerican women writers embodies as well as explores such methodological issues. While Perry discusses key theoretical challenges to the white male canon and conception of literature, Ling disputes and enlarges existing canonical boundaries in *practice* by bringing a neglected tradition to the forefront. A central theoretical issue for feminist critics, as indicated above, is the impossibility of neutral, standpointless knowledge. Ling's paper is a concrete, extended illustration of this insight, as she demonstrates how the particular historical and social experience of Chinamerican women writers has resulted in a distinctive "triple consciousness" in their work.

Phyllis Teitelbaum draws on feminist epistemological insights to excavate the androcentric model of knowledge presupposed in standardized testing. Standardized tests fulfill an important gatekeeping function in academia, playing a major role in determining who is admitted into the most prestigious programs and institutions and hence who eventually will control the dominant social definitions of knowledge. Feminists have paid some attention to these tests, noting, for instance, that the original I.Q. tests were manipulated so as to bring women's results down to the level of men's and that women's performance on several widely relied on standardized tests (the PSAT, the SAT, and the ACT) has declined since 1972, when the tests were changed to include more science and business content (Bader 1987). Teitelbaum, however, provides the most searching feminist analysis of standardized testing that we have seen, examining not only the content of the tests but the format and methodology that express their fundamental conception.

Sherry Gorelick provides a strong and provocative conclusion to the volume with a paper whose methodological explorations force a return to fundamental conceptual and ethical questions in feminist social science. Gorelick describes the attempt that she and a colleague currently are making to understand a feminist political event through a wholly feminist method. Like Linton and Narayan, whose efforts to move in the directions pointed by feminist epistemology also provide practical tests of the validity of feminist theoretical generalizations, Gorelick uses the first person singular voice. She writes frankly about her doubts and difficulties in a narrative that is vivid and immediate while exploring deep issues regarding objectivity and the relation of the feminist social scientist to the subjects of her research. The determination and seriousness of Gorelick's struggles to develop a feminist research method are both intellectually stimulating and politically inspiring.

In conclusion, we believe that the western intellectual tradition today is in a crisis even more severe than that of the seventeenth century. We are again in a period marked by economic change, social unrest, and the apparent obsolescence of traditional intellectual and political ideals. As in the seventeenth century, moreover, apparent chaos is generating new social movements and new ideas. Western and nonwestern women are prominent among the rebels who are dismantling the institutions and the ideologies in which we have been trapped for too long. The challenges to Cartesianism raised in this volume are evidence of the critical power of feminist perspectives. As they point toward alternative understandings of being and knowing, they also express the revitalizing energy of that which Cartesianism, and perhaps the entire western tradition, has marginalized as feminine and subversive.

REFERENCES

Bader, Eleanor J. 1987. "Research Reveals Bias in Testing." *Guardian*, 29 April 1987.

Part I
THE BODY, THE SELF

THE BODY
AND THE REPRODUCTION
OF FEMININITY: A FEMINIST
APPROPRIATION
OF FOUCAULT

Susan R. Bordo

RECONSTRUCTING FEMINIST
DISCOURSE ON THE BODY

The body—what we eat, how we dress, the daily rituals through which we attend to the body—is a medium of culture. The body, as anthropologist Mary Douglas has argued, is a powerful symbolic form, a surface on which the central rules, hierarchies, and even metaphysical commitments of a culture are inscribed and thus reinforced through the concete language of the body. The body may also operate as a metaphor for culture. From quarters as diverse as Plato and Hobbes to French feminist Luce Irigaray, an imagination of body-morphology has provided a blueprint for diagnosis and/or vision of social and political life.

The body is not only a *text* of culture. It is also, as anthropologist Pierre Bourdieu and philosopher Michel Foucault (among others) have argued, a *practical*, direct locus of social control. Banally, through table manners and toilet habits, through seemingly trivial routines, rules, and practices, culture is "*made* body," as Bourdieu puts it—converted into automatic, habitual activity. As such it is put "beyond the grasp of consciousness . . . [untouchable] by voluntary, deliberate transformation" (1977:94). Our conscious politics, social commitments, strivings for change may be undermined and betrayed by the life of our bodies—not the craving, instinctual body imagined by Plato, Augustine, and Freud but the docile, regulated body practiced at and habituated to the rules of cultural life.

13

Throughout his later "genealogical" works *(Discipline and Punish, History of Sexuality)*, Foucault constantly reminds us of the primacy of practice over belief. Not chiefly through "ideology," but through the organization and regulation of the time, space, and movements of our daily lives, our bodies are trained, shaped, and impressed with the stamp of prevailing historical forms of selfhood, desire, masculinity, femininity. Such an emphasis casts a dark and disquieting shadow across the contemporary scene. For women, as study after study shows, are spending more time on the management and discipline of our bodies than we have in a long, long time. In a decade marked by a reopening of the public arena to women, the intensification of such regimens appears diversionary and subverting. Through the pursuit of an ever-changing, homogenizing, elusive ideal of femininity—a pursuit without a terminus, a resting point, requiring that women constantly attend to minute and often whimsical changes in fashion—female bodies become what Foucault calls "docile bodies,"—bodies whose forces and energies are habituated to external regulation, subjection, transformation, "improvement." [1] Through the exacting and normalizing disciplines of diet, make-up, and dress—central organizing principles of time and space in the days of many women—we are rendered less socially oriented and more centripetally focused on self-modification. Through these disciplines, we continue to memorize on our bodies the feel and conviction of lack, insufficiency, of never being good enough. At the farthest extremes, the practices of femininity may lead us to utter demoralization, debilitation, and death.

Viewed historically, the discipline and normalization of the female body—perhaps the only gender oppression that exercises itself, although to different degrees and in different forms, across age, race, class, and sexual orientation—has to be acknowledged as an amazingly durable and flexible strategy of social control. In our own era, it is difficult to avoid the recognition that the contemporary preoccupation with appearance, which still affects women far more powerfully than men, even in our narcissistic and visually oriented culture,[2] may function as a "backlash" phenomenon, reasserting existing gender configurations *against* any attempts to shift or transform power-relations. Surely we are in the throes of this backlash today. In newspapers and magazines daily we encounter stories that promote traditional gender relations and prey on anxieties about change: stories about latch-key children, abuse in day-care centers, the "new woman"'s troubles with men, her lack of marriageability, and so on. A dominant visual theme in teenage magazines involves women hiding in the shadows of men, seeking solace in their arms, willingly contracting the space they occupy. The last, of course, also describes our contemporary aesthetic ideal for women, an ideal whose obsessive pursuit has become the central torment of many women's lives.[3] In such an era we desperately need an effective *political* discourse about the female body, a discourse adequate to an analysis of the insidious, and often paradoxical, pathways of modern social control.

Developing such a discourse requires reconstructing the "old" feminist body-discourse of the late 1960s and early 1970s, with its political categories of oppressors and oppressed, villains and victims. Here, I believe that a feminist appropriation of some of Foucault's later concepts can prove useful. Following Foucault, we must first abandon the idea of power as something possessed by one group and leveled against another, and we must think instead of the network of practices, institutions, and technologies that sustain positions of dominance and subordination within a particular domain. Second, we need an analytics adequate to describe a power whose central mechanisms are not repressive, but *constitutive:* "a power bent on generating forces, making them grow, and ordering them, rather than one dedicated to impeding them, making them submit, or destroying them" (Foucault 1978: 136). Particularly in the realm of femininity, where so much depends upon the seemingly willing acceptance of various norms and practices, we need an analysis of power "from below," as Foucault puts it (1978:94): for example, the mechanisms that shape and proliferate, rather than repress, desire, generate and focus our energies, construct our conceptions of normalcy and deviance. Third, we need a discourse that will enable us to account for the subversion of potential rebellion, a discourse that, while insisting on the necessity of "objective" analysis of power relations, social hierarchy, political backlash, and so forth, will nonetheless allow us to confront the mechanisms by which the subject becomes enmeshed, at times, into collusion with forces that sustain her own oppression.

This essay will not attempt to produce a "theory" along these lines. Rather, my focus will be the analysis of one particular arena where the interplay of these dynamics is striking and perhaps exemplary. It is a limited and unusual arena—a group of gender-related and historically localized disorders: hysteria, agoraphobia, and anorexia nervosa.[4] I recognize, too, that these disorders have been largely class and race specific, occurring overwhelmingly among white middle- and upper middle-class women.[5] Nonetheless, anorexia, hysteria, and agoraphobia may provide a paradigm of one way in which potential resistance is not merely undercut but *utilized* in the maintenance and reproduction of existing power relations.[6]

The central mechanism I will describe involves a transformation (or, if you wish, duality) of meaning, through which conditions that are "objectively" (and on one level, experientially) constraining, enslaving, and even murderous, come to be experienced as liberating, transforming, and life-giving. I offer this analysis, although limited to a specific domain, as an example of how various contemporary critical discourses may be joined to yield an understanding of the subtle and often unwitting role played by our bodies in the symbolization and reproduction of gender.

THE BODY AS A TEXT OF FEMININITY

The continuum between female disorder and "normal" feminine practice is sharply revealed through a close reading of those disorders to which women have been particularly vulnerable. These, of course, have varied historically: neurasthenia and hysteria in the second half of the nineteenth century; agoraphobia and, most dramatically, anorexia nervosa and bulimia in the second half of the twentieth century. This is not to say that anorexics did not exist in the nineteenth century—many cases were described, usually within the context of diagnoses of hysteria (Showalter 1985:128–129)—or that women no longer suffer from classical hysterical symptoms in the twentieth century. But the taking up of eating disorders on a mass scale is as unique to the culture of the 1980s as the epidemic of hysteria was to the Victorian era.[7]

The symptomatology of these disorders reveals itself as textuality. Loss of mobility, loss of voice, inability to leave the home, feeding others while starving self, taking up space and whittling down the space one's body takes up—all have symbolic meaning, all have *political* meaning within the varying rules governing the historical construction of gender. Working within this framework, we see that whether we look at hysteria, agoraphobia, or anorexia, we find the body of the sufferer deeply inscribed with an ideological construction of femininity emblematic of the periods in question. That construction, of course, is always homogenizing and normalizing, erasing racial, class, and other differences and insisting that all women aspire to a coercive, standardized ideal. Strikingly, in these disorders the construction of femininity is written in disturbingly concrete, hyperbolic terms: exaggerated, extremely literal, at times virtually caricatured presentations of the ruling feminine mystique. The bodies of disordered women in this way offer themselves as an aggressively graphic text for the interpreter—a text that insists, actually demands, it be read as a cultural statement, a statement about gender.

Both nineteenth-century male physicians and twentieth-century feminist critics have seen, in the symptoms of neurasthenia and hysteria (syndromes that became increasingly less differentiated as the century wore on), an exaggeration of stereotypically feminine traits. The nineteenth-century "lady" was idealized in terms of delicacy and dreaminess, sexual passivity, and a charmingly labile and capricious emotionality (Vicinus 1972:x–xi). Such notions were formalized and scientized in the work of male theorists from Acton and

Kraft-Ebbing to Freud, who described "normal," mature femininity in such terms.[8] In this context, the dissociations of hysteria, the drifting and fogging of perception, the nervous tremors and faints, the anaesthesias, and the extreme mutability of symptomatology associated with nineteenth-century female disorders can be seen to be concretizations of the feminine mystique of the period, produced according to rules governing the prevailing construction of femininity. Doctors described what came to be known as the "hysterical personality" as "impressionable, suggestible, and narcissistic; highly labile, their moods changing suddenly, dramatically, and for seemingly inconsequential reasons . . . egocentric in the extreme . . . essentially asexual and not uncommonly frigid" (Smith-Rosenberg 1985:203)—all characteristics normative of femininity in this era. As Elaine Showalter points out, the term "hysterical" itself became almost interchangeable with the term "feminine" in the literature of the period (1985:129).

The hysteric's embodiment of the feminine mystique of her era, however, seems subtle and ineffable compared to the ingenious literalism of agoraphobia and anorexia. In the context of our culture this literalism makes sense. With the advent of movies and television, the rules for femininity have come to be culturally transmitted more and more through the deployment of standardized visual images. As a result, femininity itself has come to be largely a matter of constructing, in the manner described by Erving Goffman, the appropriate surface presentation of the self. We no longer are told what "a lady" is or of what femininity consists. Rather, we learn the rules directly through bodily discourse: through images which tell us what clothes, body shape, facial expression, movements, and behavior is required.

In agoraphobia and even more dramatically in anorexia, the disorder presents itself as a virtual, though tragic, parody of twentieth-century constructions of femininity. The 1950s and early 1960s, when agoraphobia first began to escalate among women, represented a reassertion of domesticity and dependency as the feminine ideal. "Career woman" became a dirty word, much more so than it had been during the war, when the survival of the economy depended on women's willingness to do "men's work." The reigning ideology of femininity, so well described by Betty Friedan and perfectly captured in the movies and television shows of the era was childlike, nonassertive, helpless without a man, "content in a world of bedroom and kitchen, sex, babies and home" (1962:36). The house-bound agoraphobic lives this construction of femininity literally. "You want dependency? I'll give you dependency!" she proclaims with her body, "You want me in the home? You'll have me in the home—with a vengeance!" The point, which many therapists have commented on, does not need laboring. Agoraphobia, as I. G. Fodor has put it, seems "the logical—albeit extreme—extension of the cultural sex-role stereotype for women" in this era.[9]

17

The emaciated body of the anorexic, of course, immediately presents itself as a caricature of the contemporary ideal of hyperslenderness for women, an ideal that, despite the game resistance of racial and ethnic difference, has become the norm for women today. But slenderness is only the tip of the iceberg, for slenderness itself requires interpretation. "C'est le sens qui fait vendre," said Barthes, speaking of clothing styles—it's meaning that makes the sale. So, too, it is meaning that makes the body admirable. To the degree that anorexia may be said to be "about" slenderness it is about slenderness as a citadel of contemporary and historical meaning, not as an empty "fashion" ideal. As such, the interpretation of slenderness yields multiple readings, with some related to gender, some not. For the purposes of this essay I will offer an abbreviated, gender-focused reading. But I must stress that this reading illuminates only partially, and that many other currents not discussed here— economic, psychosocial, and historical, as well as ethnic and class dimensions—figure prominently.[10]

We begin with the painfully literal inscription, on the anorexic's body, of the rules governing the construction of contemporary femininity. That construction is a "double-bind" that legislates contradictory ideals and directives. On the one hand, our culture still widely advertises domestic conceptions of femininity, the ideological moorings for a rigorously dualistic sexual division of labor, with woman as chief emotional and physical nurturer. The rules for this construction of femininity (and I speak here in a language both symbolic and literal) require that women learn to feed others, not the self, and to construe any desires for self-nurturance and self-feeding as greedy and excessive. Thus, women are required to develop a totally other-oriented emotional economy.

Young women today are still being taught such a construction of the self. On television, the Betty Crocker commercials symbolically speak to men of the legitimacy of their wildest, most abandoned desires: "I've got a passion for you; I'm wild, crazy, out of control" the hungering man croons to the sensuously presented chocolate cake, offered lovingly by the (always present) female. Female hunger, on the other hand, is depicted as needful of containment and control, and female eating is seen as a furtive, shameful, illicit act, as in the Andes Candies and "Mon Cheri" commercials, where a "tiny bite" of chocolate, privately savored, is supposed to be ample reward for a day of serving others (Bordo 1986). Food is not the real issue here, of course; rather, the control of female appetite for food is merely the most concrete expression of the general rule governing the construction of femininity that female hunger—for public power, for independence, for sexual gratification—be contained, and the public space that women be allowed to take up be circumscribed, limited (Bordo 1989). On the body of the anorexic woman such rules are grimly and deeply etched.

At the same time as young, "upwardly mobile" women today continue to be taught traditionally "feminine" virtues, to the degree that the professional arena has opened up to them, they must also learn to embody the "masculine" language and values of that arena—self-control, determination, cool, emotional discipline, mastery, and so on. Female bodies now speak symbolically of this necessity in their slender spare shape and the currently fashionable menswear look. Our bodies, as we trudge to the gym every day and fiercely resist both our hungers and our desires to soothe and baby ourselves, are also becoming more and more practiced at the "male" virtues of control and self-mastery. The anorexic pursues these virtues with single-minded, unswerving dedication. "Energy, discipline, my own power will keep me going," says ex-anorexic Aimée Liu, recreating her anorexic days, "psychic fuel. I need nothing and no one else. . . . I will be master of my own body, if nothing else, I vow" (1979:123).

The ideal of slenderness, then, and the diet and exercise regimens that have become inseparable from it, offer the illusion of meeting, through the body, the contradictory demands of the contemporary ideology of femininity. Popular images reflect this dual demand. In a single issue of *Complete Woman* magazine, two articles appear, one on "Feminine Intuition," the other asking "Are You the New Macho Woman?" In *Vision Quest*, the young male hero falls in love with the heroine, as he says, because "she has all the best things I like in girls and all the best things I like in guys," that is, she's tough and cool, but warm and alluring. In the enormously popular *Aliens*, the heroine's personality has been deliberately constructed, with near comic-book explicitness, to embody traditional nurturant femininity alongside breathtaking macho-prowess and control; Sigourney Weaver, the actress who portrays her, has called the character "Rambolina."

In the pursuit of slenderness and the denial of appetite the traditional construction of femininity *intersects* with the new requirement for women to embody the "masculine" values of the public arena. The anorexic, as I have argued, embodies this intersection, this double-bind, in a particularly painful and graphic way.[11] I mean double-bind quite literally here. "Masculinity" and "femininity," at least since the nineteenth century and arguably before, have been constructed through a process of mutual exclusion. One cannot simply add the historically feminine virtues to the historically masculine ones to yield a "New Woman," a "New Man," a new ethics, or a new culture. Even on the screen or on television, embodied in created characters like the *Aliens* heroine, the result is a parody. Unfortunately, in this image-bedazzled culture, we have increasing difficulty discriminating between parodies and possibilities for the self. Explored as a possibility for the self, the "androgynous" ideal ultimately exposes its internal contradiction and becomes a war that tears the subject in two—a war explicitly thematized, by many anorexics, as a battle between male and female sides of the self (Bordo 1985).

PROTEST AND RETREAT
IN THE SAME GESTURE

In hysteria, agoraphobia, and anorexia, the woman's body may thus be viewed as a surface on which conventional constructions of femininity are exposed starkly to view, through their inscription in extreme or hyperliteral form. They are also written, of course, in languages of horrible suffering. It is as though these bodies are speaking to us of the pathology and violence that lurks just around the edge, waiting at the horizon of "normal" femininity. It is no wonder, then, that a steady motif in the feminist literature on female disorder is that of pathology as embodied *protest*—unconscious, inchoate, and counterproductive protest without an effective language, voice, or politics—but protest nonetheless.

American and French feminists alike have heard the hysteric speaking a language of protest, even or perhaps especially when she was mute. Dianne Hunter interprets Anna O's aphasia, which manifested itself in an inability to speak her native German, as a rebellion against the linguistic and cultural rules of the father and a return to the "mother-tongue": the semiotic babble of infancy, the language of the body. For Hunter, and for a number of other feminists working with Lacanian categories, the return to the semiotic level is both regressive and, as Hunter puts it, an "expressive" communication "addressed to patriarchal thought," "a self-repudiating form of feminine discourse in which the body signifies what social conditions make it impossible to state linguistically" (1985:114). "The hysterics are accusing; they are pointing," writes Catherine Clément in *The Newly Born Woman;* they make a "mockery of culture" (1986:42). In the same volume, Hélène Cixous speaks of "those wonderful hysterics, who subjected Freud to so many voluptuous moments too shameful to mention, bombarding his mosaic statute/law of Moses with their carnal, passionate body-words, haunting him with their inaudible thundering denunciations" (1986:95). For Cixous, Dora, who so frustrated Freud, is "the core example of the protesting force in women."

The literature of protest includes functional as well as symbolic approaches. Robert Seidenberg and Karen DeCrow, for example, describe agoraphobia as a "strike" against "the renunciations usually demanded of women" and the expectations of housewifely functions such as shopping, driving the children to school, accompanying their husbands to social events, and so on (1983:31). Carroll Smith-Rosenberg presents a similar analysis of hysteria, arguing that by preventing the woman from functioning in the wifely role of caretaker of others, of "ministering angel" to husband and children, hysteria "became one way in which conventional women could express—in most cases unconsciously—dissatisfaction with one or several aspects of their lives" (1983:208). A number of feminist writers, among whom Susie Ohrbach is the most articulate and forceful, have interpreted anorexia as a species of unconscious feminist protest. The anorexic is engaged in a "hunger strike," as Ohrbach calls it, stressing this as a political discourse in which the action of food refusal and dramatic transformation of body-size "expresses with [the] body what [the anorectic] is unable to tell us with words"—her indictment of a culture that disdains and suppresses female hunger, makes women ashamed of their appetites and needs, and demands women's constant work on the transformation of their bodies (1985:102).[12]

The anorexic, of course, is unaware that she is making a political statement. She may, indeed, be hostile to feminism and any other critical perspectives that she views as disputing her own autonomy and control or questioning the cultural ideals around which her life is organized. Through embodied rather than discursive demonstration she exposes and indicts those ideals, precisely by pursuing them to the point where their destructive potential is revealed for all to see. The very same gesture that expresses protest, moreover, can also signal retreat; this, indeed, may be part of the symptom's attraction. Kim Chernin argues, for example (1985), that the debilitating anorexic fixation, by halting or mitigating personal development, assuages this generation's guilt and separation anxiety over the prospect of surpassing our mothers, of living less circumscribed, freer lives. Agoraphobia, too, which often develops shortly after marriage, clearly functions in many cases as a way to cement dependency and attachment in the face of unacceptable stirrings of dissatisfaction and restlessness.

Although we may talk meaningfully of protest, then, I would emphasize the counterproductive, tragically self-defeating (indeed self-deconstructing) nature of that protest. Functionally, the symptoms of these disorders isolate, weaken, and undermine the sufferers; at the same time they turn the life of the body into an all-absorbing fetish, beside which all other objects of attention seem pale and unreal. On the symbolic level, too, the protest dimension collapses into its opposite and proclaims the utter defeat and capitulation of the subject to the contracted female world. The muteness of hysterics and their return to the level of pure, primary bodily expressivity have been interpreted, as we have seen, as rejecting the symbolic order of patriarchy and recovering a lost world of semiotic, maternal value. But *at the same time*, of course, muteness is the condition of the silent, uncomplaining woman—an ideal of patriarchal culture. Protesting the stifling of the female voice through one's own voicelessness, that is, employing the language of femininity to protest the conditions of the female world, will always involve ambiguities of this sort. Perhaps this is why symptoms crystallized from the language of femininity are so perfectly suited to express the dilemmas of women living in periods poised on the edge of gender change: the late nineteenth century, the post–World War II period, and the late twentieth century. In these periods gender has become as issue to be discussed, and discourse proliferates about "The Woman Question," "The New Woman," "What Women Want," "What Femininity Is," and so on.

Of course, such dilemmas are differently experienced, depending on class, age, and other aspects of womens' situations. Agoraphobia and anorexia are, after all, chiefly disorders of middle- and upper middle-class women— women for whom the anxieties of *possibility* have arisen, women who have the social and material resources to carry the language of femininity to symbolic excess. Clearly, we need separate analyses of the effects of homogenizing feminine practice on various class and racial groups and the different modes of protest that may be employed.

COLLUSION, RESISTANCE, AND THE BODY

The pathologies of female protest function, paradoxically, as if in collusion with the cultural conditions that produce them, reproducing rather than transforming precisely that which is being protested. In this connection, the fact that hysteria and anorexia have peaked during historical periods of cultural backlash against attempts at reorganization and redefinition of male and female roles is significant. Female pathology reveals itself here as an extremely interesting social formation, through which one source of potential for resistance and rebellion is pressed into the service of maintaining the established order.

How is this collusion established? Here, "objective" accounts of power relations fail us. For whatever the objective social conditions are that "produce" a pathology, the symptoms themselves must still be produced (however unconsciously or inadvertently) by the subject. That is, the body must become invested with meanings of various sorts. Only by examining this "productive" process on the part of the subject can we, as Mark Poster has put it, "illuminate the mechanisms of domination in the processes through which meaning is produced in everyday life" (1984:28); that is, only then can we see how the desires and dreams of the subject become implicated in the matrix of power relations.

Here, examining the context in which the anorexic syndrome is produced may be illuminating. Anorexia will erupt, typically, in the course of what begins as a fairly moderate diet regime, undertaken because someone, often the father, has made a casual critical remark. Anorexia *begins*, emerges out of what is, in our time, conventional feminine practice. In the course of that practice, for any variety of individual reasons that I cannot go into here, the practice is pushed a little farther than the parameters of moderate dieting. The young woman discovers what it feels like to crave and want and need and yet, through the exercise of her own will, to triumph over that need. In the process, a new realm of meanings is discovered, a range of values and possibilities that western culture has traditionally coded as "male" and rarely made available to women: an ethic and aesthetic of self-mastery and self-transcendence, expertise, and power over others through the example of superior will and control. The experience is intoxicating, habit-forming. Aimée Liu writes: "The sense of accomplishment exhilarates me, spurs me to continue on and on. . . . I shall become an expert [at losing weight]. . . . The constant downward trend [of the scale] somehow comforts me, gives me visible proof that I can exert control" (1979:36).

At school, she discovers that her steadily shrinking body is admired, not so much as an aesthetic or sexual object but for the strength of will and self-control it projects. At home, she discovers, in the inevitable battles her parents fight to get her to eat, that her actions have enormous power over the lives of those around her. As her body begins to lose its traditional feminine curves, its breasts and hips and rounded stomach, and begins to feel and look more like a spare, lanky male body, she begins to feel untouchable, out of reach of hurt, "invulnerable, clean and hard as the bones etched into my silhouette," as one woman described it. She despises, in particular, all those parts of her body that continue to mark her as female. "If only I could eliminate [my breasts]," says Liu, "cut them off if need be" (1979:99). For her, as for many anorexics, the breasts represent a bovine, unconscious, vulnerable, side of the self (Bordo 1985). Liu's body symbolism is thoroughly continuous with dominant cultural associations. Brett Silverstein's studies on the "Possible Causes of the Thin Standard of Bodily Attractiveness for Women," testify empirically to what is obvious from every comedy routine involving a dramatically shapely woman: namely, our cultural association of curvaceousness and incompetence. The anorexic is also quite aware, of course, of the social and sexual vulnerability involved in having a female body; many, in fact, were sexually abused as children.

Through her anorexia, on the other hand, she has unexpectedly discovered an entry into the privileged male world, a way to become what is valued in our culture, a way to become safe, above it all; for her, they are the same thing. She has discovered this, paradoxically, by pursuing conventional feminine behavior—in this case, the discipline of perfecting the body as an object—to excess, to extreme. At this point of excess, the conventionally feminine "deconstructs," we might say, into its opposite and opens onto those values our culture has coded as male. No wonder the anorexia is experienced as liberating and that she will fight family, friends, and therapists in an effort to hold onto it—fight them to the death, if need be. The anorexic's experience of power is, of course, deeply and dangerously illusory. To re-shape one's body into a male body is *not* to put on male power and privilege. To *feel* autonomous and free while harnessing body and soul to an obsessive body-practice is to serve, not transform, a social order that limits female possibilities. And, of course, for the female to become male is only to locate one-self on a different side of a disfiguring opposition. The new "power look" in female body-building, which encourages women to develop the same hulk-like, triangular shape that has been the norm for male body-builders, is no less determined by a hierarchical, dualistic construction of gender than was the conventionally "feminine" norm that tyrannized female body-builders such as Bev Francis for years.

Although the specific cultural practices and meanings are different, similar mechanisms, I suspect, are at work in hysteria and agoraphobia. In these cases too, the language of femininity, when pushed to excess—when shouted and asserted, when disruptive and demanding—deconstructs into its opposite and makes available to the woman an illusory experience of power previously forbidden to her by virtue of her gender. In the case of nineteenth-century femininity, the forbidden experience may have been the breaking out of constraint, of bursting fetters—particularly moral and emotional fetters. John Conolly, the asylum reformer, recommended institutionalization for women who "want that restraint over the passions without which the female character is lost" (Showalter 1985:48). Hysterics often infuriated male doctors for lacking just this quality. S. Weir Mitchell described them as "the despair of physicians" whose "despotic selfishness wrecks the constitution of nurses and devoted relatives, and in unconscious or half-conscious self-indulgence destroys the comfort of everyone around them" (Smith-Rosenberg 1985:207). It must have given the Victorian patient some illicit pleasure to be viewed as capable of such disruption of the staid nineteenth-century household. A similar form of power, I believe, is part of the experience of agoraphobia.

This does not mean that the primary reality of these disorders is not one of pain and entrapment. In anorexia, too, there is clearly a dimension of physical addiction to the biochemical effects of starvation. But whatever the physiology involved, the ways in which the subject understands and thematizes her experience cannot be reduced to mechanical process. The anorexic's ability to live with minimal food intake allows her to feel powerful and worthy of admiration in a "world," as Susie Ohrbach describes it, "from which at the most profound level [she] feels excluded" and unvalued (1985:103). The literature on both anorexia and hysteria is strewn with battles of will between the sufferer and those trying to "cure" her; the latter, as Ohrbach points out, very rarely understand that the psychic values she is fighting for are often more important to the woman than life itself.

TEXTUALITY, PRAXIS, AND THE BODY

The "solutions" offered by anorexia, hysteria, and agoraphobia, I have suggested, develop out of the practice of femininity itself, the pursuit of which is still presented as the chief route to acceptance and success for women in our culture. Too aggressively pursued, that practice leads to its own undoing, in one sense. For if femininity, as Susan Brownmiller has said, is at its very core a "tradition of imposed limitations" (1984:14), then an unwillingness to limit oneself, even in the pursuit of femininity, breaks the rules. But, of course, in another sense everything remains fully in place. The sufferer becomes wedded to an obsessive practice, unable to make any effective change in her life. She remains, as Toril Moi has put it, "gagged and chained to [the] feminine role" (Bernheimer and Kahane 1985:192), a reproducer of the docile body of femininity.

This tension between the psychological meaning of a disorder, which may enact fantasies of rebellion and embody a language of protest, and the practical life of the disordered body, which may utterly defeat rebellion and subvert protest, may be obscured by too exclusive a focus on the symbolic dimension and insufficient attention to praxis. As we have seen in the case of some Lacanian feminist readings of hysteria, the result of this can be a one-sided interpretation, romanticizing the hysteric's symbolic subversion of the phallocentric order while confined to her bed. This is not to say that confinement in bed has a transparent, univocal meaning—in powerlessness, debilitation, dependency, and so forth. The "practical" body is no brutely biological or material entity. It, too, is a culturally mediated form; its activities are subject to interpretation and description. The shift to the practical dimension is not a turn to biology or nature, but to another "register," as Foucault puts it (1979:136) of the cultural body: the register of the "useful body" rather than the "intelligible body." The distinction can prove useful, I believe, to feminist discourse.

The intelligible body includes our scientific, philosophic, and aesthetic representations of the body—our cultural *conceptions* of the body, norms of beauty, models of health, and so forth. But the same representations may also be seen as forming a set of *practical* rules and regulations through which the living body is "trained, shaped, obeys, responds," becoming, in short, a socially adapted and "useful body" (Foucault 1979:136). Consider this particularly clear and appropriate example: The nineteenth-century "hour-glass" figure, emphasizing breasts and hips against a wasp-waist, was an "intelligible" symbolic form, representing a domestic, sexualized ideal of femininity. The sharp cultural contrast between the female and male form, made possible by the use of corsets, bustles, and so forth, reflected, in symbolic terms, the dualistic division of social and economic life into clearly defined male and female spheres. At the same time, to achieve the specified look, a particular feminine *praxis* was required—straitlacing, minimal eating, reduced mobility—rendering the female body unfit to perform activities outside of its designated sphere. This, in Foucauldian terms, would be the "useful body" corresponding to the aesthetic norm.

The intelligible body and the useful body are two arenas of the same discourse; they often mirror and support each other, as in the above illustration. Another example can be seen in the seventeenth-century philosophic conception of the body as a machine, mirroring an increasingly more automated productive machinery of labor. But the two bodies may also contradict and mock each other. A range of contemporary representations and images, for example, have coded the transcendence of female appetite and its public display in the slenderness ideal in terms of power, will, mastery, the possibilities of success in the professional arena, and so forth. These associations are carried visually by the slender superwomen of prime-time television and popular movies and promoted explicitly in advertisements and articles appearing routinely in women's fashion magazines, diet books, and weight-training publications. The equation of slenderness and power emerges most dramatically when contemporary anorexics speak about themselves. "[My disorder] was about power," says Kim Morgan in an interview for the documentary *The Waist Land*, "that was the big thing . . . something I could throw in people's faces, and they would look at me and I'd only weigh this much, but I was strong and in control, and hey, *you're* sloppy."[13]

Yet of course the anorexic is anything *but* "strong" and "in control," and not only full-blown anorexics live such contradictions. Recent statistics—for example, the widely publicized University of California study of fourth-grade girls in San Francisco—suggest that, at least in some American cultures, more and younger girls (perhaps as many as 80 percent of the nine-year-olds surveyed) are making dedicated dieting the central organizing principle of their lives. These fourth-graders live in constant fear, reinforced by the reactions of the boys in their classes, of gaining a pound and thus ceasing to be "sexy," "attractive," or, most tellingly, "regular." They jog daily, count their calories obsessively, and risk serious vitamin deficiencies (not to mention fully developed eating disorders and delayed sexual and reproductive maturation).[14] We may be producing a generation of young women with severely diminished menstrual, nutritional, and intellectual functioning.

Exposure and cultural analysis of such contradictory and mystifying relations between image and practice is only possible if one's analysis includes attention to and interpretation of the "useful" or, as I prefer to call it, practical body. Such attention, although often in inchoate and theoretically unsophisticated form, was central to the beginnings of the contemporary feminist movement. In the late 1960s and early 1970s the objectification of the female body was a serious political issue. All the cultural paraphernalia of femininity, learning to please visually and sexually through the practices of the body—media imagery, beauty pageants, high heels, girdles, make-up, simulated orgasm—were seen as crucial in maintaining gender domination.

Disquietingly, for the feminisms of the present decade, such focus on the politics of feminine praxis, although still maintained in the work of individual feminists,[15] is no longer a centerpiece of feminist cultural critique. On the popular front, we find *Ms.* magazine presenting issues on fitness and "style," the rhetoric reconstructed for the 1980s to pitch "self-expression" and "power." Although feminist theory surely has the tools, it has not provided a critical discourse to dismantle and demystify this rhetoric. The work of French feminists has provided a powerful framework for understanding the inscription of phallocentric, dualistic culture on gendered bodies. But so far, French feminism has offered very little in the way of concrete, material analyses of the female body as a locus of practical cultural control. Among feminist theorists in this country, the study of cultural "representations" of the female body has flourished, and it has often been brilliantly illuminating and instrumental to a feminist rereading of culture.[16] But the study of cultural representations alone, divorced from consideration of their relation to the practical lives of bodies, can obscure and mislead.

Here, Helena Michie's significantly titled *The Flesh Made Word* offers a striking example. Examining nineteenth-century representations of women, appetite, and eating, Michie draws fascinating and astute metaphorical connections between female eating and female sexuality. Female hunger, she argues, and I agree, "figures unspeakable desires for sexuality and power" (1987:13). The Victorian novel's "representational taboo" against depicting women eating (an activity, apparently, that only "happens offstage," as Michie puts it) thus functions as a "code" for the suppression of female sexuality, as does the general cultural requirement, exhibited in etiquette and sex manuals of the day, that the well-bred woman eat little and delicately. The same coding is drawn on, Michie argues, in contemporary feminist "inversions" of Victorian values, inversions that celebrate female sexuality and power through images exulting in female eating and female hunger, depicting it explicitly, lushly, and joyfully.

Despite the fact that Michie's analysis centers on issues concerning women's hunger, food, and eating practices, she makes no mention of the grave eating disorders that surfaced in the late nineteenth century and that are ravaging the lives of young women today. The "practical" arena of women dieting, fasting, straitlacing, and so forth is, to a certain extent, implicit in her examination of Victorian gender ideology. But when Michie turns, at the end of her study, to consider recent feminist literature celebrating female eating and female hunger, the absence of even a passing glance at how women are *actually* managing their hungers today casts her analysis adrift from any concrete social moorings.

Michie's sole focus is on feminist literature's inevitable failure to escape "phallic representational codes" (1987:149). But the feminist celebration of the female body did not merely "deconstruct" on the written page or canvas. Largely located in the feminist counterculture of the 1970s, it has been culturally displaced by a very different contemporary reality; its celebration of female flesh now presents itself in jarring dissonance with the fact that women, feminists included, are starving themselves to death in our culture. The rising incidence of eating disorders, increasing dissatisfaction and anxiety among girls and women concerning how they look, and the compulsive regimens of bodily "improvement" in which so many of us engage suggest that a *political* battle is being waged over the energies and resources of the female body, a battle in which at least *some* feminist agendas for women's empowerment are being defeated.

I do not deny the benefits of diet, exercise, and other forms of body "management." Rather, I view our bodies as a site of struggle, where we must *work* to keep our daily practices in the service of resistance to gender domination, not in the service of "docility" and gender normalization. This requires, I believe, a determinedly skeptical attitude toward the seeming routes of liberation and pleasure offered by our culture. It also demands an awareness of the often contradictory relations between image and practice, between rhetoric and reality. Popular representations, as we have seen, may speak forcefully through the rhetoric and symbolism of empowerment, personal freedom, "having it all." Yet female bodies, pursuing these ideals, may find themselves as distracted, depressed, and physically ill as female bodies in the nineteenth century, pursuing a feminine ideal of dependency, domesticity, and delicacy. The recognition and analysis of such contradictions, and of all the other collusions, subversions, and enticements through which culture enjoins the aid of our bodies in the reproduction of gender, requires that we restore a focus on female praxis to its formerly central place in feminist politics.

NOTES

The analysis presented in this essay is part of a larger study, presently in progress (*Food Fashion and Power: The Body and the Reproduction of Gender;* forthcoming, University of California Press). Other pieces of this larger analysis appear in several other papers: "Anorexia Nervosa: Psychopathology as the Crystallization of Culture" (Bordo 1985; reprinted in Diamond and Quinby 1988), "Reading the Slender Body" (in Jacobus, Keller, and Shuttleworth 1989), and "The Contest for the Meanings of Anorexia" (in *The Body in Medical Thought and Practice,* ed. Drew Leder and Mary Rawlinson; Reidel, 1990). See also "How Television Teaches Women To Hate Their Hungers," *Mirror Images* 1986.

I wish to thank Douglass College for the time and resources made available to me as the result of my Visiting Scholarship for the Laurie Chair in Women's Studies, spring 1985. My time there, and my participation in the Women's Studies Seminar, greatly facilitated much of the initial research for this piece. Earlier versions of this paper were delivered at the philosophy department of State University of New York at Stony Brook, the University of Massachussetts conference on "Histories of Sexuality," and at the 21st Annual Conference of the Society for Phenomenology and Existential Philosophy at University of Toronto. To all those who commented on those versions I express my appreciation for stimulating suggestions and helpful criticisms.

1. On "docility," see Foucault 1979, 135–169. For a Foucauldian analysis of feminine practice, see Bartky 1988; see also Brownmiller 1984.

2. Over the last decade, there has been an undeniable increase in male concern over appearance. Study after study confirms, however, that there is still a large "gender gap" in this area. Research conducted at the University of Pennsylvania in 1985 found men to be generally satisfied with their appearance, often, in fact, "distorting their perceptions [of themselves] in a positive, self-aggrandizing way." See "Dislike of Own Bodies Found Common Among Women," *New York Times,* March 19, 1985. Women, however, were found to exhibit extreme negative assessments and distortions of body perception. Other studies have suggested that women are judged more harshly than men when they deviate from dominant social standards of attractiveness. *Psychology Today* (April 1986) reports that while the situation for men has changed recently, the situation for women has more than proportionately worsened, too. Citing results from 30,000 responses to a 1985 survey of perceptions of body image and comparing similar responses to a 1972 questionnaire, the magazine reports that the 1985 respondents were considerably more dissatisfied with their bodies than the 1972 respondents, and it notes a marked intensification of concern among men. Among the 1985 group, the group most dissatisfied of all with their appearance, however, were teen-age women. Women today are by far the largest consumers of diet products, attenders of spas and diet centers, and subjects of intestinal by-pass and other fat reduction operations.

3. On our cultural obsession with slenderness, see Chernin 1981; Ohrbach 1985; Bordo 1985, 1989. For recent research on incidence and increase in anorexia nervosa and bulimia, see Greenfeld et al. 1987; Rosenzweig and Spruill 1987.

4. On the "gendered" and historical nature of these disorders: The number of female to male hysterics has been estimated as anywhere from two to one to four to one, while as many as 80 percent of all agoraphobics are female (Brodsky and Hare-Mustin 1980:116, 122). Although more cases of male eating disorders are being reported recently, it is estimated that close to 90 percent of all anorexics are female (Garfinkel and Garner 1982:112–113). For a sociohistorical account of female psychopathology, with particular attention to nineteenth-century disorders but having, unfortunately, little mention of agoraphobia or eating disorders, see Showalter 1985. For a discussion of social and gender issues in agoraphobia, see Seidenberg and DeCrow 1983. On the clinical history of anorexia nervosa, see Garfinkel and Garner; for cultural, historical, and gender perspectives, see Bordo 1985, 1986; Ohrbach 1985, 1989.

5. There is evidence that in the case of eating disorders this is rapidly changing. Anorexia and bulimia, originally almost exclusively limited to upper- and upper middle-class white families, are now touching ethnic populations (e.g., blacks, East Indians) previously unaffected and all socioeconomic levels (Garfinkel and Garner 1982:102–103). Although there are cultural reasons for such changes, equally interesting and crucial to study are the cultural factors which have "protected" certain ethnic groups from the disorders (see, for example, Hsu's study of eating disorders among blacks).

6. In constructing such a paradigm, I do not pretend to do justice to any of these disorders in its individual complexity as "pathology" or as cultural formation. My aim is to chart some points of intersection, to describe some similar patterns, as they emerge through a particular reading of the phenomena—a "political" reading, if you will.

7. For studies suggestive of a striking increase in the frequency of eating disorders over the last twenty years, see Garfinkel and Garner 1982:100; Greenfeld et al. 1987; and Rosenzweig and Spruill 1987. On the "epidemic" of hysteria and neurasthenia, see Showalter 1985; Smith-Rosenberg 1985.

8. See Nadelson and Notman 1982:5; Vicinus 1972:82. For more general discussions, see Gay 1984, Showalter 1985. The delicate lady, an ideal that had very strong class connotations (as does slenderness today), is not the only conception of femininity to be found in Victorian cultures. But it was arguably the single most powerful ideological representation of femininity in that era, affecting women of all classes, including those without the material means to fully realize the ideal. See Michie 1987 for dicussions of the control of female appetite and Victorian constructions of femininity.

9. See Fodor 1974:119; see also Brehony 1983.

10. For other interpretive perspectives on the slenderness ideal, see Bordo 1985, 1989; Chernin 1981; Ohrbach 1985.

11. Striking, in connection with this, is Catherine Steiner-Adair's 1984 study of high-school women, which reveals a dramatic association between problems with food and body-image and emulation of the cool, professionally "together" *and* gorgeous Superwoman. On the basis of a series of interviews, the high schoolers were classified into two groups—one that expressed scepticism over the Superwoman ideal,

the other that thoroughly aspired to it. Later administration of diagnostic tests revealed that 94 percent of the Superwomen group fell into the eating disordered range of the scale. Of the other group, 100 percent fell into the noneating disordered range. Media images notwithstanding, young women today appear to sense, either consciously or through their bodies, the impossibility of simultaneously meeting the demands of two spheres whose values have been historically defined in utter opposition to each other.

12. When one looks into the many autobiographies and case studies of hysterics, anorexics, and agoraphobics, one is struck by the fact that these are, indeed, the sorts of women one might expect to be frustrated by the constraints of a specified female role. Freud and Breuer, in *Studies on Hysteria* (and Freud, in the later *Dora*) constantly remark on the ambitiousness, independence, intellectual ability, and creative strivings of their patients. We know, moreover, that many women who later became the leading social activists and feminists of the nineteenth century were among those who fell ill with hysteria or neurasthenia. It has become a virtual cliché that the typical anorexic is a perfectionist, driven to excel in all areas of her life. Though less prominently, a similar theme runs throughout the literature on agoraphobia.

One must keep in mind that in drawing on case studies, one is relying on the perceptions of other, acculturated individuals. One suspects, for example, that the popular portrait of the anorexic as a relentless "overachiever" may be colored by the lingering or perhaps resurgent Victorianism of our culture's attitudes toward ambitious women. One does not escape this hermeneutic problem by turning to autobiography. But in autobiography one is at least dealing with social constructions and attitudes that animate the subject's own psychic reality. In this regard the autobiographical literature on anorexia in particular is strikingly full of anxiety about the domestic world and other themes which suggest deep rebellion against traditional notions of femininity; see Bordo 1985.

13. "The Waist Land: Eating Disorders In America," 1985, Gannett Corporation, MTI Teleprograms.

14. "Fat or Not, 4th-Grade Girls Diet Lest They Be Teased or Unloved," *Wall Street Journal*, February 11, 1986.

15. A focus on the politics of sexualization and objectification remains central to the antipornography movement (e.g., in the work of Andrea Dworkin, Catherine MacKinnon). Feminists exploring the politics of appearance include Sandra Bartky, Susan Brownmiller, Wendy Chapkis, Kim Chernin, and Susie Ohrbach. Recently, too, a developing feminist interest in the work of Michel Foucault has begun to produce a poststructuralist feminism oriented toward practice; see, for example, Diamond and Quinby 1988.

16. See, for example, Jardine 1985; Suleiman 1986; Michie 1987.

REFERENCES

Bartky, Sandra. 1988. "Foucault, Femininity, and the Modernization of Patriarchal Power." In *Feminism and Foucault: Reflections on Resistance,* ed. Irene Diamond and Lee Quinby. Boston: Northeastern University Press.

Bernheimer, Charles, and Claire Kahane, eds. 1985. *In Dora's Case: Freud—Hysteria—Feminism.* New York: Columbia University Press.

Bordo, Susan. 1985. Anorexia Nervosa: Psychopathology as the Crystallization of Culture." *The Philosophical Forum* 17, no. 2 (Winter):73–103. Reprinted in Diamond and Quinby 1988.

———. 1986. "How Television Teaches Women To Hate Their Hungers." *Mirror Images* [newsletter of Anorexia/Bulimia Support, Syracuse, N.Y.] 4:1, 8–9.

———. 1989. "Reading the Slender Body." In *Women, Science, and the Body Politic: Discourses and Representations,* ed. Mary Jacobus, Evelyn Fox Keller, and Sally Shuttleworth. New York: Methuen.

Bourdieu, Pierre. 1977. *Outline of a Theory of Practice.* Cambridge: Cambridge University Press.

Brehony, Kathleen. 1983. "Women and Agoraphobia." In *The Stereotyping of Women,* ed. Violet Frank and Esther Rothblum. New York: Springer Press.

Brodsky, Annette, and Rachel Hare-Mustin. 1980. *Women and Psychotherapy.* New York: Guilford Press.

Brownmiller, Susan. 1984. *Femininity.* New York: Fawcett Columbine.

Chapkis, Wendy. 1986. *Beauty Secrets.* Boston: South End Press.

Chernin, Kim. 1981. *The Obsession: Reflections on the Tyranny of Slenderness.* New York: Harper & Row.

———. 1985. *The Hungry Self: Women, Eating, and Identity.* New York: Harper & Row.

Clement, Catherine, and Hélène Cixous. 1986. *The Newly Born Woman.* Trans. Betsy Wing. Minneapolis: University of Minnesota Press.

Diamond, Irene, and Lee Quinby, eds. 1988. *Feminism and Foucault: Reflections on Resistance.* Boston: Northeastern University Press.

Douglas, Mary. 1982. *Natural Symbols.* New York: Pantheon.

Fodor, I. G. 1974. "The Phobic Syndrome in Women." In *Women in Therapy,* ed. V. Franks and V. Burtle. New York: Bruner/Mazel.

Foucault, Michel. 1978. *The History of Sexuality,* Vol. I. New York: Pantheon.

———. 1979. *Discipline and Punish.* New York: Vintage.

Friedan, Betty. 1962. *The Feminine Mystique.* New York: Dell.

Garfinkel, Paul, and David Garner. 1982. *Anorexia Nervosa: A Multidimensional Perspective.* New York: Bruner/Mazel.

Gay, Peter. 1984. *The Bourgeois Experience,* Vol. I. New York: Oxford University Press.

Greenfeld, D., et al. 1987. "Eating Behavior in an Adolescent Population." *International Journal of Eating Disorders* 6:1 (January 1987):99–112.

Hsu, George. 1987. "Are Eating Disorders Becoming More Common in Blacks?" *International Journal of Eating Disorders* 6, no. 1 (January):113–124.

Hunter, Diane. 1985. "Hysteria, Psychoanalysis and Feminism." In *The (M)Other Tongue*, ed. Shirley Garner, Claire Kahane, and Madelon Sprenger. Ithaca, N.Y.: Cornell University Press.

Jardine, Alice. 1985. *Gynesis*. Ithaca, N.Y.: Cornell University Press.

Liu, Aimée. 1979. *Solitaire*. New York: Harper & Row.

Michie, Helena. 1987. *The Flesh Made Word*. New York: Oxford.

Moi, Toril. 1985. "Representations of Patriarchy: Sex And Epistemology in Freud's Dora." In *In Dora's Case: Freud—Hysteria—Feminism*, ed. Charles Bernheimer and Claire Kahane. New York: Columbia University Press.

Nadelson, Carol, and Malkah Notman. 1982. *The Female Patient*. New York: Plenum.

Ohrbach, Susie. 1985. *Hunger Strike: The Anorectic's Struggle as a Metaphor for Our Age*. New York: Norton.

Poster, Mark. 1984. *Foucault, Marxism and History*. Cambridge: Polity Press.

Rosenzweig, M., and J. Spruill. 1987. "Twenty Years After Twiggy: A Retrospective Investigation of Bulimic-Like Behaviors." *International Journal of Eating Disorders* 6, no. 1 (January):59—66.

Seidenberg, Robert, and Karen DeCrow. 1983. *Women Who Marry Houses*. New York: McGraw-Hill.

Showalter, Elaine. 1985. *The Female Malady*. New York: Pantheon.

Silverstein, Brett. n.d. "Possible Causes of the Thin Standard of Bodily Attractiveness for Women." Manuscript.

Smith-Rosenberg, Carroll. 1985. *Disorderly Conduct*. Oxford: Oxford University Press.

Steiner-Adair, C. 1987. "The Body Politic: Normal Female Adolescent Development and Eating Disorders." Ph.D. diss., Harvard University Graduate School of Education.

Suleiman, Susan, ed. 1986. *The Female Body in Western Culture*. Cambridge, Mass.: Harvard University Press.

Vicinus, Martha. 1972. *Suffer and Be Still*. Bloomington: Indiana University Press.

POWER, SEXUALITY, AND INTIMACY

Muriel Dimen

There is a familiar myth that is sometimes, and wrongly, used to explain the origins of human sexual arrangements. This is the myth of the primal horde, the primal crime, in which the patriarch keeps all the women to himself and forces his sons to work for him; finally, the sons rebel, kill and eat him, fuck the women, and then, guilt-ridden, promise to be good boys.

Many people have said a lot about what is in this myth (e.g., Brown 1959; Freud 1961; Marcuse 1955). But few have noticed what is absent from it. The original primal crime had thrée parts: first, the patriarch's domination of his wife; second, her resistance—physical, emotional, behavioral—to his power; and third, her collusion in being less than she might have been, her participation in all those unavoidable moments when, because they are physically intimidated, economically dependent, or emotionally needy, women give in to patriarchy. Missing in this myth are women, their subordination, and, indeed, all that they symbolize—personal life, reproductivity, alterity.

This myth is both description of and prescription for capitalism, patriarchy, and the state. Its silence on women focuses the problem: Where is there, in this tale of power and sex, room for intimacy, for the knowledge and expansion of self achieved through knowledge of the other? How does an economy that exploits people and nature, all the while encouraging personal enrichment, create expectations for sensual pleasure? Where the political system attempts to control the person and psyche, even while celebrating individual autonomy, whence the self-trust and hope that creativity and generativity require? Given the pervasive inequality in our society, how can intimacy, which presumes a certain democratic and reciprocal attunement between people, obtain?

THE PAST

Addressing disparate regions of experience, these questions about power, sexuality, and intimacy cannot be answered until a missing link in the theory of patriarchy is forged. Patriarchy is both a psychological-ideological—that is, representational—and a political-economic system. Although theories of mind and society abound, no present theory puts psyche and society together so that the whole story of patriarchy, including women's experience and its contradictions, can be told. The Frankfurt School's Critical Theory, in particular, has not lived up to its promise (Benjamin 1978).

Perhaps the problem is one not of *ideas* but of *bias*. Perhaps the theoretical deficiency is methodological. Most scholarship is based on "objectivity," on putatively value-free, detached, impersonal observation and analysis. However, as the feminist critique of science points out, this objectivist stance is actually very personal, based as it is not on the absence of emotions and values but on their careful restraint. In fact, orthodox scholarship lacks a certain *kind* of personal (Flax 1983; Keller 1985; Jaggar 1985:ch. 11).

In turn, then, perhaps the missing conceptual link in feminist theory is an engaged personal voice, saturated with feeling, values, and political protest, a voice such as emerges in feminist biography in which subject engages with subject.[1] But this politics of autobiography and biography should *not replace* the received patriarchal voice; rather, it should *juxtapose* it. The point is to use the different powers of both voices to generate a sense of opposition, difference, creative tension. The resultant third voice, retaining the personal power of the first and the intersubjectivity of the second, might thereby open a window on as yet unimagined, ungendered possibilities of speaking, knowing, and living.

Two such voices interweave here, a personal one telling fictionalized stories of sexuality and a public one commenting on them.[2] Sexuality is one of the most personal, engaged, and value-laden of voices. It is also one of the most theoretically demanding, for sex stands at the crossroads of nature, psyche, and culture. Accounts of sexuality, emotionally powerful and striking at cultural bedrock, beg for a response, provided here by a commentary fusing social, psychological, and feminist theory. As the commentary follows out the triple problematic of sexuality, it traces the filigreed linkages among sexuality, power, and intimacy. Essential to the filigree's design are domination, the gendering of self, the division of labor between women and men, the gendered divorce of want from need, and the use of social reproduction to control desire.

I am a thirty-seven-year-old, heterosexual, middle-class white woman, wearing junior-sized clothes a shade on the beatnik side of trendiness. I am divorced and childless, and live with my cat and my plants in New York City.

I am walking home, and this shabby, drunk man is following me, saying, "Mamma, oh mamma, baby please, I wanna fuck you, I give good tongue, oh sweetheart, PLEASE."

"Oh, leave me alone, don't you have anything better to do?" I exclaim in annoyance.

He sniggers, then turns away.

After I get inside the lobby of my building, I wonder, What was that man trying to do? Did he want to degrade me, attack me, stimulate me sexually, flatter me, or simply tease me? Should I be angry or feel sorry for him? And I ask, Why me, anyway?

The voices in my head immediately provide answers:

What do you expect when you dress like that? my mother responds rhetorically.

But it happens to me even when I'm wearing my down parka and my overalls, I explain in bewilderment, adding with some outrage, *How dare he talk to me? He doesn't even know me.*

Let me at him, I'll kill the bastard, growls my father.

Oh daddy, stop it, I reply, embarrassed by his passion.

My conscience asks, *How come you hear the pussy noises from the guys across the street? You don't know them. Yet you notice what they say.*

I don't know, I mumble.

You know you love it, insists my own analyst.

Maybe, I admit grudgingly like a patient cornered on the couch.

You must have a pretty poor opinion of yourself if you get turned on by someone like that, comments an advice columnist.

I guess so, I say, feeling a little humiliated.

Well, you know, it makes sense that you hear it, it's dangerous out there, says the indignant, rational feminist voice in no uncertain terms. *One out of two women experiences rape or an attempt at it sometime in her life. You have to be alert.*

Maybe, I think. Soothed and vindicated, I stand a little straighter.

I think your reaction is disgusting, says the politically correct line-ist in me. *This man is but a product of his environment, his class, race, ethnicity, in short, of capitalism and the state. He is attacking not you but your petit bourgeois privilege.*

I'm sorry, I'm sorry, I reply, filled with guilt.

Perhaps he's compensating for his own feelings of badness, the psychoanalyst side of me counsels empathically. *He projects his self-hatred into you who, at the same time, remain the all-powerful, all comforting mother whom he now feels good enough to make verbal love to.*

Yes, yes, okay, but, still . . . I argue in increasingly louder tones to these contradictory voices, *Still, I don't know him. He doesn't know me. Is the noise coming from a person like the noise of an ambulance siren? Do I have to hear it so I get out of the way and don't get run over?*

Don't let it upset you, dear, my kind uncle says (the one who used to engineer intense, flirtatious discussions in his den, with the door closed, with one or another of my teenage girlfriends). *Just ignore him; don't give him the benefit of your attention; don't dignify him by a response; it will just encourage him,* says my uncle, trying to calm me down and smooth things over.

I pause for breath, then, frustrated almost to tears, nearly shout, *My mind doesn't work as rationally as yours. How can it? My brain hears, my desire is stirred, I lose control of my body. On the street my body is theirs. I am a body on the street. Two tits and no head and a big ass. I am a walking Rohrschach. My body becomes a cunt and I am sore from this semiotic rape.* (Dimen 1986:1–3; slightly revised)

DOMINATION

Feminine experience is often one in which mind and body, mind and matter, are joined and, jointly, are ripped off. And at times we collude in this evisceration of our subjectivity, even as we resist. The process by which personal life slips from one's grasp as domination tears it away is coiled in women's experience. And domination makes alienation possible.

Alienation usually describes the experience of work in capitalism, in which the pacing and productivity of labor are directed not by workers but by profit needs and the extraction of surplus-value from labor-power by capital. In consequence, work life comes to seem meaningless, and people look forward to "real life," to personal life, which seems easier to arrange to one's satisfaction.

Yet, somehow, for women, alienation, or something like it, appears not only on the job but also in personal life. Every time a woman goes for a walk, her mind and her body are invaded by a social definition of her femininity that threatens to disconnect her from her own experience. This is the experience of domination, the loss of one's sense of and wish for autonomy, as a result of processes that play on one's doubts about the reality and validity of one's self, one's perceptions, and one's values.

Patriarchy is, first and last, a system of domination. But it differs from other systems of domination, whether racism, class structure, or colonialism, because it goes directly for the jugular of social relatedness and psychological integration—desire. Patriarchy attacks desire, the unconscious longing that animates all human action, by reducing it to sex and then defining sex in the politicized terms of gender. Paradoxically, however, sexuality, thus organized by gender, becomes reciprocally desire's sculptor, while gender simultaneously organizes part of desire into the self. Not only sexuality, but all manifestations of desire are thereby informed by gender; thus, the roots of desire, itself the source of personal experience, are steeped in hierarchy.[3]

In patriarchy, gender denotes a structure of political power masquerading as a system of natural difference. The invisible fulcrum of the myth of the primal horde, gender builds on a highly variable and interpretable biological given, the anatomical difference between the sexes. Thus made the lynchpin of patriarchy, gender is the way that consciousness of self, and so one's sense of empowerment, is most immediately experienced.

Or, at least, it is the way that many women become most immediately conscious of self. Insofar as this does not hold true for men, it is because human experience is linguistically, ideologically, and socially constructed as male, to wit, "mankind," not to mention the personal pronoun "he," so that men's experience of self is perhaps continuous with simply being human.

Women, in contrast, may be aware or have an unconscious sense through language that society counterposes them to men as Other. Culture makes women both human and nonhuman, and they know it, and they must both swallow and reject what they know in order to go from day to day. Where empowerment is thus unequal, intimacy cannot easily grow. But, to anticipate a bit, where experience of self is thus ambiguous, intimacy has a fighting chance.

She is eight. Her father, forty-one, and her brother, five, are about to take a shower together. "Me, too," she cries, eager to see her father's genitals. "No, no, dear, little girls don't take showers with their fathers," says her mother, forty. Since when? she wonders. She knows what she wants. They know too. Do they know that she knows that they know that she knows?

In seventh grade, if you wear green on Thursdays, they call you a dyke. If you wear a black sweater any day, they call you a whore. Somehow, she forgets and wears green on Thursday and black sweaters when she likes. At a party in a suburban basement rec-room, she finds herself suddenly alone on the couch, the only girl in the room, when the lights go out and all the boys jump her and feel her up everywhere you can imagine. The girls giggle in the laundry room.

A girl from another crowd tells her she looks nice in her black sweater. They become friends, sort of. She sleeps over at her friend's house one night. They bake chocolate chip cookies and listen to opera. Later her friend invites her into her bed to do what her friend's crowd had been doing for a while. She feels nothing, is frightened, and goes back to her own bed.

She starts kissing boys on the mouth at eleven and likes it a lot. She doesn't pet above the waist with boys until fifteen; she doesn't like it but does it anyway to be grown up. She won't pet below the waist until seventeen; then she doesn't want to admit that she has orgasms. She starts masturbating at eighteen. At twenty-one, she has intercourse for the first time; she likes the fact that she's doing it; it takes her fifteen years to like doing it. She uses her diaphragm every time for those fifteen years. (Dimen 1984:143; slightly revised)

The Division of Emotional Labor

Patriarchy constructs gender, and gender the psyche, through two divisions of labor. The first, the division of emotional labor, interrupts the fluid motion of personal experience and freezes it into two moments, "individualizing" and "relatedness." Individualizing is a mainstream cultural ideal. Connoting autonomy, agency, and singularity, it also suggests the kind of adult who is responsible for himself and no one else. Only the masculine pronoun will do here, for, in our culture, this is the masculinized part of selfhood, symbolized by the lonesome cowboy, the Marlboro man. It is associated with the universal and transcendant, with creation and achievement, with abstract rationality, with tangible and enduring products. The "self-as-individual" glows with the glamour of heroic, solitary, self-discovering travelers, from Odysseus on.[4]

Relatedness suggests Penelope, not Odysseus. While Odysseus was out adventuring with goddesses as well as monsters, Penelope was at home, weaving his shroud by day and unraveling it by night; in other words, she was doing the dishes. She was on the treadmill of relatedness, caring for things because she was caring for people (Miller 1976). Relatedness, then, connotes the personal and the interpersonal, the particular and the pragmatic, care and nurturance, and invisible, ephemeral processes and feelings—hence the symbol of relatedness, the Madonna, the woman with a child. Still, as revered as the Madonna may be and as adored the sweet child, they paradoxically represent a dependency and loss of self with which Marlboro men are notoriously uncomfortable. Relatedness pulses with ambivalence, with the love/hate for mother that starts in infancy and, in our culture, finally radiates out to all women (Dinnerstein 1976).

Yet these two tendencies of selfhood are potentially genderless and, in fact, show up in men and women alike. Indeed, to try to achieve one without the other is psychologically and socially dangerous, if possible at all. To attempt only individualizing is to become emotionally isolated; to attempt only relatedness is to lose the self by merging with someone else. Clinically speaking, the consequences of such attempts are two sides of the same pathological coin. Socially, the dangers of John Wayne in the White House have been too presently obvious to name. And the reverence for a "true woman," that is to say a wife/mother, can mutate into the scorn for someone who, because she is "only a housewife," can become a mad or bad one.

The Division of Economic Labor

Although relatedness may be essential for sociality in general and intimacy in particular, it is often disparaged because of its role in the division of economic labor. The organization of commodity production, which "division of labor" usually denotes, actually runs on an unspoken, initial premise: Whatever wage-earning work women do, they are assigned first to the domestic domain because, in ideology, they are biopsychologically suited to nurturing and, in practice, they are trained for it. There, they do the work which (a) is never done, (b) is absolutely essential to the society, (c) is not called work because it is not remunerated, and (d) is therefore denigrated, sentimentalized, and trivialized. This is the work of reproducing—physically, socially, emotionally—adult workers and the next generation.

That the first thing we want to know about a woman is whether she is married, and the second, whether she has children, testifies to the cultural conviction that all women should do this sort of work.[5] Yet in this so-called natural place women are asked to perform the most unnatural of acts. The domestic domain is meant to alleviate the alienation that everyone experiences in the public domain. It is supposed to foster autonomy and authenticity and provide pleasure and satisfaction in an atmosphere of intimacy. At the same time, it must nourish both the young and the mature so that they can not only tolerate alienated labor but also, ironically, feed their self-respect with it.

To the degree that housewifery manages to achieve the one goal, it betrays the other. In other words, housewifery is a task made virtually impossible by its contradictions. Intended as an act of love, it also serves domination. It maintains one means of production, labor-power, at no cost to the employer through the same means by which it helps the state control the labor force. Some tensions generated by this no-win arrangement find expression in the savage ridicule and subtle contempt lavished on housewives even as they stand on pedestals.

SOCIAL REPRODUCTION

Other tensions emerge in the doctor's office. The guilt and anxiety generated by their double-binding work can drive housewives a little crazy, for which reason they sometimes consult therapists, social workers, and other members of the "helping professions." Yet when they do so, they become even more entangled with the contradictions driving them there. They participate with these very professionals in "social reproduction," in the daily and crossgenerational re-creation of these three connected things—individual subjectivity, social consciousness (or "ideology"), and social relations. An intersecting personal and institutional process, social reproduction takes place, in the state, in both domestic and public domains, in kinship, educational, communicational, professional, and bureaucratic systems (Mitchell 1971; Rapp et al. 1979; Weinbaum and Bridges 1979).[6]

Social reproduction expresses and informs desire by recreating cultural contradictions within personal experience.[7] Steeped in relatedness, it is feminized by the assumption that, as the proverb in the East European stetl went, "life is with people" (Zborowski and Herzog 1952). Child rearing is central to it, both practically and symbolically, for child rearing is the raising not of monads but of beings through whose sociality and participation in social consciousness society is recreated.

Yet, at the same time that social reproduction cultivates and requires relatedness, it is equally but dissociatedly steeped in individualizing. It re-presents to us the standard model of adulthood: It cranks out an Andy Warhol silkscreen of what we have in mind when we say, "But you're not supposed to need anyone else." Through images reduplicated in speech, print, pictures, and music, it makes us long to emulate the Marlboro man—someone who may sometimes want others but who will never need them. And it makes us hate to resemble women, whose very interest in relationships and intimacy seems mired in the mud of need.

THE GENDERED DIVORCE
OF WANT FROM NEED

By the same sexist token, social reproduction sunders want and need. Merged in infancy as different aspects of desire, need and want separate out as development proceeds. Although they continue unconsciously to be kin to one another, they appear culturally as unequal strangers. Wanting, associated with adulthood, active will, and masculinity, is better than need, linked to infancy, passive dependency, and femininity. Adults therefore try to distance their dependency needs by regarding their longings for love, tenderness, and care as weak, childish, "womanish."[8]

These patriarchal judgments fuse with unconscious forces and political exigencies to make need alarming. The feeling of need is disquieting because, on the one hand, we come to know it first as a matter of life and death; it recalls unconscious memories of helplessness, of our once total, infantile dependence on others for care and love. On the other, neediness makes us anxious because in the state it signals the possibility of adult helplessness. Not only are we at the mercy of capital's vicissitudes, but when the keys to the halls of state are in the hands of those whose fingers hover over the nuclear buttons, we are nearly as weak socially as infants are physically.

Still, *feeling need* is not the same as *being needy*. When gratification is foreseeable, longing, and therefore need, is as welcome as hunger that rises with the smell of dinner cooking on the stove, as reassuringly exciting as sexual desire for a tried-and-true lover. When instead, frustration is anticipated, the *feeling of need* threatens to become a *state of neediness,* and, therefore, dangerous. And people are likely to be frustrated when unequal class, skin, and gender privileges distribute money, social know-how, and skills unevenly; when only a few may slake the thirst for success stimulated in all; and when the state disregards the quality of life, overregards the military, and lacks either work that enhances material security and self-respect or political empowerment that cultivates need-satisfying autonomy.

As need goes, so goes desire. When social conditions render the gratification of adult needs uncertain, besmirch dependency, and thwart the realization of wants, wanting can come to feel like needing; depending on others for satisfaction becomes unwelcome; consequently, longing seems altogether unpleasant. As political and unconscious forces spiral downward together, we try to get a grip on things. We try to want without needing. But, having pulled in our psychological belts, we find instead that we have diminished what we were trying to preserve—desire, and, with it, sex, hope, and intimacy. When yearnings for the Other arise nonetheless, they seem too complicated to acknowledge. As soon as such ambiguity emerges, John Wayne gets on his horse and rides off into the sunset.

When I was eighteen, I had a boyfriend with whom I was very much in love and of whom I was very much in awe, two not unconnected facts. At that time, he and his friends were in love with a book, *The Ginger Man* by J. P. Donleavy. So naturally I thought I should be in love with it too. I tried. But, somehow, it was very hard for me to see myself as the free-wheeling, woman-served, and woman-leaving main character, a great individualist who loved planting his seed, but didn't like kids or wives. No doubt I took things too literally, too personally.

This was not the first time I had difficulty with literature which portrayed the wonderful life of adult freedom in male terms. In high school, I wanted to be a beatnik. I too wanted to go on the road, but I could never figure out what would happen if, travelling in Mexico in 1958, I got my period. Were you supposed to carry a supply of Kotex with you? How many could you carry? If you took all you needed, there wouldn't be any room for all those nice jugs of wine in Jack Kerouac's car. The only beatnik I know who even considered this question was Diane diPrima in *Memoirs of a Beatnik*. She describes her first big orgy, the one with the works, including Allen Ginsburg. As she takes a deep breath and decides to plunge in, so to speak, she pulls out her Tampax and flings it across the room where somehow it gets irretrievably lost.

A grand moment, that. Do I hear you thinking, How gross? Or, How irrelevant? Gross, yes; irrelevant, no. And that's the point. Having to worry about the gross mess becomes a part of life from puberty on. A nagging, stupid worry becomes a fact of life, not quite as unnoticeable as your skin. The same nagging worry included wondering whether they had any contraceptive jelly in Mexico, just when in the seduction I was going to put my diaphragm in, once it was in whether it would stay in, and, when it was time to take it out, where I would find the water to wash it. (Dimen 1986:32–33; slightly revised)

THE STRANGE RELATIONSHIP
BETWEEN SEX AND REPRODUCTION

For every woman—heterosexual, lesbian, young, old—sexuality is inextricably entangled with reproductivity, in other words, with procreation, relatedness, and sociality as felt and as socially instituted. This entangling is experienced in various ways. When it is conscious, then either you are thinking about birth control or, if you are lesbian, postmenopausal, voluntarily sterilized, or fertile and wanting to get pregnant, you are relieved that you do not have to think about it. If you think about it a lot, you may have to stop your masturbatory sexual fantasy to figure out what kind of contraception will best fit the scene you have constructed. If you are less obsessional, and if you are heterosexual, you only have to interrupt your spontaneous passion to put in your diaphragm, if you have not already killed it off by having done so beforehand. Or you may risk your health, and so your peace of mind, by taking a pill or having an IUD inserted. And if you decide to "take a chance," as the phrase goes, you can have the thrill of forgetting about having to remember not to get pregnant.

But even if the strange relationship between sexuality and reproduction is not consciously problematic, it still rests in the unconscious experience of women who grow up in patriarchy. In our culture, women are responsible for babies, not so much because they give birth to them but because theirs is the gender made socially responsible for relatedness. This responsibility places them in fundamental conflict. It roots women's gender identity in relatedness, even as their adult identity is defined by individualizing. For women, then, every act of sex is one of a series of conflicted and contradictory decisions about contraries—self and a potential other, self and society, life and death.

These decisions, which all people face, become very ambivalent for women because of the state's abiding interest in them. The state uses women's experience to control social reproduction, which, in turn, becomes the royal road to the domestic domain, intimacy, and, finally, subjectivity itself. The state tries to control the bodies, and so the sexuality, and so the desire, and so the minds of women, thereby of the children they rear and of the men and other women for whom they are nurturers and symbols of desire.

The state has two main sources of power over women. It regulates access to the material basis of procreation, that is, to contraception, abortion, and the technology of birth, deciding by legislation who will be allowed to get them, how, and when. And the state attempts to control minds by mystifying them. For example, women appear to make independent reproductive decisions for which they feel individually responsible; they are, after all, "individualized" adults. But, because they are "in-relation" to the state, their decisions have in fact already been made for them by laws restricting their sexuality, reproductive choices, and access to jobs.

This double-binding form of domination makes alienation possible by making women, and therefore everyone they care for, feel out of touch with, split from, ill-at-ease with their bodies and their selves. Reproductive matters—periods; pregnancies; children whose impulsivity and savagery require domestication; adults whose bodies and psyches, deformed by domestication and hard labor, call out for care; the disorderly passions of intimacy and sex—these female matters seem quite chaotic, crude, even ugly. They are unappealing next to the apparently clean-cut, rational, and easily measured project of material production so central to capitalism.

In our culture, reproductive matters are to the politicoeconomic domain what, in symbol, the vagina is to the neat penis—messy. And the individual isolation asked of one and for which one hankers represents an attempt to make a neat product out of one's messy personal uniqueness. In contrast, personal development, like the rest of social reproduction—including questions of the beginning of life, the timing of death, intimacy—these are ambiguous matters.

> Drink in hand, he leaned against the wall with an air of teasing, self-mocking arrogance, eyes soft from intoxication. His sensual anticipation was all-enveloping. "When we get home, I want to fuck you," he said lovingly. "I'm going to put it in you, and go in and out, in and out, real slow, for a long time." He jerked his hips slightly. "That's how I'll fuck you," he said softly. "And when I'm done, you'll look a lot better. It'll perk things up here"—he lightly touched her breasts—"and make things smaller here"— patted her waist—"and smooth things out here"—caressed her hips.
>
> An ancient ache cramped her thoughts, and all she could do was laugh. She wished he were taller and looser. Knowing he was sensitive about his slight stature, she consciously fed his vanity, telling him of the lean precision of his proportions, the beauty of his classic face, the grace of his genitals. Indeed, his body awed her, even as his insecurity stimulated in her a luxuriant contempt.
>
> Their love-making was wonderful that night—as always. He did all the work—as always. He was hurt that she was not more grateful. (Dimen 1986:121; slightly revised)

Heterosexual experience is sometimes stained by the social evaluation of reproductivity that mutates into socially validated hatred of imperfect female flesh.

> Her tongue slid along the soft involuted folds of her labia. Her tongue slid along the soft involuted folds of her labia. She licked her clitoris, she licked her clitoris. They came together, not knowing who was who.
>
> "Your name came up," she said later, "but I told them I didn't want you in the group." "Why not?" she asked. "Because I want to keep my personal life and my public life clearly differentiated." (Dimen 1986:161; slightly revised)

Sexuality excludes neither the forces of the unconscious nor the forces of hierarchy.

> He's going to take her hand, she knows it. His palm is slightly cool and damp and soft, and her chest tightens. She will pull her hand away as soon as she can, perhaps when they must part to let some people pass on the crowded sidewalk. Her flesh crawls from him so often that you would think she might say to him, This isn't working, I'm sorry, I want to leave.

45

She has won, he has buckled. Very clearly, he needs her. And so, no longer the one ravaged by need, she becomes the strong one.

Later, she lets her denial of the waves of revulsion force her into inactivity, and she lets him make a fool of himself. This is how she can cross the line into sexual desire, and let him make love to her, and pull away abruptly from his gentle after-touch.

As we try to sever want from need, we find that sexual needs, the need for intimacy, and even the need to make meaning of life, take on an unwholesome or frivolous cast. In unavoidable consequence, life begins to make less and less sense. Life is meaningless without wanting, but there is no wanting without needing and therefore no desire without need. As need drains from desire, so does meaning bleed from life. To eliminate need is to kill desire and therefore any appetite for living.

They roll around in bed, she younger, he older, he once fat and soft now thin and hard but with a fleshly sensual aura still, she smooth and roly-poly. Perhaps the champagne from the night before fizzes their spirits still. Moments of pure delight, and finally she climbs on top and rocks into the black/silver inner spaces of realized desire where she forgets what she's doing, and, for one dizzying, bubbly, sunny moment, does not know if he is male or female, her mother or her father, and she knows that she doesn't know, and that he is who he is, and she cherishes this instant of laughing madness.

He has a pretty good time too, not the same as hers, but pretty good.

It helps them both that he's had a vasectomy. (Dimen 1986:13; slightly revised)

AMBIGUITY AND INTIMACY

Fortunately, sexual passion reunites need and want. Erotic experience is extraordinary, lying somewhere between dream and daily life. Sped by desire, it knows no shame and no bounds. In it, pleasure and power, hurt and love, mingle effortlessly. It is a between-thing, bordering psyche and society, culture and nature, conscious and unconscious, self and other. Its intrinsic messy ambiguity confers on it an inherent novelty, creativity, discovery; these give it its excitements, its pleasure, its fearsomeness. Sexual experience entails loss of self-other boundaries, the endless opening of doors to more unknown inner spaces, confusions about what to do next or who the other person is or what part of the body is being touched or what part of the body is doing the touching or where one person begins and the other ends. This is sometimes pleasurable, sometimes painful, always unsettling.

If sexuality is ambiguous, intimacy is doubly so. The lonesome Marlboro man generates his opposite number, an image of a mutual, egalitarian, empathetic, nurturing, and self-renewing relation between adults. Yet intimacy proves elusive in the very society that thus spawns, indeed, necessitates it. Individualizing that excludes relatedness makes us desperate to be close to others. But, compelled to deny need, we fear to recognize our longing. In the absence of a culturally valid image of an adult who is permitted to need, we are thrown back on infantile experience.[9] Infants, however, are unaware that bridges between separate adults must be built; they not only mistake symbiosis for intimacy but imagine that it is there for the taking, not the creating: hence the street hassler, whose desperate invasions obviate the delicate attention on which intimacy thrives; hence our lunges for intimacy and our equally passionate retreats.

Yet a model of maturity that might make intimacy more accessible stands in patriarchy's shadow, the worshipped and denigrated feminine omitted from the myth of the primal horde. Just as the personal voice juxtaposed to the scholarly can yield a creative tension, so relatedness in tension with individualizing might produce another, although rarely realized, cultural ideal of personhood: a person simultaneously distinct, autonomous, and related to others. Recognizing contradiction, this utopian model of maturity manages to accommodate the paradox of self and other, of connectedness and separateness. Built into it is the knowledge that you can experience your separateness only through knowing, sensing, and intuiting the other at the boundaries between the two, between self and other. You can care for or hate someone else only if there exists a "you" to care or to hate, a "someone else" to be cared for or hated, and the capacity to care for or hate or, more generally, be in relation to others.

In other words, this model of adulthood, emerging in the charged space between conventional masculinity and femininity, is tolerant of ambiguity, something with which women must be at ease in order to survive under patriarchy. In our culture, women symbolize ambiguity—neither of nature nor of culture but mediating them (Ortner 1974). They represent, as well, an alternate moral path, a winding one to be made, not one that, given, must be rigidly followed (Gilligan 1983; but cf. Stack forthcoming).[10] This morality of seeing "both" and "and," of grasping two points of view simultaneously, is at home with the discomfort of ambiguity. It is crucial to that called "maternal thinking," preserved by the domestic domain as a utopian vision, if not an always realized practice (Ruddick 1980).

The capacity to appreciate ambiguity is essential to intimacy as well.

Unfortunately, in patriarchy, this capacity is as absent from maturity as from the myth of the primal horde, not only because of ideals of adulthood but because of how the young mature. The primary assignment of early child care to women has guaranteed that the father, that is, the cowboy's unambiguous hardness, will institute differentiation of self from other, adulthood's beginnings, and therefore the foundations of adult intimacy (Mahler et al. 1975). Because this differentiation is stabilized by making unspeakable, and so preserving, the meltingness of Madonna and child, it makes every mother-reared person feel incomplete and unworthy. But feelings of unworth are a meager basis for the emergence of intimacy. Until differentiation by disavowal disappears and the ambiguity of self, other, and their connection is tolerable, intimacy will remain, at best, bittersweet, ambivalent, and partial, punctuated by horrid periods of distance and sweet moments of merging.

THE PRESENT ENVISIONING THE FUTURE

The myth is only of one tradition; its silence on women and intimacy bespeaks other possibilities for society and desire. Instead of the recurrent adolescent rebellion forecast by the myth; instead of the stasis that regresses to quiescent death (Freud 1961); instead of the childish return to the mother blown up into a guilt-free social order (Brown 1959); instead of a naive-passing-for-innocent belief in technologically-created abundance (Marcuse 1955); instead of a universalizing of what is merely a culturally normal heterosexuality[11]—the permanent revolution will have to be one of uncertainty, a continuous unfolding of desire. Unavoidably, therefore, it will be ambiguous. Such unfolding can emerge only in a social order that would provide the economic, political, and reproductive basis for reasonable trust and foreseeable self-esteem.

We will not see this in our time. The Oedipal drama and the pre-Oedipal passion play must change, but all we have now are reruns. Although some of us hope that Ronald Reagan's antics will have hastened the deidealization of John Wayne, the culture of death can always come up with another plastic hero. The intransigence of the patriarchal state is the reason that we must maintain a utopian vision of a society in which desire is empowering, not weakening, in which all parts of the self can come out of the closet—passion and need, will and empathy, the anger that, through a paradoxical love, can make our society realize its ideals of democracy and decency even while hell-bent on betraying them.

Sexuality is not the route to revolution. But it is a prime shaper of desire, and constraint of desire leads directly to self-betrayal and social bad faith. We suffer not from too much desire but from too little. Our failures to rebel, our incomplete revolutions, are rooted in the repression of desire that, essential to sexual opression, truncates hope. The utopian thinking of the 1960s counterculture that called for the liberation of desire is no longer fashionable, even on the left, even among feminists. We are supposed to have grown up, our eyes adjusted to the size of our stomachs. But such modish maturity mistakes the nature of desire. We must desire all we can, no matter how much it hurts or how foolish or greedy it seems. We may not be able to get everything we want, but only by wanting everything we can imagine can we get everything we need.

NOTES

This is a revised version of Dimen (1987). Portions of this paper were also published in Dimen (1984, 1986). I thank Susan Bordo and Alison Jaggar for excellent editing.

1. See, for example, Perry (essay in this volume) for a discussion of subject-subject engagement in feminist biography.

2. Dimen (1986) develops this form more fully.

3. For more complete discussions of the reduction of desire, see Dimen (1981, 1982).

4. Benjamin (1980) shows how the sex/gender hierarchy masculinizes and idealizes the individualized image of adulthood.

5. This is, of course, in addition to their work in the public domain, where over half of all adult women also work for pay. They are systematically paid less, making only sixty-four cents for every dollar that men make for full-time, year-round work (a similar proportion obtained in Brussels in 1855 [Marx 1967:671]). However, if part-time, seasonal part-time, seasonal full-time, and year-round full-time women's work are combined, the figure is about half (Sokoloff 1980). Women's jobs, furthermore, are insecure: When the economy needs more cheap labor, women, like minorities, get jobs; when it needs less, they are laid off. Finally, the cultural division of emotional labor carries into the economic world: Most women are employed in predominantly female occupations that fall into the "caring" category—teachers, nurses, secretaries, fast-food cooks, waitresses. Because these jobs are seen as feminine, they merit lesser social esteem.

6. Social reproduction may be differently organized in other cultures, as I discuss in my paper in progress, "The State's Women: Sexuality and The Classic Case for Social Reproduction." Unlike Yanigasako and Collier (1987), I have confidence in the utility of this concept, which, in contrast to Harris and Young (1981), I define to include the unconscious, inner life.

7. This phrasing begs the question of whether social reproduction must always re-create cultural contradictions in psychological life in any culture. Indeed, it raises and

then begs the question of whether there is now or ever has been any culture lacking contradictions, thus implicitly addressing a central Marxist debate about "primitive communism" and the communist utopia. A discussion of these questions is far beyond the scope of this paper.

8. In some cultures, for example, the !Kung San of Africa, where the individual is not a viable economic unit but can survive only by dependence on the extended family or community institutions, need and want may be neither so divided nor invidiously compared. In such kin-based cultures, where, if one person is homeless or hungry, it is only because everyone lacks shelter or food (Lee 1979; Shostak 1981), need may not be the source of shame that we find it to be in the state.

9. Such acknowledgment entails what Fairbairn (1953: 34–35 and *passim.*) called "mature dependency."

10. Stack's research among black people in rural North Carolina and in Washington, D.C., strongly suggests that Gilligan's thesis may be class- and race-bound. Using Gilligan's methodology, she found that adults in general tend more toward justice reasoning; among adults, men tend slightly more toward care reasoning, women to justice reasoning (Stack, forthcoming).

11. As found in the entire Marxian corpus.

REFERENCES

Benjamin, J. 1978. "Authority and the Family Revisited: A World Without Fathers?" *New German Critique* 4:35–57.

———. 1980. "The Bonds of Love: Erotic Domination and Rational Violence." *Feminist Studies* 6:144–174.

Brown, N. O. 1959. *Life Against Death*. Middletown, Conn.: Wesleyan University Press.

Dimen, M. 1981. "Variety Is the Spice of Life." *Heresies* 3, no. 4 (Issue 12):66–70.

———. 1982. "Notes toward the Reconstruction of Sexuality." *Social Text* 6:22–30.

———. 1984. "Politically Correct? Politically Incorrect?" In *Pleasure and Danger: Exploring Female Sexuality*, ed. C. S. Vance. London: Routledge and Kegan Paul.

———. 1986. *Surviving Sexual Contradictions: A Startling and Different Look at a Day in the Life of a Contemporary Professional Woman*. New York: Macmillan.

———. 1987. "Interrupting Patriarchy: Toward the Deconstruction of the Father." In *Unraveling Fatherhood*, ed. T. Knijn and A.-C. Mulder. Dordrecht, The Netherlands: Foris Publications Holland.

Dinnerstein, D. 1976. *The Mermaid and the Minotaur: Sexual Arrangements and Human Malaise*. New York: Harper & Row.

Fairbairn, W. F. D. 1953. *Psychoanalytic Studies of the Personality*. London: Routledge and Kegan Paul.

Flax, J. 1983. "Political Philosophy and the Patriarchal Unconscious: A Psychoanalytic Perspective on Epistemology and Metaphysics." In *Discovering Reality*, ed. S. Harding and M. Hintikka. Dordrecht, Holland: D. Reidel.

Freud, S. 1961 [1930]. "Civilization and Its Discontents." *The Standard Edition of the Complete Psychological Works of Sigmund Freud.* London: Hogarth Press.

Gilligan, C. 1983. *In a Different Voice: Psychological Theories and Women's Development.* Cambridge, Mass.: Harvard University Press.

Harris, O., and K. Young. 1981. "Engendered Structures: Some Problems in the Analysis of Reproduction." In *The Anthropology of Precapitalist Societies*, ed. J. S. Kahn and J. R. Llobera. London: Macmillan.

Jaggar, A. B. 1983. *Feminist Politics and Human Nature.* Totowa, N.J.: Rowman and Allenheld.

Keller, E. F. 1985. *Reflections on Gender and Science.* New Haven, Conn.: Yale University Press.

Lee, R. B. 1979. *The !Kung San: Women, Men, and Work in a Foraging Society.* Cambridge: Cambridge University Press.

Mahler, M., F. Pine, and A. Bergman. 1975. *The Psychological Birth of the Human Infant: Symbiosis and Individuation.* London: Hutchinson of London.

Marcuse, H. 1955. *Eros and Civilization.* Boston: Beacon Press.

Marx, K. 1967 [1867]. *Capital.* Vol. I. New York: International Publishers.

Miller, J. B. 1976. *Toward a New Psychology of Women.* Boston: Beacon Press.

Mitchell, J. 1971. *Women's Estate.* London: Penguin.

Ortner, S. B. 1974. "Is Female to Male as Nature Is to Culture?" In *Woman, Culture, and Society*, ed. M. Rosaldo and L. Lamphere. Stanford: Stanford University Press.

Rapp, R., E. Ross, and R. Bridenthal. 1979. "Examining Family History." *Feminist Studies* 5:181–200.

Ruddick, S. 1980. "Maternal Thinking." *Feminist Studies* 6:342–367.

Shostak, M. 1981. *Nisa.* New York: Random House.

Sokoloff, N. 1980. *Between Love and Money: The Dialectics of Women's Home and Market Work.* New York: Praeger.

Stack, C. Forthcoming. "The Culture of Gender: An Anthropologist Looks at Gilligan." In *Negotiating Gender in American Culture*, ed. F. Ginsburg and A. Tsing. Boston: Beacon Press.

Weinbaum, B., and A. Bridges. 1979. "The Other Side of the Paycheck: Monopoly Capital and the Structure of Consumption." In *Capitalist Patriarchy and the Case for Socialist Feminism*, ed. Z. Eisenstein. New York: Monthly Review Press.

Yanigasako, S. J., and J. F. Collier. 1987. "Toward a Unified Analysis of Gender and Kinship." In *Gender and Kinship: Toward a Unified Analysis*, ed. J. F. Collier and S. J. Yanigasako. Stanford: Stanford University Press.

Zborowski, M., and E. Herzog. 1952. *Life Is with People: The Jewish Little Town in Eastern Europe.* New York: International Universities Press.

THE POLITICS
OF WRITING (THE) BODY:
ÉCRITURE FÉMININE

Arleen B. Dallery

For feminism, asking whether there is, socially, a female sexuality is the same as asking whether women exist. (MacKinnon 1981:20)
Sexuality is to feminism what work is to Marxism; that which is most one's own, yet most taken away. (MacKinnon 1981:1)

These first two quotations by Catherine MacKinnon make several suggestions about female sexuality: it is alienated, given over to another, it is controlled, used, or symbolized by another; and it, like work in alienated labor, is never autonomously developed. If woman's sexuality does not exist as an independent social fact—not the product of male projections—then woman does not exist.

By contrast, consider these two short quotes from French feminist texts:

Woman has sex organs just about everywhere. (Irigaray 1981:103)
Let the priests tremble, we are going to show them our sexts (a pun on sex and texts). (Cixous 1981b:255)

These quotes suggest that women do exist *sexually;* it shall be shown as a fearful social fact, *textually*. This inscription of woman's difference in langauge is *écriture féminine* or writing (the) body.

There is a difference between MacKinnon and French feminism: MacKinnon wants a real, reified female sexuality, whereas Irigaray and Cixous see sexual difference constituting itself discursively through inscribed meanings. These quotations also sum up the differences between American academic feminism and *postmodernist* French feminism: one emphasizes the empirical, the irreducible reality of woman's experience; the other emphasizes

52

the primacy of discourse, woman's discourse, without which there is no experience—to speak of.

American academic feminism (Women's Studies) began with the perception that women's experiences, history, and voice were absent from the disciplines of western knowledge and art. Theories of behavior in the social sciences, periodizations of history in historiography, genre distinctions in literary criticism had been established without any reference to the experience of women as research subjects, as agents in history, or, as writers of literary texts. To remedy this "deafening silence" of women's experience and voice in western culture and history, feminist social scientists studied women as research subjects; feminist historians, using nontraditional sources and methods, sought to reconstruct the everyday life of women in different class locations; and feminist literary critics resurrected the works of women writers who had been marginalized by the male canon. Emphasizing *gender* differences, academic feminists charged that mainstream theories of human development as well as aesthetic or literary theories were male-biased or androcentric, often denigrating women's experiences and contributions to culture or transposing male experiences into the norms of *human* behavior.

By contrast, French feminism or *écriture féminine*, rooted in a tradition of European philosophy, linguistics, and psychoanalysis, posits the feminine as that which is repressed, misrepresented in the discourses of western culture and thought. The preconditions for the production of western knowledge, its standards of objectivity, rationality, and universality, require the exclusion of the feminine, the bodily, the unconscious. Indeed, the logical ordering of reality into hierarchies, dualisms, and binary systems presupposes a prior gender dichotomy of man/woman. Not only has women's voice or experience been excluded from the subject matter of western knowledge, but even when the discourse is "about" women, or women are the speaking subjects, (it) they still speak(s) according to phallocratic codes. French feminism, by contrast with American feminist theory, holds that a new woman's writing of discourse is necessary to retrieve the repression of the feminine unconscious in western discourse and models of subjectivity. On the basis of the radical alterity of woman's sexual difference, a new, marked writing, *écriture féminine*, *parler-femme*, is called for.

But *écriture féminine* has generated much feminist criticism, typified in Simone de Beauvoir's early reaction to French feminism. In an interview with Margaret Simons, de Beauvoir accepts this new valorization and appropriation of woman's bodily experiences in pregnancy, childbirth, menopause, the transcendence of bodily alienation in feminist praxis; but she strongly resists a cultism, a narcissism, or a mysticism of the body (Simons and Benjamin 1979:342). Yet, her pronouncements on French feminism seem to be deliberate misreadings as if "writing the body" was only a new biological reductionism, an essentialism, based on some ontological difference of woman's body or, what de Beauvoir calls, the "construction of a *counter-penis*" (Simons and Benjamin 1979:342).

But she neglects to note, along with other critics, that woman's body is always mediated by language; the human body is a text, a sign, not just a piece of fleshy matter. I shall return to this theme later. Clearly, Irigaray and Cixous are not so philosophically naive as to make this Hegelian move to an abstract opposite. The structures of language and other signifying practices that code woman's body are as equally oppressive as the material/social structures that have tended to mediate one's awareness of one's body and self and erotic possibilities. For this reason, some filmmakers, according to Mary Ann Doane (1981) have refused to film woman's body, so layered has it been with the male gaze, with male signification. In these comments, de Beauvoir completely ignores the roots of *écriture féminine* as a response to Lacanian psychoanalysis that claims sexual differences cannot be reduced to biology because woman's body is constituted through phallic symbolization.

I shall briefly explicate the major themes of *écriture féminine*, as discussed in the works of Irigaray and Cixous, and respond to some Anglo-American critics who question its political effectiveness and challenge its presumable essentialism. I shall argue that American feminist privileging of experience may lead to critical misreadings of French feminism.

ÉCRITURE FÉMININE

French feminism, *écriture féminine*, essentially deconstructs the phallic organization of sexuality and its code, which positions woman's sexuality and signified body as a mirror or complement to male sexual identity. And, correspondingly, this discourse constructs the genuine multiple otherness of woman's libidinal economy—her eroticism—which has been symbolically repressed in language and denied by patriarchal culture.

In this brief exposition I want to outline two themes: (1) the displacement of the male economy of desire for a feminine economy of pleasure or *jouissance;* and (2) the displacement of a dualistic, oppositional, heterosexuality for feminine structures of erotic embodiment where self and other are continuous, in pregnancy, childbirth, and nursing.

DECONSTRUCTION OF DIFFERENCES
TO OTHERNESS

These differences are already at work in phenomenological accounts of desire and erotic perception where woman's body is already constituted, or sexualized, as the object of desire, fragmented into erogenous zones. Cixous refers to de Beauvoir's description of woman's dependent sexuality in *The Second Sex* as the old fool's game: "I will give you your body and you'll give me mine" (Cixous 1981a:256). I will incarnate you in flesh, and you will reveal my flesh for me. Woman's body is already colonized by the hegemony of male desire; it is not *your* body.

These sexual differences are also constructed, according to Lacan, when the boy child reads the girl child's anatomy as a lack, the absence of the phallus. The boy's sexual identity is based on perception of the other—she who lacks, who is only absence. The phallus, the symbolic meanings of the penis, is the transcendental signifier, constituting difference in sameness. In response to Lacan, Cixous claims that "sexual difference is not determined merely by the fantasized relationship to anatomy, which is based on the point of view, therefore upon a strange importance accorded (by Freud and Lacan) to exteriority (the seen body of one's own and the seen body of another) and to the *specular* in the elaboration of sexuality. A voyeur's theory, of course" (Cixous 1981b:95). By speaking the body, *écriture féminine* reverses the hierarchy of male and female sexuality, this male identity-in-difference, by enunciating woman's sexual embodiment as the general model of sexuality and showing male sexuality as a variant of it, a prolonged utilization of the phallic stage. Jonathan Culler has noted this deconstructionist strategy of French feminism; instead of lack, woman's body is oversupplied: "With her, two sexual organs, one male and one female, is the general model of sexuality" (1982:172).

Irigaray expands: "Woman has sex organs just about everywhere" (1981: 103). Woman's sexuality is not one, but two, or even plural, the multiplicity of sexualized zones spread across the body: "She is neither one nor two she cannot strictly speaking be determined as one person or two. She renders any definition inadequate. Moreover, she has no proper name" (Irigaray 1981: 101). Irigaray posits woman's autoeroticism as plural, based on the primacy of *touch*.

> She experiences pleasure almost everywhere, even without speaking of the hysterization of her entire body, one can say that the geography of her pleasure in much more diversified, more multiple in its differences,

more complex, more subtle than is imagined . . . . Woman finds plea-sure more in *touch* than in sight and her entrance into a dominant scopic economy signifies, once again, her relegation to passivity. (Iriga-ray 1981:101, 103)

In constructing the radical otherness of female autoeroticism, *écriture fémi-nine* displaces the male economy of desire, the gap between desire and its object, the nexus of need, absence, and representation, for the feminine econ-omy of pleasure or *jouissance*.

No, it is at the level of sexual pleasure *(jouissance)* in my opinion that the difference makes itself most clearly apparent in as far as woman's li-bidinal economy is neither identifiable by a man nor referable to the masculine economy. . . . "How do I experience sexual pleasure?" What is feminine *sexual pleasure;* where does it take place; how is it inscribed at the level of her body, of her unconscious? And then, how is it put into writing?(Cixous 1981:95)

Woman's erotic embodiment is separate from the scopic economy of male desire which posits a dualism, an opposition of self and other, and then seeks to reduce the other to sameness or complement.

This concept of *jouissance* is central in Kristeva's writings on pregnancy and motherhood; it is the orgasmic pleasure of sexual continuity with the maternal body, of libidinal fusion.[1] Feminine *jouissance* takes place on the linguistic level of the semiotic, between physiology and speech, nature and culture, the presymbolic, before the separation of self, and other. Through motherhood one comes in contact with one's own mother before the fear of castration. "By giving birth the woman enters into contact with her Mother; she becomes, she is her own Mother. They are the same continuity differen-tiating itself" (Kristeva 1980:239). *Jouissance* does not come in quantifiable units. As Jane Gallop states:

You can have one or multiple orgasms. They are quantifiable, delimit-able. You cannot have one *jouissance* and there is no plural . . . . Femi-nine sexuality is a *'jouissance* enveloped in its own contiguity'. Such *jouissance* would be sparks of pleasure ignited by *contact* at any point, any moment along the line, not waiting for a closure, but enjoying the touching. (1983:30, 31)

And in the glossary of Kristeva's *Desire in Language* the editor explains: "*Jouissance* is a giving, expending, dispensing of pleasure without concern about ends or closure; it is sexual, spiritual, physical and conceptual, at the same time" (1980:16). *Écriture féminine* stresses the figure of the mother, *la mère qui jouît,* who experiences pleasure, bliss, *jouissance.* Irigaray criticizes Freud's analysis of the Oedipal conflict and fear of castration because the Mother never speaks; she is marginalized. Her experience of desire is never voiced; we never understand her sexual drama, although she is the object of desire for both the boy and the girl. Remember this scenario: the boy represses his desire for the mother because he fears castration, sublimates and identifies with the power of the father, whereas the girl never really gives up her attachment to the mother. *Écriture féminine* enunciates the scandal of the sexual, nonvirginal Mother.

Kristeva, in her essay on "Motherhood According to Bellini" (1980), distinguishes between the paternal/symbolic aspects of motherhood and the maternal, presymbolic aspect of motherhood:

> symbolic aspects: the desire for Motherhood is a desire to bear a child of the Father (a child of her own Father) . . . a penis substitute. . . . The father originates and justifies reproductive desire. (238)

> the pre-symbolic aspects: the Mother's body is that towards which all women aspire, just because it lacks a penis. Here women actualize the homosexual fact of Motherhood where woman is closer to her instinctual memory more negatory of the social symbolic bond. It is the reunion of a woman-Mother with the body of her Mother. This cannot be verbalized; it is a whirl of words, rhythm. (239)

Patriarchal culture seeks to repress this primordial memory of fusion with and later separation from the maternal body; this fear of the mother is masked in male sexuality. Ann Kaplan has speculated that "the extremity of patriarchal control of female sexuality may be a reaction to helplessness in the face of the threat Motherhood represents. The threat and fear of her pleasure; her sex organ, her closeness to Nature, her as the source or origin, her vulnerability, lack of the phallus" (1983:206).

This split subjectivity or elision of self and other also exists between the mother and child in pregnancy, when the pregnant woman may enjoy the heft of her body and sensations within her belly, of otherness within the self. Despite the purification and idealization of motherhood by religion and patriarchal culture, pregnancy, childbirth, and nursing are dimensions of woman's erotic embodiment. The autonomous erotic aspects of these realms are more difficult to repress or censor in patriarchal culture because women preside over them. In this regard, Iris Young (1984) has insightfully pointed out that the pregnant woman is not usually sexually objectified by the male gaze. Maternity offers what heterosexuality, as it is now historically constituted for women, cannot: libidinal fusion.

Thus, there are three overall themes of the discourse on woman's body:

1. Writing the body celebrates women as sexual subjects not objects of male desire. It undermines the phallic organization of sexuality by retrieving a presymbolic level of speech where feminine *jouissance* is disclosed. Writing the body celebrates woman's autonomous eroticism, separate from a model of male desire based on need, representation, and lack. This *jouissance* precedes self/other dualisms; it expresses the continuity of self and other.

2. Otherness of woman's body: through *écriture féminine* woman's distinct bodily geography and forms are progressively disclosed, blurring the categories of binary thought and the signifying practices of male perception. "Woman's body is not one nor two. The sex which isn't one, not a unified identity." This articulation of woman's erotic body is secured through deconstructing sexual differences based on phallomorphism à la Freud and Lacan. Through writing the body, woman's body is liberated from the objectification and fragmentation of male desire.

3. This discourse traces an archeology of woman's body from the pre-Oedipal stage. The erotogeneity of woman's body, its multiple sex organs, is repressed in the development of symbolic language because there is no one to speak it. In the beginning, the boy child interprets the girl's body as lack, as absence. Through this scopic economy he constituted his own sexual identity, based on her difference—lacking the penis. Meanwhile, as Mary Rawlinson has noted, we never hear the feminine voice in Freud's analysis; there is no *positive* reading of the feminine somatic constitution (1928:166). The silent girl remains a partial man, seeking a penis-substitute in her desire; her body only complements his. In speaking woman's body, Irigaray and Cixous signify these bodily territories that have been kept under seal, suppressed in the phallic development of male and female sexual differences.

BODY-WRITING

In an article on Irigaray, Jane Gallop refers to the "unavoidable poetics of any speaking of the body. Irigaray's *poietique du corps* is not an expression of the body but a *poiesis*, a creating of the body" (Gallop 1983:79). Speaking the body does not mirror or refer to a neutral reified body in and of itself objectively escaping all anterior significations: discourse already, always, structures the body. Gallop continues, "Belief in simple referentiality is not only unpoetic but also ultimately politically conservative, because it cannot recognize that the reality to which it appeals is a traditional ideological construction, whether one terms it phallomorphic . . . bourgeois" (1983:83).

Kaja Silverman has brilliantly explicated the relationship between the body as constructed in discourses and the "real" body (1984:320–349). Through discourse the human body is territorialized into a male or female body. The meanings of the body in discourse actually shape the materiality of the real body and its complementary desires. Male or phallocentric discursive practices have historically shaped and demarcated woman's body for herself. Indeed, woman's body is overdetermined. Accordingly, speaking the body presupposes a real body with its prior constructions to be deconstructed in the process of discursively appropriating woman's body. In speaking the body, writing is pulsed by this feminine libidinal economy and projects the meanings of a decensored body to be materially lived. A "real" body prior to discourse is meaningless.

Writing the body, then, is both *constative* and performative. It signifies those bodily territories that have been kept under seal; it figures the body. But, writing the body is also a performative utterance; the feminine libidinal economy inscribes itself in language. "Just as women's sexuality is bound up with touch, so too women use words as a form of touching. Words join in the same way as do muscles and joints. Sex and speech are contiguous; the lips of the vulva and the lips of the mouth are each figures of and for each other" (Freeman 1985:9). The characteristics of women's writing are, therefore, based on the significations of woman's body: the otherness *within* the self in pregnancy; the two lips of the labia, both one yet other, signify woman's openness to otherness in writing, her split subjectivity, not identity; her multiple polyvalent speech as homologous to the multiple sexuality of woman's body. Writing the body is writing a new text—not with the phallic pen—new inscriptions of woman's body, separate from and undermining the phallocratic coding of woman's body that produces the censure, erasure, repression of woman's libidinal economy, her *altérité*. Writing the body, then, is not access to a precultural body or precultural sexuality as some critics of *écriture féminine* assume.

POETIC IS POLITICAL

Following Gallop's suggestion, belief in a poetics of the body might be politically radical. What would be the political effects of writing the body? Would discursively establishing the otherness of a feminine sexuality change woman's desire, her sexual practices, and thus produce referentiality *in futuro?*

ARLEEN B. DALLERY

Gallop seems to think so: "For if [Irigaray] is not just writing a non-phallomorphic text (a rather common modernist practice) but actively *constructing*
a non-phallomorphic sexuality, then the gesture of a troubled but nonetheless
insistent referentiality is essential" (1983:83). For both Irigaray and Cixous,
the constitution of a feminine libidinal economy in discourse should have historical and political consequences. Writing the body is therefore both speech
and praxis:

> Write yourself, your body must be heard. . . . To write an act which will
> not only realize the decensored relation of woman to her sexuality, to
> her womanly being; it will give her back her goods, her pleasures, her
> organs, her immense bodily territories which have been kept under seal
> (Cixous 1981a:250)

> Writing is precisely the very *possibility of change,* the space that can
> serve as a springboard for subversive thought, the precursory movement
> of transformation of social and cultural structures. . . . Women *seizing*
> the occasion to speak, hence her shattering entry *into history.* (Cixous
> 1981a:249–250)

> This brings to mind the *political stake* in the restricted or generalized
> sense of this work. The fact that woman's liberation requires *trans-
> forming* the economic realm and thus necessarily transforming culture
> and its operative agency, *language.* Without such an interpretation of a
> general grammar of culture, the feminine will never take place in history,
> except as a reserve of matter and of speculation. (Irigaray 1985:155)

Yet these political consequences might appear utopian unless their analysis of
the causes of feminine oppression can be justified.

Here, critics of *écriture féminine,* especially British Marxists, are most skeptical and have mounted serious challenges to the politics of *écriture féminine*
(Moi 1985). They have attacked *écriture féminine* as an elitist, classist, narcissistic, intellectualistic, ahistorical doctrine, irrelevant to the lives of black,
poor, and third-world women. Indeed, how can this discourse on the body
liberate women from the manifold forms of material oppression in the third
world?

They question whether the economic, political, and cultural forms of oppression of women will be altered by women writing (the) body. Is the realm
of language, discourse, and symbolism the key to the oppression of women?
Is phallocracy the key to capitalist hegemony? What systematic linkages can
be made between a psychoanalytic analysis of the repression of the feminine

and a feminist (Marxist or socialist, materialist feminist) analysis of the historical forms of patriarchal control of women's labor and women's sexuality?

Although other feminists have sought to undermine patriarchal ideologies of women's difference—read inequality—by analyzing the social and therefore contingent construction of gender differences, French feminists have perversely posited a radical alterity of woman's body, pleasure, and sexuality. They doubt whether sexual "difference" or specificity can unite women across classes, races, and cultures and produce solidarity.

Gayatri Spivak, a commentator of French feminism, has responded to these sorts of criticisms. She quotes from Antoinette Fouque: "Women cannot allow themselves to deal with political problems while at the same time blotting out the unconscious. If they do, they become at best feminists capable of attacking patriarchy at the ideological level, but not on a *symbolic* level" (1981:172). Although contemporary feminists can launch their critiques of autonomy and individualism, they do not question the linguistic categories and symbolic codes they employ. French feminists, however, have unearthed the deep structures of feminine repression in the symbolic suppression of woman's subjectivity, body, and desire in the logocentrism of western knowledge.

Spivak has shown the precise relevance of the repression of women's body to third-world women, many of whom in several countries undergo clitoridectomy. Symbolically, the construction of women as exchange objects, to be exchanged by men, required effacing the clitoris as an autonomous source of sexuality, independent of reproductive purposes and patriarchal control. And we remember how Freud prescribed the normal psychosexual development of women from clitoral to vaginal sexuality, from the active-phallic stage to the stage of passivity. Clitoridectomy, the effacement of the clitoris, can be real in some cultures and symbolic in the West. Spivak calls for a crosscultural analysis of how this uterine "economy" is accomplished.

Cixous and Irigaray seem to be saying that unless woman's unconscious is liberated from repression, unless women can authentically voice their own desire and pleasure, then all forms of political liberation will be to no avail.

Politically, *écriture féminine* implies the transformation of a "hom(m)o-sexual" culture, (Irigaray) the Empire of the Self-Same, (Cixous) based on sexual difference, on the alterity of a feminine libidinal economy—keeping in mind that this economy can be found in men who do not repress their feminine side. The terms masculine/feminine do not correspond to men/women, as ideologically conceived. Both Kristeva and Cixous have explicitly stated that feminine writing can be found in male avant-garde writers—Joyce, Artaud, Genet—who also seek to undermine phallocratic discourse.

But Irigaray and Cixous do not support gaining political and economic power or equality at the cost of repressing difference. For this reason, the politics of *écriture féminine* are sharply split from contemporary Anglo-American feminism; *écriture féminine* does not belong to the feminist camp in terms of identifying with the feminist movement of ideologically conceived "women" and its historical telos. Nor does *écriture féminine* seek to construct a "gynocentrism" or the reversal of phallogocentrism, another Hegelian opposite. According to Irigaray, we cannot leap outside phallogocentrism, nor are we outside by virtue of being "women" (1985:162). But we can practice difference.

The practice of difference is precisely in gender-reading of the master discourses—Plato, Freud, Nietzsche—in moving through the masculine imaginary to show how it has marginalized the feminine. The practice of difference occurs in *écriture féminine:* symbolic codes, punning, multiple meanings, lacking closure, and linear structure. The practice of difference, displayed in other modes of reading and writing, poses a direct challenge to "the very foundation of our social and cultural order" because it is directed to "all theory, all thought, all language" (Irigaray 1985:165).

But is this psychoanalytic/semiological analysis of the *repression* of woman's body, then, the explanatory lynchpin of other forms of material *oppression?* Must we look for a unifying cause or privileged dialectical starting point for the explanation of oppression? Will the material conditions of woman's lives be altered by a change in the dominant discourse? Irigaray seems to think so, but her critics do not. Yet, her Marxist critics, in their more orthodox orientation, forget that even Marx was not an economic determinist. Although he posited the primacy of the material realm of production and the social relations of production determining the superstructures of law, ideology, and culture, he also emphasized the dialectical relationships between these spheres in the course of history. It is not a linear cause-and-effect relationship. In each historical period, the critic may ask which sphere is *dominant.* Although Marx notoriously omitted the realms of discourse, language, and symbolism—and patriarchy—from the so-called superstructures, we can insert them and claim that, at this historical moment, the realm of signifying practices and the binary categories of logocentrism used to perceive our world, ourselves, and others are the dominant spheres in contemporary society. The hegemony of patriarchy is embedded in language.

CRITIQUE: ESSENTIALISM?

Judging by the critiques of *écriture féminine*, by American, British, and French feminists, *écriture féminine* has triggered an antiessentialist paranoia. I would submit that critics of French feminism are positively terrified by the prospect of otherness, which, however, becomes concealed in rather literal-minded misreadings of *écriture féminine*. Irigaray and Cixous have been criticized as privileging subjectivity over social change, of excluding men, of lesbianism, of falling into essentialism and a metaphysics of presence, *quand même,* and of ignoring the real material forms of woman's oppression and the concrete differences among women, depending on age, class, race, and ethnic identity. But, the issue of otherness is repressed (or resisted) in these theoretical critiques.

One example of resisting the thought of otherness will suffice here. Susan Suleiman, in a recent essay (1986), expresses some personal uneasiness with the theoretical implications of Irigaray's and Cixous's writings. She claims that their discourse excludes men and constructs an "absolute nature of opposition" (15) and implies a "separatist politics" (21), at least, for Cixous and Wittig. Yet Suleiman confesses: "On one level this may be merely a heterosexual bias on my part, or even a kind of fear, the heterosexual woman's fear of being contaminated by lesbianism?" (1986:22). In her own honest attempt to deal with her own homophobia, Suleiman conceals the real question at issue: the validation of feminine nonoppositional otherness.

What, then, are the implications of woman's differentiated erotic embodiment for feminist theory? Is it liberatory for women to own their pleasure? Does *écriture féminine* posit an essentialism: an ahistorical nature of woman; a definition of woman; a *natural* body and, therefore, innate differences between men and women? Does woman's erotic body, alone, make her radically other in all respects? Is that bad? Is not the body or our relation to our body also socially mediated, open to historical shaping? On the other hand, where or how may this discourse on the body suture gaps in feminist theory and repeal the silences in feminist theory?

Both Cixous and Irigaray reject any definition of woman, any representation or categorization of woman, any Platonic universal. "For, it is no more than a question of my making woman the *subject* or the *object* of a theory than it is of subsuming the feminine under some *generic* term, such as "woman" (Irigaray 1977:156). Writing the body, then, does not mirror a Platonic essence. But the charge of essentialism is broached in a different sense: a paranoid reaction based on what patriarchy has done to women, that is, reduced women to their biological or bodily difference. *Écriture féminine* is playing into the hands of the enemy—notwithstanding the valorization of woman's erotic embodiment—because it is a reductionist doctrine.

But the antiessentialist forgets that the body is a sign, a function of discourse, in *écriture féminine,* as I have already shown. There is no fixed, univocal, ahistorical woman's body as the referent of this discourse. Here, I think Mary Ann Doane's response to the antiessentialists is on target: for want of a stake, representation is not worth anything (1981:29). There is a risk, a stake, in writing the body in its specificity, in its autonomous symbolic representation. Is it fear of otherness?

Does *écriture féminine* succumb to what Monique Wittig calls "the myth of woman" or "woman is wonderful" (Wittig 1984:150)? Here I would submit that this kind of cultural essentialism might characterize the conservative feminist theories of Jean Elshtain (1981) and Carol McMillan (1982). According to both "neo-feminists," woman's body and its biological imperatives, reproduction and sexuality, must be clearly demarcated from the male realm of production and political life and described as essentially different but human natural processes. Both writers illustrate what Kristeva has called the repression of the female unconscious in unitary categories and binary forms of thinking: private/public; production/reproduction. McMillan, for example, describes the intentional and ethical structures of childbirth, but she never dwells on the erotic aspects of these forms of embodiment. To make woman's natural experiences parallel the male norm of rational activity in the public world, McMillan (Elshtain) have de-eroticized them. The charge of cultural essentialism is misapplied to *écriture féminine* because Irigaray and Cixous have critiqued these binary spheres as based on the repression of the feminine, of women's sexual difference.

In what ways can *écriture féminine* suture the gaps and repeal the silences in feminist theory? Socialist/feminist writings, although premised on patriarchal control of woman's sexuality and woman's labor as the causes of woman's oppression, are silent on woman's erotic embodiment. Because control of woman's labor is the fundamental tenet in socialist feminism, even woman's body is positioned as an instrument of labor in patriarchy. In Hartsock's recent essay (1983:299) woman's work is described as both mental and bodily or sensuous; in pregnancy, the body is an instrument of production. For socialist feminist theory, the structures of embodiment are subsumed under the primacy of the division of labor and mediated by economic, technological, and other historical factors. Woman's body is a *material* subject, but never an erotic subject of its own discourse.

Socialist/feminists claim that sexuality and desire, too, are social constructions; our relation to our bodies is shaped by social structures, including prevailing gender ideologies in their specific historical context. Whom we desire, what we desire, what we take pleasure in, are perhaps forms of learned behavior. We become *sexed* beings. French feminism surely does not deny this latter claim, for it has shown how woman's desire has been constructed and lived in a phallocratic culture. If female sexuality and desire were *only* the social constructions of a phallocratic culture, the sites of social power, there could be no undermining or subversion of them through what has been repressed. What positions woman's discourse, *parler-femme* or *écriture fémi-*

nine, is woman's psyche-body, her libidinal economy, always already the excess of phallocratic culture, of its discourse and power.

Perhaps, it is best to locate *écriture féminine* historically and subversively as Cixous suggests. *Écriture féminine,* speaking and writing the body, is really up against the signifying practices of a culture, its androgynous advertisements, television, films, pornography—all the images and inscriptions of woman's body that reduce it "homologous to a male speaking body," through fetishizing, fragmenting, and degrading woman's body. Against the dominant discourse, the male gaze, or the scopic economy, *écriture féminine* celebrates the radical otherness of woman's erotic embodiment. As such, it poses an enormous threat to the philosophical tradition of gender-free humanism and to the treasured ideal of androgyny, itself based on fear of otherness.

Culturally, this obsession with woman's body and the phenomenon of fear of otherness seem coupled in the projected ideal of androgyny, which may be interpreted as the most recent attempt to suppress feminine alterity in the embrace of equality. The androgyne is neither one nor the other, or it is both one and the other; but the "other" is always defined in terms of identity in difference. Most doctrines of androgyny posit some sort of synthesis of masculine-identified and feminine-identified traits or gender characteristics. Yet, the so-called masculine traits—for example, rationality, objectivity, autonomy—are precisely those historically based on the suppression of woman's body, desire and difference. On the other side, the so-called feminine or nurturing traits—for example, empathy, caring, emotional responsiveness— are the epiphenomenon of structures of male domination and suppression, the virtues of the oppressed. Furthermore, it is never specified what kind of "rationality" or "objectivity" would be produced in combination with feminine-identified nurturance and emotional responsiveness. Or vice versa. So, the ideal of androgyny only repeats the suppression of woman's sexual difference.

Despite the conceptual bankruptcy of the project of androgyny, the project proceeds apace on the bodily level, where the greatest resistance to androgyny may lie: in the facticity or concreteness of woman's body. If woman's body poses a concrete resistance to the androgyny ideal, it too can be reconstituted or remetaphorized through various cultural practices. Its matter can be reformed to obliterate its geography of pleasures. It can become a muscular "sleek," "hard," almost flat surface that mirrors a male body. Here various cultural practices—fashion, dieting, jogging, weightlifting—can be interpreted as technologies of control of the body, as reconstituting woman's body to shape a sexually indeterminate body, a gender-undecidable body(?) But, *écriture féminine* makes these signifiers of woman's body slip away, and the androgyne becomes another masquerade.

NOTES

1. It is arguable whether Kristeva should be classified as a French feminist, or even postfeminist philosopher, but she is surely not a proponent of *écriture féminine*. Kristeva takes the "feminine" to signify the semiotic realm, which breaks through and subverts symbolic codes, the Law of the Father. The "feminine" can then be found in male avant-garde writers who have not repressed their presymbolic or pre-Oedipal bond with the mother; it is not gender specific. But, Irigaray, by contrast, is concerned with opening up a discursive space whereby the representation of woman's specific sexual difference becomes possible. The specification of sexual difference has no relevance in Kristeva's work because Kisteva disconnects the "feminine" from "women." See *The Kristeva Reader*, 9–12.

REFERENCES

Beauvoir, S. de 1961 [1952]. *The Second Sex*. Trans. H. M. Parshley. New York: Bantam.

Culler, J. 1982. *On Deconstruction: Theory and Criticism after Structuralism*. Ithaca, N.Y.: Cornell University Press.

Cixous, H. 1981a. "The Laugh of the Medusa." Trans. K. Cohen and P. Cohen. In *New French Feminisms*, ed. E. Marks, and I. de Courtivron. New York: Schocken.

———. 1981b. "The Newly Born Woman." Trans. A. Liddle. In *New French Feminisms*, ed. E. Marks, and I. de Courtivron. New York: Schocken.

Doane, M. A. 1981. "Woman's Stake: Filming the Female Body." *October* 17:22–36.

Elshtain, J. 1981. *Public Man, Private Woman*. Princeton, N.J.: Princeton University Press.

Freeman, B. 1985. *(Re-) Writing Patriarchal Texts: The Symposium*. Manuscript.

Gallop, J. 1983. "Quand nos lèvres s'écrivent: Irigaray's Body Politic." *Romantic Review* 74:77–83.

Hartsock, N. M. 1983. "The Feminist Standpoint." In *Discovering Reality*, ed. S. Harding, and M. B. Hintikka. Dordrecht, Holland: Reidel.

Irigaray, L. 1981. "This Sex Which is Not One." Trans. C. Reeder. In *New French Feminisms*, ed. E. Marks and I. de Courtivron. New York: Schocken.

———. 1984. *Éthique de la Différence Sexuelle*. Paris: Les Editions De Minuit.

———. 1985. *This Sex Which Is Not One*. Trans. C. Porter. Ithaca, N.Y.: Cornell University Press.

Jones, A. R. 1985. "Inscribing Femininity: French Theories of the Feminine." In *Making a Difference*, ed. G. Greene and C. Kahn. London and New York: Methuen.

Kaplan, E. A. 1983. *Women and Film*. New York: Methuen.

Kristeva, J. 1980. *Desire in Language*. Ed. L. S. Roudiez. Trans. T. Gora, A. Jardine, and L. S. Roudiez. New York: Columbia University Press.

Moi, T. 1985. *Sexual/Textual Politics*. London: Methuen.

———. 1986. *The Kristeva Reader*. New York: Columbia University Press.

MacKinnon, C. A. 1981. "Feminism, Marxism, Method and the State." In *Feminist Theory: A Critique of Ideology*, ed. N. Keohane, M. Rosaldo, and B. Gelpi. Chicago: University of Chicago Press.

McMillan, C. 1982. *Woman, Reason and Nature*. Princeton, N.J.: Princeton University Press.

Rawlinson, M. 1981. "Psychiatric Discourse and the Feminine Voice." *The Journal of Medicine and Philosophy* 7:153–177.

Silverman, K. 1984. "Histoire D'O: The Construction of a Female Subject." In *Pleasure and Danger*, ed. C. S. Vance. Boston: Routledge and Kegan Paul.

Simons, M., and J. Benjamin. 1979. "Simone de Beauvoir: An Interview." *Feminist Studies* 5, no. 2:330–345.

Spivak, G. C. 1981. "French Feminism in an International Frame." *Yale French Studies* 62:154–184.

Suleiman, S. R., ed. 1986. *The Female Body in Western Culture*. Cambridge, Mass.: Harvard University Press.

Wittig, M. 1984. "One is Not Born a Woman." In *Feminist Frameworks*, ed. A. M. Jaggar and P. S. Rothenberg. New York: McGraw-Hill.

Young, I. 1984. "Pregnant Embodiment: Subjectivity and Alienation." *Journal of Medicine and Philosophy* 9, no. 1:45–62.

(RE)PRESENTATIONS
OF EROS: EXPLORING
FEMALE SEXUAL AGENCY

Eileen O'Neill

'Agency' can be defined as "the faculty of action." According to some views, what is essential to agency is that it involves intention; according to others, that it involves responsibility (Brand 1970; Care and Landesman 1968; Feinberg 1970; Strawson 1963). In either case, agency is a property of "persons". This latter concept, as it appears in contemporary moral, political, and legal philosophy, derives from the seventeenth-century liberal tradition. Sidestepping numerous philosophical issues, we can say that a person is an entity with rights and obligations, one held responsible for its actions and one toward which we act with a certain respect. The concept is normative, not descriptive. That an entity is a human being does not imply automatically that it is a person. (Consider how it is not obvious that fetuses, the mentally deranged, or the senile have all or any of the rights or the obligations accorded to persons; perhaps they should be treated as moral patients, rather than as moral agents. However, nonhumans, like Martians, might well be persons).

The agency of persons has been, and continues to be, examined in the spheres of ethics and politics. But the model of rights and obligations often seems inappropriate for a discussion of sexual practice. This is not to say, of course, that moral or political questions do not apply to dealings within our sexual life. It is just that there seems to be something amiss in grafting on to sexuality the models taken over wholesale from ethics, law, or politics. What is needed is a theory of sexual agency.

It probably will come as no surprise that such a theory is not immediately suggested by the endeavors of contemporary women artists. Nor is it an eyebrow-raiser that many individual works are simply polemics against existing views of female sexual potency—more accurately, of female impotency. Much of their art attempts to clarify the conceptual/political/personal binds in which women find themselves when they deal with their own erotic power and efficacy.

But it is here, in the problematics of woman as sexual agent, that I find a major focus in women artists' attempts at reimaging their own sexuality. In what follows, I hope to sketch various strategies with which some women alternately are playing with, assaulting, or pulling the rug out from under Eros and envisioning a goddess of their own making.

Let me begin by reclaiming the word 'pornography' and sketching its relation to erotica. In the liberal political tradition erotica generally is considered to be a milder form of pornography: the content is more suggestive than explicit, and it aims to produce some degree of sexual interest in the viewer rather than intense sexual arousal. But recently feminist theorists have attempted to draw the distinction along moral lines (MacKinnon 1985; Kittay 1983; Steinem 1980). On this view the erotic is that which has a content deemed more sensuous than lewd and which is apt to arouse sexual interest in the viewer—where we feel that such a sexual response is legitimate. Pornography, on this analysis, is a representation apt to arouse sexual interest because of the sexual illegitimacy of what is represented, and which endorses such a response on those grounds.

I think it indispensable to have a descriptive, morally nonjudgmental term that denotes sexually explicit representations that aim at arousal.[1] And 'pornography' has functioned in this way in our liberal tradition. But, in full cognizance of the difficulty that will meet any attempt to produce a nonfascistic notion of "sexual illegitimacy," I also believe that we need to be able to apply normative distinctions to the social and cultural institutions, practices, and discourses that jointly produce the meanings that attach to sexual acts. And pornography and erotica are just such discourses.

In response, I propose the following way of treating the pornographic/erotic dichotomy: I shall use the term 'pornography' to refer to sexually explicit representations that have arousal as an aim. A few of the works of women artists that I shall discuss are pornographic in this sense and cannot hide under the comfortable term 'erotic.' The erotic has a different structure.

In my view, which has been influenced by the work of French feminists like Luce Irigaray (1985) and most notably by Audre Lorde's provocative essay "Uses of the Erotic" (1984), the erotic is what "expresses" sexual arousal and desire rather than what causes them.[2] It is what suggests it, puts me in touch with its possibility, by making me aware of myself as a physical, sexual being. The erotic reminds me, as it were, of my very fleshiness and of my capacity for sexual pleasure. Erotica may cause sexual excitement, but if so, this is a further effect and not essential to it.

Think of music, an art form that does not represent anything but which has a range of expressiveness. Music may bring to mind sadness, light-heartedness, fear, or sexual excitement, though I need not become fearful, sexually excited, and so on. Notice that on this account explicit sexual content and/or intention to arouse will work against the expressive effect of eroticism. The more sexuality is graphically represented, the more likely its intent will be to sexually arouse (i.e., cause sexual excitement) rather than to "express" sexuality.

This view is consistent with the claim that the erotic can empower us in more place than just our beds. If Audre Lorde is correct, and the erotic can energize us in our work and struggle and can be a form of knowledge, then surely putting us into a state of intense sexual need or orgasm is not essential to it. When we are in the latter states we usually can barely see beyond our lovers. Eroticism is calm passion.

Finally, we can begin to see how the erotic can be used in struggle both personal and political. An inability to easily express various aspects of our sexuality via the words and images ready to hand illustrates the epistemological possibilities of the erotic. It can vaguely point to the gaps and voids, to the silences within our sexual discourses. In addition, on this view of the erotic it makes sense to speak of the "eroticization of pain." A tenor sax may express sadness and simultaneously eroticize it; through the music I am made aware of the possibility of sexual healing. To put this another way, the "lived-body" can revitalize itself in order to face long bouts of struggle by being put in touch with its own undeniable sources of pleasure within itself. Many works of women artists at which I have looked have this property of expressing, rather than representing, points of pain in their lives. And part of these works' eroticism is the concomittant healing and empowering quality.

I shall use 'obscene pornography' (and 'obscene erotica') to refer to pornography (erotica) that violates particular sexual customs or mores. Of course, the obscene is not subjective in the sense that it arises from ahistorically grounded preferences of individuals. Instead, what is found disgusting, offensive, or indecent will be relative to the value systems of particular groups or communities of interest within specific cultures at a given time. I do not find any of the works that I shall discuss to be obscene, but some are pornographic. This is a distinction that I want to draw.

Pornography and erotica that violate universalizable moral maxims about respect for personhood I shall call 'noxious.' This type of pornography (erotica) aims at sexual arousal (sexual expression) via represented (intimated) "harm" to a person—where this must be distinguished from "hurt." A doctor who removes an infected limb in order to save a life may cause hurt to the body, but (s)he does not harm the person. (This distinction between hurt and harm will be used in the third section when I raise some questions concerning lesbian S/M pornography.) Noxious representations, for example, might suggest that certain persons are really nonpersons, that they are creatures undeserving of the liberties and respect accorded to agents—conceived of in their social, political, moral, or sexual capacities.

Feminists like Rosemarie Tong (1982) and Eva Feder Kittay (1983) have used the expression 'thanatica' to refer to such pornography. I resist the use of this term for conceptual reasons. 'Thanatica' comes from the Greek for "death" as opposed to "life, lust, or joy." But death is not at all the same thing as harm or disrespect for personhood. Death can befall one without bringing about humiliation, loss of integrity, or damage to one's sense of identity. In many instances the prospect of death brings a sense of completion; death is imagined as a resting point to which one may look forward unparadoxically. Sometimes death is seen as a kind of sanctuary, a place of forgetfulness where the pain of life may be left behind. But the still point, the process gone full-circle, the unified whole, the retreat from the anguish of Being, these are traditional metaphors for eros as well. Especially after recently reading Marguerite Duras's *The Lover*, I would be hard put to disallow important connections between women's feelings about death and their own imaging of sexuality.[3]

But if harm is essential to the representations that violate our universalizable maxims about personhood, as Tong and Kittay seem to concede, then I think we need a term to mark this. I suggest 'noxious,' which derives from the Latin *nocere*, meaning "to harm."

A final point about both obscene and noxious pornography and erotica: They are not detected by a quick perusal of what is explicitly depicted in an image. Consider, for example, the painting, *The Broken Column* (1944), by Mexican surrealist artist Frida Kahlo. Its pictorial content is in some respects similar to that which I have seen in the magazine *Tit and Body Torture Photos*. But Kahlo's self-portrait depicts the pain she suffered as the result of a broken spine. In the context of Kahlo's artistic corpus, this work signifies the personal strength she needed to survive her painful physical existence. The obscene or noxious quality of pornography and erotica derives from its contextual meaning, not from the representation alone. Although it is beyond the scope of this paper to fully flesh out the notion of "contextual meaning," let me simply say that the meanings a viewer is able to attribute to an image will be a function of the viewer's beliefs about the production of the image, the manner in which the image functions aesthetically, culturally, and politically, and the ways it relates to facts about the world.

THE FEMALE NUDE

One major category of pornographic and erotic classical art in the West, perhaps its primary, has been the female nude. She was the object of the male artist's gaze, passive result of his active intellect and libido, creation of his subjectivity. And given the conventions of classical painting, the female nude, in most cases, was reduced to a "sexual object."

But, it might be argued, are not all nudes, including male nudes, objects for the spectator's gaze? How can a representation not be an object of possible perception? The only other option that seems open is for that which is imaged to be a subject. But that seems ridiculous. Let's pause for some clarification.

A painting, as a material entity, can be an object of perception. Many paintings, however, have a dual nature. They are not only things in and of themselves, they also have a "representational character"—they purport to refer to something outside themselves.[4] Paintings typically termed "representational paintings" are *of* something. The thing the painting is of (the purportedly represented entity, *qua* represented) also can be an object of our perception. For example, if I show you a picture of a tree and ask you what you see, you can either say "a painting" or "a tree."

But a further concept is needed before we can return to nudes. It is the concept of "representation-as" (Goodman 1968). When a painting represents an entity there need be no similarity or likeness between the painting and the entity. For a painting to represent an entity it is simply necessary for it to denote the object. Thus, one of Manet's sketches is a representation of Baudelaire's mistress because it denotes Jeanne Duval. I might want to say further that Jeanne Duval is "represented-as" a lifeless doll in Manet's sketch. What I mean here is that Jeanne Duval is denoted by the figure in the sketch, and that the sketch belongs to the classification of lifeless doll images.

Returning to our nudes, when I say that in classical painting the female nude is reduced to a sexual object, what I mean is that the nude women represented, or purportedly represented, in the paintings are represented-as sexual objects.

Kenneth Clark's distinction between "the naked" and "the nude" is relevant here (Clark 1956). The latter is not simply a bit of subject matter; it is a "way of seeing" and of celebrating the human form according to sets of historically specific formal conventions. The naked body is turned into an aesthetic object—it is turned into a "sight"—in the nude. This is true in the cases of both male and female nudes. The substantive question, then, still remains: What is the specific way in which female nudes are represented-as objects?

Classical male nudes, in their stance and gesture, generally convey a physical and sexual potency. What is more, these nudes often evoke a sense of religious and political potency (Walters 1979). For, the male nudes stand guard and express action in public space; they also are used to represent what some believe to be the most potent force of all: the Deity.

But notice that we cannot make a simple equation of sexual agency and visible activity. The body of Christ on the cross is characteristically rendered in a passive pose: a vertical supine position analogous to the lateral supine position of the traditional female nude. (Recall that 'supine' also means "indisposed to act or object; lethargic; passive." Yet the theological backdrop that, in part, gives meaning to the figure, makes it difficult to read this nude simply as a passive object for the viewer's delectation. Similarly in Michelangelo's sculpture, *Dying Slave,* we see the nude's arm posed in the submissive gesture of the classical Greek sculpture of the wounded *Daughter of Niobe*— a gesture that has come to signify female sexuality in traditional female nudes. Consider also the countless sleeping fauns and gods, male corpses, dying or tortured saints, martyrs, heroes, warriors, and athletes. Nonetheless, I would argue that in these instances the forces outside the control of the male figures explain the passiveness of the poses. To read these sleeping, dying, pained male bodies as per se passive is problematic at best. Although it is true, then, that classical male nudes, qua nudes, are displayed for the spectator (who, historically, has been presumed to be male), males characteristically are represented-as agents. And in those cases where they are not, other techniques are employed to intimate the agency essential to the male figure.[5]

The case of classical female nudes is quite different. These figures frequently are depicted in a private or fantasy space wherein their nudity is addressed to the male spectator. Their nudity, the placement of their bodies, their gestures, glances, and movements (if any) rarely express sexual agency. In fact, in classical European painting, woman's own sexual potencies are minimized precisely in order to enhance the feelings of potency and "power over" that the male spectator achieves in viewing the nudes.

For example, regardless of what we might take to be the demands of an erotic narrative sequence or a tableau of passion, female nudes are frequently contorted so as to offer frontal, or provocative side, or posterior views of themselves to the external (male) viewer. This is almost always the case in classical treatments of sexual exchanges between two or more women, and it is often true even in those cases where the image shows sexual exchanges taking place between a woman and a man. Of course, there are instances where the glance of the female figure remains within the space of the canvas. Sometimes it is focused on her male lover or on other male viewers within the represented space. And sometimes her body is arranged so as to make sense of the erotic interaction depicted. But, traditionally, the male spectator simply identifies with the lover or voyeur in such paintings, and through fantasy he once again visually possesses the nude.

Some specific conventions that circumscribed the creation of the female nude in classical art changed in the modern period. From at least Manet's *Olympia* on, the display of a generalized female form in a blatantly passive pose slowly begins to wane. Individualized, formidable women come to be depicted. But who are these women? Frequently they are studio models, femme fatales, and whores—women who are deemed at once threatening and powerless (Duncan 1977; 1982).

I have merely stated these claims about the female nude in classical and modern western art because, to my mind, they have been argued for persuasively by numerous art historians and social theorists (e.g., Berger 1979; Broude and Garrad 1982; Hess and Nochlin 1972; Parker and Pollock 1981; Walters 1979). Their detailed, historically grounded studies suggest that essential to erotic art in our tradition have been the images geared to male sexuality so as to enhance the male spectators' sense of potency. The changing personas of the female nude have been a function of the fluctuating economy of heterosexual male desires, fears, and needs.[6]

How, then, can a woman artist paint a female nude without merely providing a passive object for male delectation? One solution, which by now has a long history, is for the artist, the subject, who is about to depict her object of thought, to paint herself. In this way the nude is, in a sense, the subject. More exactly, the nude denotes the artist-agent. Joan Semmel has elaborated on this technique by giving us not merely nude self-portraits but ones literally from the artist's point of view. By means of this technique it is more difficult for the image to be seen as a passive object for the viewer, rather than as a reflection of the woman artist's subjectivity.

But woman's nude body has not been the only focus of erotic and lust-inducing art in the West; her bodily parts, or indeed any intimation of her body or parts, have also been central. Even woman's clothed body falls prey to the subject/object problematic.

Cindy Sherman, in her self-portrait film stills and photographs, has used clothing and disguise as both an erotic ploy and a way of questioning Cartesian subjectivity. The point here is not that Sherman is simultaneously both artist (hence subject or agent) and object of our gaze in the representation. It is that the scores of utterly different looking depictions of Sherman force us to ask: Which is her? Then: Is any really her? And finally: Is she the subject/agent generating these representations, or is she the composite result of the logically prior representations? In Sherman's work an unambiguous reference to the artist/agent disappears in the midst of a proliferation of representations-as: sex-symbol, coed, working girl, ingenue, and so on. The images entice us to say that if anything is denoted it is a female stereotype. As a paradigmatic case of postmodernist art, these images do not represent a particular woman but the problematics of representation itself. Consequently, the images are only borderline or quasi erotica. What seems to be given as a sexual offering is forthwith deconstructed.

Many of Meredith Lund's paintings also contain self-portraiture. But neither this feature alone, nor a polemical questioning of traditional representation blocks the viewer from reading the nudes as "represented-as" passive vis-à-vis his or her own desire. At first it would seem that the treatment of nudes derives from the modernist tradition: We are given individual women who stare self-possessively at us from the canvas. But our sense that we have completely grasped the signification of these figures (namely as nudes, at whom we can stare back) is thwarted by the virtually medieval organization of the artist's canvas.

Lund's work is an attempt to revision the world as it was before "the Cartesian masculinization of thought," as philosopher Susan Bordo (1986) puts it. It stands in opposition to the world view of detached observers, fixed in specific spatio-temporal locales, who gain access to the objective realm of external bodies or their painted representations. Here we have a medieval sense of relatedness to the world. The viewer is continuous with the represented objects, spirits, personages, and fabulous creatures, through elaborate layerings of allegorical signs and associations. Modern spatial, temporal, and causal relations partially give way to relations of metaphor and metonymy or more properly to the medieval relations of "convenience," "emulation," "analogy," and "sympathy" (see Foucault 1970). And in this world view, in which all things "express" each other and stand in relations of similitude, the viewer becomes just another sign in this sea of meaning relations. The gold paint, then, is a metaphor for gold ground space—a space in which figures are to be viewed *sub specie aeternitatis*. They may become objects of contemplation. But this requires us to conform our thought and emotion to them, rather than imposing upon them our appetites.

Lund's painting *Bathtub*, reproduced in O'Neill 1987, is paradigmatically erotic in the sense I have discussed. What we see is the slight contact of sponge upon knee, which expresses, through a variety of similitudes, the pleasures of the body: the soothingness of water, the sensuality of being sponged, the possibility of intimacy. There is a great tentativeness in this work, a precariousness, and a sense of sexual tension. Here we have the erotics of the possible.

In her *Woman On Cross* the pain of the woman, the artist, brings to mind another aspect of our fleshy essence: the shutdown of our erotic nature. This is expressed in the turned-in legs of the figure, the vulva closing in upon itself. However, we are also invited to see a woman in the aftermath of orgasm, evidenced by the still curled toes. Pain and pleasure, death and resurrection, caught up in the webs of "sympathies" and "antipathies" are yet again reflected through the relation of emulation in the sign of the cross. The work is a psalm of erotic healing.

In addition to the problem of women being represented-as sexually passive vis-à-vis the viewer, depictions of the female nude traditionally have reflected the underlying assumption in western thought of a nature/culture distinction. Woman has been associated with nature—that which is to be subdued, dominated, plowed, or fertilized by means of male physical power, technology, or sexual potency.

The paintings of Asian-American artist, Margo Machida, challenge this distinction and attempt to simultaneously assert woman's affinity with nature, and her sexual/political (i.e., cultural) powerfulness and dangerousness. *Watch and Wait* and *On the Alert* can be read as visual parallels to Susan Griffin's *Woman and Nature: The Roaring Inside Her* (1978). The dog or wolf heads are no mere phallic symbols; these are images of wildness and power that Machida reclaims for women. In the latter painting the artist's arms are bound; but this lack of control, this helplessness, is balanced by the erotic power that literally leaps out from her womb. This icon functions as a revolutionary call for women to ready themselves for the release of the potency within them.

It is important, in this context, to note the difference between Machida's nudes and most of the "dangerous women" and femme fatales that we have seen in much modern art. For we might well be able to imagine her nudes as expressing male fears of castrating females, or of Nature untamed. A crucial difference, as I see it, is that the figures represent the female artist. And this is not to say that representations of dangerous looking women provide us with a new image of eros if they are painted by women while they are just part of the old male bias if they are painted by men. What is new about Machida's nudes is the special combination: They are self-portraits, and they represent the woman artist as sexually and (as the title suggests) politically formidable. Through denoting the artist/agent, the agency of the female nudes can be combined with their representation-as erotically vigorous.

EROTIC (RE)PRESENTATIONS

After the nude, I suppose the second most common theme in traditional erotic or pornographic art is the depiction of sexual acts. Lee Stoliar's ceramic wall sculptures do not simply bring to mind our corporeality; they are erotica pushed nearer to its limits. These are explicit representations that aim at quickening the pulse; thus, they begin to approach the pornographic. In *One*

Figure 1. Margo Machida, *On the Alert*, acrylic on paper, 22 x 30", 1985. Reproduced courtesy of the artist.

of the Ways the question of who is active in heterosexual intercourse is reappraised. Here the male lover does not so much act upon the female, as he is enveloped by the embrace of the woman's legs, hands, and sex. The piece invites us to reconsider what sexuality, indeed what our world, would be like if the central metaphor for heterosexual intercourse were female engulfing rather than male penetration (Baker 1984). The design of *Getting It* follows from the premise, once again, of making clear female sexual agency. The man's head or brain, traditionally symbolic of what is essentially male, gives

77

Figure 2. Lee Stoliar, *One of the Ways*, terra cotta, 7½ x 9½ x 6¾″, 1986. Reproduced courtesy of Carlo Lamagna Gallery. Photo: Avenue B Galleries.

way for a view of the facial expressions of the woman active in lovemaking. *Calling It* captures sexual passion between two women in a way that has few counterparts in traditional male art. (Recall Courbet's *Sleep* or the cool poses of lesbians in many of Schiele's drawings.) And finally, in *Dancing It* Stoliar expands a traditional notion of eroticism that primarily is genitally oriented. The "it" that is gotten, called, and even danced in Stoliar's work is sexual energy.

This theme of breaking out of the single, genital locus of the erotic in order to adapt it to the female "sex which is not one," as Irigarary has put it, has been taken up by many women artists. For example, in the photograph of Darquita and Denyeta from Joan E. Biren's series, *Eye To Eye: Portraits of Lesbians* (1979) we are faced with the question: Why do we hesitate to call this passionate tableau of lips and skin, of nourishment and nurturance between mother and daughter, 'erotic'? And at the 1986 Women's Caucus for

Figure 3. JEB (Joan E. Biren), "Darquita and Denyeta," from *Eye to Eye: Portraits of Lesbians*, silver print, 8 x 10″, 1979. Copyright JEB (Joan E. Biren), 1979. Reproduced courtesy of the artist.

Art, Nancy Fried asked why her works were always read as lesbian scenes. For her, a lesbian artist, such works are about female physical intimacy—be it between friends, lovers, sisters, or mothers and daughters. Why are women hestitant to think of the whole range of these intimacies as erotic?

Consider Meredith Lund's recent painting, *The First Free Generation*. The representation of the artist/spirit on the right of the canvas leads us into a meshwork of signifiers. The figures on the left, which the spirit has painted, provide one gloss on the linguistic signs in the title: these are lovers or inti-mate friends of the same generation. But further reflection upon the title suggests that the figures may be of different generations; here we may have a mother bringing a daughter into a world at last free. The lyric eroticism in the facial expressions and gestures of the two figures is in no way under-mined by the layering of significations. On the contrary, the play of simili-tudes—particularly those of "sympathy" and "antipathy" between lover and beloved *qua* sexual partners, *qua* parent and child, and *qua* friends—requires us to consider the ways in which these distinct relations, in turn, "emulate" each other, reflecting the breadth of human sexuality. The analytical im-pulse to discover what is essential to *the* love relation is stifled in this erotic

Figure 4. Meredith Lund, *The First Free Generation*, oil and enamel on canvas, 72 x 64″, 1986. Reproduced courtesy of the artist. Photo: Avenue B Galleries.

palimpsest. (Interestingly enough, Lund's paintings are literally palimpsests; the surfaces of her works generally are built up out of multiple radically different compositions.)

The topic of anxiety or fear concerning sexual acts has been expressed in classical and modern western art by a particular range of visual metaphors: decapitation (St. John the Baptist, Holofernes), loss of hair (Samson), the *vagina dentata*, the vampiress, and the femme fatale, to name just a few. But the theme of rape, for example, is almost never treated from the point of view of the victim, nor is the anguish of a woman pressured into sexual service, nor the distress of a woman bound sexually and emotionally by her own internal sense of powerlessness.

Margo Machida, whose icons I discussed earlier, deals with many of these issues in her narrative, autobiographical work. In *Snapshots* a series of traumatic events in the life of the artist—psychosexual rites of passage—are depicted. The central panel of the triptych is a graphic image of male sexual aggression. The hand that will suppress, the penis that will penetrate, are seen from a point of view not identical to but certainly sympathetic with that of the victim. In *No Choice* Machida recalls her life in Hawaii, where U.S. soldiers expected to be serviced by local women. Here the female body, shown in all its voluptuousness, is literally up against a wall. A feeling of despair is expressed: to be heterosexually active in a phallocratic society is often to be a sexual servant. *Bird in a Cage* is an ambiguous and evocative work. The body of Machida lies vulnerably before us. But between her body and us are hands. Will these hands harm the woman? On closer inspection these are rather gentle hands. Perhaps there is no danger at all. Perhaps the bird in the cage is not the woman but the hands that may gently enter her. But finally, these hands may well be the woman's own, as they would be found placed under her head. Perhaps the woman constrains herself, holds herself back from experiencing her full sensuality. These musings remain open-ended. The painting asks us to consider the degree to which fear of our own sexuality comes from sources external or internal to ourselves.

Finally, in an oil on paper piece, *Seduced and Abandoned* (reproduced in O'Neill 1987), Barrie Karp depicts her rape several decades earlier at the age of thirteen. This example, like much of her work, contains an illusive tension: it is at once light, tender, and quiet, as well as wrenching and emotionally piercing. As both the title and the formal qualities of the painting suggest, this is an attempt to express the feelings of a young girl in the aftermath of her attack—a theme quite rare in western painting.

Women artists have been using a variety of strategies to question the conceptual distinctions which underlie the classification of sexual symbols in classical and modern art. These distinctions include the binary polarities of mind/body, culture/nature, active/passive, and reason/emotion, among others. In some cases, however, the artists have been reacting not so much to the usefulness of the distinctions, as to what Alison Jaggar (1983) calls "normative dualism." This is the bifurcation of mind and body and its attendant polarities along normative lines. As far back as Plato, the active mind had been deemed more noble than the inert body. And since that time, but especially since the rise of the New Science in the late Renaissance, this higher realm of "pure reason" had become the sphere of man (Lloyd 1984; Bordo 1986).

In her 1982–1983 performance piece, *This Is My Body*, Cheri Gaulke attempted to exorcize the misogynist meanings out of a number of Judeo-Christian representations. Performance, readings, music, and slides were used to illustrate and dialectically interact with the central text, Mary Daly's

Gyn/Ecology (1978), as well as other feminist writings. Following Daly's prescription, Gaulke journeyed through the value and symbol system of "God the Father." She became Christ crucified, Eve, the serpent, the tree of life, and finally a woman hung for practicing witchcraft. Through eroticized reenactments, she deconstructed her roles and ultimately danced upon their ruins. For example, in one part of the performance, Gaulke plays Eve in front of a projected slide of Hugo van der Goes's *The Original Sin* (1476). But this is an Eve who will not be shamed by her body and its desires. To the music of the Pretenders' song, "The Adulteress," Gaulke "gradually devours the apples with a sexual passion almost as though [she] were eating [herself]."[7] Later, when the artist plays Christ on the cross, in front of a slide of Antonella da Messina's *Crucifixion* (1475), she provocatively writhes like a serpent.

Through ritualized eroticization, Gaulke is able symbolically to break the spell of the hocus pocus of male inscriptions on the female body. She is freed by the end of the piece to dance ecstatically to matrilineal African music. Dressed as the serpent, the artist is now transfigured in gold and jewels. Gaulke has reclaimed the older, pre-Judeo-Christian signification of the snake—that of female wisdom and potency. This, then, is our body: knowing, powerful, dangerous, passionate, divine. Through the agency of ourselves as body, and not by its denial, woman is capable of transcendent experience.

The critique of western religious and secular symbols that are rooted in attempts to deny the female body and its desires has a feminist history of its own. Anita Steckel has been a visual pioneer of feminist sexual politics since the 1960s. In 1977, Steckel did a color xerox collage series, *The Journey*, in which the image of the artist's face is grafted onto the nude body of Woman. The artist/Woman, seated on a bird, flies to various places in western history where the female body has been forbidden. *Creation Revisited*, from the series, shows Michelangelo's rendition of the crucial moment, in the time before woman, when God the Father imbues the inert matter of man's body with life. Steckel inserts herself and Woman into this confraternity, as she soars with utter abandon between God and man. In a joyous, celebrational manner, Steckel provides a biting critique of western art and culture: How audacious of patriarchy to make the body of woman absent at this paradigmatic occasion of parturition. And women will not stand for this absence; they will fly in, cackling all the way. For only through our bodies, through sexual coupling with us, is man given life.

Steckel's *Giant Woman On the Empire State Building* (reproduced in O'Neill 1987) similarly depicts the artist/woman positioning herself with ease and utter abandon within the patriarchal landscape. Here woman takes hold of the phallic city, which is the source of her physical pleasure and the material means for her ability to paint the heavens.

But we must not think that Steckel is unaware of the dangers and problems that face women when they grab at the phallic sources of pleasure and power. In her painting, *Woman Looking Into a Mirror*, she uses a ubiquitous theme in classical and modern paintings of the female nude. But here the mirror is a penis. Steckel is really just using a metonymical device (penis for man) in order to express a familiar notion. Philosophy, the rational mind, and, by sexist extension, man constitute the "mirror of nature"—nature, of course, being a woman. Woman, then, sees herself and gains her identity through men. But this can put Woman in a bind, or more precisely in a corset. If she is not careful, the mirror will show her that her waist is not slender enough, her skin not smooth enough. Woman risks being bewitched by an image of herself that she in no way actively creates.

In her much earlier collage, *Solo*, Steckel deals sensitively with the tensions that heterosexuality pose for women in a sexist society. Here the symbol of woman as instrument of man's sexual pleasure is reconsidered. Clearly if this is a metaphor for sexuality between a man and a woman, there are not two persons engaged in sexual intimacy; there is only one. There is the man and an object that he uses to gain his pleasure. Thus, it is a solo performance. But in this work, the female presence, which by means of collage technique is the presence of the artist, cannot be erased. This is not a solo but a duet. Or is it? On closer inspection we can see that the hand holding the bow is the woman/artist's hand, not that of the male. The woman, via the body of man, performs acts of pleasure for herself. Whose solo is this? Steckel's image forces us to reconsider heterosexual agency.

In a corpus of otherwise largely abstract work, Chris Costan uses figures of eggs, teacups, fruit, and vessels in order to call into question gender symbols and, more specifically, the mind/body distinction underlying this system. In her color xerox magazine cover we see some classical and modern symbols of the intellect: geometrical forms (material approximations to the Platonic Forms), light bulbs, and devices for scientific measurement. But here these figures, traditionally designated as masculine, are bursting out of their "female" shells. Similarly, in her sculpture, *Container With Bulbs*, woman is presented as an "enlightened vessel." And in Costan's xerox collage placemat we get Judy Chicago's *The Dinner Party* with a twist. Instead of Chicago's vaginal images, the central image here is what emerges from the womb: a child's head, symbolic again of mind and intelligence. The womb is presented as a causal agent of rationality.

Bonnie Lucas's surrealist collages, which come out of the feminist art tradition of Miriam Schapiro and Joyce Kozloff, have focused on reappropriating and revaluing the symbols of female sexuality. In *Cut* the lettering for the word 'cute' is literally cut off, leaving just the letters 'c','u','t'. And the cut or slit that we are shown is constructed out of intricate layers of fabric and women's clothing, mostly underapparel. The bra straps, pink blouse, and silky panties are all reclaimed and made into a powerfully erotic image. For they lead us to a vaginal construction that is not cute, it is rich, evocative, and overflowing. The very physicality of Lucas's layerings invites us to slip a hand in here or there, to explore these hidden recesses of treasure.

On one level *Terrible Two* confronts us with the repression and binding of female sexuality as it begins to develop in our early prelatency stage, the "terrible two" stage. On another level we are presented with a vaginal image as erotically compelling as Louise Bourgeoise's *Femme Couteau,* although constructed out of what our culture deems to be girlish frippery.

(RE)PRESENTATION OF THE PORNOGRAPHIC AND PORNOGRAPHIC (RE)PRESENTATION

Like Lucas, Deborah Kruger's assemblages have a source in Schapiro and Kozloff, and they also focus sharply on feminist political issues. Her decorative 1984 series, *Crosses to Bear,* explores the degradation of woman's body as the reality that underlies the idealization and worship of it by culture and, especially, religion.

The background surface is composed of pastel paints applied over xeroxes of actual ads from hard-core magazines geared toward a male heterosexual audience. The crosses are composed of wallpaper strips and paint. The flowers at the centers are made from xeroxes of photographs of women's genitals, again taken from the hard-core magazines. Kruger's original intent was to show the degrading quality of these literal "cunt shots," as well as that of the written texts in the background. But she came to see the erotic potential of these images in the politicized context she had created. As reclaimed through the agency of the artist, via the formal qualities of the artwork, and the context of the display, the obscene and noxious pornography could be read as erotic and empowering.

Similarly we could conceive of portions of Tee Corrine's photographs in her series, *Yantras of Womanlove* (1982), as appearing in magazines devoted to obscene or noxious pornography. But the meanings of these sexually explicit images are transformed as much through the accompanying texts as technically through solarization and photomontage. Words and pictures combine to form a whole devoted to celebrating lesbian sexuality.

Of course, it would be an oversimplification simply to assume that the placement of an image in a context directed toward feminist or lesbian interests absolved it of all complicity with culture's view of woman's body as fetish and commodity. It is, I think, partly for this reason that many women photographers are reluctant to produce pornography—the material considered by many to have degraded woman's image most egregiously. I am quite sympathetic, yet I believe that women can be empowered by pornography, that is, by sexually explicit representations that aim at arousal. I have no neat solution to the general problem. But I do want to raise a few questions about a subset of women's pornography that has come under a particular form of attack: lesbian S/M photography.

The photographers Morgan Gwenwald and Honey Lee Cottrell, frequent contributors to a magazine called *On Our Backs: Entertainment for the Adventurous Lesbian,* have each produced a group of images for the book, *Coming To Power: Writings and Graphics On Lesbian S/M* (SAMOIS 1982). These photographs are pornographic insofar as they are images in a larger artistic work that aims, in part, at turning us on to lesbian S/M. For me, these images are not obscene. Nor do I think they constitute noxious pornography: they do not undermine the personhood of women. Because I know that this may be controversial, let me briefly hint at why I hold the latter view.

The book, *Coming To Power,* may well be describing the contributors' personal practices or fantasies, as opposed to the bulk of actual practice. Be that as it may, the type of S/M that the book attempts to represent through text and image constitutes a body of sexual practices in which woman is sexual agent through and through. This description is appropriate for not only the sadist, but also the masochist. On this account, the masochist acts out her sexuality, constructs scenarios, takes on roles, sets limits. The sadist also acts out her sexuality and takes on roles, but her activity alone dictates neither the scenario nor the limits. Lesbian S/M, then, is matter of the teamwork of female sexual agents. Set in this context, it is hard to read the images of the bound woman simply as a representation of a victim, as a sexual slave, as fetishized object. It is harder to read the code of whips, chains, and knives as one of "harm" to the personhood of women.[8] Some degree of physical hurt may be intimated, but this is quite different from harm to persons.

In no way am I suggesting that, even in context, these photographs have a single reading as images of female sexual empowerment. What I do want to say is that the photographs, in the context of the book, call for a reexamination of what constitutes a representation of harm to women or a threat to their personhood. Difficult moral and political questions need to be addressed concerning the eroticization of both power differentials and their parodies. In the process we will need to ask whether one and the same type of S/M act might be more readily read as play within lesbian practice than it would be when a man is acting as "top" to the woman as "bottom." (The aggressively wielded dildo can be a tool or a prop to be toyed with, tried on for size, as it were, and discarded; but a man has no such relation to his penis.) Similar

Figure 5. Honey Lee Cottrell, *Beloved*, black and white photograph, 8 x 10″, 1982. Reproduced courtesy of the artist.

kinds of questions need to be raised substituting racial, class, and age differences for ones of gender.[9]

FROM PAIN TO HUMOR:
THE SCOPE OF THE EROTIC

As several of the works I have discussed demonstrate, humor has played a key role in women artists' struggles with sexual (re)presentation. In the past, the humorous sometimes has been seen as antithetical to the seriousness taken to characterize the erotic. But this need not be so. Consider the photograph from the series, *People In Places Doing Things*, by Vicki Stephens. It is one among many of her erotic images of life as it is lived. And it is humor that, in part, both eroticizes the scene and draws our attention to its eroticism. Notice that the visual pun, provided by the lettering on the steps, largely gets us to look more closely at the position of the feet, and thus at passion at work. Here we have an erotic joke created by the tension between the strident sexuality of the text and the innocent intimacy of the bodily parts.

An eroticism of humor and tension, pain and healing, pleasure and fear, ecstasy and poignancy—in this essay I have attempted to open up some traditional notions of the erotic and pornographic in order to encompass the reimagings of some contemporary women artists, whose visions, in turn, derive from the reality of their own experiences. I am reminded of Luce Irigaray's words:

> (Re)discovering herself, for a woman, thus could signify the possibility of sacrificing no one of her pleasures to another, of identifying herself

Figure 6. Vicki Pearson Stephens, *Cummings*, black and white photograph, 4 x 8½", 1984. Reproduced courtesy of the artist.

with no one of them in particular, of never being simply one. A sort of
expanding universe to which no limits could be fixed and which would
not be incoherence nonetheless. (Irigaray 1985, 30–31)

NOTES

The original version of this essay was delivered at the Women, Art, and Power sym-
posia at Rutgers University (February 1986), sponsored by the Institute for Research
on Women. The paper profited greatly from the criticisms and suggestions of the
cospeakers, Joanna Freuh and Sandy Langer, and those of the executive officer of
IRW, Ferris Olin. I wish to acknowledge the students and faculty of the Parsons
School of Design, Le Moyne College, and Queens College, especially Lucia Lermond
and Barrie Karp, for their comments on revised manuscripts. I thank Martha Gever
for raising important questions about what it is for a representation to "aim at sexual
arousal" and about the social and cultural role that feminist erotic and pornographic
art *qua* art can and does play. Unfortunately these complicated issues have been beyond the scope of the present study. Most of all, I am indebted to the women artists,
whose work provided the initial impulse for the paper and whose reactions to my
views stimulated further reflection. Selections from the present essay appear in O'Neill
1987.

1. Of course the very notion of "sexual explicitness" is itself normative, as anyone
who has followed the pornography and censorship debates will know.
2. The notion of the "expressive" quality of erotica derives from a suggestion by
Antonia Philipps to the 1970 British Government Committtee on Obscenity and Film
Censorship. See an excerpt of this report in Copp and Wendell (1983).
3. I make these remarks in full appreciation of the work of feminists who have
shown the ways in which much heterosexual male pornography does tie the representations of sex, and female sexuality, to those of death. Still, I believe that a close
reading of these feminist analyses makes clear that the element of harm to persons
constitutes the "noxious" quality of the pornography. See, for example, Dworkin
(1981); Griffin (1978, 1981).
4. I say that all such paintings "purport to refer" rather than simply refer because it
is beyond the scope of this paper to address the issue of whether depictions of fictional
entities refer to (i.e., denote) anything.
5. There do seem to be some male nudes that resist my account. Several of Caravaggio's paintings, particularly his *Bacchus*, Perugino's *Apollo and Marsyas*, Michelangelo's *Athlete* from the Sistine ceiling, his *Apollo-David* sculpture, to some extent
Donatello's *David*, but most of all Girodet's nudes provide us with true examples of
the male body represented-as sexual object. In part, such a reading of the nudes is
made possible by the artists' use of traditional codes for female sexuality. For example, Michelangelo's athlete takes on the pose of the daughter of Niobe. In Girodet's
Endymion, the prone body is in a dreamlike space, twisted almost ninety degrees

to provide a full frontal view to the spectator; the arm is positioned à la the daughter of Niobe, and the head is thrown back exposing the neck in the manner of Ingres's *Roger Delivering Angelica*. These works demonstrate that there are alternative codings of the male body in traditional western art. I think it would be misleading to say simply that the canon as I described it earlier in this essay is a heterosexual coding of the male nude, but Caravaggio, Donatello, Michelangelo, Perugino, and Girodet make use of a homosexual system of signifiers. First of all, such an analysis would appear to depend upon anachronistically applying a contemporary homosexual/heterosexual distinction. I suggest that a thorough examination of how the conventions of the classical male nude relate to the variety of codes of male sexuality as they existed in ancient Greece, the Renaissance, the neo-classical era, and so on is needed. These codes, as they existed from the classical Greek period until the Middle Ages, are explored in Foucault (1978–). Compare Walters (1979). My discussion here has profited greatly from conversations with Terri Cafaro.

6. The work of feminist film theorists has also contributed to a better understanding of how ideology gets coded into artistic conventions. See the writings of Molly Haskell, Kate Millet, and Linda Nochlin in the journal *Women in Film* (1972–1975), and the articles, written throughout the seventies by Mary Ann Doane, Laura Mulvey, and other feminists, in *Screen* and *Camera Obscura*.

7. This is Gaulke's description of herself, as quoted in Raven (1986).

8. See Frye and Shafer (1978) for a partial analysis of "harm to the personhood of women". They carefully distinguish this harm from simple injury to women's bodies.

9. Given my understanding of "contextual meaning," however, the meanings that I ascribe to an image will be a function of not only the larger artistic work in which the image appears but also, among many other things, my beliefs about the world. Thus, if data about widespread, nonconsensual violence (e.g., assault, battery, rape) within the lesbian S/M community surfaced, they would certainly erode my confidence in reading the bound women in the images as agents rather than victims. But precisely my belief that, for example, rape (as opposed to partners jointly choosing to enact a fantasy of rape) is not typical within the lesbian S/M community but a common act men perform on women in our society, leads me to read lesbian S/M images differently from certain heterosexual S/M representations. My remarks here have profited from discussion with Lynne Arnault.

REFERENCES

Baker, Robert. 1984. "'Pricks' and 'Chicks': A Plea For Persons." In *Philosophy and Sex*, ed. Robert Baker and Frederick Elliston, 249–267. New York: Prometheus Books.

Berger, John. 1979. *Ways of Seeing*. New York: Penguin Books.

Bordo, Susan. 1986. "The Cartesian Masculinization of Thought." *Signs* 11, no. 3:439–456.

Brand, Myles, ed. 1970. *The Nature of Human Action*. Glenview, Ill.: Scott, Foresman.

Broude, Norma, and Mary D. Garrard, eds. 1982. *Feminism and Art History: Questioning the Litany.* New York: Harper & Row.

Care, Norman, and Charles Landesman, eds. 1968. *Readings in the Theory of Action.* Bloomington: Indiana University Press.

Chicago, Judy. 1980. *Embroidering Our Heritage: The Dinner Party Needlework.* Garden City, N.Y.: Anchor Books.

Clark, Kenneth. 1956. *The Nude: A Study in Ideal Form.* New York: Doubleday Anchor.

Copp, David, and Susan Wendell, eds. 1983. *Pornography and Censorship.* New York: Prometheus.

Corrine, Tee, Jacquiline Lapidus, and Margaret Sloan-Hunter. 1982. *Yantras of Womanlove.* Tallahassee, Fla.: The Naiad Press.

Daly, Mary. 1978. *Gyn/Ecology: The Metaethics of Radical Feminism.* Boston: Beacon Press.

Duncan, Carol. 1977. "The Esthetics of Power in Modern Erotic Art." *Heresies* 1: 46–50.

———. 1982. "Virility and Domination in Early Twentieth-Century Vanguard Painting." In *Feminism and Art History: Questioning the Litany,* ed. Norma Broude and Mary D. Garrard, 293–313. New York: Harper & Row.

Dworkin, Andrea. 1981. *Pornography: Men Possessing Women.* New York: Perigee Books.

Feinberg, Joel. 1970. *Doing and Deserving.* Princeton: Princeton University Press.

Foucault, Michel. 1970. *The Order of Things.* New York: Vintage Books.

———. 1978–. *The History of Sexuality,* vol. 1–4. New York: Pantheon.

Frye, Marilyn, and Carolyn M. Shafer. 1978. "Rape and Respect." In *Feminism and Philosophy,* ed. Mary Vetterling Braggin, Frederick Elliston, and Jane English, 333–346. Totowa, N.J.: Littlefield, Adams.

Goodman, Nelson. 1968. *Languages of Art.* New York: Bobbs-Merrill.

Griffin, Susan. 1978. *Woman and Nature: The Roaring Inside Her.* New York: Harper Colophon.

———. 1981. *Pornography and Silence.* New York: Harper & Row.

Hammond, Harmony. 1984. *Wrappings: Essays on Feminism, Art and the Marital Arts.* New York: TSL Press.

Hess, Thomas, and Linda Nochlin, eds. 1972. *Woman As Sex Object.* New York: Newsweek.

Irigarary, Luce. 1985. "This Sex Which Is Not One." In *This Sex Which Is Not One,* trans. Catherine Porter, 23–33. Ithaca, N.Y.: Cornell University Press.

Jaggar, Alison. 1983. *Feminist Politics and Human Nature.* Totowa, N.J.: Rowman and Allanheld.

JEB (Joan E. Biren). 1979. *Eye to Eye: Portraits of Lesbians.* Washington, D.C.: Glad Hag Books.

Kittay, Eva Feder. 1983. "Pornography and the Erotics of Domination." In *Beyond Domination,* ed. Carol Gould, 145–174. Totowa, N.J.: Rowman and Allanheld.

Lippard, Lucy. 1976. *From the Center: Feminist Essays on Women's Art.* New York: E. P. Dutton.

Lloyd, Genevieve. 1984. *The Man of Reason: Male and Female in Western Philosophy*. Minneapolis: University of Minnesota Press.

Lorde, Audre. 1984. "Uses of the Erotic." In *Sister Outsider*, 53–59. Trumanburg, N.Y.: The Crossing Press.

MacKinnon, Catharine. 1985. "Pornography, Civil Rights, and Speech." *Harvard Civil Rights-Civil Liberties Law Review* 20, no. 1 (Winter):1–70.

O'Neill, Eileen. 1987. "The Re-Imaging of Eros: Women Construct Their Own Sexuality." *IKON* 7:118–126.

Parker, Roszika, and Griselda Pollack, eds. 1981. *Old Mistresses: Women, Art, and Ideology*. New York: Pantheon.

Raven, Arlene. 1986. "Passion/Passage." *High Performance* 2:14–17.

SAMOIS, ed. 1982. *Coming To Power: Writings and Graphics On Lesbian S/M*. Boston: Alyson Publications.

Steinem, Gloria. 1980. "Erotica and Pornography: A Clear and Present Difference." In *Take Back the Night: Women On Pornography*, ed. Laura Lederer, 35–39. New York: William Morrow.

Strawson, P. F. 1963. *Individuals*. New York: Doubleday.

Tong, Rosemarie. 1982. "Feminism, Pornograph, and Censorship." *Social Theory and Practice* 8, no. 1:1–17.

Walters, Margaret. 1979. *The Nude Male: A New Perspective*. New York: Penguin Books.

THE USES OF MYTH, IMAGE, AND THE FEMALE BODY IN RE-VISIONING KNOWLEDGE

Donna Wilshire

Western epistemology is both hierarchical and pyramidal. This system gives some kinds of knowing more value than others, demeans some, and elevates one kind to a position of highest value and independence from the others. Science and philosophy strive to achieve and defend this ultimate, most desirable kind of cognition: objective, factual, Pure Knowledge.

This system needs to be rethought and re-visioned, for in my experience knowledge, or a healthy awareness of the world, comes from many kinds of knowing working together or taking turns, with no one kind ultimately more valuable than any other. Knowledge is, in a sense, like diet, for many food ingredients—vitamins, amino acids, minerals, proteins—must also all work together to provide us with proper nourishment. With knowledge, as with diet, each component or ingredient is essential to goodness; no one manner of knowing—not disinterested cognition, intuition, inspiration, sensuous awareness, nor any other—is sufficient unto itself to satisfy our need to know ouselves and the world.

The following is a critique of our traditional western theory of Knowledge and a format for revising this exclusive or Apollonic model into a field or matrix model that welcomes and esteems all forms of human cognition, even the primal ways of knowing of our Myth-making ancestors, ways that I feel are essential to acquiring a full store of knowledge.

MYTH AND KNOWLEDGE

Some current definitions and familiar assumptions:

myth: an ill-founded belief or story; legend; a false belief belonging to the dark, distant, superstitious past; fabricated, invented, imaginary; an *unverifiable* assumption (certainly not considered Knowledge).

Knowledge: what is known; publicly *verifiable,* provable, objective structure of reality (as in mathematics); facts, information; enlightenment; casts a light on a subject; the result of coming *up* out of darkness and ignorance (*low-down* things) into the light of Truth.

This model of Knowledge is at least 2,500 years old. In classical Greece it was epitomized by Apollo, sky deity, god of the sun and enlightenment, god of Reason. From that ancient time to this, this system has held Reason to be of *highest* value, for Reason is *up,* of the mind, ordered, cool, controlled, objective—all positive things, all associated with ideas, with maleness and Apollo[1]—and all lead our eyes and hearts *up*ward, "out there" as they whisper of ultimate achievement . . . holiness . . . heaven. Notice that value judgments frequently attend spatial assumptions.[2]

The opposite of Truth and Knowledge is, of course, *ignorance:* unknowing; being unaware; an undesirable thing; to be in darkness; a *lowly* (negative) state, to be avoided at all costs for it feels "fallen" and pulls us *down*ward, whispering of superstition, the occult, of taboo, of the unholy . . . perhaps of hell.[3]

Aristotle wrote that Reasoned Knowledge is the *highest* human achievement, therefore men (who he claims are more "active" and capable of achieving in this strictly mental area) are "superior" (*Politics* I, 2:1254b) and "more divine" (*De Generatione Animalium* [G.A.] II, 1:732a), a *higher* species than women whom he describes as "monsters . . . deviated from the generic human type" (G.A., I, 4:2, 767B5–15). He calls women "mutilated males," (G.A. II, 3:737a) "emotional," "passive" captives of their "body functions" and therefore a *lower* species, more like animals than like men. To him, a woman is not parent to the child; female bodies are mere vessels for male (the true parent) sperm. He sees nothing positive about women's life-giving wombs, nothing valuable about the feeding-nurturing functions of our bodies.

Aristotle's world is characterized by hierarchical dualisms—that is, polar opposites within which one side rules *over* the other; for him Soul rules *over* body, Reason *over* emotion, Male *over* female, and so on. For him, Pure Mind ("Nous," only possible for males) is connected with "divine" Soul, which is supreme of all earthly things. The male Mind is therefore *higher* and *holier* than all matter, even higher than the beloved Apollonian (ideal, male) body; certainly the male Mind and Reason rule over and are "more divine" than the female body because she (being ruled by emotions and body functions) is not as capable of Mind or Reason, and so on.

Later these same hierarchies appear in Aquinas, his rankings and rulings extending "out there" through nine angelic choirs, with Mind always having dominion over matter and bodies, which he considers innately sinful. The Great Chain of Being of the Renaissance was really a Chain of Command, a continuation of the ranking that put Pure Spirit "out there" on high, supreme over bodies and pure matter, which were demeaned by being "down below": God ruled over angels who ranked higher than men who ruled over women who ruled over children . . . over animals . . . over earth . . . .

The history of western civilization and philosophy is varied to the extent that each era stresses its favored, characteristic aspect of knowledge and its acquisition, but each era in this history has in common with every other era *the explicit devaluing of earth and body*—most especially the female body along with female-associated ways of knowing and being-in-the-world. Even Christians like St. Paul and St. Augustine, who despise pagan gods like Apollo, nevertheless continue to extol and keep central to their theorizing the hierarchical Apollonian dualisms that demean the human body, the *female* body being most especially sinful, Eve (and all subsequent women) being blamed for the fall of Man and for Original Sin, and everything else. Augustine's misogyny is often blatant, as in: "man is the image and glory of God," and therefore he "ought not to cover his head"; but the woman is "not the image of God" and "she is instructed for this very reason to cover her head" (*On the Trinity*, b. 12, chap. 7, p. 814), following Paul's lead from I Corinthians (11:7, 5).

During the scientific revolution Soul and Mind were still thought to be fulfillable only in males, still experienced as striving to conquer the *body*. Descartes ushered in the Modern Age describing the human Mind as Spirit that has nothing in it of matter or body. Like the ancients he associated the male Mind with divinity and Soul, defining Soul "by precisely and only those qualities which the human shares with God" (Bordo 1987:94), that is, having no matter or body. He added to the age-old list of powerful images aimed at disassociating the body from God by calling it a machine. Determined to remove his Self as much as possible from the lowliness of his body and its matter (matter from *mater*, the Greek word for mother), he labored in his Mind to disassociate himself from his own infancy and mother, "to give birth to himself" out of his own Reason-head (Bordo 1987:105) (just as Zeus had bypassed Mother Goddess Metis and birthed Wisdom, Athena, from his own head). Descartes and his times continued the classical attempt to extricate Knowledge and Reason from any bodily contamination, from Mother Earth and all things female, to totally free Logos from Sophia, man and his Mind from Nature, and so on (Merchant 1980).

Returning to the current definitions with which I began this essay, one sees that the more things change the more they stay the same, for the philosophical tradition *continues* to extol things culturally perceived as male (e.g., knowledge in the mind) and to demean and suppress things culturally perceived as female (e.g., knowing in the body). Note here, briefly but pointedly, that *maleness and femaleness in this context often have nothing to do with being a woman or a man.*[4]

Hierarchical dualisms—with their prejudice for Mind (i.e., maleness) and bias against body and matter (i.e., femaleness)—lie at the foundations of western epistemology and moral thought. These prejudices have become the core of our philosophical and scientific traditions and cannot easily be weeded out for at least two powerful reasons. First, the positive and negative *images* that go with our words and concepts, of male and female, are strong and have accumulated over millennia of use. They are an integral part of the sacred stories we have learned from childhood, the profane stories, the fables; they are part and parcel of the standard jests; the associated *images have become a part of the way we think.* Second, *sexist value judgments are inherent in the very words we use.* The tradition must finally be seen for what it is: intrinsically one-sided and partial. And therefore its claims to Knowledge must be labeled a *myth,* meaning "an ill-founded belief or story." Let me detail some of its presumptions and failings as I experience them.

The following columns of basic words contain many of our thought system's core dualisms. You will recognize key words from the definitions of *myth* and *Knowledge* I cited earlier. The columns reveal clusters of meanings, spatial assumptions, and the misogyny of both the words and the system. They expose value judgments that have unnecessarily brought about human alienation from self, other, and planet and that have disastrously limited what we think is desirable and worth knowing.

KNOWLEDGE (accepted wisdom) / IGNORANCE (the occult and taboo)

higher (up) /	lower (down)
good, positive /	negative, bad
mind (ideas), head, spirit /	body (flesh), womb (blood), Nature (Earth)
reason (the rational) /	emotion and feelings (the irrational)
cool /	hot
order /	chaos
control /	letting-be, allowing, spontaneity
objective (outside, "out there") /	subjective (inside, immanent)
literal truth, fact /	poetic truth, metaphor, art
goals /	process
light /	darkness
written text, Logos /	oral tradition, enactment, Myth
Apollo as sky-sun /	Sophia as earth-cave-moon[5]

KNOWLEDGE (accepted wisdom)	IGNORANCE (the occult and taboo)
public sphere /	private sphere
seeing, detached /	listening,[6] attached
secular /	holy and sacred
linear /	cyclical
permanence, ideal (fixed) forms, "changeless and immortal" /	change, fluctuations, evolution,[7] process, ephemeras (performance)
hard /	soft
independent, individual, isolated /	dependent, social, interconnected, shared
dualistic /	whole
MALE /	FEMALE[8]

The discussion that follows seeks to redeem all words and concepts in the right column of the above list, to reclaim as valuable the idea of the body as knowing,[9] to reclaim female-associated things that were anciently, unfairly relegated to lowly status. Much of what I am doing can be called "valorizing the female," but I am actually seeking to make *human* experience whole by reclaiming the value and knowledge in the *human* body, in human emotion and sharing—the value in everything in the right column, the value in things perceived as unmanly and therefore unworthy for three millennia. But these things were so judged by ancient patriarchs, not by me. I will demonstrate how such things as long-derided "ignorance," "taboo," "low-down," "subjective," "private and inside" things—right down the list—can enhance and enrich the search for truth and knowledge.

A feminist vision of knowledge must not continue the dualistic *either/or* PATTERN, so I will not eliminate or devalue any items in the first column. I am suggesting a nondualistic *both/and* PATTERN of utilization, in which items in both columns either cooperate or alternate just as one can alternate one's focus between the field and the ground of a graphic or see both together easily and at will. Rather than choosing or demeaning one column or the other, I suggest we mine the *warmth* of women's experience and ways of knowing (*dark, interior, female* wisdom) as well as the *cool, bright* en*light*enment of public, male Apollo-Logos.[10]

As I go down the second-place column reclaiming its concepts, I will show that primal Myth, far from being synonymous with superstition and backwardness, is a vital, positive force and can open doors long-closed on the riches of the so-called "female" perspective (Lauter and Rupprecht 1985). Unlike the heroic myths that made an appearance after the politically-instigated Archetypal Reversals of the late Bronze Age,[11] primal Myth exposes a way of thinking and being in the world that dissolves dualisms, neutralizes coercive hierarchies, and puts some old taboos (especially about women's blood and bodies with their dark interiors) into new and positive frameworks, creating exciting possibilities for the future, for knowing about our human nature, and for revealing a more accurate (nondualistic) view (PATTERN) of the world we live in.

I will argue that the method and subject matter of primal Myth correctly understood, *not* as defined by the western scientific tradition, is synonymous with and indispensable to the feminist quest for knowledge that I wish to foster. This feminist quest seeks to validate the social, bonding, community experiences, for therein lie the highest human values and the solution to alienation for all of us on this planet. Thus, individuality must be seen as properly manifested only within a sharing community, the individual's quest being not to become top dog or ruler over others but rather to acquire wholeness and an ecological balance, an interconnectedness between the fully developed individual self and all other forms of life.

We can discover from Myths much about how such things were an integral part of the lives and world views of our earliest human ancestors. Mircea Eliade (1971), among other scholars in the field, shows how Myths reveal profound universal truths,[12] describing what all humans share rather than what individuates and isolates us from one another (Gebser 1985). An integral part of the knowledge revealed when Myth is properly interpreted is that the meaning of life for its tellers was in wholeness, in interconnectedness, and in a cyclical experience of time—not in dualisms and not in linearity. From Myths of the distant past come examples of human attitudes toward the earth, nature, time, women, and women's bodies (all interconnected) matching those attitudes that many feminists and ecologists, like myself, now struggle to create for our present and future. The techniques of Myth making are available to us to help us discover and describe how such things can function profitably in our lives today.

Traditionally it is claimed that only knowledge from a *public* place can be verified. But some of the knowledge in primal, archaic Myth, created from *private* places like dreams and women's bodies, can be communicated and understood across vast geographic distances and cultural differences—with the creators separated from their modern audience by thousands of years.

The ancient wisdom of Myth is, unfortunately, locked in code, hidden from most modern readers. Although the words are recognizable and seemingly intelligible, the value escapes us. Myth, like our dreaming, uses the symbolic language of *Image* and *Metaphor* (from the debased column above) to reveal its truths, rather than the language of *Literalness*, which is the only language we expect and respect in this age of mathematical and scientific exactitude. A different consciousness, a change in mental focus away from the literal, is required to unlock the meaning of Myth. Only a nonliteral, dilated consciousness can read Myth's Images and Metaphors.

One kind of consciousness, one focus, is sharp; it narrows our attention to one point in the way of traditional science and epistemology, indeed one of our valuable human skills. Another kind of consciousness is our less appreciated ability to unfocus—to utilize our peripheral vision, to widen out to include many ideas and images *all at once*—the same way the eye's iris narrows its focus for certain feats of seeing and widens for others. These two essential, valuable methods should not fall into the either/or PATTERN of dualism. Both are good, acceptable, usable behaviors. We must learn to treasure and utilize at appropriate times the technique of widening and blurring the mental field of vision so that it does not focus on any one thing, not even on what is straight in front. Called "splatter vision" by trackers, this is an essential skill in the wilds where one must constantly be alert and guard one's safety by attending to the entire surroundings, not focusing even on the place where one will step.[13] Among many other uses for such a consciousness psychologists have devised a technique for problem solving called the "Aha!" experience; it utilizes being temporarily out-of-focus and in-ignorance to move one from "controling" the status-quo to "allowing" change, the "allowing" attitude enabling one to move from an insoluble difficulty onto the edge of discovery. These untouted skills, from the list's right column, are valuable for knowledge gathering and necessary for perceiving the overall PATTERNS and knowledge lodged in Myth.

This other kind of consciousness, the kind that does not focus on separate details and always opens up to a wide spectrum of data all at once, belongs to art and science (Heisenberg 1970) as well as to Myth, and mothering. It is very much like the mental activity of a woman who is tending to sewing and hearth while simultaneously listening to a friend, watching the clock, planning dinner, and minding the children. This inclusive method of minding—whether its tasks be those of homekeeping or science—does not deal with isolated data. Instead it looks at the data all together *in situ,* in the surroundings in which they naturally occur. Neither does the minder exert great control in assembling and selecting the data. Rather, she sets up her field of minding deliberately as broad as possible in order to receive—to *allow* all that *spontaneously* presents itself (chosen and unchosen) to come into the picture. And even then, rather than analyzing or focusing on any details assembled in the clear light, the minder *looks through them.* The minding, the consciousness, is aimed beyond the facts into the murky darkness and uncertainty; concentration is on the misty, fuzzy, unfocused disorder of the collage, attending without prejudice to the chaos it temporarily presents, letting the assemblage form itself into its own PATTERN. When its own PATTERN emerges, the seeker-of-knowledge will know then and only then the proper questions to ask in order to produce an effective interpretation or answer. By contrast, in the pursuit of the more conventional methods of scientific investigation it is possible to focus on isolated data to such an extent that the seeker-of-knowledge loses sight of which data are truly worth investigating.

Like the tracker who hopes someday to see a bear and therefore must wait in the wilds (in the chaos?) for a bear to present itself, the deliberately unfocused thinker positions herself within the assembling information, waiting unhurriedly for an unforced understanding of the large picture to present itself. She waits uninflated, without ego, without control—content to be in ignorance for an unspecified time, willing to be not-knowing until the elusive essential PATTERNS appear in their own good time. Although ignorance and lack of control are not part of the "accepted wisdom" of our times, deeper wisdom recommends a place for them in a full human epistemology. Sensible, mindful, thinking people have always known that sometimes worthwhile knowledge is vague, unclear, subterranean. And because there are uses for such knowing, there must also be room, recognition, and respect for it.

The knowledge in Myth is often expressed in an abundance of inexact, constantly shifting, seemingly illogical metaphors. Myths, like dreams, follow a meandering thread. But if one is willing to stick with the script until the larger PATTERNS begin to fall in place, the images of Myth will begin to make sense. Admittedly, it differs from the kind of sense we are used to because Myth, like modern physics, has no unbending obligation to logic (Heisenberg 1970). It is PATTERN—overall PATTERN and ever-recurring cycles—that myth seeks to reveal. In the PATTERNS lie Myth's special kind of truth and knowledge.

A Myth's Image is most often that of a deity, but the divinity, the sacred Image, always represents fundamental PATTERNS and Principles, not Personhoods. It was the PATTERN and the Principle that was seen as divine and immanent in Nature. But a deity was not a Person; a deity was the Image of a PATTERN exhibited within the *anima mundi* that governed the workings of the universe.[14] Herein is a significant difference between transcendent (Person) deities, like Yahweh, and immanent (PATTERN) deities (Eliade 1971), like the Great Mother Goddess. This difference results in totally different kinds of worship and holds one important key to understanding Myth, thus, I suggest it for a feminist epistemology.

The divinity within the seed is a good example of this immanence. The earliest inventors of agriculture, most likely women (Boulding 1976:97–114), were able to plant crops because they discovered the dead seeds had the innate power to be Born Again—and therefore must be divine. So that people could celebrate and speak intimately about the divinity in the seed, they gave it a humanlike form and a name. Archaic Greeks called the Divinity-within-seeds "Kore, daughter of Mother Earth . . . Kore, She who is born out of De-Meter's womb, the Earth." Kore, called Persephone by later Greeks, was the personification of the divine creative power within the seed and had no raison d'etre, no importance, no Personhood or story or biography in earliest times other than as that simple personification of the seed. But all who participated in the religious rituals of Kore understood that the divinity was *within the seed*, and that Kore was *not* a Person existing in Her own right with any Her-story separate from the seed.

By the time of Homer in Greece and Moses in the Near East deities had become important as Persons, laying claims to individualistic feats and personalities; but their descriptions and myths resembled heroes and legendary adventurers more than the universal PATTERNS of primal, archaic Myth (Kerenyi 1975:42–43). These deities' achievements in their own Persons as individuals made them different from ordinary people and nature, whereas Myth tells of what all people, nature, and deities share with each other. The areas of jurisdiction of heroic deities were separate from their Persons and often only incidential to their nature. For example, the three sons of Kronos, Zeus, Poseidon, and Hades, acquired their various jurisdictions (sky, sea, and underworld) only after winning a war with their father. But none of them had from conception an essence innate to the realm he eventually acquired in the spoils of war, as Kore (Persephone) had.

Kore *was* the Seed, Child of the Earth, born and reborn from Earth Mother's womb. Period. From the beginning. She did not acquire seeds as Her jurisdiction later on. Life, Kore, Seed—each was identical with the divine, eternal cycle.

Keeping any distinction between past and future at a minimum (any dualism at a minimum), our early ancestors perceived themselves and all things as divine and as cycling eternally from birth, death, to rebirth. And they personified that eternal PATTERN, that cycling Process, as "The Great Mother Goddess who gives birth to all the universe and all life out of Her Cosmic Womb." She gave birth to the earth itself; then, once the earth was in existence, earth and its caves became an extension of Her cosmic womb out of which was born the sun on Winter Solstice, as well as the animals, people . . . all of Her creation. The earth was the Mother's body out of which we are born and to which we return at death (by burial) for rebirth, just as the seeds when dead are returned to (buried in) the earth whence they receive the gift of rebirth from Her body and are born again in the eternal divine cycle of birth-death-and-rebirth. The Mother's body, the earth, was perceived both as the womb out of which we are born and the tomb into which we are buried—that automatically again is the womb out of which we are reborn in the unending cycle. *Both* womb *and* tomb. Not either/or.

Sometimes our ancestors perceived the form of life as continuing unchanged through the cycle of birth-death-and-rebirth—as with, say, a pomegranate that dies (goes to seed) and is reborn again as a pomegranate. But earliest humankind also witnessed forms of life in flux, one form constantly becoming another in magical transformations—forms flowing, interchanging, intermingling, one into another. The vulture ate dead fish, transforming the fish into vulture (rebirth in a different form), leaving the bones to be transformed by the divine work of the Mother as Wind, Water, and Weather into soil (rebirth of fish and beast into still another form), then soil into plant, and plant into animal or human, and so on. Each transformation, each stage of the cycling from death to rebirth-into-another-form was seen as equally important, equally valuable in the overall scheme or cycle of life in the universe. *Our long-ago ancestors did not need to anticipate being reborn as human. To them there were no ideal forms, no fixed forms; no one form was perceived as closer to deity or "more divine" than any other.* The deity was immanent in all forms. Divine PATTERN was in the common cycling; the PATTERN itself was the ultimate divinity. Such a vision of the holy working in nature has within it an ecological respect for all nature that the earth would surely appreciate at this moment in history in linear time.

The PATTERN of birth-death-and-rebirth was itself divine—*and Female.* Birth and rebirth were seen as its primordial essence, the core of the PATTERN, and recognized as the significant and distinguishing characteristics of "female." The dictionary's minimal definition of "female" is that sex that gives birth or lays eggs or divides parthenogenetically. The Goddess had within Her nature the characteristics of all to which She gave birth; hence, because she gave birth to sons and daughters, She Herself had to be Male as well as Female, just as She was also Tree, Stone, Sea, Bird, and so forth. She was bisexual but never It. She was always She—thought of at base as the Primordial Female, as Primordial Mother and Creatrix.

Care must be taken not to think of the Great Mother Goddess literally: as a big birth-giving Woman "out there" somewhere. The personification of a Mythic or divine PATTERN comes out of immanence and metaphoric thought. Thinking of these divine Images as "out there" to be taken literally reduces them to masquerade; interpreted literally, the images become too individual or specific—too trivial, even if heroic—to speak profoundly, universally, and with impersonal truth about the nature of the world and all humanity, as the Metaphor of Myth can.

Literalness/Metaphor. In traditional epistemology one of these two languages is privileged; only one is acceptable for determining knowledge. But *both* the literal and the metaphoric are true and have value for knowledge. *Both*, not either/or. The language of Literalness is good for logic and sometimes for mathematics, and Apollo is a metaphor and Image for its values. The language of Metaphor, on the other hand, does not translate into logic, but it is good for many tasks in science as well as for translating Myth and its subject matter of wholeness, universals, and what people share. I will now examine the Metaphor-Image of the Great Mother deity to find the knowledge in it.

RE-VISIONING KNOWLEDGE
THROUGH FEMALE IMAGERY

Archaic deities were *imaged* Metaphors for the perceived essense of timeless, sacred Principles and PATTERNS. It is, however, not appropriate to say the Goddess was "*merely* a metaphor." Mary Daly is emphatic: "When I say 'metaphor' I mean something tremendous!" [15] And James Hillman writes that the importance of deity as Metaphor and PATTERN cannot be overstressed: "An archetypal image operates like the original meaning of idea (from the Greek *eidos* and *eidolon*): not only 'that which' one sees but also the 'means by which' [the PATTERN through which] one sees" (1983:12). In other words, the Images of archaic immanent deities ("What-is-seen") always included the world view the worshipper brought to the seeing. The Image appeared as a sacred "What" to the Neolithic worshipper who saw it as a manifest Divinity; "what" the same image is to one of us viewing it today as an unendowed, secular object is quite different. When the worshipper saw the Image, it was seen to have "immanent" in it something of the Divinity she or he believed it contained. The worshipper looked *through* the Image and saw on the other side certain "truths" that typified the PATTERN they believed made the world go round . . . cycle.

Specifically, the Image of the Goddess is a "What-is-seen." But Her worshippers saw not only the "What" of Her statue or Image, they also saw and understood the cyclical PATTERN She embodied (whether a circle or spiral was a part of the Image or not). For She personified a gestalt, a whole cyclical world view, the PATTERN or "means-by-which" Her worshippers experienced the entire world. [16] Always immanent to the Image was a perception of the whole eternal cycle of birth-death-and-rebirth in which all forms of creation were "seen" to be eternally turning and evolving, all equally divine and important. Part of the "What" of the Image they saw was the idea of the Female Body as divine. Through the ubiquitous Image of the Goddess they experienced the Female as Primordial Creatrix. They "saw" in Her Image the idea of Wholeness and Cooperation as the PATTERN shared throughout the universe—in both the macrocosm and the microcosm.

The Myth says: "Demeter gives birth to Kore." What is the profound truth in that? Let's see. First, we know that this is a Metaphoric way of speaking about *something perceived to be universal* (see note 12). We know the Image of Demeter is the Mother Goddess whose womb is the Earth; and the Image of Kore is young girl, Demeter's divine daughter, the Seed. The external present tense of the Myth—"Demeter *gives* birth . . ."—means this event goes on now, always has, always will, now and evermore, cycle without end; it relates an unending universal truth.

Knowing that the Mother Goddess was conceived as a trinity helps us decipher the Myth; her three divine Persons represent the phases of women's lives—Kore, the young Daughter; Demeter, Mother and Queen of Heaven; Persephone, the wise old Crone and Ruler of the Underworld and Death. It also aids understanding if we realize that Kore later came to be known as Persephone. Persephone, in archaic times, was the Death Goddess of the Under-Earth, which was to Her worshippers a womblike place of healing and rebirth, the vessel out of which came Creation. As you can see, the three seemingly distinct Persons in the trinity of the Mother are actually inseparable, all connected, mixed up, and cannot be neatly categorized or cleanly distinguished from one another. The trinity is One—a Whole. Kore, the Seed, died and was buried (planted) under the Earth (in the womb of Death Goddess Persephone) where the Seed came into contact with (became One with) the deep, dark, magically transforming powers of Her Mother's Body the Earth. And out of that sacred Womb place Kore the Seed came to life again, She rose from the dead, She was reborn! When we seek en*light*enment and shun the darkness, we might remember that most forms of life—even ideas— require "close and holy Darkness" in which to germinate and gestate before they receive the gift of life. It is testimony of our ancestors' deep conviction that Death is but a transformation into further life to learn that even Persephone (Death Herself) eventually cycled and became "the newly reborn," the Daughter Herself.

Our age sees the normal desirable human life span as linear. The Myth tells us that archaic peoples saw the normal desirable human life span as cyclical. Kore and Demeter and Persephone, the evercycling Trinity that represents the eternal PATTERN of birth-death-and-rebirth, em*body* their believers' philosophy that in cyclicalness is universality and therefore the meaningful, eternal life, but that what falls into linear or individual time will end when it dies, for it is profane and insignificant and will therefore not be reborn (Eliade 1971:35). Kore and Demeter and Persephone. The cyclical PATTERN or world view comes to us as embodied in the Images themselves—an immanent, integral part of those Images. The Mythic Images contain both a "What" *and* a PATTERN, that is, the "means-by-which" or the "way-in-which-the-What-was-seen."

As various writers have pointed out in various ways, this is the way that all people make sense out of their world—today's scientists and philosophers as well as our Myth-making ancestors. All of the "whats", all descriptions of "that which is seen"—whether in a scientific or a Mythic system—all contain the assumptions of the PATTERN *through which* they are seen. All the "whats" described by science and philosophy, all of those supposedly objective truths, have been determined by the point of view, the world view, the PATTERN *through which* the observer has been looking. Every human carries within her or him the PATTERN through which she or he sees the world; the PATTERN—the describer's (subjective) world view—will always be inseparable from "what-is-seen." So there really cannot be such a thing as "an objective reality" "out there" with one and only one correct description made by a detached observer, as the accepted wisdom of the West has claimed. Although objectivity has been the sacrosanct, one-and-only valid stance from which to acquire knowledge, one branch of our tradition from time immemorial has been impelled by the urge to "know thyself," which is a subjective quest, surely. It becomes an impossible quest, prima facie, when we limit epistemology and our notion of what is good to the realm of objectivity.

There are many already-existing models for the new science and epistemology I propose. One is Barbara McClintock's work on the genetic structure of corn seeds, research that beautifully exemplifies the way of Myth as the way of Science. Interestingly, Persephone was not just any seed; She was specifically the corn seed. I am reminded of our early foremothers and their belief that divinity (Knowledge) is immanent in nature and how that led them to discover that seeds can be reborn. When doing her revolutionary experiments, McClintock abstained from the traditional scientific, legalistic, pharisaical method: that determines objectively with one's detached mind what the rules of science are and then superimposes them on one's work. Instead McClintock became emotionally involved with her corn seed kernels. She listened and watched patiently, without ego, letting the corn reveal itself to her, "allowing" what was immanent within the seed kernel to teach her about itself. She imposed no preconceived notions onto the PATTERNS the corn exhibited. Rather, the corn told her what its Nature was; she, having her ears open, heard (see note 6 regarding difference between seeing and listening).

The revolutionary work in physics that went on at the Max Planck Institute in the 1920s (Heisenberg 1970), resulted from the observation that the usual understanding of "objective reality" and "detached observer" as *separate* notions was incorrect and that such an idea caused fundamental problems in doing science.[17] The apparent contradiction dissolved when these notions were conceived of as *not separate;* rather, the physicists said, observation is an *event,* or *process of change,* in which "observed" and "observer" are united, and in which the PATTERN imposed by the "observer" plays an essential role. To attain this quantum-physical way of understanding events, physicists had to explore and accept radically new ways of knowing—a new epistemology. For "quantum" does not refer to isolated facts. "The word 'quantum' refers to a whole amount of something. Thus, the body quantum refers to a whole amount of something important governing the whole human body. That something is consciousness . . . [which] acts in a quantum manner inside our bodies" (Wolf 1986).

Werner Heisenberg and Niels Bohr have written that what happened in the discovery of quantum physics *united the methods of science and art,* an important statement about their perception of the goals and methods of science. According to Bohr, sometimes before one can see or know the "what" that science is investigating, the scientist, like the artist, must examine the *process* and try to discern a PATTERN. And very importantly, he says, the scientific method at certain points in the work must proceed by image, parable, and metaphor—as in poetry and art. Science, literature, art must value one another and incorporate and share one another's methods and forms. In this theory emotion, passion, and wild speculation become essential to science. I anticipate the day when all discussions of ideas and science will include poetry, oral history, literary and emotional allusions. I am eager to read the astronomer-mathematician who gives as much attention to the rhythms, music, and dance she experiences in her body while she is observing as she gives to the observed: the cosmic dance, flow, and energy she is reducing to formula or speculating about.

Wolfgang Pauli's discovery of "wavicles" contradicts the laws and basic assumptions of Newtonian physics and traditional philosophy of science. In the 1930s Pauli urged a new description of science as a "wildly illogical" field that deals with both mathematical precision and paradox and contradiction. Bohr stated, unequivocally, that although in Logic the opposite of a truth is a falsehood (a dualism), "in physics the opposite of a profound truth is often another profound truth" (not a dualism). Thus, if the first-placed word in each dualism is profoundly true (e.g., literalness, mind, reason, cool, etc.) their opposites are also profoundly true (metaphor, body, emotion, hot, etc.)—a good tenet for physics, a good tenet for feminist epistemology.

Lévi-Strauss looks at certain archaic peoples and declares that the basic PATTERN of their lives and world is competition; other scholars look at the same peoples and see them exhibiting cooperation and interdependence (Pratt 1985:122). Traditional epistemology sees the world as a place beset by unsolvable dualistic problems; many feminist scholars, like people in gatherer-hunter cultures, do not experience the world dualistically. Clearly, "what-is-seen" comes in large part from an a priori PATTERN of seeing carried within the beholder. The Goddess's Image contains within Her an assumption (PATTERN) of wholeness, of the oneness of mind-body and earth, of a nondualistic, cooperative, caring way of being in the world.

RECLAIMING THE POWER INHERENT
IN THE IMAGE OF THE GODDESS

The western philosophical, scientific tradition, symbolized by Apollo, perceives the world *through* a dualistic PATTERN, the dualisms having a valued (male-associated) side and a debased (female-associated) side. In my opinion the feminist effort to revise, re-vision, this system of PATTERNING has a dual task: (1) showing the prized column to be inadequate *by itself* for gathering knowledge; and (2) redeeming the other column that has for so long been shunned or "second-best." But as Carol Christ warns, "Symbol systems cannot simply be rejected, they must be replaced. When there is no replacement, the mind will revert to familiar structures at times of crisis, bafflement or defeat" (1979:275) and grab for the old gods, images, PATTERNS.

So the list's second column must not just be rethought; it must be re-*vision*ed. A new Image must replace the beloved Image of Apollo as the symbol of knowledge, for this Image glorifies male superiority and all dualistic heirarchies, unacceptable as both an Image/metaphor for knowledge and as a means by which knowledge is obtained. The new Image must be a deity that embodies the male-associated items in the left column and the essence of those female-associated ideas in the right column; this Image, a "What," will include an acceptable means-by-which, that is, the PATTERNS *through which* we might wish ourselves and others to perceive the world.

No one needs to invent or concoct such an Image. A powerful Image already exists—the Great Mother Goddess. Much of the religion of Zeus-Apollo (father-son sky gods) and the sacrosanctness of traditional epistemology came into being specifically to counter the authority and inherent wisdom in this Goddess. Zeus was invented by the conquerors of Her people (Ionians, Archaeans, Dorians) around 1580 B.C.E. (Kerenyi 1975:38). The conquerors knew the image well; through the processess of defamation and "masculine overlay" they put Her down (as with Helle who went from "Underearth Source of Knowledge" to "Accursed") while stealing much of Her essence and power for their male deities (e.g., Zeus giving birth out of his body!—recall note 11).

All other Goddesses are later derivations or forms of the Great Mother Goddess (Gimbutas 1982:236–237). The later, classical goddesses have little of the divine power the Great Mother enjoyed[18] in heaven, earth, and below, although it must be remembered that any power She had was immanent in Nature, intrinsic to Her being, not derived from acquired authority over others. Once perceived as Wholeness itself—once praised as the Creatrix whose Oneness manifested in Manyness—Her nature by classical times had been divided (the best way to conquer) into different aspects of Her Manyness, into separate Images, such as Goddess of Love, Goddess of Wisdom, Goddess of Music, and so on. But it is not difficult to image Her as *whole* and *holy* again.

The Goddess's divine Image represented a way of seeing that acknowledged women as beings with innate powers of knowing to be reckoned with. Women's blood and women's bodies were witnessed as knowing, as actually being connected to the most mysterious, cycling, life-giving powers of the cosmos. The first human calendars were lunar, and they unambiguously related women's menstrual periods to the moon's periods, each having a dark period of withdrawal. Biology can now explain the phenomenon of women having their periods at the same time; it is due to the ecto-hormones called pheromones that transmit between bodies (McClintock 1971:244–245). Thus, archaic peoples saw women and the moon actually cycling together. And as long as they *saw* women's bodies rhythmically synchronized with the heavens, women were considered beings with wisdom and authority, in both the earthly community and the sacred realm.

Archaeologist Marija Gimbutas in one of many researchers who finds strong evidence that women's authority equaled men's in Goddess-worshipping cultures. She reports that in Neolithic cultures "A division of labor between the sexes is indicated, but not a superiority of either" (1980:32). "The role of a woman was not subject to that of a man" (1982:237), for both women and men had responsbile, if different, work in governance and maintenance; and each was respected and valued.[19] Women were esteemed leaders and priestesses who took charge of religious rituals in this "generally unstratified and basically equalitarian society with no marked distinctions based on either class or sex" (Eisler 1987:14). Myth and society were both dominated by the M/mother, but this was not domination in the sense of tyrannical *power-over* others; "this dominance [had] the character of centrality and experience" (French 1985:35), for all life was seen as created and *empowered* from within *by* H/her.

The task of redeeming women's bodies in the service of knowing means redeeming women's blood. One must leave behind the notion of menstrual blood as curse or something to be ignored and go back to the Neolithic's perception of it as something to be celebrated, regarded as the Sacred Source of Life containing the Wisdom of the Ages in it, passed from Mother to Daughter. Women's womb blood has been considered sacred and related to Wisdom from earliest times—for example, red ochre is often found on places where rebirth was devoutly wished, at entrances to caves and on dead bodies. Hot, red, blood, womb, dark—these "down inside" menses words all stand for vigor, life, excitement, passion. They come from the tabooed right column but belong in any epistemology, for they are essential to knowing about human life and existence.

When a woman grew old and no longer bled, she was called Crone, a *"wise* old Crone," for the "Blood of Wisdom" (as menstrual blood was called) was being kept inside (Walker 1985:49). Athena, a Goddess of Wisdom, wears the Gorgon's severed, bleeding head on Her chest because the bleeding woman was related to Wisdom even into classical times. Athena bears other remnants too that identify Her as a derivative of the earliest Goddess of Wisdom: Gaia, She of deep Earth Wisdom. From the crevice in the Earth (Gaia's body) at Her temple at Delphi came the voices and snakes of Prophecy, Python being Gaia's Truth-speaking Daughter. The oracular snake wraps around Athena's legs and the wise old oracular owl perches on Her shoulder.

The Myths tell an interesting story: before a certain time in the Myths female blood sanctified the soil, symbolized cosmic fertility and kinship. Then suddenly the stories no longer speak of sacred female womb-blood; suddenly the sacred genital blood of castrated males like Dionysos is spilled to renew the soil, or Adonis's sacred genital blood is spilled to save humankind, and so forth. And the spill of woman's wise sacred womb blood? It and the Gorgon became the Curse.

I believe that women's blood is not a peripheral issue in devising a feminist epistemology. It is central to the issue of women's esteem—the way we are perceived in the culture-at-large, as well as how our attributes are valued and what importance our special *knowing* and ways have. Woman's blood also concerns an information-gathering method that is the opposite of conscious control, that is, with allowing, with letting-be—something women experience in the "periods" that come on them and that has little or no parallel in the lives of men. "Allowing" is the "means-by-which" a different kind of knowledge comes. Respecting the "private" and "down inside" (not just "out there") as places where knowledge is, respecting the minding body, respecting the way a woman "is-in-the-world," respecting being female as a method and technique for gathering and defining what can be or ought to be known, and respecting being female and the female body as a way of *knowing* cooperativeness and community (the opposite of competitiveness)—all these respects are essential ways in which *humans* know; they should be accounted for in an epistemology.

Women's blood and women's periodicity direct our attention to a different consciousness and to an acceptance of fluctuating, changing forms as paradigms. Listen to how the Navajo Goddess, Changing Woman, creates. She is the opposite of all that our Judeo-Greek tradition reveres and expects from a creating deity. We are used to Zeus and Yahweh who do their divine things with the speed of lightning and the suddenness of thunderbolts. "Let it be!" and "Kah-zam!" there it is—like magic, instantly—and it's perfect too! complete, and never needs modification! Yahweh—changeless, the Unmoved

Mover—creates not only quickly but in so final a form that he needs never create anything again. Is this a proper model-form for human knowledge?

Not so with Changing Woman. She does not take Herself that seriously. She is sometimes in cahoots with Coyote, the trickster. She tinkers. She plays. She tries it this way, that way. She may like it fine one way but just for variety might change it anyway. She is so good at creating that She never stops, but She goes on and on, continually bringing new PATTERNS and new ideas into existence[20] (maddening for any one who thinks he has to keep everything all categorized and systematized). It is interesting to look back at the dualism columns with these two creating models in mind. Which is more human?

By suggesting we use "Myth, Image, and the Female Body in Re-Visioning Knowledge," I am not only proposing that we enlarge our data base considerably to include the experience of half of humanity. But I am also suggesting several other things: that we employ different methods of looking at data; that we analyze it differently and from a new perspective—our own (Gilligan 1982); that we seek a different PATTERN in it, utilize *different kinds of consciousness,* and learn to go from one to the other at will; that we learn to listen with empathy when we have been taught only to look with detachment; and that we employ ways of thinking and seeing that for the most part have been excluded from western science and epistemology.

If we are to know in new and better ways, we must also acquaint ourselves with the so-far bypassed knowledge in our bodies, not just in our minds. Actually I wish to suggest that we let *our bodies take the lead in the new learning.* "Accepted wisdom" has said that Myth, metaphor, art, and one's bodily being-in-the-world are not fully respectable in the context of knowledge because they belong culturally to a realm of unesteemed, disdained, dark, unacceptable stuff—a realm associated with world and matter, lowly forms of being associated with sin and femaleness. Understandably, even women may wish to disassociate themselves from it.

James Hillman understands the extraordinary damage the exclusions of such "psychologically female things" have caused:

Even the determination of what constitutes appropriate data, the very questions asked . . . are determined by the specific consciousness we call scientific, Western, modern, and which is the long-sharpened tool of the masculine mind that has discarded part of its own substance, calling it "Eve," "female," and "inferior." This kind of consciousness [Apollonic] . . . is driven to repeat the same misogynist views century after century, because of its archetypal base. . . . *Until another archetypal structure or cosmos informs our view of things* and our vision of what it is "to be conscious" with another, we shall remain endlessly repeating and help-lessly confirming with ever more subtle scientific observation our misog-ynist [world view]. (1972:250–251; emphasis mine)

The Great Goddess is what Carol Christ and James Hillman are asking for: an archetypal female image that can inform and reform our view of the world. Bohr and Heisenberg, as I have indicated, had to discount formal "ob-jectivity" (the view from "out there," Apollo's realm) in order to achieve a coherent view of physics. If this is true of the "hardest" of sciences, then phi-losophy and the social sciences can also benefit by dethroning Apollo as the exclusive model and symbol for knowledge. The Mother Goddess, better than Apollo, captures our actual situation, which is *in the world* rather than "out there" like Apollo. She, with Her earth-body wisdom, is an Image, Para-ble, and Metaphor that in*corpo*rates ("has in the body") our "what" and at the same time the "means-by-which" we must proceed to acquire knowledge.

NOTES

1. Apollo is "the main symbol bearer of classical civilization. . . . Whether it be the body of a god or a man, [this Ideal Male] is *changeless and immortal*" (Redner 1986:350; my emphasis).
2. Developed more fully in Donna Wilshire and Bruce Wilshire's "Spatial Arche-types and the Gender Stereotypes Inherent in Them," *Anima—An Experiential Journal* (Spring 1989).
3. Hell is named for *Hel*, once-beloved Goddess of the Underworld.
4. For clarification of this idea, read "On Psychological Femininity" in Hillman (1972:215–298). For a discussion of how the Divine Female (e.g., Wisdom as Sophia) was demeaned and suppressed in Greek, Hebrew, and Christian philoso-phy, read Joan C. Engelsman's *The Feminine Dimension of the Divine* (1987). See also Catherine Keller's *From a Broken Web: Separation, Sexism, and Self* (1987).
5. For an analysis of texts showing Sophia rooted in Gaia, Goddess of Earth Wis-dom, see Engelsman 1987.
6. As in: "Sight and hearing use our intelligence in two completely different ways. . . . Our optic intelligence forms an image in our mind. Hearing, on the other hand . . . evoking a response from the emotive centres" (Lawlor 1982:14).
7. The presence of "evolution" in this column opposite "permanence" and "ideal [fixed] forms" may account for both the difficulty that evolution still meets in some quarters and the reluctance of mainstream philosophers of science to embrace other theories of unfixedness, such as Nobel physicist Ilya Prigogine's Chaos The-ory (1984) and his work on emerging patterns (1980), or the illogic of quantum theories.

8. Carol Gilligan would likely add "justice and rights" to the left column, as part of "the typical male voice." And she would add "caring relationships" to the right column as "the typical female voice." Her research shows that although the care perspective and deep regard for relationships most typically describe female experience, they are not solely women's province; they belong to all humans. "The different voice I describe is chararcterized not by gender but theme" (1982:2).

9. Much has recently been written on body knowledge. See Feldenkrais 1972, Rosenfeld 1981, Wilshire 1982, Steinman 1986, and their bibliographies.

10. Although the entire spectrum of human experience is available to all humans, one cannot rule out the possibility that there may be a genetic predisposition of one sex to certain aspects. Such differences are irrelevant to the need to redeem the right-hand column, however.

11. This observation is made frequently by mythographers and other scholars in pre–Iron Age studies. Some have called the Archetypal Reversal phenomenon "masculine overlay," with the Freudian overtones intended. Samuel Noah Kramer, the distinguished linguist who first deciphered the cuneiform tablets of Sumer, calls the third millennium B.C.E. a time of "priestly piracy" when "male theologians manipulated the order of the deities in accordance with their chauvinistic predilections" and stole the goddesses' perogatives to give to their sons (Kramer 1979: 27, 29).

12. Truth imposed from "on high" rarely turns out to be universal. It becomes possible to talk about universal truths, however, when the seeker goes to and through *immanence*, as all preheroic Myths do. For those who wish to explore how Myth reveals these truths more fully than I am doing in this piece, read James Hillman's *Archetypal Psychology* (1983), Mircea Eliade's *The Eternal Return* (1971), and Jean Gebser's *Ever-Present Origin* (1985).

13. This means teaching the bottom of the foot, bare or in moccasins, to feel and test *before* accepting weight. In this kind of tracking the whole body contributes to the minding, to the thinking and the knowing.

14. *Anima mundi* literally means *the soul of the world* with "world" being a good translation of *mundi*, for the *anima* is definitely of the world—it "permeates all things of the world" (Hillman 1983:18); *anima* can mean "soul" only in a special sense because it is not "spirit"; it cannot mean spirit because it is totally "worldly," of the "world," "squarely in the midst of the world" (26); it means "soul" as in "soul food," food that gives evidence of the eater's perspective on life—so *anima* as "soul" means "a perspective," a PATTERN through which life is viewed, a *means by which* and not a "what," not a "substance"—a subjective outlook, not an object (16). Seeing ourselves as being within and interconnected with the great workings of Nature—understanding the *anima mundi*, the Soul of Nature itself not as a something, but as a *Way*-of-Being-and-Seeing—certainly does away with the dualistic dilemma of human alienation and isolation from the world.

15. From Merlin Stone's interview of Mary Daly for Canadian Broadcasting Company's 1986 four-hour radio series, "Return of the Goddess." (Audio Tape Cassettes, CBC Audio Products, Box 500-Station A, Toronto, Ontario M5W 1E6)

16. I think of my performance work—enacting stories and history of "The

Goddess and Her Myths"—as doing this, as "embodying ideas," combining a live "what" with the nondualistic "way-in-which" I see the world.

17. I am indebted to physicist Bruce Bush, Ph.D., for his careful readings of this paper and for his generous, instructive notes on the parts pertaining to physics and scientific method. The ideas and statements are, however, my own.

18. The same demotion of the Goddess went on in Europe (Berger 1985).

19. Many anthropologists, especially Marla Powers (1986) and Eleanor Leacock (1981), have made findings similar to those of Gimbutas (1982). "The empirical status of women" in cultures studied by Powers "is frequently clouded" by the false claim of Euramericans "that reproductive roles cause women to be subordinate; [and] that males are somehow intrinsically and universally dominant." Actually "women are neither inferior nor superior to men, merely different" in the Oglala culture. "Both sexes are valued for the contribution they make to the society" (Powers 1986:6).

20. Prigogine's work reveals that new patterns and structures, the physical bases of life, emerge constantly and randomly (1984).

REFERENCES

Aristotle. 1912. *De Generatione Animalium*. In *The Works of Aristotle*. Trans. J. A. Smith and W. D. Ross. London: Oxford. Cited G.A.

———. 1921. *Politica*. Trans. Benjamin Jowett. In *The Works of Aristotle*, ed. W. D. Ross. London: Oxford.

Augustine. 1948. *On the Trinity*. Trans. A. W. Haddan, revised W. G. T. Shedd. In *Basic Writings of Saint Augustine*, ed. Whitney J. Oates. Vol. 2. New York: Random House.

Berger, Pamela. 1985. *The Goddess Obscured: Transformation of the Grain Protectress from Goddess to Saint*. Boston: Beacon Press.

Bordo, Susan. 1987. *The Flight to Objectivity: Essays on Cartesianism and Culture*. Albany, N.Y.: SUNY Press.

Boulding, Elise. 1976. *The Underside of History*. Boulder, Colo.: Westview Press.

Christ, Carol, and Judith Plaskow, eds. 1979. *Womanspirit Rising*. San Francisco: Harper & Row.

Daly, Mary. 1986. Radio interview with Merlin Stone. Part of "Return of the Goddess" series. Canadian Broadcasting Company.

Eisler, Riane. 1987. *The Chalice and the Blade: Our History, Our Future*. San Francisco: Harper & Row.

Eliade, Mircea. 1971. *The Myth of the Eternal Return: Or Cosmos and History*. Princeton, N.J.: Princeton University Press.

Engelsman, Joan Chamberlain. 1987. 2d ed. *The Feminine Dimension of the Divine*. Willmette, Ill.: Chiron Publishers.

Feldenkrais, Moshe. 1972. *Awareness Through Movement*. New York: Harper & Row.

French, Marilyn. 1985. *Beyond Power: On Women, Men, and Morals*. New York: Summit Books.

Gebser, Jean. 1985. *The Ever-Present Origin*. Trans. by Noel Barstad with Algis Mickunas. Athens: Ohio University Press.

Gilligan, Carol. 1982. *In a Different Voice: Psychological Theory and Women's Development*. Cambridge, Mass.: Harvard University Press.

Gimbutas, Marija. 1980. *The Early Civilization of Europe*. Monograph for Indo-European Studies 131. Los Angeles: University of California Press.

————. 1982. *Goddesses and Gods of Old Europe, 6500–3500 B.C.: Myths and Cult Images*. Berkeley: University of California Press.

Heisenberg, Werner. 1970. *Physics and Beyond—Encounters and Conversations*. New York: Harper & Row.

Hillman, James. 1972. *The Myth of Analysis: Three Essays in Archetypal Psychology*. New York: Harper & Row.

————. 1983. *Archetypal Psychology*. Dallas: Spring Publications.

Keller, Catherine, 1987. *From a Broken Web: Separation, Sexism, and Self*. Boston: Beacon Press.

Kerenyi, Carl. 1975. *Zeus and Hera: Archetypal Image of Father, Husband and Wife*. Princeton, N.J.: Princeton University Press.

Kramer, Samuel Noah. 1979. *From the Poetry of Sumer*. Berkeley: University of California Press.

Lauter, Estelle, and Carol S. Rupprecht. 1985. *Feminist Archetypal Theory— Interdisciplinary Re-Visions of Jungian Thought*. Knoxville: University of Tennessee Press.

Lawlor, Robert. 1982. *Sacred Geometry*. New York: Crossroad.

Leacock, Eleanor. 1981. *Myths and Male Dominance*. New York: Monthly Review Press.

McClintock, Martha K. 1971. "Menstrual Synchrony and Suppression." *Nature* 229, no. 5285:244–245.

Merchant, Carolyn. 1980. *The Death of Nature: Women, Ecology and the Scientific Revolution*. San Francisco: Harper & Row.

Powers, Marla. 1986. *Oglala Women: Myth, Ritual, and Reality*. Chicago: University of Chicago Press.

Pratt, Annis V. 1985. "Spinning Among Fields: Jung, Frye, Lévi-Strauss and Feminist Archetypal Theory." In Lauter and Rupprecht, *Feminist Archetypal Theory*.

Prigogine, Ilya. 1980. *Being to Becoming*. San Francisco: W. H. Freeman.

Prigogine, Ilya, and Isabel Stengers. 1984. *Order out of Chaos*. New York: Bantam.

Redner, Harry. 1986. *The Ends of Philosophy*. Totowa, N.J.: Rowman and Allanheld.

Rosenfeld, Albert. 1981. "Teaching the Body how to Program the Brain is Moshe [Feldenkrais]'s 'Miracle.'" *Smithsonian* (Jan. 1981):52–58.

Spretnak, Charlene. 1984. *Lost Goddesses of Early Greece: A Collection of Pre-Hellenic Myths*. Boston: Beacon Press.

Steinman, Louise. 1986. *The Knowing Body*. Boston: Shambhala.

DONNA WILSHIRE

Walker, Barbara. 1985. *The Crone: Woman of Age, Wisdom and Power*. San Francisco: Harper & Row.

Wilshire, Bruce W. 1982. *Role Playing and Identity: The Limits of the Theatrical Metaphor*. Bloomington: Indiana University Press.

Wilshire, Donna, and Bruce Wilshire. 1989. "Spatial Archetypes and the Gender Stereotypes Inherent in Them." *Anima—An Experiental Journal* 15, no. 2 (Spring): 77–86.

Wolf, Fred Alan. 1986. *The Body Quantum*. New York: Macmillan.

HEALING THE WOUNDS: FEMINISM, ECOLOGY, AND NATURE/CULTURE DUALISM

Ynestra King

No part of living nature can ignore the extreme threat to life on earth. We are faced with worldwide deforestation, the disappearance of hundreds of species of life, and the increasing pollution of the gene pool by poisons and low-level radiation. We are also faced with biological atrocities unique to modern life—the existence of the AIDS virus and the possibility of even more dreadful and pernicious diseases caused by genetic mutation as well as the unforeseen ecological consequences of disasters such as the industrial accident in India and nuclear meltdown in the Soviet Union. Worldwide food short-ages, including episodes of mass starvation, continue to mount as prime agri-cultural land is used to grow cash crops to pay national debts instead of food to feed people.[1] Animals are mistreated and mutilated in horrible ways to test cosmetics, drugs, and surgical procedures.[2] The stockpiling of ever greater weapons of annihilation and the horrible imagining of new ones con-tinues. The piece of the pie that women have only begun to sample as a result of the feminist movement is rotten and carcinogenic, and surely our feminist theory and politics must take account of this however much we yearn for the opportunities within this society that have been denied to us. What is the point of partaking equally in a system that is killing us all?[3]

The contemporary ecological crisis alone creates an imperative that femi-nists take ecology seriously, but there are other reasons ecology is central to feminist philosophy and politics. The ecological crisis is related to the systems of hatred of all that is natural and female by the white, male western formu-lators of philosophy, technology, and death inventions. I contend that the sys-tematic denigration of working-class people and people of color, women, and animals are all connected to the basic dualism that lies at the root of western civilization. But this mindset of hierarchy originates within human society, its material roots in the domination of human by human, particularly women by men. Although I cannot speak for the liberation struggles of people of color, I believe that the goals of feminism, ecology, and movements against racism and for the survival of indigenous peoples are internally related; they must be understood and pursued together in a worldwide, genuinely prolife,[4] movement.

At the root of western society exist both a deep ambivalence about life itself, our own fertility and that of nonhuman nature, and a terrible confusion about our place in nature. Nature did not declare war on humanity; patriarchal humanity declared war on women and on living nature. Nowhere is this transition more hauntingly portrayed than by the Chorus in Sophocles' *Antigone:*

Many the wonders but nothing more wondrous than man.
This thing crosses the sea in the winter's storm,
making his path through the roaring waves.
And she, the greatest of gods, the Earth—
deathless she is, and unwearies—he wears her away
as the ploughs go up and down from year to year
and his mules turn up the soil.

So far have we gone from our roots in living nature that the living, not the dead, perplexes us. The pannaturalism of ancient and ancestral culture has given way to panmechanism, the norm of the lifeless.

But for a long time after the first echoes of this transition, the inroads human beings made on living nature were superficial and unable to fundamentally upset the balance and fecundity of the nonhuman natural world. Appropriately ethics and the ideas about how people should live that took their instrumental form in politics concerned the relationships of human beings to one another, especially in cities. But with the arrival of modern technologies the task of ethics and the domain of politics change drastically. The consideration of the place of human beings in nature, formerly the terrain of religion, becomes a crucial concern for all human beings. And with modern technologies, the particular responsibilities of human beings for nature must move to the center of politics. As biological ethicist Hans Jonas writes, "A kind of metaphysical responsibility beyond self-interest has devolved in us with the magnitude of our powers relative to this tenuous film of life, that is, since man has become dangerous not only to himself but to the whole biosphere."[5]

Yet around the world, capitalism, the preeminent culture and economics of self-interest, is homogenizing cultures and simplifying life on earth by disrupting naturally complex balances within the ecosystem. Capitalism depends upon expanding markets; therefore, ever greater areas of life must be mediated by sold products. From a capitalist standpoint, the more things that can be bought and sold, the better. Capitalism requires a rationalized world-view, asserting both that human science and technology are inherently progressive, which systematically denigrates ancestral cultures, and that human beings are entitled to dominion over nonhuman nature.

Nonhuman nature is being rapidly simplified, undoing the work of organic evolution. Hundreds of species of life disappear forever each year, and the figure is accelerating. Diverse, complex, ecosystems are more stable than simple ones. They have had longer periods of evolution, and they are necessary to support human beings and many other species. Yet in the name of civilization, nature has been desecrated in a process of rationalization sociologist Max Weber called "the disenchantment of the world."

The diversity of human life on the planet is also being undermined. This worldwide process of simplification impoverishes all humanity. The cultural diversity of human societies around the world developed over thousands of years; it is part of the general evolution of life on the planet. Homogenizing culture turns the world into a giant factory and facilitates top-down authoritarian government. In the name of helping people, the industrial countries export models of development that assume the American way of life is best for everyone. In this country, McDonald's and shopping malls cater to a uniform clientele, which is becoming more uniform all the time. To "go malling" has become a verb in American English; shopping has become our national pastime, as prosperous American consumers seek to scratch an itch that can never be satisfied by commodities.[6]

A critical analysis of and opposition to the uniformity of technological, industrial culture—capitalist and socialist—is crucial to feminism, ecology, and the struggles of indigenous peoples. At this point in history, there is no way to unravel the matrix of oppressions within human society without at the same time liberating nature and reconciling the human and the nonhuman parts of nature. Socialists do not have the answer to these problems; they share the antinaturalism and basic dualism of capitalism. Although developed by capitalism, the technological means of production utilized by capitalist and socialist states are largely the same. All hitherto existing philosophies of liberation, with the possible exception of some forms of social anarchism, accept the anthropocentric notion that humanity should dominate nature and that the increasing domination of nonhuman nature is a precondition for true human freedom.[7] No socialist revolution has ever fundamentally challenged the basic prototype for nature/culture dualism—the domination of men over women.

This old socialism has apparently ended by deconstructing itself in the academy, as the white male principals of academic Marxism proclaim the end of the subject. In this sense, socialism may be in its death throes, but, I will argue, the old socialist spirit of history, a valuable legacy, is not dead. It has passed on to new subjects—feminists, greens, and other bearers of identity politics, including movements against racism and for national liberation and the survival of indigenous peoples. And in this sense, these most anti-modern of movements are modern, not postmodern. In response to the modern crisis, they argue for more, not less, heart, taking the side of Pascal against Descartes, "The heart hath its reasons which the reason knows not."

THE PROBLEM OF NATURE FOR FEMINISM

From its inception, feminism has had to wrestle with the problem of the projection of human ideas onto the natural, where these human ideas of what is natural have then been projected back onto human society as natural law and used to reinforce male ideas about female nature.[8] Because ideas reinforcing the relationship between women and nature have been used to limit and oppress women in western society, feminists have looked to social constructionism. They are understandably wary of any theory that appears to reinforce the woman/nature relationship as biological determinism by another name. At the same time, ecologists have been busy reinforcing the humanity/nature relationship and demonstrating the perilous situation of life on earth brought about by human attempts to master nature. This has led other feminists to assert that the feminist project should be freeing nature from men, rather than freeing women from nature.

Thus, in taking up ecology feminism necessarily begins to try and understand what it has meant for us as women to be represented as closer to nature than men in a male-dominated culture that defines itself in opposition to nature. I will first explore current feminist thinking about nature/culture dualism, arguing that each side of the debate capitulates to the false opposition stated above, which is itself a product of patriarchal dualism. Next I will articulate what I believe to be a way past this division appropriating from the feminist perspectives that have so far dominated the public discourse about nature/culture dualism. I will argue that the serious consideration of ecology by feminists suggests critical directions for theory and creates an imperative for a feminist epistemology based on a noninstrumental way of knowing. This implies a reformulation, not a repudiation, of reason and science. I will also address the new forms of politics emerging from the antidualistic, eco-feminist imperative. This praxis is embodied and articulate—passionate and thoughtful. It connects political issues to one another, connects different cul-

tures of women, and continually connects the fate of human beings to the
fate of the rest of life on this planet.

Liberal Feminism, Rationalization, and the Domination of Nature

Liberalism, with its assertion of "liberty, equality, and fraternity" provided
the conceptual tools for feminists to argue that no people are naturally meant
to rule over other people, including men over women.[9] This rationalization
of difference has worked *for* women and other dehumanized peoples because
it calls into question the idea of any "natural" roles or destinies. In a liberal
framework "difference" itself must be obliterated to achieve equality.[10] In
other words, if women were educated like men they would *be* like men. To
argue that women are capable of mindful activity—that women reason and
think—was and is a liberatory argument.

Mary Wollstonecraft drew on liberal Enlightenment ideas in her germinal
Vindication of the Rights of Women, the first feminist work in English. It
suggested that women could attain "the virtues of man" if she were extended
"the rights of reason." In this framework, it is obviously preferable for
women to be like men. Wollstonecraft writes:

> Asserting the rights which women in common with men ought to con-
> tend for, I have not attempted to extenuate their faults; but to prove
> them to be the natural consequences of their education and station in so-
> ciety. If so, it is reasonable to suppose that they will change their charac-
> ter, and correct their vices and follies, when they are allowed to be free
> in a physical, moral, and civil sense.[11]

Obviously, women are mindful human beings, capable of reason, who should
be extended the vote, educational opportunities, and public political power.
But the problem is basing the extension of full personhood to women (and
other persons) on an enforced sameness.

So the version of feminism least able to appropriately address ecology is
liberal feminism with its rationalist, utilitarian bias and underlying assumption that "male is better." By and large, liberal feminism is a white middle-
class movement, concerned with the extension of male power and privilege to
women like themselves, not the fate of women as a whole. To the extent that
they address ecological concerns, liberal feminists will be "environmentalists"
rather than "ecologists." The difference between environmentalists and ecolo-

gists is revealed in the terminology itself: environmentalists refer to either nonhuman nature as "the environment," the environment of human beings, or "natural resources," those resources for human use. "Environmental management" seeks to make sure that these resources are not depleted to a degree that slows human productivity. Environmentalists accept the anthropocentric view that nature exists solely to serve human ends and purposes. In this instrumentalist view, concerned more with efficacy than with ends, it is to the good that everything be rationalized and quantified so that we might manage it better for human ends.

One could argue from the perspective of liberal feminism that women contribute to the military and industrial ravage of nature and receive proportionately few of the supposed benefits—profits and jobs. Men are drafted and may be injured or even die in combat, but they also get jobs and have the opportunity to take part in one of the great person-making dramas of our civilization, war. For this reason contemporary liberal feminists have supported the draft, just as suffragists supported their governments in World War I to prove that they were loyal citizens, contributing to the war effort and deserving of a full franchise. Many of these feminists had an internationalist, antimilitarist perspective, just as many feminists who opposed the Vietnam War now support the drafting of women so we will stand alongside men in identical relationship to the state.

Liberal feminists since Harriet Taylor Mill and John Stuart Mill[12] have emphasized the similarities of women to men as the basis for the emancipation of women. But trying to maintain this stance in a contemporary context leads liberal feminists into absurdly unsisterly positions. The limitations of liberalism as a basis for feminism are especially obvious as we approach the so-called new reproductive technologies. I was recently at a meeting of feminist writers called to draft a response to the Mary Beth Whitehead surrogacy case. Although these feminists disagreed about surrogacy, all agreed that this particular woman had been wronged and should get her baby back.

One woman, a solid liberal feminist who also supports the draft, refused to publicly side with Whitehead; she thought that injustice had definitely been done, but she refused to take a public stance for two reasons. Her primary concern was maintaining women's contract credibility. It did not matter to her that Whitehead had not understood the contract she signed and had entered into this contract because she needed $10,000 desperately and had no other way to get it. Her other reason for opposing Whitehead is more insidious from an ecofeminist standpoint and represents the fundamental biases of liberalism toward a denatured sameness as a condition for equality, or subjectivity. She opposed any policy recognizing that men and women stand in different relationship to a baby at the moment of its birth, thereby giving a woman a greater initial claim to the child of her flesh. Such claims may appear to reinforce the idea that women are more creatures of nature than men or that "biology is destiny." But women do bear children, and in virtually all cultures they take major responsibility for caring for and acculturating them. To a greater degree than men, women are the repository of human fertility and the possibility of future generations. And so far that fact does not stop with the biological bearing of children determined by sex, but it extends into the social division of human activity, the realm of gender.

Feminists who have argued against any special relationship between mothers and their children, believing that the emphasis on this biological bond is the ideological basis for the oppression of women, have had their arguments used in court to take children away from their mothers.[13] In a sense they have given away what little social power women as a group have had without receiving an equal share of male power and privilege, however it might be defined. Obviously, I do not argue that abusive mothers should be given custody of their children over loving fathers; rather, I argue that women should seek to hold on to reproductive and procreative powers as a political strategy and a recognition of the biological fact that women bear children out of our own bodies and therefore have a particular claim to control how this process is carried out.

Radical Feminism's Patriarchal Root: To Embrace or Repudiate Nature?

Radical feminists, or feminists who believe that the biologically based domination of women by men is the root cause of oppression, have considered ecology from a feminist perspective more often than liberal or socialist feminists because nature is their central category of analysis. Radical feminists believe that the subordination of women in society is the root form of human oppression, closely related to the association of women with nature, hence the word "radical."

Radical feminists root the oppression of women in biological difference itself. They see "patriarchy," by which they mean the systematic dominance of men in society, as preceding and laying the foundation for other forms of human oppression and exploitation. Men identify women with nature and seek to enlist both in the service of male "projects" designed to make men safe from feared nature and mortality. The ideology of women as closer to nature is essential to such a project. If patriarchy is the archetypal form of human oppression, then it follows that if we get rid of that, other forms of oppression will likewise crumble. But there is a basic difference between the two schools of radical feminists: Is the woman/nature connection potentially emancipatory? Or does it provide a rationale for the continued subordination of women.[14]

How do women who call themselves radical feminists come to opposite conclusions?[15] The former implies a separate feminist culture and philosophy from the vantage point of identification with nature and a celebration of the woman/nature connection—this is the position of *radical cultural feminists,* which I will address later.

Radical rationalist feminists take the second position, repudiating the woman/nature connection. For these feminists, freedom is being liberated from the primordial realm of women and nature, which they regard as an imprisoning female ghetto. They believe that the key to the emancipation of women lies in the dissociation of women from nature and the end of what they believe to be a "female ghetto," an inherently unfree realm of necessity. In this sense, liberal feminism is similar to radical rationalist feminism.

Radical rationalist feminists deplore the appropriation of ecology as a feminist issue and see it as a regression bound to reinforce sex-role stereotyping. Anything that reinforces gender differences or makes any kind of special claim for women is problematic. Rationalist feminists think that feminists should not do anything that would restimulate traditional ideas about women. They celebrate the fact that we have finally begun to gain access to male bastions by using the political tools of liberalism and the rationalization of human life, mythically severing the woman/nature connection as the humanity/nature connection has been severed.

The mother of modern feminism, Simone de Beauvoir, represents this position. Recently she came out against what she calls "the new femininity":

"An enhanced status for traditional feminine values, such as woman and her rapport with nature, woman and her maternal instinct, woman and her physical being . . . etc. This renewed attempt to pin women down to their traditional role, together with a small effort to meet some of the demands made by women—that's the formula used to try and keep women quiet. Even women who call themselves feminists don't always see through it. Once again, women are being defined in terms of 'the other', once again they are being made into the 'second sex.'" . . .

She goes on to say of women and peace, and feminism and ecology:

"Why should women be more in favour of peace than men? I should think it a matter of equal concern for both! . . . being a mother means being for peace. Equating ecology with feminism is something that irritates me. They are not automatically one and the same thing at all."[16]

She reiterates the position she took almost forty years ago in *The Second Sex*—that it is a sexist ploy to define women as beings who are closer to nature than men. She claims that such associations divert women from their struggle for emancipation and channel their energies "into subsidiary concerns," such as ecology and peace.

The best-known contemporary explication of this position is Shulamith Firestone's *The Dialectic of Sex*,[17] which concludes with a chapter advocating test tube reproduction and the removal of biological reproduction from women's bodies as a condition for women's liberation.

Following de Beauvoir, rationalist radical feminism is the version of radical feminism most socialist-feminists are attempting to integrate with Marxist historical materialism;[18] it asserts that the woman-nature identification is a male ideology and a tool of oppression that must itself be overcome.[19] Therefore, if women are to be allowed full participation in the male world we should not do anything in the name of feminism that reinforces the woman/nature connection. Socialist feminists seek to maintain liberal feminism commitment to equality, combining it with a socialist analysis of class.

The other form of radical feminism seeks to address the root of women's oppression with the opposite theory and strategy; this *radical cultural feminism* is usually called cultural feminism. Cultural feminists resolve the problem not by obliterating the difference between men and women but by taking women's side, which as they see it is also the side of nonhuman nature. Cultural feminism grows out of radical feminism, emphasizing the differences rather than the similarities between men and women. And not surprisingly, *they* have taken the slogan "the personal is political" in the opposite direction, personalizing the political. They celebrate the life experience of the "female ghetto," which they see as a source of female freedom, rather than subordination. Cultural feminists argue, following Virginia Woolf, that they do not want to enter the male world with its "procession of professions."[20] Cultural feminists have attempted to articulate and even create a separate women's culture; they have been major proponents of identifying women with nature and feminism with ecology. The major strength of cultural feminism is that it is a deeply woman-identified movement. It celebrates what is distinct about women, challenging male culture rather than strategizing to become part of it. Cultural feminists have celebrated the identification of women with nature in music, art, literature, poetry, covens, and communes. Although there are feminists of every stripe who are lesbians and cultural feminists who are not lesbians, lesbian cultural feminists have developed a highly political, energetic visible culture that allows women to live every aspect of their lives among women. Much of this culture intentionally identifies with women and nature against (male) culture.

For example, cultural feminists have often been in the forefront of feminist antimilitarist activism. They blame men for war and point out the masculine preoccupation with death-defying deeds as constitutive of man(person)hood. Men who are socialized in this way have little respect for women, or for life, including their own. Since Vietnam, even in the popular culture, the glorification of the military and the idea that soldiering is great preparation for a successful manly life has been tarnished. At the same time, the Rambo industry (films, dolls, toys, games, etc.) is immensely successful, and efforts to "reconstruct" the history of the Vietnam War as the emasculation of America proceed. Not only have cultural feminists criticized male and military culture, but males themselves have challenged the masculine construction of personhood, with its idealization of war. The most popular adventure show on U.S. television is Magnum P.I., where four friends (three Vietnam vets and a long-time British army officer) live in Hawaii, trying to recover from and make sense of their personally devastating military experiences. Films like *Platoon* portray the dehumanization of soldiering, rather than romanticizing the battlefield and furthering the idea of hero/soldier as human ideal. In this way, antimilitary art and culture share the cultural feminist project, suggesting that the imperatives of manhood are destructive to men as well as to women and nature.

In her book *Gyn/ecology: The Metaethics of Radical Feminism*, a major work of cultural feminist theory, Mary Daly calls herself an ecofeminist and implores women to identify with nature against men and live our lives separately from men. For Daly the oppression of women under patriarchy and the pillage of the natural world are the same phenomenon, and consequently she does not theoretically differentiate the issues.[21] In the political realm, Sonia Johnson recently waged a presidential campaign as a candidate for the Citizens Party, translating a perspective very much like Mary Daly's into conventional political terms.[22] My ecofeminism differs from that of Daly; I think *Gyn/ecology* stands as a powerful phenomenology of the victimization of women, but it is ultimately dualistic. Hers is a work of metaphysical naturalism or naturalistic metaphysics—either way dualistic. She has turned the old misogynist Thomas Aquinas on his head. Although she is more correct than he, she has *reified* the female over the male. She does not take us past dualism, which I believe to be the ecofeminist agenda.

Susan Griffin's book *Women and Nature: The Roaring Inside Her,* is another cultural feminist classic. A long prose poem, it is not intended to spell out a precise political philosophy and program but to let us know and feel how the woman/nature connection has played out historically in the dominant western culture. It suggests a powerful potentiality for a feminist movement that links feminism and ecology, with an immanent, or mystical, relationship to nature. Griffin does not mean to trade history for mystery, although her work has been interpreted that way. Griffin's work, located ambiguously between theory and poetry, has been read much too literally and at times invoked wrongly to collapse the domination of women and the domination of nature into a single, timeless phenomenon.[23] Griffin collapses the rigid boundaries of the subject and the object, suggesting a recovery of mysticism as a way of knowing nature immanently.

But one problem that white cultural feminists, like other feminists, have not adequately faced is that in celebrating the commonalities of women and emphasizing the ways in which women are universal victims of male oppression, they have inadequately addressed the real diversity of women's lives and histories across race, class, and national boundaries. For women of color, opposing racism and genocide and encouraging ethnic pride are agendas they often share with men in a white-dominated society, even while they struggle against sexism in their own communities. These complex, multidimensional loyalties and historically divergent life situations require a politics that recognizes those complexities. This connecting of women and nature has lent itself to a romanticization of women as good, separate from all the dastardly deeds of men and culture. The problem is that history, power, women, and nature are all a lot more complicated than that.

In the last ten years, the old cultural feminism has given birth to "the feminist spirituality movement,"[24] an eclectic potpourri of beliefs and practices, with an immanent goddess (as opposed to the transcendent god). I believe there has been a greater racial diversity in this movement than in any other form of feminism; this is due in part to the fact that this is a spiritual movement, based on the ultimate unity of all living things and a respect for diversity. There is no particular dogma in this movement, only a recognition of a woman as an embodied, earth-bound living being who should celebrate her connection to the rest of life and, for some, invoke this connection in her public political protest actions. These beliefs have their scientific corollaries: for example, the Gaia hypothesis, the idea that the planet is to be conceived as one single living organism; and the thesis of scientist Lynn Margolis, whose research corroborates Peter Kropotkin's mutualism,[25] that cooperation was a stronger force in evolution than competition.[26]

Cultural feminism and the women's spirituality movement have been subjected to the same critique feminists of color have made of the ethnocentricity of much white feminism,[27] as women of color have become a powerful presence in its circles. This critique comes from women of color who draw on indigenous spiritual traditions; Native American and African women argue that these white western feminists are inventing and originating an earth-centered prowoman spirituality while they are defending their indigenous spirituality against the imperialism of western rationalism.[28] For example, Louisah Teish, the first voodoo priestess to attempt to explain her tradition to the public, advocates a practice that integrates the political and spiritual, bringing together a disciplined understanding of the African spiritual tradition with contemporary feminist and black power politics. Members of her group in Oakland are planning urban gardening projects both to help the poor feed themselves and to supply the herbs needed for the holistic healing remedies of her tradition while they engage in community organizing to stop gentrification. Women in the Hopi and Navaho traditions are also attempting to explain their traditions to a wider public while they orginize politically to keep their lands from being taken over by developers or poisoned by industry.

The collision of modern industrial society with indigenous cultures has decimated these ancestral forms, but it may have brought white westerners into contact with forms of knowledge useful to us as we try to imagine our way beyond dualism, to understand what it means to be embodied beings on this planet. These traditions are often used as examples of nondualistic ways of life, at least which overcome nature/culture dualism.[29] But human beings cannot simply jump off or out of history. These indigenous, embodied, earth-centered spiritual traditions are planting seeds in the imaginations of people who are the products of dualistic cultures, but, as pointed out by their original practitioners, they are not ways of being or systems of thought that can be adopted whole cloth by white westerners who want to avoid the responsibility of their own history.

The movement has changed in recent years, becoming more sophisticated and diverse as women of color articulate a powerful survival-based feminism emerging from their experience at the crucible of multiple oppressions. From both the feminism of women of color, sometimes called "womanist" as opposed to "feminist" in order to convey the different priorities of women of color from white women, and ecofeminism has come the urging of a more holistic feminism, linking all issues of personal and planetary survival.[30] The critique of cultural feminism advanced by women of color—that it is often ahistorical in that white women, in particular, need to take responsibility for being oppressors as well as oppressed and for having been powerful as white people or as people with class or national privileges—is crucial. In other words, women have a complexity of historical identities and therefore a complexity of loyalties. Instead of constantly attempting to make our identities less complex by emphasizing what we have in common as women, as has been the tendency of women who are feminists first and foremost, we should attend to the differences between us.

Socialist Feminism, Rationalization, and the Domination of Nature

Socialist feminism is an odd hybrid—an attempt at a synthesis of the rationalist feminism, radical and liberal, and the historical materialism of the Marxist tradition. Socialist feminism is not a mass movement, just as socialism is not a mass movement. However, the existence of a women's movement has assured that the feminists are the liveliest presence at otherwise tepid socialist gatherings.[31] This version of feminism has dominated the academy, while radical feminism, cultural feminism, and more recently ecofeminism are popular movements with a political base. Both Marxism and rationalist feminism subscribe to the domination of nature; thus, ecology has not been on the socialist feminist agenda. Some socialist feminists argued that socialist feminism should be differentiated from Marxist feminism. They may be a valid distinction, but so far socialist feminism has shared many of Marxism's blind spots.

In taking "labor" as its central category, Marxists have reduced the human being to homo laborans, and the history of capitalism cries out with the resistance of human beings not only to being exploited but to being conceived of as essentially "workers." In Marxism, revolutionary discourse has been reduced to a "language of productivity"[32] where a critique of the mode of production does not necessarily challenge the principle of production, shared by political economy and Marxism. This functionalist, rationalist idea of persons has been a central theoretical and political weakness of the post-Marxist socialist tradition, including socialist feminism.

The socialist feminist theory of the body as socially constructed (re)producer has informed a public discourse of "reproductive freedom"—the freedom to (re)produce or not (re)produce with your own body. In this area socialist feminists have been a political force. But socialist feminists have an inadequate theory with which to confront the new reproductive technologies. Arguing that women have a right to "control our own bodies" does not prepare one to confront the issue of whether our reproductive, like our productive capacities, should be bought and sold in the marketplace, as one more form of wage labor.[33]

Socialist feminists have criticized liberal feminists, just as socialists have criticized liberalism, for not going far enough in a critique of the political economy and class differences. They are right to the extent that liberal feminists cannot take account of systematic inequalities in our liberal democracy that discriminate against women and the poor and prevent everyone from having equal opportunity. They have rightfully pointed out that as long as we earn on the average fifty-nine cents to the dollar earned by men, women

are not equal. This would still be the case even if the Equal Rights Amendment had passed.

But socialist feminists have shared the rationalist bias of liberal feminism,
depicting the world primarily in exchange terms—whether production or
reproduction—and have agreed with the liberal feminist analysis that we
must strive in all possible ways to demonstrate that we are more like men
than different. Some socialist feminists have even argued that liberal feminism
has a radical potential.[34] For such feminists, the dualistic, overly rationalized
premises of liberal feminism are not a problem. For them too, severing the
woman/nature connection is a feminist project.

In a sense the strength and weakness of socialist feminism lie in the same
premise: the centrality of economics in their theory and practice. Socialist
feminists have articulated a strong economic and class analysis, but they have
not sufficiently addressed the domination of nature.[35] The socialist feminist
agenda would be complete if we could overcome systematic inequalities of
social and economic power. Socialist feminists have addressed one of the
three forms of domination of nature, domination between persons, but they
have not seriously attended to the domination of either nonhuman nature or
inner nature.

Socialist feminism draws on but goes beyond socialism, demonstrating the
independent dynamic of patriarchy and fundamentally challenging the total-
izing claims of Marxist economistic approach. In socialist feminism, women
seek to enter the political world as articulate, historical subjects, capable of
understanding and making history. And some socialist feminists have drawn
on historical materialism in very creative ways, such as the standpoint theories of Alison Jaggar and Nancy Hartsock,[36] which attempt to articulate a
position from which women can make special historical claims without being
biologically determinist. But even Hartsock, Jaggar, and other socialist feminists who are attempting a multifactored historical analysis of the oppression
of women do not treat the domination of nature as a significant category for
feminism, although they notice it in passing.

In general, socialist feminists are very unsympathetic to "cultural feminism."[37] They accuse it of being ahistorical, essentialist, which they define as
believing in male and female essences (male = bad, female = good), and anti-
intellectual. This debate partakes of the ontology versus epistemology debate
in western philosophy, where "being" is opposed to "knowing," and implicitly women are relegated to the realm of "being," the ontological slums.
From an ecological (i.e., antidualistic) standpoint, essentialism and ontology
are not the same as biological determinism. In other words, we are neither
talking heads nor unselfconsciousness nature.

Although certain aspects of this critique may be correct, socialist feminists
are avoiding the important truths being recognized by cultural feminism,

among them the female political imagination manifesting itself in the political practice of a feminism of difference. They also forget that no revolution in human history has succeeded without a strong cultural foundation and a utopian vision emerging from the life experience of the revolutionary subjects. In part, I believe the myopia of socialist feminism with respect to cultural feminism is rooted in the old Marxist debate about the primacy of the base (economics/production) over the superstructure (culture/reproduction). This dualism must also be overcome, as a condition for a dialectical or genuinely ecological feminism.

The socialist feminist fidelity to a theory of history where women seek to understand the past in order to make the future is crucial to feminism. Also the project of a feminist reconstitution of reason has been largely undertaken by socialist feminists who do not wish to throw the baby out with the bath water in critiquing instrumental reason. But belief in a direct relationship between the rationalization and domination of nature and the project of human liberation remains a central tenet of socialism. The question for socialist feminists is whether they can accommodate their version of feminism within the socialist movement, or whether they will have to move in a "greener" direction with a more radical critique of all forms of the domination of nature. That would involve considering the recessive form of socialism—social anarchism—that finds its contemporary manifestation in green politics and among feminists in ecofeminism.[38]

ECOFEMINISM: ON THE NECESSITY OF HISTORY AND MYSTERY

Women have been culture's sacrifice to nature. The practice of human sacrifice to outsmart or appease a feared nature is ancient. And in resistance to this sacrificial mentality—on the part of both the sacrificer and the sacrificee—some feminists have argued against the association of women with nature, emphasizing the social dimension to traditional women's lives. Women's activities have been represented as nonsocial, as natural. Part of the work of feminism has been asserting that the activities of women, believed to be more natural, are in fact absolutely social. This process of looking at women's activities has led to a greater valuing of women's social contribution; it is part of the antisacrificial current of feminism. Giving birth is natural, although how it is done is very social, but mothering is an absolutely social activity.[39] In bringing up their children, mothers face ethical and moral choices as complex as those considered by professional policitians and ethicists. In the wake of feminism, women will continue to do these things, but the problem of connecting humanity to nature will have to be acknowledged and solved in a different way. In our mythology of complementarity, men and women have led vicarious lives, where women had feelings and led instinctual lives and men engaged in the projects illuminated by reason. Feminism has exposed the extent to which it was all a lie; thus, it has been so important to feminism to establish the mindful, social nature of mothering.

But just as women are refusing to be sacrificed, nonhuman nature is requiring even more attention; it is revolting against human domination in the ecological crisis. Part of the resistance to contemporary feminism is that it embodies the return of the repressed, those things men put away to create a dualistic culture founded on the domination of nature. Now, nature moves to the center of the social and political choices facing humanity.

It is as if women were entrusted with and kept the dirty little secret that humanity emerges from nonhuman nature into society in the life of the species, and the person. The process of nurturing an unsocialized, undifferentiated human infant into an adult person—the socialization of the organic—is the bridge between nature and culture. The western male bourgeois subject then extracts himself from the realm of the organic to become a public citizen, as if born from the head of Zeus. He puts away childish things. Then he disempowers and sentimentalizes his mother, sacrificing her to nature. The coming of age of the male subject repeats the drama of the emergence of the polis, made possible by banishing the mother, and with her the organic world. But the key to the historic agency of women with respect to nature/culture dualism lies in the fact that the mediating traditional conversion activities of women—mothering, cooking, healing, farming, foraging—are as social as they are natural.

The task of an ecological feminism is the organic forging of a genuinely antidualistic, or dialectical, theory and praxis. No previous feminism can address this problem adequately from within the framework of their theory and politics, hence the necessity of ecofeminism. Rather than succumb to nihilism, pessimism, and an end to reason and history, we seek to enter into history, to habilitate a genuinely ethical thinking—where one uses mind and history to reason from the "is" to the "ought" and to reconcile humanity with nature, within and without. This is the starting point for ecofeminism.

Each major contemporary feminist theory—liberal, social, cultural—has taken up the issue of the relationship between women and nature. Each in its own way has capitulated to dualistic thinking, theoretically conflating a reconciliation with nature by surrendering to some form of natural determinism. As I have demonstrated, we have seen the same positions appear again and again in extending the natural into the social (cultural feminism) or in severing the social from the natural (socialist feminism). Each direction forms two sides of the same dualism, and from an ecofeminist perspective both are wrong because they have chosen between culture and nature. I contend that this is a false choice, leading to bad politics and bad theory on each side and that we need a new, dialectical way of thinking about our relationship to nature to realize the full meaning and potential of feminism, a social ecological feminism.

Absolute social constructionism on which socialist feminism relies is disembodied. The logical conclusion is a rationalized, denatured, totally deconstructed person. But socialist feminism is the antisacrificial current of feminism, with its insistence that women are social beings, whose traditional work is as social as it is natural. The fidelity to the social aspects of women's lives found in socialist feminism makes a crucial contribution to ecofeminism.

It is for ecofeminism to interpret the historical significance of the fact that women have been positioned at the biological dividing line where the organic emerges into the social. It is for ecofeminism to interpret this fact historically and to make the most of this mediated subjectivity to heal a divided world. The domination of nature originates in society and therefore must be resolved in society. Therefore, the embodied woman as social historical agent, rather than product of natural law, is the subject of ecofeminism.

But the weakness of socialist feminism's theory of the person is serious from an ecofeminist standpoint. An ecological feminism calls for a dynamic, developmental theory of the person—male and female—who emerges out of nonhuman nature, where difference is neither reified or ignored and the dialectical relationship between human and nonhuman nature is understood.

Cultural feminism's greatest weakness is its tendency to make the personal into the political, with its emphasis on personal transformation and empowerment. This is most obvious in cultural feminists' attempt to overcome the apparent opposition between spirituality and politics. For cultural feminists spirituality is the heart in a heartless world, whereas for socialist feminists it is the opiate of the people. Cultural feminists have formed the "beloved community" of feminism—with all the power, potential, and problems of a religion. For several years spiritual feminism has been the fastest growing part of the women's movement, with spirituality circles often replacing consciousness-raising groups as the place that women meet for personal empowerment.

As an appropriate response to the need for mystery and attention to personal alienation in an overly rationalized world it is a vital and important movement. But by itself it does not provide the basis for a genuinely dialectical ecofeminist theory and praxis, addressing history as well as mystery. For this reason, cultural/spiritual feminism, sometimes even called "nature feminism," is not synonymous with ecofeminism in that creating a gynocentric culture and politics is a necessary but insufficient condition for ecofeminism.

Healing the split between the political and the spiritual cannot be done at the expense of either repudiating the rational or developing a historically informed, dynamic political program. Socialist feminists have often mistakenly ridiculed spiritual feminists for having "false consciousness" or being "idealist." Socialism's impoverished idea of personhood, which denies the qualitative dimensions of subjectivity, is a major reason socialism, including socialist-feminism, has no political base.[40] But many practitioners of feminist spirituality have eschewed thinking about politics and power, arguing that personal empowerment is in and of itself a sufficient agent of social transformation.

Both feminism and ecology embody the revolt of nature against human domination. They demand that we rethink the relationship between humanity and the rest of nature, including our natural, embodied selves. In ecofeminism, nature is the central category of analysis. An analysis of the interrelated dominations of nature—psyche and sexuality, human oppression, and nonhuman nature—and the historic position of women in relation to those forms of domination is the starting point of ecofeminist theory. We share with cultural feminism the necessity of a politics with heart and a beloved community, recognizing our connection with each other, and nonhuman nature. Socialist feminism has given us a powerful critical perspective with which to understand and transform history. Separately, they perpetuate the dualism of "mind" and "nature." Together they make possible a new ecological relationship between nature and culture, in which mind and nature, heart and reason, join forces to transform the internal and external systems of domination that threaten the existence of life on earth.

Practice does not wait for theory; it comes out of the imperatives of history. Women are the revolutionary bearers of this antidualistic potential in the world today. In additional to the enormous impact of feminism on western civilization, women have been at the forefront of every historical, political movement to reclaim the earth. A principle of reconciliation, with an organic praxis of nonoppositional opposition, provides the basis for an ecofeminist politics. The laboratory of nonoppositional opposition is the action taken worldwide by women, women who do not necessarily call themselves feminists.

For example, for many years in India poor women who came out of the Gandhian movement have waged a nonviolent land reform and forest preservation campaign, called the Chipko Andolan (the Hugging Movement). Each woman has a tree of her own to protect, to steward, by wrapping her body around a tree as bulldozers arrive.[41] When loggers were sent in, one movement leader said, "Let them know they will not fell a single tree without the felling of us first. When the men raise their axes, we will embrace the trees to protect them."[42] These women have waged a remarkably successful nonviolent struggle, and their tactics have spread to other parts of India. Men have joined this campaign, although it was originated and continues to be led by women. Yet this is not a sentimental movement; lives depend on the survival of the forest. For most women of the world, interest in the preservation of the land, water, air, and energy is no abstraction but a clear part of the effort to simply survive.

The increasing militarization of the world has intensified this struggle. Women and children make up 80 percent of war refugees. Land they are left with is often burned and scarred in such a way as to prevent cultivation for many years after battle so starvation and hardship follow long after the fighting has stopped.[43] And here too women—often mothers and farmers —respond to necessity. They become the guardians of the earth in an effort to eke out a small living on the land to feed themselves and their families.

Other areas of feminist activism also illuminate an enlightened ecofeminist perspective.[44] Potentially, one of the best examples of an appropriately mediated, dialectical relationship to nature is the feminist health movement. The medicalization of childbirth in the first part of the twentieth century and the later redesign and appropriation of reproduction both create new profit-making technologies for capitalism and make heretofore natural processes mediated by women into arenas controlled by men. Here women offered themselves up to the ministrations of experts,[45] internalizing the notion they do not know enough, and surrender their power. They also accepted the idea that the maximum intervention in and the domination of nature is an inherent good.

But since the onset of feminism in the 1960s, women in the United States have gone quite a way in reappropriating and demedicalizing childbirth. As a result of this movement, many more women want to be given all their options, choosing invasive medical technologies only under unusual and informed circumstances. They do not necessarily reject these technologies as useful in some cases, but they have pointed a finger at motivations of profit and control in their widespread application. Likewise, my argument here is not that feminism should repudiate all aspects of western science and medicine; rather, I assert that we should develop the sophistication to decide for ourselves when intervention serves our best interest.

A related critical area for a genuinely dialectical praxis is a reconstruction of science, taking into account the critique of science advanced by radical ecology and feminism.[46] Feminist historians and philosophers of science are demonstrating that the will to know and the will to power need not be the same thing. They argue that there are ways of knowing the world that are not based on objectification and domination.[47] Here again, apparently antithetical epistemologies, science and mysticism, coexist. We shall need all our ways of knowing to create life on this planet that is both ecological, sustainable, and free.

As feminists, we shall need to develop an ideal of freedom that is neither antisocial nor antinatural.[48] We are past the point of a Rousseauian throwing off of our chains to reclaim our ostensibly free nature, if such a point ever existed. Ecofeminism is not an argument for a return to prehistory. The knowledge that women were not always dominated and that society was not always hierarchical is a powerful inspiration for contemporary women, so long as such a society is not represented as a "natural order" apart from history to which we will inevitably return by a great reversal.

From an ecofeminist perspective, we are part of nature, but neither inherently good or bad, free or unfree. No one natural order represents freedom. We are *potentially* free in nature, but as human beings that freedom must be intentionally created by using our understanding of the natural world of which we are a part in a noninstrumental way. For this reason we must develop a different understanding of the relationship between human and nonhuman nature. To do this we need a theory of history where the natural evolution of the planet and the social history of the species are not separated. We emerged from nonhuman nature, as the organic emerged from the inorganic.

Here, potentially, we recover ontology as the ground for ethics.[49] We thoughtful human beings must use the fullness of our sensibility and intelligence to push ourselves intentionally to another stage of evolution—one where we will fuse a new way of being human on this planet with a sense of the sacred, informed by all ways of knowing, intuitive *and* scientific, mystical *and* rational. It is the moment where women recognize ourselves as agents of history—yes, even unique agents—and knowingly bridge the classic dualisms between spirit and matter, art and politics, reason and intuition. This is the potentiality of a *rational* reenchantment. This is the project of ecofeminism.

At this point in history, the domination of nature is inextricably bound up with the domination of persons, and both must be addressed, without arguments over "the primary contradiction" in search of a single Archimedes point for revolution. There is no such thing. And there is no point in liberating people if the planet cannot sustain their liberated lives or in saving the planet by disregarding the preciousness of human existence, not only to ourselves but to the rest of life on earth.

NOTES

1. One major issue at the United Nations Decade on Women Forum held in Nairobi, Kenya, in 1985 was the effect of the international monetary system on

women and the particular burdens women bear because of the money owed the "first world" particularly U.S. economic interests, by developing countries.

2. The animal liberation movement is more developed in the United Kingdom than in the United States. One of its major publications is a periodical called *Beast: The Magazine That Bites Back*. See Peter Singer, *Animal Liberation: A New Ethics For Our Treatment of Animals* (New York: Avon Books, 1975).

3. The National Organization for Women (NOW) is caught in the myopia of this position, supporting the draft of women because men are drafted rather than taking an antimilitarist position and opposing the draft for anyone. At their Denver convention held in June 1986 NOW began to evalulate its prodraft position, but it will be a while before this process proceeds through the state committee structures and takes on national significance. Even then, there is no guarantee that it will change its position.

4. It is one of the absurd examples of newspeak that the designation "pro-life" has been appropriated by the militarist right to support forced child bearing.

5. Hans Jonas, *The Imperative of Responsibility: In Search of an Ethics for the Technological Age* (Chicago: University of Chicago Press, 1984), 136.

6. For a fuller discussion of this point, see William Leiss, *The Limits to Satisfaction: An Essay on the Problem of Needs and Commodities* (Toronto: University of Toronto Press, 1976).

7. In *The German Ideology* Marx cut his teeth on the "natural order" socialism of Feuerbach, although he had tended toward a "naturalistic socialism" himself in his early "Economic and Philosophic Manuscripts." See T. B. Bottomore, *Karl Marx: Early Writings* (New York: McGraw-Hill, 1964).

Since Marx, scientific socialists have argued that socialism is the culmination of reason understood as the domination of nature, and have argued against utopianism. For Marxists "utopian" is a bad word; it means unrealistic, unscientific, anti-instrumental, by definition naive. Social anarchists have maintained a much more ambivalent relationship to the domination of nature and a fidelity to the cultural dimensions of pre-Marxist utopian socialism. Although both scientific socialism and social anarchism are parts of the historical socialist tradition, in a contemporary context the term "socialism" applies to the Marxists, as distinct from the "anarchists." Lately, there is a move afoot among socialists to "recover" the pre-Marxist utopian tradition and to utilize this forgotten history to save contemporary socialism. I think this is ahistorical in that it begs the problem of the need to critique the history (and theory) of anti-utopian Marxist socialism. Socialists and anarchists have had crucial ideological differences with respect to the domination of nature, the base/superstructure distinction, power and the state, sexuality and the individual. The contemporary "green" movement grows out of the social anarchist utopian socialist tradition, where the conditions for human freedom depend on *ending* the domination of nonhuman nature. It is crucial that socialists be honest about the shortcomings of their own movement, and, if they make a major historic shift in a direction they have scorned for over a century, this change should be acknowledged and examined. I also do not mean to suggest here either that social anarchism is a fully adequate theory or that the proper strategy for rectifying the domination of nature is a simple reversion. But the critique of socialism advanced through this work is illuminated by, but not limited to, that of social anarchism, and it is aimed at anti-utopian socialism.

8. For a full discussion of the relationship between feminist politics and ideas about human nature, see Alison M. Jaggar, *Feminist Politics and Human Nature* (Totowa, N.J.: Rowman and Allanheld, 1983).

9. See Christine DiStefano, "Gender and Political Theory: Gender as Ideology," for a fuller treatment of the problem of "deep masculinity" in political thought. Her section on the problematic relationship between feminism and liberalism is especially instructive. Ph.D. diss., University of Massachusetts, Amherst, 1985.

10. See Alison Jaggar, "Difference and Equality," (unpublished paper) for an exposition of the difference versus equality problem in feminist theory. She concludes by arguing that feminists must be able to argue our case based on either, or both.

11. Mary Wollstonecraft, *A Vindication of the Rights of Woman* (New York: W. W. Norton, 1967), 286.

12. Harriet Taylor Mill and John Stuart Mill, *On the Subjugation of Women* (London: Virago, 1983).

13. If the mother is given no special preference and both parents are presumed equally suited before the law, then the decision may be made on other grounds. Men generally have a larger income than women, especially women who have left the work force to mother children, and can arguably provide greater economic and cultural advantages.

14. See Alice Echols, "The New Feminism of Yin and Yang," in *The Powers of Desire,* ed. Ann Snitow, Sharon Thompson, and Christine Stansell (New York: Monthly Review Press, 1983).

15. See Alison M. Jaggar, *Feminist Politics and Human Nature.*

16. Alice Schwarzer, *After the Second Sex: Conversations With Simone de Beauvoir* (New York: Pantheon, 1984), 103.

17. See Shulamith Firestone, "Conclusion: The Ultimate Revolution," in *The Dialectic of Sex* (New York: Bantam Books, 1971).

18. This is evident in Zillah Eisenstein, *The Radical Future of Liberal Feminism* (New York: Longman, 1981), and Zillah Eisenstein, ed., *Capitalist Patriarchy and the Case for Socialist Feminism* (New York: Monthly Review Press, 1979).

19. See Sherry Ortner, "Is Female to Male as Nature is to Culture?" in *Woman, Culture and Society,* ed. Michele Rosaldo and Louise Lamphere (Palo Alto: Stanford University Press, 1974).

20. See Virginia Woolf, *Three Guineas* (New York: Harcourt, Brace & World, 1938).

21. See Mary Daly, *Gyn/ecology.* (Boston: Beacon Press, 1979). In response to her critics, Daly's position in her later work is intentionally ambiguous on these points. See *Pure Lust* (Boston: Beacon Press, 1985).

22. Johnson was solicited by the Citizens Party, a political party made up of both men and women, founded primarily to advocate "environmentalism" from a socialist perspective. It is interesting that a mixed party with an environmental (not ecological) emphasis, not a leftist party, drafted Johnson to run. Her analysis of all the political issues was basically an analysis of male power, and Mary Daly worked very hard for her candidacy. Prior to her campaign it was difficult to imagine how radical feminism would translate into the jargon and iconography of the American political arena, but Johnson did a very good job of this. She was widely criticized for having a naive un-

derstanding or being evangelical, but she articulated a woman centered perspective that had not previously been heard in presidential politics. Her message was basically simple—that women are different and therefore can make a difference if elected to public office. And she used the device of the imaginary cabinet to suggest department heads such as Barbara Deming for secretary of state. Barbara Deming was a well-known feminist pacifist whose essays are collected in a volume, *We Are All Part of One Another* (Philadelphia: New Society Publishers, 1983). She was alive at the time of Johnson's candidacy and also supported her.

23. It is a good example of the care the reader must take in interpreting the medium of the artist. See Susan Griffin, *Women and Nature: The Roaring Inside Her* (New York: Harper & Row, 1978). Her later work on pornography *Pornography and Silence: Culture's Revenge Against Nature* (New York: Harper & Row, 1981). Her forthcoming work on war, "A Woman Thinks About War" (manuscript), is an explicitly theoretical, ecofeminist work.

24. Much iconography of the contemporary radical feminist peace movement is inspired by the feminist spirituality movement, devising political actions that use the imagery of embodied female spirituality. Actions have featured guerrilla theater where the Furies ravage Ronald Reagan, women encircle military bases and war research centers with pictures of children, trees, brooks in preparation for civil disobedience, and weave shut the doors of the stock exchange.

25. See Peter Kropotkin, *Mutual Aid: A Factor in Evolution* (Boston: Porter Sargent, 1914).

26. See the works of scientists Lynn Margolis and James Lovelock, especially J. E. Lovelock, *Gaia: A New Look at Life on Earth* (New York: Oxford University Press, 1982).

27. See "The Cumbahee River Collective Statement," in Zillah Eisenstein, ed., *Capitalist Patriarchy*; Cherrie Moraga and Gloria Anzuldua, *This Bridge Called My Back* (New York: Kitchen Table Press, 1983); Gloria Joseph and Jill Lewis, *Common Differences: Conflicts in Black and White Feminist Perspectives* (Garden City, N.Y.: Anchor Press, 1981); and Bell Hooks, *Feminist Theory: From Margin to Center* (Boston: South End Press, 1984). Audre Lorde has written eloquently of the problems of attempting to "use the master's tools to disassemble the master's house" and the implicit racism of heretofore definitions of "theory." See Audre Lorde, *Sister Outsider* (Trumansburg, N.Y.: The Crossing Press, 1986).

28. See Louisah Teish, *Jambalaya* (San Francisco: Harper & Row, 1986).

29. These traditions are complex, and there are critical differences among them. Each has an ancient and total cosmology and set of practices, and, although it is possible to find commonalities, creating a willy-nilly, random patchwork is not a brilliant new synthesis. That is the problem with the incoherent mush called "new age spirituality" or its slightly more secular version "the human potential movement." Each religious tradition requires instruction, which may be in an oral or written tradition, or both, study, and the discipline of practice. I also do not know that traditions and cultures that apparently have an antidualistic perspective when it comes to the relationship between human and nonhuman nature are *necessarily* not sexist, xenophobic, or hierarchical in a contemporary context, even if they once were.

30. See Ynestra King, "Thinking About Seneca," *Ikon* (Summer 1984). In this

piece I addressed the contradictions of the mostly white women's peace movement, which grew out of an ecofeminist perspective. In response to the concern that the feminist peace movement up to that point was mostly white, I explored what I believed to be underlying commonalities between the "womanist" feminism of women of color, which affirms the traditional lives and struggles of women, and a feminism that up to that point had been mostly articulated by white women who believed feminism should associate itself with ecology and peace, adopting rather than repudiating the traditional concerns of women.

31. I am thinking here of the annual "Socialist Scholars Conference," held each spring in New York City, or the socialist caucus offerings at academic conferences.

32. See Jean Baudrillard, *The Mirror of Production* (St. Louis: Telos Press, 1975).

33. In raising these issues I am in no way advocating the criminalization of women who market their eggs or wombs. And obviously, there are critical economic and class issues here.

34. See especially Eisenstein, *The Radical Future of Liberal Feminism.*

35. One exception is Carolyn Merchant, who has written a socialist feminist analysis of the scientific revolution, *The Death of Nature: Women, Ecology and the Scientific Revolution* (New York: Harper & Row, 1979). See also Carolyn Merchant, "Earthcare: Women and the Environmental Movement," *Environment* 23, no. 5 (June 1981):6.

36. See Nancy Hartsock, *Money, Sex and Power* (Boston: Northeastern University Press, 1983), and Jaggar, *Feminist Politics and Human Nature.*

37. Cultural feminism is a term invented by feminists who believe in the primacy of economic, as opposed to cultural, forces in making history, but cultural feminists are proud of their emphasis.

38. See note 8.

39. On the social, mindful nature of mothering see the work of Sara Ruddick, especially "Maternal Thinking," *Feminist Studies* 6, no. 2 (Summer 1980):342–367; and "Preservative Love and Military Destruction: Some Reflections on Mothering and Peace," in *Mothering: Essays in Feminist Theory,* ed. Joyce Trebilcot (Totowa, N.J.: Rowman and Allanheld, 1983), 231–262.

40. The most vital socialism in the world today is liberation theology, with its roots in the Catholic base communities of the poor in Latin America.

41. Catherine Caufield, *In the Rainforest* (Chicago: University of Chicago Press, 1984), 156–158.

42. Ibid., 157.

43. See Edward Hyams, *Soil and Civilization* (New York: Harper & Row, 1976).

44. West German green Petra Kelly outlines a practical, feminist green political analysis and program, with examples of ongoing movements and activities in her work. Petra Kelly, *Fighting for Hope* (Boston: South End Press, 1984).

45. See Barbara Ehrenreich and Dierdre English, *For Her Own Good: 150 Years of the Experts Advice to Women* (Garden City, N.Y.: Anchor Press, 1979).

46. See Elizabeth Fee, "Is Feminism a Threat to Scientific Objectivity?" *International Journal of Women's Studies* 4, no. 4, (1981). See also Sandra Harding, *The Science Question in Feminism* (Ithaca, N.Y.: Cornell University Press, 1986) and Evelyn

Fox Keller, *Reflections on Gender and Science* (New Haven, Conn.: Yale University Press, 1985).

47. See Evelyn Fox Keller, *A Feeling for the Organism: The Life and Work of Barbara McClintock* (San Francisco, W. H. Freeman, 1983).

48. The crosscultural interpretations of personal freedom of anthropologist Dorothy Lee are evocative of the possibility of such an ideal of freedom. See Dorothy Lee, *Freedom and Culture* (New York: Prentice Hall, 1959).

49. I am aware that this is a controversial point, one that I am developing more explicitly in a work on ecofeminist ethics.

REFERENCES

Baudrillard, Jean. 1975. *The Mirror of Production*. St. Louis: Telos Press.

Bookchin, Murray. 1982. *The Ecology of Freedom*. Palo Alto, Calif.: Cheshire Books.

Bottomore, T. B. 1964. *Karl Marx: Early Writings*. New York: McGraw-Hill.

Caufield, Catherine. 1984. *In the Rainforest*. Chicago: University of Chicago Press.

Cumbahee River Collective. 1979. "Cumbahee River Collective Statement." In *Capitalist Patriarchy*, ed. Zillah Eisenstein.

Daly, Mary. 1979. *Gyn/ecology*. Boston: Beacon Press.

———. 1985. *Pure Lust*. Boston: Beacon Press.

Deming, Barbara. 1983. *We Are All Part of One Another*. Philadelphia: New Society Publishers.

DiStefano, Christine. 1985. "Gender and Political Theory: Gender as Ideology." Ph.D. diss., University of Massachusetts, Amherst.

Echols, Alice. 1983. "The New Feminism of Yin and Yang." In *The Powers of Desire*, ed. Snitow, Thompson, and Stansell.

Ehrenreich, Barbara, and Dierdre English. 1978. *For Her Own Good*. Garden City, N.Y.: Anchor Press.

Eisenstein, Zillah, ed. 1979. *Capitalist Patriarchy and the Case for Socialist Feminism*. New York: Monthly Review Press.

———. 1981. *The Radical Future of Liberal Feminism*. New York: Longman.

Fee, Elizabeth. 1981. "Is Feminism a Threat to Scientific Objectivity?" *International Journal of Women's Studies* 4, no. 4.

Firestone, Shulamith. 1971. *The Dialectic of Sex*. New York: Bantam Books.

Griffin, Susan. 1978. *Woman and Nature: The Roaring Inside Her*. New York: Harper & Row.

———. 1981. *Pornography and Silence: Culture's Revenge Against Nature*. New York: Harper & Row.

———. 1988. "A Woman Thinks About War." Manuscript.

Harding, Sandra. 1986. *The Science Question in Feminism*. Ithaca, N.Y.: Cornell University Press.

Hartsock, Nancy. 1983. *Money, Sex and Power*. Boston: Northeastern University Press.

Hooks, Bell. 1984. *Feminist Theory: From Margin to Center*. Boston: South End Press.

Hyams, Edward. 1976. *Soil and Civilization*. New York: Harper & Row.

Jaggar, Alison M. 1983. *Feminist Politics and Human Nature*. Totowa, N.J.: Rowman and Allanheld.

Jonas, Hans. *The Imperative of Responsibility: In Search of an Ethics for the Technological Age*. Chicago: University of Chicago Press.

Joseph, Gloria, and Jill Lewis. *Common Differences: Conflicts in Black and White Feminist Perspectives*. Garden City, N.Y.: Anchor Press, 1981.

Keller, Evelyn Fox. 1983. *A Feeling for the Organism: The Life and Work of Barbara McClintock*. San Francisco: W. H. Freeman.

_____. 1985. *Reflections on Gender and Science*. New Haven, Conn.: Yale University Press.

Kelly, Petra. 1984. *Fighting for Hope*. Boston: South End Press.

King, Ynestra. 1982. "Feminism and the Revolt of Nature." *Heresies* 13.

_____. 1982. "Toward An Ecological Feminism and a Feminist Ecology." In *Machina Ex Dea*, ed. Joan Rothschild. New York: Pergamon Press.

_____. 1984. "Thinking About Seneca." *Ikon*.

Kropotkin, Peter. 1914. *Mutual Aid: A Factor in Evolution*. Boston: Porter Sargeant.

Lee, Dorothy. 1959. *Freedom and Culture*. New York: Prentice-Hall.

Leiss, William. 1976. *The Limits to Satisfaction: An Essay on the Problem of Needs and Commodities*. Toronto: University of Toronto Press.

Lorde, Audre. 1986. *Sister Outsider*. Trumansburg, N.Y.: The Crossing Press.

Lovelock, James E. 1982. *Gaia: A New Look at Life on Earth*. New York: Oxford University Press.

Merchant, Carolyn. 1979. *The Death of Nature: Women, Ecology and the Scientific Revolution*. New York: Harper & Row.

_____. 1981. "Earthcare: Women and the Environmental Movement." *Environment* 23, no. 5 (June).

Mill, Harriet Taylor, and John Stuart Mill. 1983. *On the Subjugation of Women*. London: Virago.

Moraga, Cherrie, and Gloria Anzuldua. 1983. *This Bridge Called My Back*. New York: Kitchen Table Press.

Ortner, Sherry. 1974. "Is Female to Male as Nature is to Culture?" In *Woman, Culture and Society*, ed. Michele Rosaldo and Louise Lamphere.

Rosaldo, Michele, and Louise Lamphere. 1974. *Woman, Culture and Society*. Palo Alto: Stanford University Press.

Ruddick, Sara. 1980. "Maternal Thinking." *Feminist Studies* 6, no. 2 (Summer).

_____. 1983. "Preservative Love and Military Destruction: Some Reflections on Mothering and Peace." In *Mothering: Essays in Feminist Theory*, ed. Joyce Tribilcot.

Schwarzer, Alice. 1984. *After the Second Sex: Conversations With Simone de Beauvoir*. New York: Pantheon.

Singer, Peter. 1975. *Animal Liberation: A New Ethics For Our Treatment of Animals*. New York: Avon Books.

Snitow, Ann, Sharon Thompson, and Christine Stansell, eds. 1983. *The Powers of Desire*. New York: Monthly Review Press.

Teish, Louisah. 1986. *Jambalaya*. San Francisco: Harper & Row.

Tribilcot, Joyce, ed. 1983. *Mothering: Essays in Feminist Theory*. Totowa, N.J.: Rowman and Allanheld.

Wollstonecraft, Mary. 1967. *A Vindication of the Rights of Woman*. New York: W. W. Norton.

Woolf, Virginia. 1983. *Three Guineaus*. New York: Harcourt, Brace and World.

Part II
FEMINIST WAYS OF KNOWING

LOVE AND KNOWLEDGE:
EMOTION IN FEMINIST
EPISTEMOLOGY

Alison M. Jaggar

Within the western philosophical tradition, emotions usually have been considered as potentially or actually subversive of knowledge.[1] From Plato until the present, with a few notable exceptions, reason rather than emotion has been regarded as the indispensable faculty for acquiring knowledge.[2]

Typically, although again not invariably, the rational has been contrasted with the emotional, and this contrasted pair then has often been linked with other dichotomies. Not only has reason been contrasted with emotion, but it has also been associated with the mental, the cultural, the universal, the public, and the male, whereas emotion has been associated with the irrational, the physical, the natural, the particular, the private, and, of course, the female.

Although western epistemology has tended to give pride of place to reason rather than emotion, it has not always excluded emotion completely from the realm of reason. In the *Phaedrus*, Plato portrayed emotions, such as anger or curiosity, as irrational urges (horses) that must always be controlled by reason (the charioteer). On this model, the emotions were not seen as needing to be totally suppressed but rather as needing direction by reason: for example, in a genuinely threatening situation, it was thought not only irrational but foolhardy not to be afraid.[3] The split between reason and emotion was not absolute, therefore, for the Greeks. Instead, the emotions were thought of as providing indispensable motive power that needed to be channeled appropriately. Without horses, after all, the skill of the charioteer would be worthless.

The contrast between reason and emotion was sharpened in the seventeenth century by redefining reason as a purely instrumental faculty. For both the Greeks and the medieval philosophers, reason had been linked with value insofar as reason provided access to the objective structure or order of reality, seen as simultaneously natural and morally justified. With the rise of modern science, however, the realms of nature and value were separated: nature was stripped of value and reconceptualized as an inanimate mechanism of no intrinsic worth. Values were relocated in human beings, rooted in their preferences and emotional responses. The separation of supposedly natural fact from human value meant that reason, if it were to provide trustworthy insight into reality, had to be uncontaminated by or abstracted from value. Increasingly, therefore, though never universally,[4] reason was reconceptualized as the ability to make valid inferences from premises established elsewhere, the ability to calculate means but not to determine ends. The validity of logical inferences was thought independent of human attitudes and preferences; this was now the sense in which reason was taken to be objective and universal.[5]

The modern redefinition of rationality required a corresponding reconceptualization of emotion. This was achieved by portraying emotions as nonrational and often irrational urges that regularly swept the body, rather as a storm sweeps over the land. The common way of referring to the emotions as the "passions" emphasized that emotions happened to or were imposed upon an individual, something she suffered rather than something she did.

The epistemology associated with this new ontology rehabilitated sensory perception that, like emotion, typically had been suspected or even discounted by the western tradition as a reliable source of knowledge. British empiricism, succeeded in the nineteenth century by positivism, took its epistemological task to be the formulation of rules of inference that would guarantee the derivation of certain knowledge from the "raw data" supposedly given directly to the senses. Empirical testability became accepted as the hallmark of natural science; this, in turn, was viewed as the paradigm of genuine knowledge. Epistemology was often equated with the philosophy of science, and the dominant methodology of positivism prescribed that truly scientific knowledge must be capable of intersubjective verification. Because values and emotions had been defined as variable and idiosyncratic, positivism stipulated that trustworthy knowledge could be established only by methods that neutralized the values and emotions of individual scientists.

Recent approaches to epistemology have challenged some fundamental assumptions of the positivist epistemological model. Contemporary theorists of knowledge have undermined once rigid distinctions between analytic and synthetic statements, between theories and observations, and even between facts and values. However, few challenges have thus far been raised to the purported gap between emotion and knowledge. In this essay, I wish to begin bridging this gap through the suggestion that emotions may be helpful and even necessary rather than inimical to the construction of knowledge.

My account is exploratory in nature and leaves many questions unanswered. It is not supported by irrefutable arguments or conclusive proofs; instead, it should be viewed as a preliminary sketch for an epistemological model that will require much further development before its workability can be established.

EMOTION

1. What Are Emotions?

The philosophical question: What are emotions? requires both explicating the ways in which people ordinarily speak about emotion and evaluating the adequacy of those ways for expressing and illuminating experience and activity. Several problems confront someone trying to answer this deceptively simple question. One set of difficulties results from the variety, complexity, and even inconsistency of the ways in which emotions are viewed, in both daily life and scientific contexts. It is, in part, this variety that makes emotions into a "question" at the same time that it precludes answering that question by simple appeal to ordinary usage. A second set of difficulties is the wide range of phenomena covered by the term "emotion": these extend from apparently instantaneous "knee-jerk" responses of fright to lifelong dedication to an individual or a cause; from highly civilized aesthetic responses to undifferentiated feelings of hunger and thirst,[6] from background moods such as contentment or depression to intense and focused involvement in an immediate situation. It may well be impossible to construct a manageable account of emotion to cover such apparently diverse phenomena.

A further problem concerns the criteria for preferring one account of emotion to another. The more one learns about the ways in which other cultures conceptualize human faculties, the less plausible it becomes that emotions constitute what philosophers call a "natural kind." Not only do some cultures identify emotions unrecognized in the West, but there is reason to believe that the concept of emotion itself is a historical invention, like the concept of intelligence (Lewontin 1982) or even the concept of mind (Rorty 1979). For instance, anthropologist Catherine Lutz argues that the "dichotomous categories of 'cognition' and 'affect' are themselves Euroamerican cultural constructions, master symbols that participate in the fundamental organization of our ways of looking at ourselves and others (Lutz 1985, 1986), both in and outside of social science" (Lutz 1987:308). If this is true, then we have even more reason to wonder about the adequacy of ordinary western ways of talking about emotion. Yet we have no access either to our emotions or to those of others, independent of or unmediated by the discourse of our culture.

In the face of these difficulties, I shall sketch an account of emotion with the following limitations. First, it will operate within the context of western discussions of emotion: I shall not question, for instance, whether it would be possible or desirable to dispense entirely with anything resembling our concept of emotion. Second, although this account attempts to be consistent with as much as possible of western understandings of emotion, it is intended to cover only a limited domain, not every phenomenon that may be called an emotion. On the contrary, it excludes as genuine emotions both automatic physical responses and nonintentional sensations, such as hunger pangs. Third, I do not pretend to offer a complete theory of emotion; instead, I focus on a few specific aspects of emotion that I take to have been neglected or misrepresented, especially in positivist and neopositivist accounts. Finally, I would defend my approach not only on the ground that it illuminates aspects of our experience and activity that are obscured by positivist and neopositivist construals but also on the ground that it is less open than these to ideological abuse. In particular, I believe that recognizing certain neglected aspects of emotion makes possible a better and less ideologically biased account of how knowledge is, and so ought to be, constructed.

2. Emotions as Intentional

Early positivist approaches to understanding emotion assumed that an adequate account required analytically separating emotion from other human faculties. Just as positivist accounts of sense perception attempted to distinguish the supposedly raw data of sensation from their cognitive interpretations, so positivist accounts of emotion tried to separate emotion conceptually from both reason and sense perception. As part of their sharpening of these distinctions, positivist construals of emotion tended to identify emotions with the physical feelings or involuntary bodily movements that typically accompany them, such as pangs or qualms, flushes or tremors; emotions were also assimilated to the subduing of physiological function or movement, as in the case of sadness, depression, or boredom. The continuing influence of such supposedly scientific conceptions of emotion can be seen in the fact that "feeling" is often used colloquially as a synonym for emotion, even though the more central meaning of "feeling" is physiological sensation. On such accounts, emotions were not seen as being *about* anything: instead, they were contrasted with and seen as potential disruptions of other phenomena that *are* about some thing, phenomena, such as rational judgments, thoughts, and observations. The positivist approach to understanding emotion has been called the Dumb View (Spelman 1982).

The Dumb View of emotion is quite untenable. For one thing, the same feeling or physiological response is likely to be interpreted as various emotions, depending on the context of its experience. This point is often illustrated by reference to the famous Schachter and Singer experiment; excited feelings were induced in research subjects by the injection of adrenalin, and the subjects then attributed to themselves appropriate emotions depending on their context (Schachter and Singer 1969). Another problem with the Dumb View is that identifying emotions with feelings would make it impossible to postulate that a person might not be aware of her emotional state because feelings by definition are a matter of conscious awareness. Finally, emotions differ from feelings, sensations, or physiological responses in that they are dispositional rather than episodic. For instance, we may assert truthfully that we are outraged by, proud of, or saddened by certain events, even if at that moment we are neither agitated nor tearful.

In recent years, contemporary philosophers have tended to reject the Dumb View of emotion and have substituted more intentional or cognitivist understandings. These newer conceptions emphasize that intentional judgments as well as physiological disturbances are integral elements in emotion.[7] They define or identify emotions not by the quality or character of the physiological sensation that may be associated with them but rather by their intentional aspect, the associated judgment. Thus, it is the content of my associated thought or judgment that determines whether my physical agitation and restlessness are defined as "anxiety about my daughter's lateness" or "anticipation of tonight's performance."

Cognitivist accounts of emotion have been criticized as overly rationalist, inapplicable to allegedly spontaneous, automatic, or global emotions, such as general feelings of nervousness, contentedness, angst, ecstasy, or terror. Certainly, these accounts entail that infants and animals experience emotions, if at all, in only a primitive, rudimentary form. Far from being unacceptable, however, this entailment is desirable because it suggests that humans develop and mature in emotions as well as in other dimensions; they increase the range, variety, and subtlety of their emotional responses in accordance with their life experiences and their reflections on these.

Cognitivist accounts of emotion are not without their own problems. A serious difficulty with many is that they end up replicating within the structure of emotion the very problem they are trying to solve—namely, that of an artificial split between emotion and thought—because most cognitivist accounts explain emotion as having two "components": an affective or feeling component and a cognition that supposedly interprets or identifies the feelings. These accounts, therefore, unwittingly perpetuate the positivist

distinction between the shared, public, objective world of verifiable calculations, observations, and facts and the individual, private, subjective world of
idiosyncratic feelings and sensations. This sharp distinction breaks any conceptual links between our feelings and the "external" world: if feelings are
still conceived as blind or raw or undifferentiated, then we can give no sense
of the notion of feelings fitting or failing to fit our perceptual judgments, that
is, being appropriate or inappropriate. When intentionality is viewed as intellectual cognition and moved to the center of our picture of emotion, the affective elements are pushed to the periphery and become shadowy conceptual
danglers whose relevance to emotion is obscure or even negligible. An adequate cognitive account of emotion must overcome this problem.

Most cognitivist accounts of emotion thus remain problematic insofar as
they fail to explain the relation between the cognitive and the affective aspects
of emotion. Moreover, insofar as they prioritize the intellectual over the feeling aspects, they reinforce the traditional western preference for mind over
body.[8] Nevertheless, they do identify a vital feature of emotion overlooked
by the Dumb View, namely, its intentionality.

3. Emotions as Social Constructs

We tend to experience our emotions as involuntary individual responses to
situations, responses that are often (though, significantly, not always) private
in the sense that they are not perceived as directly and immediately by other
people as they are by the subject of the experience. The apparently individual
and involuntary character of our emotional experience is often taken as evidence that emotions are presocial, instinctive responses, determined by our
biological constitution. This inference, however, is quite mistaken. Although
it is probably true that the physiological disturbances characterizing emotions—facial grimaces, changes in the metabolic rate, sweating, trembling,
tears, and so on—are continuous with the instinctive responses of our pre-
human ancestors and also that the ontogeny of emotions to some extent re-
capitulates their phylogeny, mature human emotions can be seen as neither
instinctive nor biologically determined. Instead, they are socially constructed
on several levels.

Emotions are most obviously socially constructed in that children are
taught deliberately what their culture defines as appropriate responses to certain situations: to fear strangers, to enjoy spicy food, or to like swimming in
cold water. On a less conscious level, children also learn what their culture
defines as the appropriate ways to express the emotions that it recognizes. Although there may be crosscultural similarities in the expression of some apparently universal emotions, there are also wide divergences in what are

recognized as expressions of grief, respect, contempt, or anger. On an even deeper level, cultures construct divergent understandings of what emotions are. For instance, English metaphors and metonymies are said to reveal a "folk" theory of anger as a hot fluid, contained in a private space within an individual and liable to dangerous public explosion (Lakoff and Kovecses 1987). By contrast, the Ilongot, a people of the Philippines, apparently do not understand the self in terms of a public/private distinction and consequently do not experience anger as an explosive internal force: for them, rather, it is an interpersonal phenomenon for which an individual may, for instance, be paid (Rosaldo 1984).

Further aspects of the social construction of emotion are revealed through reflection on emotion's intentional structure. If emotions necessarily involve judgments, then obviously they require concepts, which may be seen as socially constructed ways of organizing and making sense of the world. For this reason, emotions are simultaneously made possible and limited by the conceptual and linguistic resources of a society. This philosophical claim is borne out by empirical observation of the cultural variability of emotion. Although there is considerable overlap in the emotions identified by many cultures (Wierzbicka 1986), at least some emotions are historically or culturally specific, including perhaps *ennui, angst,* the Japanese *amai* (in which one clings to another, affiliative love) and the response of "being a wild pig," which occurs among the Gururumba, a horticultural people living in the New Guinea Highlands (Averell 1980:158). Even apparently universal emotions, such as anger or love may vary crossculturally. We have just seen that the Ilongot experience of anger apparently is quite different from the modern western experience. Romantic love was invented in the Middle Ages in Europe and since that time has been modified considerably; for instance, it is no longer confined to the nobility, and it no longer needs to be extramarital or unconsummated. In some cultures, romantic love does not exist at all.[9]

Thus, there are complex linguistic and other social preconditions for the experience, that is, for the existence of human emotions. The emotions that we experience reflect prevailing forms of social life. For instance, one could not feel or even be betrayed in the absence of social norms about fidelity: it is inconceivable that betrayal or indeed any distinctively human emotion could be experienced by a solitary individual in some hypothetical presocial state of nature. There is a sense in which any individual's guilt or anger, joy or triumph, presupposes the existence of a social group capable of feeling guilt, anger, joy, or triumph. This is not to say that group emotions historically precede or are logically prior to the emotions of individuals; it is to say that individual experience is simultaneously social experience.[10] In later sections, I shall explore the epistemological and political implications of this social rather than individual understanding of emotion.

4. Emotions as Active Engagements

We often interpret our emotions as experiences that overwhelm us rather than as responses we consciously choose: that emotions are to some extent involuntary is part of the ordinary meaning of the term "emotion." Even in daily life, however, we recognize that emotions are not entirely involuntary, and we try to gain control over them in various ways, ranging from mechanistic behavior modification techniques designed to sensitize or desensitize our feeling responses to various situations to cognitive techniques designed to help us to think differently about situations. For instance, we might try to change our response to an upsetting situation by thinking about it in a way that will either divert our attention from its more painful aspects or present it as necessary for some larger good.

Some psychological theories interpret emotions as chosen on an even deeper level—as actions for which the agent disclaims responsibility. For instance, the psychologist Averell likens the experience of emotion to playing a culturally recognized role: we ordinarily perform so smoothly and automatically that we do not realize we are giving a performance. He provides many examples demonstrating that even extreme and apparently totally involving displays of emotion in fact are functional for the individual and/or the society.[11] For example, students requested to record their experiences of anger or annoyance over a two-week period came to realize that their anger was not as uncontrollable and irrational as they had assumed previously, and they noted the usefulness and effectiveness of anger in achieving various social goods. Averell, notes, however, that emotions are often useful in attaining their goals only if they are interpreted as passions rather than as actions, and he cites the case of one subject led to reflect on her anger who later wrote that it was less useful as a defence mechanism when she became conscious of its function.

The action/passion dichotomy is too simple for understanding emotion, as it is for other aspects of our lives. Perhaps it is more helpful to think of emotions as habitual responses that we may have more or less difficulty in breaking. We claim or disclaim responsibility for these responses depending on our purposes in a particular context. We could never experience our emotions entirely as deliberate actions, for then they would appear nongenuine and inauthentic, but neither should emotions be seen as nonintentional, primal, or physical forces with which our rational selves are forever at war. As they have been socially constructed, so may they be reconstructed, although describing how this might happen would require a long and complicated story.

Emotions, then, are wrongly seen as necessarily passive or involuntary responses to the world. Rather, they are ways in which we engage actively and even construct the world. They have both mental and physical aspects, each of which conditions the other. In some respects, they are chosen, but in others they are involuntary; they presuppose language and a social order. Thus, they can be attributed only to what are sometimes called "whole persons," engaged in the on-going activity of social life.

5. Emotion, Evaluation, and Observation

Emotions and values are closely related. The relation is so close, indeed, that some philosophical accounts of what it is to hold or express certain values reduce these phenomena to nothing more than holding or expressing certain emotional attitudes. When the relevant conception of emotion is the Dumb View, then simple emotivism certainly is too crude an account of what it is to hold a value; on this account, the intentionality of value judgments vanishes, and value judgments become nothing more than sophisticated grunts and groans. Nevertheless, the grain of important truth in emotivism is its recognition that values presuppose emotions to the extent that emotions provide the experiential basis for values. If we had no emotional responses to the world, it is inconceivable that we should ever come to value one state of affairs more highly than another.

Just as values presuppose emotions, so emotions presuppose values. The object of an emotion—that is, the object of fear, grief, pride, and so on—is a complex state of affairs that is appraised or evaluated by the individual. For instance, my pride in a friend's achievement necessarily incorporates the value judgment that my friend has done something worthy of admiration.

Emotions and evaluations, then, are logically or conceptually connected. Indeed, many evaluative terms derive directly from words for emotions: "desirable," "admirable," "contemptible," "despicable," "respectable," and so on. Certainly it is true (pace J. S. Mill) that the evaluation of a situation as desirable or dangerous does not entail that it is universally desired or feared but it does entail that desire or fear is viewed generally as an appropriate response to the situation. If someone is unafraid in a situation generally perceived as dangerous, her lack of fear requires further explanation; conversely, if someone is afraid without evident danger, then her fear demands explanation; and, if no danger can be identified, her fear is denounced as irrational or pathological. Thus, every emotion presupposes an evaluation of some aspect of the environment while, conversely, every evaluation or appraisal of the situation implies that those who share that evaluation will share, *ceteris paribus,* a predictable emotional response to the situation.

The rejection of the Dumb View and the recognition of intentional elements in emotion already incorporate a realization that observation influences and indeed partially constitutes emotion. We have seen already that distinctively human emotions are not simple instinctive responses to situations or events; instead, they depend essentially on the ways that we perceive those situations and events, as well on the ways that we have learned or decided to respond to them. Without characteristically human perceptions of and engagements in the world, there would be no characteristically human emotions.

Just as observation directs, shapes, and partially defines emotion, so too emotion directs, shapes, and even partially defines observation. Observation is not simply a passive process of absorbing impressions or recording stimuli; instead, it is an activity of selection and interpretation. What is selected and how it is interpreted are influenced by emotional attitudes. On the level of individual observation, this influence has always been apparent to common sense, noting that we remark on very different features of the world when we are happy or depressed, fearful or confident. This influence of emotion on perception is now being explored by social scientists. One example is the so-called Honi phenomenon, named after a subject called Honi who, under identical experimental conditions, perceived strangers' heads as changing in size but saw her husband's head as remaining the same.[12]

The most obvious significance of this sort of example is illustrating how the individual experience of emotion focuses our attention selectively, directing, shaping, and even partially defining our observations, just as our observations direct, shape, and partially define our emotions. In addition, the example has been taken further in an argument for the social construction of what are taken in any situation to be undisputed facts, showing how these rest on intersubjective agreements that consist partly in shared assumptions about "normal" or appropriate emotional responses to situations (McLaughlin 1985). Thus, these examples suggest that certain emotional attitudes are involved on a deep level in all observation, in the intersubjectively verified and so supposedly dispassionate observations of science as well as in the common perceptions of daily life. In the next section, I shall elaborate this claim.

EPISTEMOLOGY

6. The Myth of Dispassionate Investigation

As we have already seen, western epistemology has tended to view emotion with suspicion and even hostility.[13] This derogatory western attitude toward emotion, like the earlier western contempt for sensory observation, fails to recognize that emotion, like sensory perception, is necessary to human survival. Emotions prompt us to act appropriately, to approach some people and situations and to avoid others, to caress or cuddle, fight or flee. Without emotion, human life would be unthinkable. Moreover, emotions have an intrinsic as well as an instrumental value. Although not all emotions are enjoyable or even justifiable, as we shall see, life without any emotion would be life without any meaning.

Within the context of western culture, however, people have often been encouraged to control or even suppress their emotions. Consequently, it is not unusual for people to be unaware of their emotional state or to deny it to themselves and others. This lack of awareness, especially combined with a neopositivist understanding of emotion that construes it just as a feeling of which one is aware, lends plausibility to the myth of dispassionate investigation. But lack of awareness of emotions certainly does not mean that emotions are not present subconsciously or unconsciously or that subterranean emotions do not exert a continuing influence on people's articulated values and observations, thoughts and actions.[14]

Within the positivist tradition, the influence of emotion is usually seen only as distorting or impeding observation or knowledge. Certainly it is true that contempt, disgust, shame, revulsion, or fear may inhibit investigation of certain situations or phenomena. Furiously angry or extremely sad people often seem quite unaware of their surroundings or even their own conditions; they may fail to hear or may systematically misinterpret what other people say. People in love are notoriously oblivious to many aspects of the situation around them.

In spite of these examples, however, positivist epistemology recognizes that the role of emotion in the construction of knowledge is not invariably deleterious and that emotions may make a valuable contribution to knowledge. But the positivist tradition will allow emotion to play only the role of suggesting hypotheses for investigation. Emotions are allowed this because the so-called logic of discovery sets no limits on the idiosyncratic methods that investigators may use for generating hypotheses.

When hypotheses are to be tested, however, positivist epistemology imposes the much stricter logic of justification. The core of this logic is replicability, a criterion believed capable of eliminating or canceling out what are conceptualized as emotional as well as evaluative biases on the part of individual investigators. The conclusions of western science thus are presumed "objective," precisely in the sense that they are uncontaminated by the supposedly "subjective" values and emotions that might bias individual investigators (Nagel 1968:33−34).

But if, as has been argued, the positivist distinction between discovery and justification is not viable, then such a distinction is incapable of filtering out values in science. For example, although such a split, when built into the western scientific method, is generally successful in neutralizing the idiosyncratic or unconventional values of individual investigators, it has been argued that it does not, indeed cannot, eliminate generally accepted social values. These values are implicit in the identification of the problems considered worthy of investigation, in the selection of the hypotheses considered worthy of testing, and in the solutions to the problems considered worthy of acceptance. The science of past centuries provides sample evidence of the influence of prevailing social values, whether seventeenth-century atomistic physics (Merchant 1980) or, competitive interpretations of natural selection (Young 1985).

Of course, only hindsight allows us to identify clearly the values that shaped the science of the past and thus to reveal the formative influence on science of pervasive emotional attitudes, attitudes that typically went unremarked at the time because they were shared so generally. For instance, it is now glaringly evident that contempt for (and perhaps fear of) people of color is implicit in nineteenth-century anthropology's interpretation and even construction of anthropological facts. Because we are closer to them, however, it is harder for us to see how certain emotions, such as sexual possessiveness or the need to dominate others, currently are accepted as guiding principles in twentieth-century sociobiology or even defined as part of reason within political theory and economics (Quinby 1986).

Values and emotions enter into the science of the past and the present, not only on the level of scientific practice but also on the metascientific level, as answers to various questions: What is science? How should it be practiced? and What is the status of scientific investigation versus nonscientific modes of enquiry? For instance, it is claimed with increasing frequency that the modern western conception of science, which identifies knowledge with power and views it as a weapon for dominating nature, reflects the imperialism, racism, and misogyny of the societies that created it. Several feminist theorists have argued that modern epistemology itself may be viewed as an expression of certain emotions alleged to be especially characteristic of males in certain periods, such as separation anxiety and paranoia (Flax 1983; Bordo 1987) or an obsession with control and fear of contamination (Scheman 1985; Schott 1988).

Positivism views values and emotions as alien invaders that must be repelled by a stricter application of the scientific method. If the foregoing claims are correct, however, the scientific method and even its positivist construals themselves incorporate values and emotions. Moreover, such an incorporation seems a necessary feature of all knowledge and conceptions of knowledge. Therefore, rather than repressing emotion in epistemology it is necessary to rethink the relation between knowledge and emotion and construct conceptual models that demonstrate the mutually constitutive rather than oppositional relation between reason and emotion. Far from precluding the possibility of reliable knowledge, emotion as well as value must be shown as necessary to such knowledge. Despite its classical antecedents and like the ideal of disinterested enquiry, the ideal of dispassionate enquiry is an impossible dream but a dream nonetheless or perhaps a myth that has exerted enormous influence on western epistemology. Like all myths, it is a form of ideology that fulfils certain social and political functions.

7. The Ideological Function of the Myth

So far, I have spoken very generally of people and their emotions, as though everyone experienced similar emotions and dealt with them in similar ways. It is an axiom of feminist theory, however, that all generalizations about "people" are suspect. The divisions in our society are so deep, particularly the divisions of race, class, and gender, that many feminist theorists would claim that talk about people in general is ideologically dangerous because such talk obscures the fact that no one is simply a person but instead is constituted fundamentally by race, class, and gender. Race, class, and gender shape every aspect of our lives, and our emotional constitution is not excluded. Recognizing this helps us to see more clearly the political functions of the myth of the dispassionate investigator.

Feminist theorists have pointed out that the western tradition has not seen everyone as equally emotional. Instead, reason has been associated with members of dominant political, social, and cultural groups and emotion with members of subordinate groups. Prominent among those subordinate groups in our society are people of color, except for supposedly "inscrutable orientals," and women.[15]

Although the emotionality of women is a familiar cultural stereotype, its grounding is quite shaky. Women appear more emotional than men because they, along with some groups of people of color, are permitted and even required to express emotion more openly. In contemporary western culture, emotionally inexpressive women are suspect as not being real women,[16] whereas men who express their emotions freely are suspected of being homosexual or in some other way deviant from the masculine ideal. Modern western men, in contrast with Shakespeare's heroes, for instance, are required to present a facade of coolness, lack of excitement, even boredom, to express emotion only rarely and then for relatively trivial events, such as sporting occasions, where expressed emotions are acknowledged to be dramatized and so are not taken entirely seriously. Thus, women in our society form the main group allowed or even expected to feel emotion. A woman may cry in the face of disaster, and a man of color may gesticulate, but a white man merely sets his jaw.[17]

White men's control of their emotional expression may go to the extremes of repressing their emotions, failing to develop emotionally, or even losing the capacity to experience many emotions. Not uncommonly these men are unable to identify what they are feeling, and even they may be surprised, on occasion, by their own apparent lack of emotional response to a situation, such as death, where emotional reaction is perceived appropriate. In some married couples, the wife implicitly is assigned the job of feeling emotion for both of them. White, college-educated men increasingly enter therapy in order to learn how to "get in touch with" their emotions, a project other men may ridicule as weakness. In therapeutic situations, men may learn that they are just as emotional as women but less adept at identifying their own or others' emotions. In consequence, their emotional development may be relatively rudimentary; this may lead to moral rigidity or insensitivity. Paradoxically, men's lacking awareness of their own emotional responses frequently results in their being more influenced by emotion rather than less.

Although there is no reason to suppose that the thoughts and actions of women are any more influenced by emotion than the thoughts and actions of men, the stereotypes of cool men and emotional women continue to flourish because they are confirmed by an uncritical daily experience. In these circumstances, where there is a differential assignment of reason and emotion, it is easy to see the ideological function of the myth of the dispassionate investigator. It functions, obviously, to bolster the epistemic authority of the currently dominant groups, composed largely of white men, and to discredit the observations and claims of the currently subordinate groups including, of course, the observations and claims of many people of color and women. The more forcefully and vehemently the latter groups express their observations and claims, the more emotional they appear and so the more easily they are discredited. The alleged epistemic authority of the dominant groups then justifies their political authority.

The previous section of this chapter argued that dispassionate enquiry was a myth. This section has shown that the myth promotes a conception of epistemological justification vindicating the silencing of those, especially women, who are defined culturally as the bearers of emotion and so are perceived as more "subjective," biased, and irrational. In our present social context, therefore, the ideal of the dispassionate investigator is a classist, racist, and especially masculinist myth.[18]

8. *Emotional Hegemony and Emotional Subversion*

As we have seen already, mature human emotions are neither instinctive nor biologically determined, although they may have developed out of presocial, instinctive responses. Like everything else that is human, emotions in part are socially constructed; like all social constructs, they are historical products, bearing the marks of the society that constructed them. Within the very language of emotion, in our basic definitions and explanations of what it is to feel pride or embarrassment, resentment or contempt, cultural norms and expectations are embedded. Simply describing ourselves as angry, for instance, presupposes that we view ourselves as having been wronged, victimized by the violation of some social norm. Thus, we absorb the standards and values of our society in the very process of learning the language of emotion, and those standards and values are built into the foundation of our emotional constitution.

Within a hierarchical society, the norms and values that predominate tend to serve the interest of the dominant group. Within a capitalist, white supremacist, and male-dominant society, the predominant values will tend to serve the interests of rich white men. Consequently, we are all likely to develop an emotional constitution quite inappropriate for feminism. Whatever our color, we are likely to feel what Irving Thalberg has called "visceral racism"; whatever our sexual orientation, we are likely to be homophobic; whatever our class, we are likely to be at least somewhat ambitious and competitive; whatever our sex, we are likely to feel contempt for women. The emotional responses may be so deeply rooted in us that they are relatively impervious to intellectual argument and may recur even when we pay lip service to changed intellectual convictions.[19]

By forming our emotional constitution in particular ways, our society helps to ensure its own perpetuation. The dominant values are implicit in responses taken to be precultural or acultural, our so-called gut responses. Not only do these conservative responses hamper and disrupt our attempts to live in or prefigure alternative social forms, but also, and insofar as we take them to be natural responses, they blinker us theoretically. For instance, they limit our capacity for outrage; they either prevent us from despising or encourage us to despise; they lend plausibility to the belief that greed and domination are inevitable universal human motivations; in sum, they blind us to the possibility of alternative ways of living.

This picture may seem at first to support the positivist claim that the intrusion of emotion only disrupts the process of seeking knowledge and distorts the results of that process. The picture, however, is not complete; it ignores the fact that people do not always experience the conventionally acceptable emotions. They may feel satisfaction rather than embarrassment when their leaders make fools of themselves. They may feel resentment rather than gratitude for welfare payments and hand-me-downs. They may be attracted to forbidden modes of sexual expression. They may feel revulsion for socially sanctioned ways of treating children or animals. In other words, the hegemony that our society exercises over people's emotional constitution is not total.

People who experience conventionally unacceptable, or what I call "outlaw," emotions often are subordinated individuals who pay a disproportionately high price for maintaining the status quo. The social situation of such people makes them unable to experience the conventionally prescribed emotions: for instance, people of color are more likely to experience anger than amusement when a racist joke is recounted, and women subjected to male sexual banter are less likely to be flattered than uncomfortable or even afraid.

When unconventional emotional responses are experienced by isolated individuals, those concerned may be confused, unable to name their experience; they may even doubt their own sanity. Women may come to believe that they are "emotionally disturbed" and that the embarrassment or fear aroused in them by male sexual innuendo is prudery or paranoia. When certain emotions are shared or validated by others, however, the basis exists for forming a subculture defined by perceptions, norms, and values that systematically oppose the prevailing perceptions, norms, and values. By constituting the basis for such a subculture, outlaw emotions may be politically because epistemologically subversive.

Outlaw emotions are distinguished by their incompatibility with the dominant perceptions and values, and some, though certainly not all, of these outlaw emotions are potentially or actually feminist emotions. Emotions become feminist when they incorporate feminist perceptions and values, just as emotions are sexist or racist when they incorporate sexist or racist perceptions and values. For example, anger becomes feminist anger when it involves the perception that the persistent importuning endured by one woman is a single instance of a widespread pattern of sexual harassment, and pride becomes feminist pride when it is evoked by realizing that a certain person's achievement was possible only because that individual overcame specifically gendered obstacles to success.[20]

Outlaw emotions stand in a dialectical relation to critical social theory: at least some are necessary to develop a critical perspective on the world, but they also presuppose at least the beginnings of such a perspective. Feminists need to be aware of how we can draw on some of our outlaw emotions in constructing feminist theory and also of how the increasing sophistication of feminist theory can contribute to the reeducation, refinement, and eventual reconstruction of our emotional constitution.

9. Outlaw Emotions and Feminist Theory

The most obvious way in which feminist and other outlaw emotions can help in developing alternatives to prevailing conceptions of reality is by motivating new investigations. This is possible because, as we saw earlier, emotions may be long-term as well as momentary; it makes sense to say that someone continues to be shocked or saddened by a situation, even if she is at the moment laughing heartily. As we have seen already, theoretical investigation is always purposeful, and observation is always selective. Feminist emotions provide a political motivation for investigation and so help to determine the selection of problems as well as the method by which they are investigated. Susan Griffin makes the same point when she characterizes feminist theory as following "a direction determined by pain, and trauma, and compassion and outrage" (Griffin 1979:31).

As well as motivating critical research, outlaw emotions may also enable us to perceive the world differently from its portrayal in conventional descriptions. They may provide the first indications that something is wrong with the way alleged facts have been constructed, with accepted understandings of how things are. Conventionally unexpected or inappropriate emotions may precede our conscious recognition that accepted descriptions and justifications often conceal as much as reveal the prevailing state of affairs. Only when we reflect on our initially puzzling irritability, revulsion, anger, or fear may we bring to consciousness our "gut-level" awareness that we are in a situation of coercion, cruelty, injustice, or danger. Thus, conventionally inexplicable emotions, particularly, though not exclusively, those experienced by women, may lead us to make subversive observations that challenge dominant conceptions of the status quo. They may help us to realize that what are taken generally to be facts have been constructed in a way that obscures the reality of subordinated people, especially women's reality.

But why should we trust the emotional responses of women and other subordinated groups? How can we determine which outlaw emotions are to be endorsed or encouraged and which rejected? In what sense can we say that some emotional responses are more appropriate than others? What reason is there for supposing that certain alternative perceptions of the world, perceptions informed by outlaw emotions, are to be preferred to perceptions informed by conventional emotions? Here I can indicate only the general direction of an answer, whose full elaboration must await another occasion.[21]

I suggest that emotions are appropriate if they are characteristic of a society in which all humans (and perhaps some nonhuman life, too) thrive, or if they are conducive to establishing such a society. For instance, it is appropriate to feel joy when we are developing or exercizing our creative powers, and it is appropriate to feel anger and perhaps disgust in those situations where humans are denied their full creativity or freedom. Similarly, it is appropriate to feel fear if those capacities are threatened in us.

This suggestion obviously is extremely vague, verging on the tautologous. How can we apply it in situations where there is disagreement over what is or is not disgusting or exhilarating or unjust? Here I appeal to a claim for which I have argued elsewhere: the perspective on reality available from the standpoint of the oppressed, which in part at least is the standpoint of women, is a perspective that offers a less partial and distorted and therefore more reliable view (Jaggar 1983:chap. 11). Oppressed people have a kind of epistemological privilege insofar as they have easier access to this standpoint and therefore a better chance of ascertaining the possible beginnings of a society in which all could thrive. For this reason, I would claim that the emotional responses of oppressed people in general, and often of women in particular, are more likely to be appropriate than the emotional responses of the dominant class. That is, they are more likely to incorporate reliable appraisals of situations.

Even in contemporary science, where the ideology of dispassionate enquiry is almost overwhelming, it is possible to discover a few examples that seem to support the claim that certain emotions are more appropriate than others in both a moral and epistemological sense. For instance, Hilary Rose claims that women's practice of caring, even though warped by its containment in the alienated context of a coercive sexual division of labor, nevertheless has generated more accurate and less oppressive understandings of women's bodily functions, such as menstruation (Rose 1983). Certain emotions may be both morally appropriate and epistemologically advantageous in approaching the nonhuman and even the inanimate world. Jane Goodall's scientific contribution to our understanding of chimpanzee behavior seems to have been made possible only by her amazing empathy with or even love for these animals (Goodall 1987). In her study of Barbara McClintock, Evelyn Fox Keller describes McClintock's relation to the objects of her research—grains of maize and their genetic properties—as a relation of affection, empathy, and "the highest form of love: love that allows for intimacy without the annihilation of difference." She notes that McClintock's "vocabulary is consistently a vocabulary of affection, of kinship, of empathy" (Keller 1984:164). Examples like these prompt Hilary Rose to assert that a feminist science of nature needs to draw on heart as well as hand and brain.

10. *Some Implications of Recognizing the Epistemic Potential of Emotion*

Accepting that appropriate emotions are indispensable to reliable knowledge does not mean, of course, that uncritical feeling may be substituted for supposedly dispassionate investigation. Nor does it mean that the emotional responses of women and other members of the underclass are to be trusted without question. Although our emotions are epistemologically indispensable, they are not epistemologically indisputable. Like all our faculties, they may be misleading, and their data, like all data, are always subject to reinterpretation and revision. Because emotions are not presocial, physiological responses to unequivocal situations, they are open to challenge on various grounds. They may be dishonest or self-deceptive, they may incorporate inaccurate or partial perceptions, or they may be constituted by oppressive values. Accepting the indispensability of appropriate emotions to knowledge means no more (and no less) than that discordant emotions should be attended to seriously and respectfully rather than condemned, ignored, discounted, or suppressed.

Just as appropriate emotions may contribute to the development of knowledge, so the growth of knowledge may contribute to the development of appropriate emotions. For instance, the powerful insights of feminist theory often stimulate new emotional responses to past and present situations. Inevitably, our emotions are affected by the knowledge that the women on our faculty are paid systematically less than the men, that one girl in four is subjected to sexual abuse from heterosexual men in her own family, and that few women reach orgasm in heterosexual intercourse. We are likely to feel different emotions toward older women or people of color as we reevaluate our standards of sexual attractiveness or acknowledge that black is beautiful. The new emotions evoked by feminist insights are likely in turn to stimulate further feminist observations and insights, and these may generate new directions in both theory and political practice. The feedback loop between our emotional constitution and our theorizing is continuous; each continually modifies the other, in principle inseparable from it.

The ease and speed with which we can reeducate our emotions unfortunately is not great. Emotions are only partially within our control as individuals. Although affected by new information, these habitual responses are not quickly unlearned. Even when we come to believe consciously that our fear or shame or revulsion is unwarranted, we may still continue to experience emotions inconsistent with our conscious politics. We may still continue to be anxious for male approval, competitive with our comrades and sisters, and possessive with our lovers. These unwelcome, because apparently inappropriate emotions, should not be suppressed or denied; instead, they should be acknowledged and subjected to critical scrutiny. The persistence of such recalcitrant emotions probably demonstrates how fundamentally we have been constituted by the dominant world view, but it may also indicate superficiality or other inadequacy in our emerging theory and politics.[22] We can only start from where we are—beings who have been created in a cruelly racist, capitalist, and male-dominated society that has shaped our bodies and our minds, our perceptions, our values and our emotions, our language and our systems of knowledge.

The alternative epistemological models that I would suggest display the continuous interaction between how we understand the world and who we are as people. They would show how our emotional responses to the world change as we conceptualize it differently and how our changing emotional responses then stimulate us to new insights. They would demonstrate the need for theory to be self-reflexive, to focus not only on the outer world but also on ourselves and our relation to that world, to examine critically our social location, our actions, our values, our perceptions, and our emotions. The models also show how feminist and other critical social theories are indispensable psychotherapeutic tools because they provide some insights necessary to a full understanding of our emotional constitution. Thus, the models would explain how the reconstruction of knowledge is inseparable from the reconstruction of ourselves.

A corollary of the reflexivity of feminist and other critical theory is that it requires a much broader construal than positivism accepts of the process of theoretical investigation. In particular, it requires acknowledging that a necessary part of theoretical process is critical self-examination. Time spent in analyzing emotions and uncovering their sources should be viewed, therefore, neither as irrelevant to theoretical investigation nor even as a prerequisite for it; it is not a kind of clearing of the emotional decks, "dealing with" our emotions so that they not influence our thinking. Instead, we must recognize that our efforts to reinterpret and refine our emotions are necessary to our theoretical investigation, just as our efforts to reeducate our emotions are necessary to our political activity. Critical reflection on emotion is not a self-indulgent substitute for political analysis and political action. It is itself a kind of political theory and political practice, indispensable for an adequate social theory and social transformation.

Finally, the recognition that emotions play a vital part in developing knowledge enlarges our understanding of women's claimed epistemic advantage. We can now see that women's subversive insights owe much to women's outlaw emotions, themselves appropriate responses to the situations of women's subordination. In addition to their propensity to experience outlaw emotions, at least on some level, women are relatively adept at identifying such emotions, in themselves and others, in part because of their social responsibility for caretaking, including emotional nurturance. It is true that women, like all subordinated peoples, especially those who must live in close proximity with their masters, often engage in emotional deception and even self-deception as the price of their survival. Even so, women may be less likely than other subordinated groups to engage in denial or suppression of outlaw emotions. Women's work of emotional nurturance has required them to develop a special acuity in recognizing hidden emotions and in understanding the genesis of those emotions. This emotional acumen can now be recognized as a skill in political analysis and validated as giving women a special advantage in both understanding the mechanisms of domination and envisioning freer ways to live.

11. CONCLUSION

The claim that emotion is vital to systematic knowledge is only the most obvious contrast between the conception of theoretical investigation that I have sketched here and the conception provided by positivism. For instance, the alternative approach emphasizes that what we identify as emotion is a conceptual abstraction from a complex process of human activity that also involves acting, sensing, and evaluating. This proposed account of theoretical construction demonstrates the simultaneous necessity for and interdependence of faculties that our culture has abstracted and separated from each other: emotion and reason, evaluation and perception, observation and action. The model of knowing suggested here is nonhierarchical and antifoundationalist; instead, it is appropriately symbolized by the radical feminist metaphor of the upward spiral. Emotions are neither more basic than observation, reason, or action in building theory, nor are they secondary to them. Each of these human faculties reflects an aspect of human knowing inseparable from the other aspects. Thus, to borrow a famous phrase from a Marxian context, the development of each of these faculties is a necessary condition for the development of all.

In conclusion, it is interesting to note that acknowledging the importance of emotion for knowledge is not an entirely novel suggestion within the western epistemological tradition. The archrationalist Plato himself came to accept that in the end knowledge required a (very purified form of) love. It may be no accident that in the *Symposium* Socrates learns this lesson from Diotima, the wise woman!

NOTES

I wish to thank the following individuals who commented helpfully on earlier drafts of this chapter or made me aware of further resources: Lynne Arnault, Susan Bordo, Martha Bolton, Cheshire Calhoun, Randy Cornelius, Shelagh Crooks, Ronald De Sousa, Tim Diamond, Dick Foley, Ann Garry, Judy Gerson, Mary Gibson, Sherry Gorelick, Marcia Lind, Helen Longino, Andy McLaughlin, Uma Narayan, Linda Nicholson, Bob Richardson, Sally Ruddick, Laurie Shrage, Alan Soble, Vicky Spelman, Karsten Struhl, Joan Tronto, Daisy Quarm, Naomi Quinn, and Alison Wylie. I am also grateful to my colleagues in the fall 1985 Women's Studies Chair Seminar at Douglass College, Rutgers University, and to audiences at Duke University, Georgia University Centre, Hobart and William Smith Colleges, Northeastern University, the University of North Carolina at Chapel Hill, and Princeton University, for their responses to earlier versions of this chapter. In addition, I received many helpful comments from members of the Canadian Society for Women in Philosophy and from students in Lisa Heldke's classes in feminist epistemology at Carleton College and Northwestern University. Thanks, too, to Delia Cushway, who provided a comfortable environment in which I wrote the first draft.

A similar version of this essay appeared in *Inquiry: An Interdisciplinary Journal of Philosophy* (June 1989). Reprinted by permission of Norwegian University Press.

1. Philosophers who do not conform to this generalization and constitute part of what Susan Bordo calls a "recessive" tradition in western philosophy include Hume and Nietzsche, Dewey and James (Bordo 1987:114–118).

2. The western tradition as a whole has been profoundly rationalist, and much of its history may be viewed as a continuous redrawing of the boundaries of the rational. For a survey of this history from a feminist perspective, see Lloyd 1984.

3. Thus, fear or other emotions were seen as rational in some circumstances. To illustrate this point, Vicky Spelman quotes Aristotle as saying (in the *Nichomachean Ethics*, Bk. IV, ch. 5): "[Anyone] who does not get angry when there is reason to be angry, or who does not get angry in the right way at the right time and with the right people, is a dolt" (Spelman 1982:1).

4. Descartes, Leibnitz, and Kant are among the prominent philosophers who did not endorse a wholly stripped-down, instrumentalist conception of reason.

5. The relocation of values in human attitudes and preferences in itself was not grounds for denying their universality because they could have been conceived as grounded in a common or universal human nature. In fact, however, the variability, rather than the commonality, of human preferences and responses was emphasized; values gradually came to be viewed as individual, particular, and even idiosyncratic rather than as universal and objective. The only exception to the variability of human desires was the supposedly universal urge to egoism and the motive to maximize one's own utility, whatever that consisted in. The value of autonomy and liberty, consequently, was seen as perhaps the only value capable of being justified objectively because it was a precondition for satisfying other desires.

6. For instance, Julius Moravcsik has characterized as emotions what I would call "plain" hunger and thirst, appetites that are not desires for any particular food or drink (Moravcsik 1982:207–224). I myself think that such states, which Moravcsik also calls instincts or appetites, are understood better as sensations than emotions. In other words, I would view so-called instinctive, nonintentional feelings as the biological raw material from which full-fledged human emotions develop.

7. Even adherents of the Dumb View recognize, of course, that emotions are not entirely random or unrelated to an individual's judgments and beliefs; in other words, they note that people are angry or excited *about* something, afraid or proud *of* something. On the Dumb View, however, the judgments or beliefs associated with an emotion are seen as its causes and thus as related to it only externally.

8. Cheshire Calhoun pointed this out to me in private correspondence.

9. Recognition of the many levels on which emotions are socially constructed raises the question whether it makes sense even to speak of the possibility of universal emotions. Although a full answer to this question is methodologically problematic, one might speculate that many of what we westerners identify as emotions have functional analogues in other cultures. In other words, it may be that people in every culture might behave in ways that fulfil at least some social functions of our angry or fearful behavior.

10. The relationship between the emotional experience of an individual and the emotional experience of the group to which the individual belongs may perhaps be clarified by analogy with the relation between a word and the language of which it is a part. That the word has meaning presupposes it's a part of a linguistic system without which it has no meaning; yet the language itself has no meaning over and above the meaning of the words of which it is composed together with their grammatical ordering. Words and language presuppose and mutually constitute each other. Similarly, both individual and group emotion presuppose and mutually constitute each other.

11. Averell cites dissociative reactions by military personnel at Wright Paterson Air Force Base and shows how these were effective in mustering help to deal with difficult situations while simultaneously relieving the individual of responsibility or blame (Averell 1980:157).

12. These and similar experiments are described in Kilpatrick 1961:ch. 10, cited by McLaughlin 1985:296.

13. The positivist attitude toward emotion, which requires that ideal investigators be both disinterested and dispassionate, may be a modern variant of older traditions in western philosophy that recommended people seek to minimize their emotional responses to the world and develop instead their powers of rationality and pure contemplation.

14. It is now widely accepted that the suppression and repression of emotion has damaging if not explosive consequences. There is general acknowledgment that no one can avoid at some time experiencing emotions she or he finds unpleasant, and there is also increasing recognition that the denial of such emotions is likely to result in hysterical disorders of thought and behavior, in projecting one's own emotions on to others, in displacing them to inappropriate situations, or in psychosomatic ailments. Psychotherapy, which purports to help individuals recognize and "deal with" their

emotions, has become an enormous industry, especially in the United States. In much conventional psychotherapy, however, emotions still are conceived as feelings or passions, "subjective" disturbances that afflict individuals or interfere with their capacity for rational thought and action. Different therapies, therefore, have developed a wide variety of techniques for encouraging people to "discharge" or "vent" their emotions, just as they would drain an abscess. Once emotions have been discharged or vented, they are supposed to be experienced less intensely, or even to vanish entirely, and consequently to exert less influence on individuals' thoughts and actions. This approach to psychotherapy clearly demonstrates its kinship with the "folk" theory of anger mentioned earlier, and it equally clearly retains the traditional western assumption that emotion is inimical to rational thought and action. Thus, such approaches fail to challenge and indeed provide covert support for the view that "objective" knowers are not only disinterested but also dispassionate.

15. E. V. Spelman (1982) illustrates this point with a quotation from the well-known contemporary philosopher, R. S. Peters, who wrote "we speak of emotional outbursts, reactions, upheavals and women" (*Proceedings of the Aristotelian Society*, New Series, vol. 62.).

16. It seems likely that the conspicuous absence of emotion shown by Mrs. Thatcher is a deliberate strategy she finds necessary to counter the public perception of women as too emotional for political leadership. The strategy results in her being perceived as a formidable leader, but an Iron Lady rather than a real woman. Ironically, Neil Kinnock, leader of the British Labour Party and Thatcher's main opponent in the 1987 General Election, was able to muster considerable public support through television commercials portraying him in the stereotypically feminine role of caring about the unfortunate victims of Thatcher economics. Ultimately, however, this support was not sufficient to destroy public confidence in Mrs. Thatcher's "masculine" competence and gain Kinnock the election.

17. On the rare occasions when a white man cries, he is embarrassed and feels constrained to apologize. The one exception to the rule that men should be emotionless is that they are allowed and often even expected to experience anger. Spelman (1982) points out that men's cultural permission to be angry bolsters their claim to authority.

18. Someone might argue that the viciousness of this myth was not a logical necessity. In the egalitarian society, where the concepts of reason and emotion were not gender-bound in the way they still are today, it might be argued that the ideal of the dispassionate investigator could be epistemologically beneficial. Is it possible that, in such socially and conceptually egalitarian circumstances, the myth of the dispassionate investigator could serve as a heuristic device, an ideal never to be realized in practice but nevertheless helping to minimize "subjectivity" and bias? My own view is that counterfactual myths rarely bring the benefits advertised and that this one is no exception. This myth fosters an equally mythical conception of pure truth and objectivity, quite independent of human interests or desires, and in this way it functions to disguise the inseparability of theory and practice, science and politics. Thus, it is part of an antidemocratic world view that mystifies the political dimension of knowledge and unwarrantedly circumscribes the arena of political debate.

19. Of course, the similarities in our emotional constitutions should not blind us to

systematic differences. For instance, girls rather than boys are taught fear and disgust for spiders and snakes, affection for fluffy animals, and shame for their naked bodies. It is primarily, though not exclusively, men rather than women whose sexual responses are shaped by exposure to visual and sometimes violent pornography. Girls and women are taught to cultivate sympathy for others: boys and men are taught to separate themselves emotionally from others. As I have noted already, more emotional expression is permitted for lower-class and some nonwhite men than for ruling-class men, perhaps because the expression of emotion is thought to expose vulnerability. Men of the upper classes learn to cultivate an attitude of condescension, boredom, or detached amusement. As we shall see shortly, differences in the emotional constitution of various groups may be epistemologically significant in so far as they both presuppose and facilitate different ways of perceiving the world.

20. A necessary condition for experiencing feminist emotions is that one already be a feminist in some sense, even if one does not consciously wear that label. But many women and some men, even those who would deny that they are feminist, still experience emotions compatible with feminist values. For instance, they may be angered by the perception that someone is being mistreated just because she is a woman, or they may take special pride in the achievement of a woman. If those who experience such emotions are unwilling to recognize them as feminist, their emotions are probably described better as potentially feminist or prefeminist emotions.

21. I owe this suggestion to Marcia Lind.

22. Within a feminist context, Berenice Fisher suggests that we focus particular attention on our emotions of guilt and shame as part of a critical reevaluation of our political ideals and our political practice (Fisher 1984).

REFERENCES

Averell, James R. 1980. "The Emotions." In *Personality: Basic Aspects and Current Research*, ed. Ervin Staub. Englewood Cliffs, N.J.: Prentice-Hall.

Bordo, W. R. 1987. *The Flight to Objectivity: Essays on Cartesianism and Culture*. Albany, N.Y.: SUNY Press.

Fisher, Berenice. 1984. "Guilt and Shame in the Women's Movement: The Radical Ideal of Action and its Meaning for Feminist Intellectuals." *Feminist Studies* 10:185–212.

Flax, Jane. 1983. "Political Philosophy and the Patriarchal Unconscious: A Psychoanalytic Perspective on Epistemology and Metaphysics." In *Discovering Reality: Feminist Perspectives on Epistemology, Metaphysics, Methodology and Philosophy of Science*, ed. Sandra Harding and Merrill Hintikka. Dordrecht, Holland: D. Reidel Publishing.

Goodall, Jane. 1986. *The Chimpanzees of Bombe: Patterns of Behavior*. Cambridge, Mass.: Harvard University Press.

Griffin, Susan. 1979. *Rape: The Power of Consciousness*. San Francisco: Harper & Row.

Hinman, Lawrence. 1986. "Emotion, Morality and Understanding." Paper presented at Annual Meeting of Central Division of the American Philosophical Association, St. Louis, Missouri, May 1986.

Jaggar, Alison M. 1983. *Feminist Politics and Human Nature*. Totowa, N.J.: Rowman and Allanheld.

Keller, E. F. 1984. *Gender and Science*. New Haven, Conn.: Yale University Press.

Kilpatrick, Franklin P., ed. 1961. *Explorations in Transactional Psychology*. New York: New York University Press.

Lakoff, George, and Zoltan Kovecses. 1987. "The Cognitive Model of Anger Inherent in American English." In *Cultural Models in Language and Thought*, ed. N. Quinn and D. Holland. New York: Cambridge University Press.

Lewontin, R. C. 1982. "Letter to the editor." *New York Review of Books*, 4 February:40–41. This letter was drawn to my attention by Alan Soble.

Lloyd, Genevieve. 1984. *The Man of Reason: 'Male' and 'Female' in Western Philosophy*. Minneapolis: University of Minnesota Press.

Lutz, Catherine. 1985. "Depression and the Translation of Emotional Worlds." In *Culture and Depression: Studies in the Anthropology and Cross-cultural Psychiatry of Affect and Disorder*," ed. A. Kleinman and B. Good. Berkeley: University of California Press, 63–100.

———. 1986. "Emotion, Thought and Estrangement: Emotion as a Cultural Category." *Cultural Anthropology* 1:287–309.

———. 1987. "Goals, Events and Understanding in Ifaluck and Emotion Theory." In *Cultural Models in Language and Thought*, ed. N. Quinn and D. Holland. New York: Cambridge University Press.

McLaughlin, Andrew. 1985. "Images and Ethics of Nature." *Environmental Ethics* 7:293–319.

Merchant, Carolyn M. 1980. *The Death of Nature: Women, Ecology and the Scientific Revolution*. New York: Harper & Row.

Moravcsik, J. M. E. 1982. "Understanding and the Emotions." *Dialectica* 36, 2–3: 207–224.

Nagel, E. 1968. "The Subjective Nature of Social Subject Matter." In *Readings in the Philosophy of the Social Sciences*, ed. May Brodbeck. New York: Macmillan.

Quinby, Lee. 1986. Discussion following talk at Hobart and William Smith colleges, April 1986.

Rorty, Richard. 1979. *Philosophy and the Mirror of Nature*. Princeton, N.J.: Princeton University Press.

Rosaldo, Michelle Z. 1984. "Toward an Anthropology of Self and Feeling." In *Culture Theory*, ed. Richard A. Shweder and Robert A. Levine. New York: Cambridge University Press.

Rose, Hilary. 1983. "Hand, Brain, and Heart: A Feminist Epistemology for the Natural Sciences." *Signs: Journal of Women in Culture and Society* 9, 1:73–90.

Schachter, Stanley, and Jerome B. Singer. 1969. "Cognitive, Social and Psychological Determinants of Emotional State." *Psychological Review* 69:379–399.

Scheman, Naomi. "Women in the Philosophy Curriculum." Paper presented at the Annual Meeting of Central Division of the American Philosophical Association, Chicago, April 1985.

Schott, Robin M. 1988. *Cognition and Eros: A Critique of the Kantian Paradigm.* Boston, Mass.: Beacon Press.

Spelman, E. V. 1982. "Anger and Insubordination." Manuscript; early version read to midwestern chapter of the Society for Women in Philosophy, spring 1982.

Wierzbicka, Anna. 1986. "Human Emotions: Universal or Culture-Specific?" *American Anthropologist* 88:584–594.

Young, R. M. 1985. *Darwin's Metaphor: Nature's Place in Victorian Culture.* Cambridge: Cambridge University Press.

WOMEN AND CARING: WHAT CAN FEMINISTS LEARN ABOUT MORALITY FROM CARING?

Joan C. Tronto

Embedded in our notions of caring we can see some of the deepest dimensions of traditional gender differentiation in our society. The script runs something like this: Men care about money, career, ideas, and advancement; men show they care by the work they do, the values they hold, and the provisions they make for their families (see Ehrenreich 1983). Women care for their families, neighbors, and friends; women care for their families by doing the direct work of caring. Furthermore, the script continues, men care about more important things, whereas women care about less important.

Some writers have begun to challenge this script. Caring has been defended in the first instance as a kind of labor, the "labor of love" (Finch and Groves 1983). Others have looked behind the work involved in women's caring to the attitudes and thinking involved in it. Sara Ruddick (1980) began the rehabilitation of one part of caring with her description of "maternal thinking" as a difficult and demanding practice. Further rehabilitation of caring has taken an explicitly moral direction (Elshtain 1982). The most widely read work on women's moral development, Carol Gilligan's *In a Different Voice* (1982), is often associated with the language of "an ethic of care." Other writers have suggested that caring grounds women in the world in such a way that they become and should remain immune from the appeals of abstract principles (McMillan 1982) or of religion (Noddings 1984:97).

In this essay I not only continue challenging the traditional script about men's and women's caring, but I also suggest that feminists must be careful about the direction their analysis of care takes. I shall argue that feminists cannot assume that any attribute of women is automatically a virtue worthy of feminists embracing it. Unless we adopt an uncritically profeminine position and say whatever women do is fine because women do it, we need to take a closer look at caring. In this essay I attempt to explore what a feminist approach to caring could be.

The task of disentangling feminine and feminist aspects of caring is not simple. First, we must clarify the nature of caring as understood today in the West. Then we will be in a position to evaluate how caring challenges contemporary notions in moral theory about what is desirable and virtuous. In both regards, feminine and feminist analyses of caring may overlap. In the final analysis, however, moral categories take on meaning in a broader context. Feminine analyses of caring can be distinguished in that they assume that the traditional script about caring is more or less correct. The truly transformative and feminist aspects of caring cannot be recognized unless we also revise our view of the political context in which we situate caring as a moral phenomenon.

TWO TYPES OF CARING:
CARING ABOUT AND CARING FOR

The language of caring appears in many settings in our daily language. Caring includes myriad actors and activities. Doing household tasks is taking care of the house. Doctors, nurses, and others provide medical care. We might ask whether a corporation cares for its workers. Someone might ask, who is taking care of this account? Historians care about the past. Judges care about justice. We usually assume that mothers care for their children, that nurses care for their patients, that teachers care for their students, that social workers care for their clients.

What all of these examples share can be distilled: Caring implies some kind of on-going responsibility and commitment. This notion accords with the original meaning of "care" in English, where care meant a burden; to care is to assume a burden. When a person or a group cares about something or someone, we presume that they are willing to work, to sacrifice, to spend money, to show emotional concern, and to expend energy toward the object of care. Thus, we can make sense of statements such as: he only cares about making money; she cares for her mother; this society does not care about the homeless. To the challenge, You do not care, one responds by showing some evidence of work, sacrifice, or commitment.

If caring involves a commitment, then caring must have an object. Thus, caring is necessarily relational. We say that we care for or about something or someone. We can distinguish "caring about" from "caring for" based on the objects of caring.[1] Caring about refers to less concrete objects; it is characterized by a more general form of commitment. Caring for implies a specific, particular object that is the focus of caring. The boundaries between caring about and caring for are not so neat as these statements imply. Nonetheless, this distinction is useful in revealing something about the way we think of caring in our society because this distinction fits with the engendered category of caring in our society.

Caring for involves responding to the particular, concrete, physical, spiritual, intellectual, psychic, and emotional needs of others. The self, another person, or a group of others can provide care. For example, I take care of myself, a mother cares for the child, a nurse for hospital patients, the Red Cross for victims of the earthquake. These types of care are unified by growing out of the fact that humans have physical and psychic needs (food, grooming, warmth, comfort, etc.) that require activity to satisfy them. These needs are in part socially determined; they are also met in different societies by different types of social practices.

In our society, the particular structures involving caring for grow especially out of the family; caring professions are often construed as a buttress to, or substitute for, care that can no longer be provided within a family. The family may no longer be intact, as a result of death, divorce, distance. Or the family may not be able to provide help; some caring requires expertise. The family may be or may be seen as the source of the problem—for example, families with patterns of substance abuse, incest, violence. Increasingly, then, care has been provided for by the state or in the market. Americans eat fewer meals at home, hire housekeepers, contract for others to wait in a line for them. In response to this increasingly market-oriented version of caring, some thinkers have pulled back in horror and suggested that caring cannot be provided if it disturbs the integrity of the self-other relationship (Elshtain 1981:330; Noddings 1984). The result is that in modern market society the illusion of caring is often preserved: providers of services are expected to feign caring (Hochschild 1983).

Caring is engendered in both market and private life. Women's occupations are the caring occupations, and women do the disproportionate amount of caretaking in the private household. To put the point simply, traditional gender roles in our society imply that men care about but women care for.

Because not all caring is moral, another distinction between caring about and caring for becomes obvious. When we wish to know if "caring about" is a moral activity, we inquire about the nature of the object of the care. To care about justice is a moral activity because justice is a moral concern; to care about one's accumulation of vacation days presumably is not a moral activity.

Caring for takes on moral significance in a different way. When we inquire about caring for, it is not enough to know the object of the care; presumably we must know something about the context of care, perhaps especially about the relationship between the caregiver and recipient of care. A dirty child is not a moral concern for most people, but we might morally disapprove of such a child's mother, who we might think has failed to meet her duty to care for her child. Note, of course, that such judgments are deeply rooted in social, classist, and cultural assumptions about mother's duties, about standards of cleanliness, and so on. The assignment of the responsibility of caring for someone, something, or some group, then might be a moral question. Thus, what typically makes "caring for" perceived as moral is not the activity per se but how that activity reflects upon the assigned social duties of the caretaker and who is doing the assigning.

The actual *activity* of caring for another person seems far removed from what we usually consider moral. Caring as an activity seems more tied to the realm of necessity than to the realm of freedom where moral judgments presumably have a place (see Arendt 1958; Aristotle 1981). One way in which recent theorists have tried to describe the value of caring is to deny that caring is simply banal activity devoid of judgment. Sara Ruddick (1980) describes maternal thinking as a kind of practice, that is, as a prudential activity where emotions and reason are brought to bear to raise a child. Like the theorists of care, Ruddick stresses that maternal thinking is a particular practice; the maternal thinker focuses on the single child before her or him. In order for children to grow, Ruddick explains, they must be preserved, they must grow physically and mentally, and they must be made aware of the norms and practices of the society of which they are a part. These goals will actually be in conflict in individual instances; for example, the toddler learning to climb threatens its preservation at the same time it develops its strength. Because raising children involves conflicting goals, the maternal thinker cannot simply rely upon instincts or receptivity to the child's wishes to achieve the ultimate goal or raising the child. Instead, a complex set of prudential calculations are involved, which Ruddick calls maternal thinking. Ruddick's point suggests that it might be worthwhile to explore at length the ways in which the practice of caring involves moral issues.

From the standpoint of much contemporary moral theory, caring poses a moral question only in deciding whether one ought to care, not in determining how one engages in the activity of caring. The "moral point of view," as described by moral philosophers such as William Frankena (1973), involves attributes of impartiality and universalizability. We might agree, universally, that special relationships such as being a parent entail certain duties toward our children, but this moral precept cannot then bring us any closer to how to engage in the practice of caring in a moral way. Furthermore, we often assume that morality concerns our interaction with other morally autonomous actors; in caring, the relationships between the caretakers and those cared for are often relations between unequals, where some amount of dependency exists.

Thus, in order to determine the moral dimensions of caring for others, the kind of caring most closely associated with women in our society, we must consider two aspects of caring for others. First, we must consider whether the activity of caring raises moral questions in and of itself. Second, and here a feminist analysis of caring will differ from a simply "feminine" analysis of caring, we must consider how the duties of caring for others are given moral significance in society as a whole. I shall explore these two concerns in the next two sections of this essay.

MORAL DIMENSIONS OF THE ACTIVITY OF CARING FOR OTHERS

In this section I shall suggest three ways in which caring for another raises questions about moral life. First, I shall discuss some aspects of moral life posed by the necessary attentiveness to other's needs when caring for another. Second, I shall consider the way in which caring for another raises questions about authority and autonomy between carer and cared-for. And third, I shall examine how caring for another raises problems that grow out of the particularity of caring.

Attentiveness

Caring suggests an alternative moral attitude. From the perspective of caring, what is important is not arriving at the fair decision, understood as how the abstract individual in this situation would want to be treated, but at meeting the needs of particular others or preserving the relationships of care that exist (see Gilligan 1982). In this way, moral theory becomes much more closely connected to the concrete needs of others. How we come to know these needs raises several dimensions of concern for moral theory.

KNOWLEDGE. In order to engage in the practice of caring the nature of knowledge needed to act morally changes. At the most obvious level, the mode of philosophical discussion that starts from a philosopher's introspection is an inappropriate starting place to arrive at caring judgments. In the first instance one needs knowledge about others' needs, knowledge that comes from others.

It is not that contemporary moral theory ignores the needs of others, but in most moral discussion the needs of others are taken to reflect the understood needs of the thinking self if only he or she were in another's situation. In contrast, caring rests on knowledge completely peculiar to the particular person being cared for. Proper action for a nurse, faced with a patient who will not finish a meal, depends upon knowing the patient's medical condition, usual eating habits, and tastes. There is no simple way one can generalize from one's own experience to what another needs.

To provide such knowledge, the caring person must devote much attention to learning what the other person might need. Accounts of caring stress that an important part of the process of caring is attentiveness to the needs of others (see Weil 1951: 72–73; Ruddick 1980: 357–358). To achieve the proper frame of mind in which to care, Noddings stresses the need to be receptive to the needs of others (1984:24). At the moment when one wishes to care, it is impossible to be preoccupied with the self. This kind of selflessness is a key element of what Noddings calls the crucial moral question in caring, that is, how to meet the other morally.

How radically different the epistemological notion of attentiveness is from contemporary ways of thinking can be illustrated by reexamining the long-standing issue about the relationship of knowledge and interests from this perspective. Liberals commonly assume that no one knows your interests as well as you yourself do (see Mill 1975:187). Marxists and those inspired by Marx believe that a person's interests arise out of the objective circumstances in which one finds oneself or that one can posit some universal, or nearly universal, human interests for example, "emancipatory interests" (Marx and Engels 1978; Habermans 1971; Cohen 1978). But from the standpoint of caring, these views are equally incomplete. There is some relationship between what the cared-for thinks he or she wants and his or her true interests and needs, although it may not be a perfect correspondence. A patient in the hospital who refuses to get up may be forced to do so. A child who wishes only to eat junk food may be disappointed by parents' reluctance to meet this wish. Genuine attentiveness would presumably allow the caretaker to see through these pseudo-needs and come to appreciate what the other really needs.

Such a commitment to perceiving the genuine needs of the other, though, is not so easy. Alice Miller suggests that many parents act not so much to meet the needs of their children as to work out unmet needs they continue to carry from when they were children (Miller 1981). If a caretaker has deficient self-knowledge about his or her own needs, then there is no way to guarantee that those needs have been removed in looking to see what the other's needs are. It may be very difficult to achieve the state of attentiveness, requiring first a tremendous self-knowledge so that the caretaker does not simply transform the needs of the other into a projection of the self's own needs.[2]

THE ATTENTIVE SELF. To say that attentiveness requires a profound self-knowledge, though, does not yet capture how deeply attentiveness affects the self. The concern with attentiveness, with losing one's own concerns in order to see clearly the concerns of the cared-for, raises some difficult questions for the moral theory of caring: How much must one disregard's one's own needs in order to be sufficiently attentive? How does one become adept at creating the condition of receptivity? If one is being solely receptive to the needs of others, how can one judge whether the needs are genuine, as serious as the one cared-for believes they are, and so on?

Furthermore, attentiveness involves a commitment of time and effort that may be made at a high price to the self. Noddings asserts that caring is not complete unless recognized by the cared-for person (1984: 73–74), but this position is clearly wrong. As Noddings herself suggests, such recognition depends upon whether the cared-for person has the capacity to respond to caring. Although a mother's child may develop what Noddings would consider the proper responsiveness to caring over time, others, such as teachers and nurses, who provide care over a shorter duration, cannot expect that their commitment will be recognized and rewarded. Nodding's argument (1984:86) is seductive in its suggestion that we are always recognized for our sacrifices, but it also dangerous in encouraging us to restrict caring only to those near to us on a continuing basis. For the rest of us, though, who are willing to attempt to care at some greater distance, attentiveness has a cost.

Another potential cost to the self is that caring is risky. As Sara Ruddick notes, the contingencies of the world will often cause disasters to befall those for whom we care (Ruddick 1980: 350–351). If the self has become too committed to caring for the other, then the loss of the other may destroy the self. Thus caring cannot simply be a romanticized notion of selflessness, nor can it occur if the self remains aloof. A connection between the self and the other is necessary for the self to care, and the nature of this connection is a problem for any ethic of care.

ATTENTIVENESS AND MARKET RELATIONS. These questions about self-other relations and knowledge are not restricted to relations among individuals; there is a social and political dimension to attentiveness as well. I have noted that in order to be attentive to the needs of others one must relinquish the absolute primacy of the needs of the self. In this regard, attentive care is incompatible with the paradigmatic relationship of modern society, exchange (Hartsock 1983). The paradigm of market relations, of exchange, involves putting one's own interests first. It involves the assertion that one knows one's own interests best, another assumption inconsistent with the attitude of caring. It involves reducing complex relationships into terms that can be made equivalent. None of these premises is compatible with attentiveness.

The seriousness of this point depends upon whether market relationships and attentive care can coexist, and if so, how (see Lane 1986; Hardwig 1984; Walzer 1983; Schaar 1983). Theorists differ about how much the metaphors of exchange permeate all social relationships. Virtually all social relationships in modern life can be described in terms of exchange, but whether that means it is the only or the most illuminating way in which individuals conceive of those relationships is another matter.

If individuals are capable of using and discarding exchange and caring modes of thought at will, then to recognize a caring dimension provides important depth to our picture of moral life. If one cannot move easily from one mode to the other, however (see Hardwig 1984), then to suggest that caring is of value suggests several other disturbing possibilities. If people must either be predominantly caring or exchange-oriented, then the simplest way to arrange social institutions would be to create separate spheres for each mode of life. The ideological glorification of men in the cruel business world and women in the caring home is one obvious solution.

The advocate of caring might respond, that if caring and market society cannot coexist, let us abolish market relations. The radicalness of this claim is immediately obvious, but the obviousness of its replacement to conduct life in a complex society is not.

Authority and Autonomy

The second area where caring raises fundamental questions opposed to contemporary moral theory is another issue that grows out of caring as providing help to meet the needs of others. Because caring occurs in a situation where one person is helping to meet the concrete needs of another, caring raises questions that cannot be easily accommodated by the starting assumption in most contemporary moral philosophy that we are rational, autonomous actors. Many conditions that we usually associate with care-giving belie this view because society does not consider all people we take care of to be rational and autonomous, either in an abstract moral sense (e.g., children) or in a concrete, physical sense (e.g., a bed-ridden parent, a disabled person) (see Fisher and Galler 1988). Furthermore, if the care-giver is considered rational and autonomous, then the relationship between the parties is unequal, and relationships of authority and dependency are likely to emerge. As I noted earlier, if the care-giver's needs are themselves met by providing care, then the care-giver might desire to keep the cared-for person dependent. How should care-givers understand their authoritative position in relation to those for whom they care?

However, the image of equal adults who rely upon other equal adults for care, not exchange, once again raises questions about what it means to be rational and autonomous. Two people in an equal relationship of care share an awareness of the concrete complications of caring. To maintain such a relationship will often entail making judgments that, from a more abstract point of view, might seem questionable. Is one wrong if one refuses to move for a better job because of an on-going situation for caring? Again one is forced to consider what autonomy actually means.

Previous writers about an ethic of care vary in whether they perceive authority and autonomy as an issue. The work of Carol Gilligan and Nona Lyons is useful in that it poses the nature of autonomy as an issue. Gilligan has identified an "ethic of care" characterized by a commitment to maintaining and fostering the relationships in which one is woven (Gilligan 1982: 19). Her analysis leads her to suggest that without this dimension the account of morality found in enumeration of rights would be incomplete. Kohlberg's cognitive model of moral development, which Gilligan criticizes, stresses that a sense of the autonomous self, clearly differentiated from others, is crucial to developing a moral sense. In contrast, this ethic of care is based upon a different account of the self. Lyons's research suggests that only individuals who view themselves as connected to others, rather than as separate and objective, are able to use both an ethic of care and claims about justice to resolve real-life moral dilemmas. (Lyons 1983:140–141). Gilligan stresses that there may well be tension between the maintenance of self and of relationships; by her account moral maturity arrives when an individual can correctly balance concerns for the self and for others (Gilligan 1983:41–45).

Noddings's approach, on the other hand, seems to leave too little autonomy to the self and is unable to discern that relations of care might also be relations of authority. Noddings analyzes care as the relationship between the one caring and the one cared-for. The essential aspect of caring is that it involves a displacement from one's own interests to the interests of the one cared-for. "Our attention, our mental engrossment is on the cared-for, not on ourselves" (Noddings 1984:24). Caring affects both the one caring and the one cared-for. It affects the one caring because she must become engrossed in the other; it affects the cared-for because that individual's needs are met and because that individual must somehow respond and accept the care offered.

Caring challenges the view that morality starts where rational and autonomous individuals confront each other to work out the rules of moral life. Instead, caring allows us to see autonomy as a problem that people must deal with all the time, in their relations with both equals and those who either help them or depend upon them.

Particularity

Finally, let us consider how the particularity of caring challenges contemporary moral theory. Most contemporary moral theorists require universal moral judgments, that is, that if it is moral for a person to act in a given way in a given situation then it must be moral for any person so situated to act the same way[3] (Kohlberg 1981). Yet the decision we must make about how much care to provide and to whom cannot be so easily generalized or universalized. It is theoretically possible to spend all of one's time caring for others (see Blum 1976); the real decisions everyone will face then are decisions about both when to provide care and when to stop providing care. Because caring varies with the amount of time and kind of effort that a caring individual can expend as well as with the needs of the ones who need care, it is difficult to imagine that rules could ever be specified allowing us to claim that we had applied universal moral principles.

Consider, for example, a rule: always give aid to a person whose car is broken down on the highway. Suppose you are a nonmechanical woman alone and the stranger is a male? Always take care of your mother. Suppose she and your children rely on your income to keep the household together and caring for her will cost you your job? Thus, the moral judgments made in offering and providing care are much more complex than any set of rules can take into account. Any rule sufficiently flexible to cover all the complexities would probably have to take a form such as "do all that you can to help someone else." Such a form, though, does not serve as any guide to what morality requires. What may be "too much" care for a child to provide an elderly parent may seem too selfishly skimpy to another. This logical objection about the limits of rule-governed morality is familiar, yet it remains a practical difficulty.

The reason that rule-governed behavior is so often associated with moral life, though, is that if we are bound to follow the rules then we are bound to act impartially, not giving special favors to those nearest us. Another problem with caring from a moral point of view, then, is that we might, because of our caring relationship, provide special treatment to those closest to us and ignore others more deserving of care.

Nel Noddings pursues this problem in a disturbing way. Noddings is very restrictive about the conditions under which caring occurs. Although Noddings argues that it is natural for us to care for our children, when we extend care beyond our own children it becomes an ethical act (Noddings 1984:79–80). Noddings also suggests that caring must take place in a limited context or it is not properly understood as caring: Noddings's description of caring is very personal; her examples include caring for cats and birds, children and husbands, students and strangers who arrive at the door.

Mother-child and teacher-pupil are paradigmatic caring relationships. But any expansion of caring beyond this sphere is dangerous because caring cannot be generalized. Thus, Noddings wishes to separate caring from many of its broader social connotations; she seems to exclude caretaking from caring for:

> The danger is that caring, which is essentially nonrational in that it requires a constitutive engrossment and displacement of motivation, may gradually or abruptly be tranformed into abstract problem solving. There is, then, a shift of focus from the cared-for to the "problem." Opportunities arise for self-interest, and persons entrusted with caring may lack the necessary engrossment in those to be cared for. (Noddings 1984:25–26; compare Finch and Groves 1983)

Such caring can only be provided for very limited number of others, and Noddings would probably exclude many relationships we might otherwise think of as caring. By Noddings's understanding of caring nurses in hospitals do not necessarily care; indeed, by this view there are probably many mothers who would not qualify as carers. In this case, a moral question arises about the needs of the particular others we care for weighed against the needs of others more distant from us. To Noddings this problem is solved by saying that because everyone will be cared for by someone, it is not any one else's concern to wonder about who is caring for whom in society.

To say that we should only care for those things that come within our immediate purview ignores the ways in which we are responsible for the construction of our narrow sphere. When Noddings says that she will respond with caring to the stranger at her door but not to starving children in Africa, she ignores the ways in which the modern world is intertwined and the ways in which hundreds of prior public and private decisions affect where we find ourselves and which strangers show up at our doors. In an affluent community, where affluence is maintained by such decisions as zoning ordinances, the stranger at the door is less of a threat than in a dense city, where the stranger may wish to do you harm. Perhaps Noddings would have no problem with this point because in the city you do not have to care for strangers at the door. But the question then becomes, who does? Questions about the proximity of people to us are shaped by our collective social decisions. If we decide to isolate ourselves from others, we may reduce our moral burden of caring. Yet if moral life is only understood narrowly in the context of the exhibition of caring, then we can be absolved from these broader responsibilities.

One way to answer this objection is to say that the task of moral theory is to set out what the parameters of caring should be. Such an approach would soon blend into questions of social and political life. For caring to be an on-going activity, it is necessarily bounded by the activities of daily life because the entire complex of social institutions and structures determine with whom we come into contact on a regular enough basis to establish relationships of care.[4]

If caring is used as an excuse to narrow the scope of our moral activity to be concerned only with those immediately around us, then it does have little to recommend it as a moral theory. But the question of whom we should care for is not left entirely to individuals in our society.

A FEMINIST APPROACH TO CARING: CARING ABOUT WHAT WE CARE FOR

In the second section of this essay I explored some ways in which caring chal-lenges contemporary moral theory. In each case, I realized that caring seems to provide a richer account of people's moral lives. Nevertheless, caring seems to suffer a fatal moral flaw if we allow it to be circumscribed by deciding that we shall only care for those closest to us. From this perspective, it is hard to see how caring can remain moral, rather than becoming a way to justify in-consideration of others at the expense of those for whom we care.

To solve this problem I must return to the way in which the activity of caring is situated in contemporary society. I noted at the beginning of this essay that the problem of who should care for whom is rooted in (often ques-tionable) social values, expectations, and institutions. We do not hold every-one (anyone?) individually responsible for the homeless. Similarly, we do not hold just anyone responsible for the appearance of a child, but we do hold her mother (and father?) responsible. Nonetheless, I can make at least one generalization about caring in this society: men care about; women care for. Thus, by definition the traditional script on caring reenacts the division of male and female worlds into public and private. To raise the question about whether caring for is inevitably too particularistic is thus to return as well to the engendered nature of caring in our society and to a consideration of the difference between a feminist and feminine account of caring.

What does it mean to assert, as Nel Noddings does, that caring is a "fem-inine" approach to ethics? For Noddings, it means the celebration and le-gitimation of a part of women's lives. Yet we have seen that Noddings's formulation of caring cannot be satisfying as a model for moral theory. As Genevieve Lloyd (1984) argues about reason, the category of the feminine is quite problematic (see also Gilman 1979). Femininity is constructed as the antithesis of masculinity. Thus, what is constructed as the masculine, as the normal, is constructed in opposition to what is feminine. In this case, the construction of women as tied to the more particular activity of caring for others stands in opposition to the more public and social concerns about which men care.

I can make this argument still more pointed. Insofar as caring is a kind of attentiveness, it may be a reflection of a survival mechanism for women or others who are dealing with oppressive conditions, rather than a quality of intrinsic value on its own. Another way to understand caring is to see it as an ethic most appropriate for those in a subordinate social position. Just as women and others who are not in the central corridors of power in this society adopt a variety of deferential mannerisms (e.g., differences in speech, smiling, other forms of body language, etc.), so too it may have served their purposes of survival to have adopted an attitude that Noddings may approvingly call "attentiveness" but might otherwise be understood as the necessity to anticipate the wishes of one's superior.[5]

A feminine approach to caring, then, cannot serve as a starting point for a broader questioning of the proper role of caring in society. As with Temma Kaplan's (1982) description of "female consciousness," the feminine approach to caring bears the burden of accepting traditional gender divisions in a society that devalues what women do. From this perspective, caring will always remain as a corrective to morality, as an "extra" aspect of life, neither suggesting nor requiring a fundamental rethinking of moral categories.

A feminist approach to caring, in contrast, needs to begin by broadening our understanding of what caring for others means, both in terms of the moral questions it raises and in terms of the need to restructure broader social and political institutions if caring for others is to be made a more central part of the everyday lives of everyone in society. It is beyond the scope of this essay to spell out fully a feminist theory of care, but some points seem to suggest a starting place for further analysis.

In this essay I noted the way in which caring involves moral acts not usually comprehended in the framework of contemporary moral theory. The moral relevance of attentiveness belies the adequacy of the abstract, exchange-oriented individual as the moral subject. We noted earlier that to take attentiveness seriously questions our assumptions about our autonomy, the self, our knowledge of our interests, the effectiveness of the market. These issues are already topics that feminist political and moral philosophers consider. Caring may prove an especially useful way for feminist thinkers to try to ground their thoughts on these subjects.

Feminist theory will also need to describe what constitutes good caring. We have already noted that this task will be difficult because caring is so much tied to particular circumstances. Yet we need to rethink as well how those particular circumstances are socially constructed. Perhaps the impoverishment of our vocabulary for discussing caring is a result of the way caring is privatized, thus beneath our social vision in this society. The need to rethink appropriate forms for caring also raises the broadest questions about the shape of social and political institutions in our society.

To think of the social world in terms of caring for others radically differs from our present way of conceiving of it in terms of pursuing our self-interest. Because caring emphasizes concrete connections with others, because it evokes so much of the daily stuff of women's lives, and because it stands as a fundamental critique of abstract and often seemingly irrelevant moral theory, it is worthy of the serious attention of feminist theorists.

NOTES

I gratefully acknowledge in writing this essay the help I received from Annmarie Levins, Mary Dietz, George Shulman, Berenice Fisher, and Alison Jaggar.

1. Note that my distinction between caring for and caring about differs from the distinction drawn by Meyeroff (1971) and Noddings (1984). Meyeroff wishes to conflate caring for ideas with caring for people. Not only does this parallel mask the traditional gender difference, but, as will become clear later, the kinds of activities involved in caring for other people cannot be easily used in this same sense. Noddings distinguishes caring for from caring about on a dimension that tries to get at the degree of commitment. We care more for what we care for than for what we care about (1984:86, 112), but Noddings also wishes to claim that we can care for ideas. I believe that the way I have formulated the distinction reveals more about caring and traditional assumptions of gender difference.

2. Nonetheless, in order for caring to occur, there must be more than good intentions and undistorted communication; the acts of caring must also occur. I believe this point may help to distinguish this approach from (at least early versions of) Habermas's approach. For the criticism that Habermas's work is too intellectualized, see Henning Ottmann (1982:86).

3. See, among other recent authors who question the dominant Kantian form of morality, Lawrence Blum (1980), Alasdair MacIntyre and Stanley Hauerwas (1983), John Kekes (1984), and Peter Winch (1972).

4. I am indebted here to Berenice Fisher's suggestion that one important element of a theory of care is the specification of the limits of caring.

5. Jack H. Nagel refined earlier analyses of power to include what C. J. Friedrich had called the "rule of anticipated reactions," the situation where "one actor, B, shapes his behavior to conform to what he believes are the desires of another actor, A, without having received explicit messages about A's wants or intentions from A or A's agents" (1975:16). See also Dahl (1984:24–25).

REFERENCES

Aristotle. 1981. *The Politics.* Harmondsworth: Penguin Books.
Arendt, H. 1958. *The Human Condition.* Chicago: University of Chicago Press.
Blum, L. 1980. *Friendship, Altruism, and Morality.* Boston: Routledge and Kegan Paul.
Blum, L., M. Homiak, J. Housman, and N. Scheman. 1976. "Altruism and Women's Oppression." In *Women and Philosophy,* ed. L. Gould and M. W. Wartofsky. New York: G. P. Putnam.
Cohen, G. A. 1978. *Karl Marx's Theory of History: A Defence.* Princeton, N.J.: Princeton University Press.
Dahl, R. A. 1984. *Modern Political Analysis.* 4th ed. Englewood Cliffs, N.J.: Prentice-Hall.
Ehrenreich, B. 1983. *The Hearts of Men.* Garden City, N.Y.: Anchor Books.
Elshtain, J. B. 1981. *Public Man, Private Woman.* Princeton, N.J.: Princeton University Press.
———. 1982. "Antigone's Daughters." *democracy* 2:46–59.
Finch, J., and D. Groves, eds. 1983. *A Labour of Love: Women, Work and Caring.* London: Routledge and Kegan Paul.
Fisher, B., and R. Galler. 1988. "Friendship and Fairness: How Disability Affects Friendship Between Women." In *Women with Disabilities: Essays in Psychology, Politics and Policy,* ed. A. Asch and M. Fine. Philadelphia: Temple University Press.
Frankena, W. 1973. *Ethics.* Englewood Cliffs, N.J.: Prentice-Hall.
Gilligan, C. 1982. *In a Different Voice.* Cambridge: Harvard University Press.
———. 1983. "Do the Social Sciences Have an Adequate Theory of Moral Development?" In *Social Science as Moral Inquiry,* ed. N. Haan, et al. New York: Columbia University Press.
Gilman, C. P. 1979. *Herland.* New York: Pantheon.
Habermas, J. 1971. *Knowledge and Human Interests.* Boston: Beacon Press.
Hardwig, J. 1984. "Should Women Think in Terms of Rights?" *Ethics* 94:441–455.
Hartsock, N. C. M. 1983. *Money, Sex and Power: Toward a Feminist Historical Materialism.* New York: Longman.
Hochschild, A. 1983. *The Managed Heart: Commercialization of Human Feeling.* Berkeley: University of California Press.
Kaplan, T. 1982. "Female Consciousness and Collective Action: The Case of Barcelona, 1910–1918." In *Feminist Theory: A Critique of Ideology,* eds. N. Keohane, M. Rosaldo, B. Gelpi. Chicago: University of Chicago Press.
Kekes, J. 1984. "Moral Sensitivity." *Philosophy* 59:3–19.
Kohlberg, L. 1981. "From *Is* to *Ought:* How to Commit the Naturalistic Fallacy and Get Away With It In the Study of Moral Development." In his *The Philosophy of Moral Development: Moral Stages and the Idea of Justice.* Vol. 1 of *Essays in Moral Development.* New York: Harper & Row.
Lane, R. E. 1986. "Market Justice, Political Justice." *American Political Science Review* 80:383–402.

Lloyd, G. 1984. *The Man of Reason: "Male" and "Female" in Western Philosophy.* Minneapolis: University of Minnesota Press.

Lyons, N. P. 1983. "Two Perspectives: On Self, Relationships, and Morality." *Harvard Educational Review* 53:125–144.

MacIntyre, A., and S. Hauerwas, eds. 1983. *Revisions: Changing Perspectives in Moral Philosophy.* Notre Dame, Ind.: University of Notre Dame Press.

Marx, K., and F. Engels. 1978. "The German Ideology." In *The Marx-Engels Reader,* ed. R. C. Tucker. 2d ed. New York: Norton.

McMillan, C. 1982. *Women, Reason, and Nature: Some Philosophical Problems With Feminism.* Princeton, N.J.: Princeton University Press.

Meyeroff, M. 1971. *On Caring.* New York: Harper & Row.

Mill, J. S. 1975. "Considerations on Representative Government." In *Three Essays,* ed. R. Wollheim. Oxford: Oxford University Press.

Miller, A. 1981. *The Drama of the Gifted Child.* New York: Basic Books.

Nagel, J. H. 1975. *The Descriptive Analysis of Power.* New Haven, Conn.: Yale University Press.

Noddings, N. 1984. *Caring: A Feminine Approach to Ethics.* Berkeley: University of California Press.

Ottmann, H. 1982. "Cognitive Interests and Self-Reflection." In *Habermas: Critical Debates,* eds. J. B. Thompson and D. Held. Cambridge, Mass.: MIT Press.

Ruddick, S. 1980. "Maternal Thinking." *Feminist Studies* 6:342–367.

Schaar, J. 1983. "The Question of Justice." *Raritan Review* 3:107–129.

Walzer, M. 1983. *Spheres of Justice.* New York: Basic Books.

Weil, S. 1951. "Reflection on the Right Use of School Studies With a View to the Love of God." In *Waiting for God.* Trans. E. Craufurd. New York: Harper.

Winch, P. 1972. *Ethics and Action.* London: Routledge and Kegan Paul.

THE RADICAL FUTURE
OF A CLASSIC
MORAL THEORY

Lynne S. Arnault

For many philosophers in the American-British analytic tradition, radical feminist moral theory seems way out in left field. Feminist repudiation of essentialism and the autonomous self, its rejection of the "standpoint of exchange" and mind-centered definitions of moral reasoning, its emphasis on the influence of gender and gender politics in the construction of knowledge, including moral theory—all suggest to many analytic philosophers a radically different and problematic meta-ethical orientation. In this essay, I hope to gain support for radical feminist moral theory by taking a classic theory of moral reasoning—R. M. Hare's universal prescriptivism—and exposing its radical future.[1] I will attempt to show that in order to meet its own criteria of universalizability and prescriptivity, this formalist-dispositional account of morals must abandon the liberal conception of the self and its accompanying, monological model of moral deliberation. Maintaining the internal coherence of Hare's ideal of universal prescriptivism, I will argue, requires a trip to left field, endorsing a more radicalized conception of autonomy and allowing for the possibility that social divisions may be so embedded in the structure of things as to infect even the means of discourse.

I call Hare's theory of universal prescriptivism a "classic" moral theory for two reasons. First, American-British analytic philosophers generally regard it as a major contribution to the development of "the novel issues and methods introduced into ethical theory in the twentieth century" (Kerner 1966:2). With the publication of G. E. Moore's *Principia Ethica* in 1903, American-British moral philosophy took a linguistic turn, involving itself with the logical analysis of moral terms, judgments, and modes of reasoning. Because Hare's theory that "the language of morals is one sort of prescriptive language" (Hare 1952:I) is usually included in analytic philosophy's canon of great theories, I have applied the honorific term "classic" to it.

Second, I call Hare's theory of universal prescriptivism a "classic" because I believe that if we put aside the particularities of the relatively new "linguistic turn" and the importance of Hare's theory within it, we find that the deep assumptions underlying Hare's theory are not really novel at all but have dominated western philosophy since the seventeenth century. Hare's moral theory embodies commitments to universalism, impersonality, detachment, dispassion, neutrality, and the social transcendency of language. It is representative of a tradition with certain enduring, dominating beliefs: that morality consists in respect for rules; that moral decision making is a matter of using the proper moral calculus; and that meta-ethics consists in identifying precisely the correct method for justifying moral judgments. These assumptions, I would argue, have systematically privileged the point of view of a particular group of people (white, middle-class males of European descent) and have reinforced dualistic ideologies of masculinity and femininity. By attempting to decenter some of Hare's fundamental theoretical assumptions and thereby to expose the radical future of a classic moral theory, I hope to encourage the reclamation of modalities too long suppressed.

To uncover the radical future of Hare's universal prescriptivism, we must first understand why Hare holds that universalizability and prescriptivity are the sine qua non of moral discourse and why he proposes that utilitarianism, which he views as a logical extension of universal prescriptivism, provides the proper method for resolving interpersonal moral disagreements. Hare contends that the logical properties of universalizability and prescriptivity[2] generate the rules that govern moral thinking at the critical level. By "universalizability" Hare means that "if we make different moral judgements about situations which we admit to be identical in their universal descriptive properties, we contradict ourselves" (1981:21). As he puts it more informally elsewhere, universalizability means that "if I now say that I ought to do a certain thing to a certain person, I am committed to the view that the very same thing ought to be done to me, were I in exactly his situation, including the same personal characteristics and in particular the same motivational states" (1981:108).

Hare insists that prescriptions must be universalizable to qualify as moral because he conceives of moral judgments as necessarily requiring "reasons" and sees this requirement as equivalent to requiring universalizability. One reason Hare insists that moral judgments have a reason-requiring function is that he believes they are prescriptive or action-guiding speech-acts, and he recognizes that a moral "prescriber" is able to influence conduct in a guiding rather than goading or coercive way only if "the answering of moral questions is . . . a rational activity" (1963:2).

By claiming that evaluative expressions are prescriptive, Hare wants to establish that normative judgments are necessarily connected with action; the common function of words like "ought" and "good," he believes, is to guide conduct, commend behavior. On Hare's view, then, accepting a moral judgment is necessarily connected with doing, or at least attempting to do, what the judgment enjoins. It is important, therefore, that he characterize moral judgments as necessarily requiring reasons because, although he wants to maintain that moral judgments involve assent to an imperative, he nevertheless wants to deny that these utterances are merely attempts at persuasion or goading; moral judgments, for Hare, involve a willingness to prescribe courses of action to others as rational self-guiding agents (1952:sec.1.7).

I will argue that Hare's theory of moral reasoning does not really secure the autonomy of the persons prescribed to, especially if they are members of a subordinated group. But before moving on to this critique, it is important to note that Hare gives a dispositional account of the criteria for right and wrong. The source of moral criteria, he believes, resides in the overriding dispositions or inclinations of the individual moral deliberator. What are to count as criteria for right conduct, he feels, ultimately boil down to a matter of individual choice. *Any* set of prescriptions subjected to the requirements of universalizability and prescriptivity constitutes a morality in good logical standing: as long as the moral deliberator has assumed the burden of universalizability, it is open to him or her to decide without logical error that a given set of facts does or does not constitute sufficient grounds for action (1963:195–196). Thus, for example, as long as a Nazi has assumed the burden of universalizability, he may decide without logical error that a person's being Jewish constitutes sufficient grounds for extermination. This follows from the fact that, on Hare's account, every moral judgment involves an implicit autonomous legislation of criteria.

Hare recognizes, of course, that people's inclinations may differ and thereby occasion moral dispute. People disagree about what ought to be done "because their different inclinations make one reject some singular prescription which the other can accept" (1963:97). According to Hare, moral disagreement can be resolved by rational deliberation in the majority of cases because "people's inclinations about most of the important matters in life tend to be the same (very few people, for example, like being starved or run over by motor-cars)" (1963:97). In particular, most human beings share the inclination or desire to have their own interests satisfied; as a result, they will not universalize prescriptions that disregard the desires of other people.

With the understanding that most people share the inclination to want their own interests respected, Hare claims that moral disagreements can be resolved by rational deliberation because the rules of moral reasoning, universalizability and prescriptivity, can be "generalized" to include the utilitarian principle "Everyone to count for one, nobody for more than one" (1963:118):

For if my action is going to affect the interests of a number of people, and I ask myself what course of action I can prescribe universally for people in just this situation, then what I shall have to do, in order to answer this question, is to put myself imaginatively in the place of the other parties. . . . And the considerations that weigh with me in this inquiry can only be, How much (as I imagine myself in the place of each man in turn) do I want to have this, or to avoid that? But when I have been the round of all the affected parties, and come back, in my own person, to make an impartial moral judgment giving equal weight to the interests of all parties, what can I possibly do except advocate that course which will, taken all in all, least frustrate the desires which I have imagined myself having? But this (it is plausible to go on) is to maximize satisfactions. (1963:123)

According to Hare, then, whenever there is a conflict of inclinations or interests, we must fully represent to ourselves the situation of each other party (1981:111); we must imagine ourselves in the place of the affected parties, not with our own likes and dislikes but with each of their likes and dislikes (1963:113). We must then accept only those prescriptions that impartially maximize satisfactions. By saying that our moral judgments must be impartial, Hare means that "whoever is in which role in the situation being judged . . . [must not be] treated as relevant" (1981:211). Thus, according to Hare, whenever there is a moral dispute, we must "put ourselves in the shoes of each of the affected persons" (1981:101), and we must accept only those prescriptions that count equal preferences equally, whatever their content (1981:145).

Hare argues that this procedure of implementing the ideal of universal prescriptivism is imposed on us by the logical properties of the moral concepts (1981:91). The steps in the argument from universal prescriptivism to utilitarianism are all based, he contends, on the logic of the concepts involved (1981:176).

The claim that utilitarian methodology follows from the logical features of moral discourse is not, I will argue, a well-founded claim, but it clearly reveals Hare's commitment to liberal individualism. Consider, for example, one assumption underlying Hare's account of interpersonal moral reasoning: most people will not universalize prescriptions that disregard the interests of others because they want to have their own interests satisfied. This implicitly articulates what Nancy Hartsock calls "the standpoint of exchange": it constitutes people as rational, self-interested, fundamentally isolated individuals who interact with one another when there is a momentary conjuncture of interest (1985:ch. 2). Despite their interdependence, individuals, as this model conceptualizes them, have no intrinsically fundamental relations with one another; interpersonal interactions are between Person and Other—the latter remaining "someone to whom Person has only instrumental and extrinsic ties and to whom he relates only to gain his own ends" (Hartsock 1985:24).

Hare seems to make allowances for the fact that we may have ties of affection and loyalty toward certain people that bind us less instrumentally to them than to humanity in general (1981:135–137). For example, Hare recognizes that mothers take an interest in the interests of their newborn children in a way that they do not with other people's children. But we should note that Hare endorses this partiality only because it "can be defended on utilitarian grounds by critical thinking, as having a high acceptance-utility" (1981:137). As he puts it:

> If mothers had the propensity to care equally for all the children in the world, it is unlikely that children would be as well provided for even as they are. The dilution of the responsibility would weaken it out of existence. . . . And evidently Evolution (if we may personify her) has had the same idea; there are, we are told, a great many of these particular loyalties and affections which are genetically transmitted, and have no doubt favoured the survival of the genes which transmit them (1981:137).

What is striking about this discussion, among other things, is that Hare ends up articulating the mother-child relationship from the standpoint of exchange. On his view, the "special" tie that binds a mother and her young child is not really so special after all. A mother's interest in the interests of her child turns out, upon critical inspection, to be a contingent feature of their relation: satisfying her child's interest in good care is a way for the mother to ensure that her own interests (in this case, her genes' "preference" for survival) will be satisfied.

It is not surprising, of course, that Hare ends up giving a kind of sociobiological account of the "special" connectedness of mothers and children in the modern nuclear family. A theory that constitutes people as rational, solitary, interest-driven monads whose every interpersonal action is an effort to maximize personal interests is not especially well suited for representing experiences involving ongoing dependency. Nor, we should note, is it particularly well suited for giving voice to the forms of connectedness and solidarity that members of a subordinated group experience. Thus, in moral deliberation with members of dominant groups, women, people of color, and the poor would be at a disadvantage because they would be hindered from representing their experience, interests, and needs in a nondistorted, nonrepressed way.

Because Hare's theory of moral reasoning instructs us to imagine ourselves in the place of the affected parties, with each of their likes and dislikes, and to count equal preferences equally, it may seem as though everyone's interests—including those of women, people of color, and the poor—are equally well represented in his model of moral deliberation. But the fact that Hare presents "taking the standpoint of others" as a monological process belies that impression.

Hare characterizes "putting oneself in the shoes of others" as a matter of hypothetical role-playing, done singly by the moral deliberator. Getting to know the preferences of the people whom our actions will affect is a process, he suggests, of coming to identify with them: it involves imagining ourselves in the place of the affected parties and of representing to ourselves, by analogy with our own experience, what the experiences of these people would be like for them (1981:127).[3]

Hare gives what he calls a prescriptivist account of "extended" or "sympathetic identification" (1981:96f.). Identifying with another person, he claims, involves *acquiring* that person's inclinations, motivations, and preferences:

> If I have full knowledge of the other person's preferences, I shall myself have acquired preferences equal to his regarding what should be done to me were I in his situation; and these are the preferences which are now conflicting with my original prescription. So we have in effect not an interpersonal conflict of preferences or prescriptions, but an intrapersonal one; both the conflicting preferences are mine. I shall therefore deal with the conflict in exactly the same way as with that between two original preferences of my own. (1981:110)

Even taken at his own word, that is, given his commitment to the liberal conception of the self and to a mind-centered definition of sympathetic identification, Hare's reduction of interpersonal moral conflict to intrapersonal conflict is a bold move. If I understand him correctly, Hare is claiming that it is possible *in practice* for me to acquire your preferences and dispositions. He admits that there are some "practical difficulties in getting to know the states of mind of other sentient beings, which increase with the remoteness of their experiences from ours," but he recommends that they are "to be overcome by getting as closely acquainted as we can with their circumstances, verbal and other behaviour, anatomies, etc., and comparing them with our own"; and he dismisses the practical problem as secondary to the philosophical problem of other minds (1981:127).

On the grounds that it is possible in practice for me to acquire your preferences and dispositions, Hare claims that I can singly and impartially solve our interpersonal moral conflict by using a moral calculus: if I have gained full knowledge of your preferences, I have acquired your preferences as intensely or moderately as you hold them. The moral conflict, now, is therefore not as much *between us* as *within me*. The problem of being impartial in effect disappears: I can "impartially" determine how to maximize satisfactions because all that this procedure entails at this point is comparing the strengths of my own preferences.[4]

Because Hare characterizes the process of "putting oneself in the shoes of others" as a monological process, his model of moral deliberation articulates the liberal conception of the self. That is, it constitutes the social identity of the moral agent as being epistemically insignificant; the moral self is a disembodied and disembedded entity. We can acquire knowledge of other people's situations by a process of solitary hypothetical role-playing because membership in a particular social group or groups is an "accidental" or contingent feature of social life. Thus, on Hare's view, human beings approach the task of gaining knowledge of other people's situations, not as socially constituted members of historically changing groups, which have epistemologically distinctive vantage points, but as solitary individuals with essentially the same vantage point.

By discounting the effects of a person's social experience upon his or her motivations, interests, needs, and understandings of the world, Hare's monological model of moral deliberation makes no allowances for the possibilities that the forms of discourse may privilege the view point of dominant groups in society and that such forms could themselves become contested in moral deliberation. To be sure, Hare recognizes the difficulty, even the impossibility, of human beings reasoning in a perfectly unbiased manner. He explicitly acknowledges that his model of moral reasoning obligates us to try to think like "ideal observers" or "archangels," that is, like beings with superhuman powers of thought, superhuman knowledge, and no human weaknesses, in particular, no partiality to self, friends, or relations (1981:44). And he emphasizes the point that archangelic moral thinking is unattainable. But the fact that his model requires us to try to transcend human finitude is evidence of Hare's implicit commitment to viewing human individuals in abstraction from social circumstances. And it is significant, I want to suggest, that, although Hare acknowledges that archangelic thinking is unattainable, he does not recognize the possibility that the epistemological ideal embodied in "the archangel" reflects the experience and point of view of a particular social group, specifically, white male bourgeois property owners of European descent.

For Hare, the archangel's "virtue" consists precisely in his lack of social embeddedness: the ideal observer is ideal because "he" lacks a particular point of view. "His" is a disinterested, disembodied, value-neutral standpoint. In short, "his" is "a view from nowhere"[5]—a standpoint that bears no "social fingerprints." And, of course, if "his" point of view is really socially unsituated, then it is gender-neutral, and we could easily refer to him as "her."

The epistemological mandate embodied in the "ideal observer"—that the standpoint of the moral deliberator be "no-where"—has been criticized by radical feminists as both containing a deep gender bias and being highly implicated in projects of social domination, including projects of gender domination. According to feminist epistemologists,[6] what is problematic about the notion of a nonsituated, disembedded, disinterested standpoint is not simply that there can actually be no ideal observers. True, human individuals cannot be abstracted from their social circumstances, but what is more fundamentally problematic about the ideal observer, they believe, is that it is a masculinist ideal whose deployment structurally hinders members of subordinated groups from participating on a par with members of dominant groups in communicative interactions.

As Sandra Harding points out, for many feminist epistemologists, the gender-specificity of point-of-viewlessness is evidenced by the fact that this criterion of objectivity, with its emphasis on detachment, dispassion, and noninvolvement, relies upon three characteristically male conceptualizations: of *self* "as autonomous, individualistic, self-interested, fundamentally isolated from other people and from nature"; of *community* "as a collection of similarly autonomous, isolated, self-interested individuals having no intrinsically fundamental relations with one another"; and of *nature* as "an autonomous system from which the self is fundamentally separated and which must be dominated to alleviate the threat of the self's being controlled by it" (Harding 1986:171).[7] Underlying the epistemology embodied in the ideal of point-of-viewlessness, feminists have argued, are the dualisms of mind versus body, reason versus emotion, culture versus nature, fact versus value, knowing versus being, objectivity versus subjectivity; these Cartesian dualisms historically have been regarded as gender-linked and have served, because of gender stratification, to stigmatize women's epistemic agency and to legitimize projects of gender domination.

Because the modalities against which reason has been defined—body, emotions, instincts, subjectivity—have traditionally been associated with the female and because the division of labor in western class societies is gender-based where women take primary responsibility for bodily processes, we should undoubtedly note that because the ideal observer functions in Hare's theory as a (disembodied) embodiment of "pure" reason, it is not easily referred to as a female. More important, however, we should recognize that the Cartesian ideal of point-of-viewlessness embodied in "the ideal observer" or "archangel" puts women and other subordinated people at a disadvantage in moral deliberation. By discounting the effects of people's social identity upon their understandings of the world, including theory of knowledge, Hare's archangel ideal obscures and mystifies the privileged relation that members of dominant groups occupy with respect to the sociocultural means of discourse.

From a radical perspective—that is, from a perspective that denies the autonomy or social transcendency of reason and the language of morals—a critical appreciation of the different levels of moral reflexivity is therefore crucial to moral theory. This brings us to the question of whether there is potential in Hare's theory, considered on its own terms, for a radicalization of its deepest assumptions. Given its monological form, its liberal conception of the self, and its commitment to both "the standpoint of exchange" and the neutrality of the forms of discourse, where, if at all, does the radical future of Hare's moral theory lie?

In what follows, I want to suggest that because Hare's notion of "taking the standpoint of others" is epistemically incoherent and because his argument for a utilitarian mode of reasoning contains a non sequitur—the fallacious inference that universal prescriptivism logically dictates utilitarianism—certain revisions are necessary that yield a more radicalized model of moral reasoning. I will argue that in order to make universalizability a viable criterion of morality and in order to take full account of the multiple ways of implementing the ideal of universal prescriptivism, Hare must abandon the liberal conception of the self and its accompanying, monological model of moral deliberation. These revisions, in turn, redefine the task of meta-ethics and call for a more radicalized, feminist notion of autonomy.

The epistemic incoherency of Hare's concept of "taking the standpoint of the other" is due, I want to argue, to his commitment to a liberal conception of the self. Given his emphasis on universalizability as a logical property of moral language, Hare clearly wants to maintain that adopting the moral point of view requires taking the preferences of others into account. The starting point for reflection and action in Hare's moral theory *seems* to be difference. But, as discussed above, Hare is implicitly committed to viewing the moral agency of human individuals in abstraction from social circumstances and all that belongs to them as embodied, historically situated beings. By bracketing the social experience of individuals, their historical situatedness and connectedness to specific human groups, Hare constitutes selves as being epistemologically and metaphysically prior to their individuating characteristics. This yields the following difficulty: how—if individuals are generalized abstractions—can the motivations, desires, needs, and interests of Person and Other be individuated? By assuming the standpoint of a disembodied, disembedded other means abstracting from the particularities that form an individual's identity, the difference between self and other disappears—and with it, the coherency of Hare's concept of "taking the standpoint of the other."

Not surprisingly, Hare makes the essentialist statement that "people's inclinations about most of the important matters in life tend to be the same" (1963:97). But this claim, besides being empirically dubious, does not dissolve the problem of individuation that infects Hare's procedure of universalizability.

As I noted earlier, universalizability construed as a rule of moral reasoning requires that "if I now say that I ought to do a certain thing to a certain person, I am committed to the view that the very same thing ought to be done to me, were I in exactly his situation" (1981:108). The problem of individuating situations—of knowing that this situation is like or unlike that situation—arises for Hare because, on the one hand, situations do not have prepackaged descriptions or "people-independent" constructions and, on the other hand, Hare discounts the effects of a person's social experience upon his or her definition of a situation. Individuals define what the situation is, and their constructions depend upon their life-history, social experience and social situatedness. Thus, for example, a male manager may define the situation as simple flirtation, but a female secretary may construct it as sexual harrasment. Similarly, a white male student may define his school's implementation of an affirmative action program as reverse discrimination, but a black student may construe the situation as the school's way of attempting to live up to egalitarian ideals.

There is interesting evidence in the research of Carol Gilligan that the way people see or understand a moral situation depends upon how they construe self, others, and the relationship between them—whether they assume that self and other are interdependent or whether, like classic liberals, they assume that the self is fundamentally isolated. Gilligan's findings suggest, moreover, that these constructions correlate according to gender. Hare's liberal understanding of the self and its connection with others, for example, may be characteristic of privileged white males. Important to the issue at hand is that the problem of individuation that infects Hare's procedure of universalizability cannot be dissolved by an a priori privileging of what is, according to Gilligan, a characteristically male orientation toward self and others. If one assumes the soundness of Gilligan's empirical findings, most women, and some men,[8] construe the self as fundamentally connected with others; this affects the way they frame or define a moral situation.

Because people may, and often do, dispute the definition of a moral situation, the universalizability requirement that we treat like situations alike can only be viable if the task of defining what constitutes a "like" situation is articulated as involving the viewpoints of moral deliberators who are not solitary, disembedded, point-of-viewless beings but rather who are socially constructed, embodied members of historically changing groups with epistemologically distinctive vantage points. This, in turn, requires characterizing "taking the standpoint of others" as an actual dialogic interaction with concrete others, rather than as a matter of hypothetical role-playing done singly by the moral deliberator. If the social identity of the moral deliberator is viewed as epistemologically significant, a moral theory must eschew a mono-logical characterization of moral reasoning in order to ensure that taking the standpoint of others does not reduce de facto to projecting one's own per-spective onto others, to defining others in one's own terms by putting oneself in their place.

I will argue that there is more to endorsing a dialogical model of moral de-liberation than stipulating that moral agents sit down and talk to one an-other: unless one recognizes that the fairness of the conditions under which dialogue takes places is itself subject to dispute and evaluation, one's moral theory does not, I will contend, secure the moral autonomy of all the affected parties, especially members of subordinated groups. Before I turn to this point, however, I would like to demonstrate that it is necessary for Hare to articulate a dialogical ethic, not only to make universalizability a viable crite-rion of morality but also to take account of the fact that utilitarianism is not the only way of implementing the ideal of universal prescriptivism. Because the method of universalization, as well as conceptions of the good and definitions of the moral situation, can be the subject of moral disputation, the viability of Hare's moral theory depends, I want to argue, upon his charac-terizing moral reasoning as a dialogical process.

Because Hare asserts that moral thinking on the critical level consists "in making a choice under the constraints imposed by the logical properties of the moral concepts and by the non-moral facts, and by nothing else" (1981: 40) and because he designates utilitarianism as the proper expedient for re-solving moral conflicts, it is crucial to his theory that he demonstrate that a utilitarian mode of reasoning is logically generated by the requirement that we universalize our prescriptions. As the following passage reveals, Hare be-lieves that utilitarianism is imposed on us by the logical properties of moral expressions because "the effect of universalizability is to compel us to find principles which impartially maximize the satisfaction of . . . [people's] prefer-ences" (1981:226):

We retain, all of us, the freedom to prefer whatever we prefer, subject to the constraint that we have, *ceteris paribus,* to prefer that, were we in others' exact positions, that should happen which *they* prefer should happen. The requirement of universalizability then demands that we ad-just these preferences to accommodate the hypothetical preferences gen-erated by this constraint, as if they were not hypothetical but for actual cases; and thus, each of us, arrive at a universal prescription which rep-resents our total impartial preference (i.e., it is that principle which we prefer, all in all, should be applied in situations like this regardless of what position we occupy). What has happened is that the logical constraints have, between them, compelled us, if we are to arrive at a moral judgement about the case, to coordinate our individual preferences into a total preference which is impartial between us. The claim is that this impartial preference will be the same for all, and will be utilitarian. (1981:227)

It is a mistake, I believe, for Hare to infer that accommodating the preferences of others means counting equal preferences equally or, as he puts it, arriving "at a universal prescription which represents our total impartial preference." Because he believes that moral principles are universal in application, Hare must hold—on pain of contradiction—that to advance a moral principle as universal is to prescribe that the principle be consistently followed by all parties. It does not follow from the claim that moral principles are binding on all people, however, that to advance a moral principle is to prescribe a principle that "coordinates our individual preferences into a total preference which is impartial between us" (1981:227). The mistake consists in overlooking the fact that universalizability is methodologically instantiable in more than one way. Insisting that principles of morality be universal in application does not commit us a priori to what the mode or way of operationalizing universalizability must be. As Kenneth Goodpaster points out, in principle there are no limits to the sorts of methods that a community of moral deliberators might agree upon as a way of operationalizing universalizability:

One might resolve the conflict so as to maximize the satisfactions of the most gifted. Or the most influential. Or the most virtuous. Or, in the spirit of Rawls' recent theory of justice, the least advantaged. Or again, one might seek to maximize *average* utility, as against *total* utility. And the suggestions could be multiplied indefinitely. . . . At the very best, it seems to me, Hare might maintain plausibly that utilitarianism provides *one effective way* of implementing the ideal of universal prescriptivism. But it is more than exaggeration to claim that universal prescriptivism in any way 'dictates' an utilitarian mode of reasoning or that such a mode of reasoning in any sense 'follows from' the logical features of moral expressions. For this suggests at the very least that one who rejects utilitarianism is in some way committed to rejecting universalizability (as a logical property)—and this is as implausible as it is unargued. (1974:14, 15)

The objection, then, is that utilitarianism is not an expedient that *follows from* the logical properties of prescriptivity and universalizability. It is not, therefore, the only expedient that can be used to make prescriptivity and universalizability, construed as rules for moral reasoning, jointly sufficient in providing a method of moral reasoning. This consequence implies that moral reasoning may not be a single method for resolving conflicts of interest but rather a set of methods, each giving rise to principles of conduct that are prima facie justified (Goodpaster 1974:20–22). Without changing the rules of moral reasoning or ceasing to insist upon a monistic way of implementing the ideal of universal prescriptivism, then, Hare is not really warranted in designating utilitarianism as *the* method for resolving moral disagreements.

Of course, utilitarianism may provide one of the best ways of implementing the ideal of universal prescriptivism, and it might be chosen as the preferred method of universalization. But because universalizability is methodologically instantiable in more than one way, it would seem that in order to secure the autonomy[9] of the persons prescribed to, as well as the autonomy of the prescriber, Hare must add the proviso that if a set of facts is to constitute a reason or justification for moral action, it must be universalizable *and* the universalization must be intersubjectively acceptable. As I mentioned earlier, Hare wants to maintain that although moral judgments involve assent to an imperative, they are not merely attempts at persuasion or goading. Unless he introduces intersubjective constraints on the choice of a method or methods of universalization, however, it is difficult to see how Hare can coherently maintain that moral judgments involve a willingness to prescribe courses of action to others as rational self-guiding agents. The process of moral deliberation would turn out, ultimately, to be an act of solipsistic freedom on the part of individual moral prescribers. Thus, once one recognizes that no single method of universalization is guaranteed (or precluded) a priori by the requirement that moral principles be universalizable, in order to secure the autonomy of all affected parties, one must construe the process of choosing a method or methods of universalization as an actual dialogue in which the involved parties communicate with one another.

I would add, furthermore, that once one recognizes the different levels on which moral disputation may take place and the effects of a person's social experience upon his or her motivations, interests, needs, and understandings of the world, one must go deeper into "left field" and radicalize one's conceptions of both autonomy and meta-ethics. In the interests of showing that maintaining the internal coherence of Hare's theory of universal prescriptivism requires radicalizing some of its deep assumptions, I have followed Hare in privileging universalizability and prescriptivity as the rules of moral reasoning and in defining meta-ethics as the attempt "to give an account of the logical properties of . . . [moral language], and thus of the canons of rational thinking about moral questions" (1981:4). In the following discussion, I want to point out that the assumption that the forms of discourse are socially neutral underlies Hare's understanding of meta-ethics and the derivation of the rules of moral reasoning. This assumption, I will argue, is not tenable once we abandon the liberal conception of the self and a monological model of moral deliberation.

Hare maintains that when we operate on the meta-ethical level—that is, when we discuss the meanings of moral words and the logic of moral reasoning—we are not concerned with moral questions of substance (1981:26). Thus, according to Hare, because universalizability and prescriptivity are established as rules of moral reasoning by philosophical logic, they cannot be the subject matter of moral reasoning and dispute. Hare's theory, therefore, makes no allowances for the possibility that the meanings of moral expressions may themselves be entangled in a web of power relationships. He assumes the social neutrality of the means of discourse—in this particular case, the neutrality of the kinds of linguistic intuitions appealed to by contemporary empirical linguists and philosophical logicians in the Anglo-American world (1981:11).

This assumption of neutrality is tenable, I would argue, only if we conceptualize the knowing subject as an individualistic, isolated, disembedded entity. If we discount the influence of social factors and social politics in the construction of the knowing subject, then we need not make allowances for the possibilities that there may be biases in the forms of discourse and that these forms could themselves become the subject matter of moral reasoning and dispute. By "biases in the forms of discourse" I mean, for example, that in a society that values dispassionate, abstract argumentation and principled reasoning, those who argue in an emotional, vibrant, physically expressive way or who make appeals from the heart and personal experience are easily discredited and readily excluded from defining the terms of the debate. What I am contending here is that once we abandon the liberal conception of the self—as I have argued Hare must do in order to establish the viability in his model of moral reasoning—we must recognize the possibility that social divisions may infect even the means of discourse and, therefore, may privilege the point of view of the dominant groups within society.

The fact that members of subordinated groups may be disadvantaged in giving voice to their experience, interests, and needs has far-reaching ramifications for moral theory. It means, first, that genuine dialogical interaction does not happen by verbal fiat ("Can we talk?"). Unless the very conditions and constraints that govern dialogical interactions are themselves subject to on-going thematization, critique, and change and until members of subordinated groups are able to represent their experience, interests, and needs in a nondistorted, nonrepressed way, one has, at least from the perspective of the subordinated, not a dialogical determination of the right but a heteronomic[10] or "other-imposed" determination.

Recognizing the possibility that the dominant groups within society may enjoy a privileged relation to the means of discourse means recognizing, then, that for genuine dialogical interaction to occur, the central discursive institutions of society must be capable of giving voice to many different kinds of people. This, in turn, means recognizing that, *pace* Hare, moral autonomy is not the private, inner capacity of individuals to form and express their own opinions about moral questions (1963:2). Having moral autonomy, rather, is being a member of a group that has sufficient collective control over the sociocultural forms of discourse that one is able to express one's point of view in a nondistorted, nonrepressed way without having it marginalized or discounted.[11]

A more radicalized conception of moral autonomy is called for, then, once we allow for the possibility that social divisions may permeate the means of discourse. We are also required to recognize, I would argue, that meta-ethics is partly social theory. If one major objective of meta-ethics is "to formulate precisely the correct method for justifying normative statements or opinions, and to show that this method is the correct method" (Brandt 1959:8), and if, as I have suggested, the forms of discourse are not socially neutral, then the task of the meta-ethician must include articulating the social conditions and constraints necessary to enable members of subordinated groups to represent their interests and interpretations in a nondistorted, nonmarginalized way. And because meta-ethicians are as socially situated as the rest of us, *their* theoretical activity must also be subject to dialogical constraints, especially given the field's domination by white, middle-class males of European descent. Hence, moral theory involves *critical* social theory, and there cannot be any closure of moral reflexivity. No aspect of moral reasoning should be privileged or shielded from critical scrutiny—whether it be the conditions that ought to govern dialogical interchanges, Hare's rules of moral reasoning, which are arguably androcentric,[12] or the very objectives of meta-ethics.[13]

Recognizing the possibility that there may be biases in the forms of discourse, then, entails acknowledging how radical analytic moral philosophy must become. This essay, obviously, has provided only a limited defense of Hare's moral theory—a defense of its radical future. It is a defense most liberals could do without because it calls for abandoning cherished assumptions. But from a feminist perspective, relinquishing assumptions that are implicated in projects of gender, race, and class domination is de rigueur for anyone claiming commitment to emancipatory goals. In fact, if my argument in this paper is sound, relinquishing assumptions that systematically privilege the point of view of a particular group of people is an essential aspect of moral thinking.

With the recognition that moral theory involves critical social theory and an absence of reflexive closure comes the possibility, I would point out, of reclaiming that which is seen in classic liberal moral theory as hindrances to moral knowing, namely, passion and emotion, subjectivity, the self's contingent existence, partiality, and special connectedness to particular others—all those modalities traditionally associated with "the feminine." In the process of dialogical critical reflection, one *discovers* that our disdaining attitudes toward these modalities are socially produced, not reflections of something "real" and universal about the nature of moral knowing.

In this essay I have tried to encourage the reclamation of modalities historically conceptualized as distinctively "feminine" by deconstructing some fundamental theoretical assumptions of classic liberal moral theory. This approach has the virtue, I hope, of escaping a dualistic confrontation between modalities traditionally conceptualized as "masculine" and modalities traditionally conceptualized as "feminine"—something of utmost importance to feminists because ultimately what most needs reconstruction are not particular qualities and values but the structuring of reality in terms of hierarchial binary oppositions. Besides possessing theoretical value, this deconstructive approach also has practical strategic value: a paradigm shift is more likely effected, or at least assisted, not by trying to make one's opponents "see the light," [14] but—as Thomas Kuhn has argued—by exposing the problems generated internally by the old paradigm and by exploiting the sense its adherents may have that something has gone wrong with the old paradigm. [15]

NOTES

I would like to thank Susan Bordo for her invaluable comments and suggestions and for her supportive friendship and constant encouragement.

1. This expression is borrowed from the title of Zillah Eisenstein's book, *The Radical Future of Liberal Feminism* (New York: Longman, 1981).

2. Hare regards "overridingness" as another logical property of moral expressions, but I do not include discussion of it because it is not germane to my purposes.

3. Hare's characterization of "identifying with others" or "putting oneself in the shoes of others" as involving a hypothetical thought process reveals his deep commitment to a mind-centered approach to moral reasoning. For a feminist critique of this rationalist bias, see Alison Jaggar's essay in this volume.

4. If empathetic connection were not conceptualized simply as a cognitive process and if the relationship between self and others were construed as fundamentally interdependent, not instrumental and extrinsic, I could imagine cases in which Hare's assumption that it is possible for a person to acquire another person's preferences and desires would not seem so empirically implausible. Mother-child relationships in the modern nuclear family come to mind. But Hare's commitment to a liberal conception of the self precludes this construction (see below.)

5. This expression is borrowed from the title of Thomas Nagel's book, *A View From Nowhere* (New York: Oxford University Press, 1986).

6. See, for example, Bordo 1987; Fee 1983; Harding 1986; Hartsock 1983, 1985; and Smith 1974, 1977, 1979.

7. To explain why objectivity as detachment and noninvolvement is the epistemological stance to which men are predisposed some feminists make recourse to feminist revisions of "object-relations" theory. See, for example, Bordo 1987; Chodorow 1978; Flax 1983; Hartsock 1983, 1985; and Keller 1984. Less psychoanalytically oriented feminists account for the gender specificity of the Cartesian ideal in terms of a post-Marxist theory of labor and its effects upon mental life. See, for example, Rose 1983 and Smith 1974, 1977, 1979.

8. Although Gilligan does not elaborate a theory of gender difference in her book, *A Different Voice*, and although the correlations she draws between gender and epistemological constructions of the self, others, and relationships are historically and ethnocentrically circumscribed, her work does not rest, I would contend, upon essentialist notions of male and female. We can explain the gender correlations she discovers in terms of the effects that particular historical and social factors have had upon mental life.

9. In his work Hare is implicitly committed to a liberal conception of moral autonomy—as the private, inner capacity of individuals to form and express preferences about moral issues. Although I argue in a later section that Hare needs to radicalize his conception of autonomy, my argument here does not depend upon any particular definition of moral autonomy.

10. This term is borrowed from Kenneth Goodpaster's "Morality and Dialogue" (1975).

11. This understanding of autonomy construes it not so much as an entitlement or something simply given but as an ideal or goal that must be achieved politically through successful coalition-building and a refusal to suppress difference in the interests of forging a collective understanding of the world.

12. With its emphasis upon the division of self and other, impersonality, and the logic of reciprocity, the universalizability criterion embodies a calculative approach to moral decision making that may be characteristic of privileged white males (see Gilligan 1982).

13. The ideas that morality consists in respect for rules, that solving moral problems is a matter of using the proper moral calculus, and that meta-ethics thus consists in identifying precisely the correct method for justifying moral judgments may suppress differences in social life and therefore warrant critical dialogical evaluation.

14. See Donna Wilshire's essay in this volume for a discussion of some of the gender implications of this metaphor.

15. Thomas Kuhn, *The Structure of Scientific Revolutions*, 2d ed. (Chicago: University of Chicago Press, 1970).

REFERENCES

Bordo, Susan R. 1987. *The Flight to Objectivity: Essays on Cartesianism and Culture.* Albany: SUNY Press.

Brandt, Richard B. 1959. *Ethical Theory: The Problems of Normative and Critical Ethics.* Englewood Cliffs, N.J.: Prentice-Hall.

Chodorow, Nancy. 1978. *The Reproduction of Mothering.* Berkeley: University of California Press.

Fee, Elizabeth. 1983. "Women's Nature and Scientific Objectivity." In *Women's Nature: Rationalizations of Inequality,* ed. M. Lowe and R. Hubbard. New York: Pergamon Press.

Flax, Jane. 1983. "Political Philosophy and the Patriarchal Unconscious: A Psychoanalytic Perspective on Epistemology and Metaphysics." In *Discovering Reality: Feminist Perspectives on Epistemology, Metaphysics, Methodology and Philosophy of Science,* ed. S. Harding and M. Hintikka. Dordrecht: Reidel.

———. 1986. "Gender as a Social Problem: In and For Feminist Theory." *American Studies/Amerika Studien,* 193–213.

Gilligan, Carol. 1982. *In a Different Voice: Psychological Theory and Women's Development.* Cambridge, Mass.: Harvard University Press.

Goodpaster, Kenneth E. 1974. "Universal Prescriptivism and/or Utilitarian Methodology." Manuscript.

———. 1975. "Morality and Dialogue." *Southern Journal of Philosophy* 13:55–70.

Harding, Sandra. 1986. *The Science Question in Feminism.* Ithaca, N.Y.: Cornell University Press.

Hare, R. M. 1952. *The Language of Morals.* Oxford: Oxford University Press/Clarendon.

———. 1963. *Freedom and Reason.* Oxford: Oxford University Press/Clarendon.

———. 1981. *Moral Thinking: Its Levels, Method, and Point.* Oxford: Oxford University Press/Clarendon.

Hartsock, Nancy. 1983. "The Feminist Standpoint: Developing the Ground for a Specifically Feminist Historical Materialism." In *Discovering Reality: Feminist Perspectives on Epistemology, Metaphysics, Methodology and Philosophy of Science,* ed. S. Harding and M. Hintikka. Dordrecht: Reidel.

———. 1985. *Money, Sex and Power: Toward a Feminist Historical Materialism.* Boston: Northeastern University Press.

Keller, Evelyn Fox. 1984. *Reflections on Gender and Science.* New Haven, Conn.: Yale University Press.

Kerner, George C. 1966. *The Revolution in Ethical Theory.* New York: Oxford University Press.

Kuhn, Thomas. 1970. *The Structure of Scientific Revolutions.* 2d ed. Chicago: University of Chicago Press.

Moore, G. E. 1903. *Principia Ethica.* Cambridge: Cambridge University Press.

Rose, Hilary. 1983. "Hand, Brain and Heart: A Feminist Epistemology for the Natural Sciences." *Signs: Journal of Women in Culture and Society* 9, no.1:73–90.

Smith, Dorothy. 1974. "Women's Perspective as a Radical Critique of Sociology." *Sociological Inquiry* 44:7–13.

———. 1977. "Some Implications of a Sociology for Women." In *Women in a Man-Made World: A Socioeconomic Handbook*, ed. N. Glazer and H. Waehrer. Chicago: Rand-McNally.

———. 1979. "A Sociology For Women." In *Prism of Sex: Essays on the Sociology of Knowledge*, ed. J. Sherman and E. T. Beck. Madison: University of Wisconsin Press.

FEMINISM
AND THE RECONSTRUCTION
OF SOCIAL SCIENCE

Sondra Farganis

In their introduction to this collection of essays, Alison Jaggar and Susan Bordo list the embedded assumptions of western science, explicitly arguing that knowledge of the world is socially constructed and, within the world in which we live, gendered; for if gender patterns who we are, it also patterns how we think, and our views on science cannot escape this. The Jaggar/ Bordo critique of science questions the traditional view that something called an *objective* nature exists, corresponding to some clearly discernible *reality* that the human mind can understand through the rather simple and direct process known as *reason*. The scientific method has come to be regarded as the vehicle through which the mind, unencumbered by factors of class or status (religion, race, nationality, gender) can know or understand that objective reality. One must question the Cartesian ideal on which the contemporary notion of science is based, Jaggar and Bordo argue, for it disregards the role that politics and history play in this ethereal search for truth; furthermore, it disregards the ways in which reason, emotion, and passion mean different things and are valued in different ways by different people.

Contemporary feminist epistemology is part of the current critique of the Cartesian model of science, distinguishing itself from other challenges to science by its attribution of gender bias to both the scientific method and the western epistemological tradition of which that method is a part. The feminist challenge is not to argue that women can reason or "do" science as now practiced just as well as men can. Rather, its position is that women who have come to recognize and accept feminist assumptions about the world will practice science differently in a world that legitimates those assumptions: they will use a different methodology, or set of practices, to observe and understand the world around themselves; they will be conscious of the intent of their studies and the uses to which their researches will be put; and they may even rename, and thus transform, the heretofore blacklisted or outlawed emotions which have been kept out of scientific inquiry, those suspect "'non-rational' approaches to reality" (See Jaggar and Bordo, introduction to this volume).

At the root of the Jaggar/Bordo position, which I share, is a belief in the sociality of personhood. Turning away from the idealism and abstraction of much contemporary thought, those who share this belief argue that individuals are not divorced from time and place, housed in some conflict-free world populated only by themselves. Instead, individuals, men and women, are historically embodied, concrete persons whose perspective is a consequence of who they are; therefore, in a society divided by gender, women will see and know differently from men. The gendered sociality of their existence gives women a different perspective, and the place at which they stand—their activity within the world and how they are esteemed in a gender-stratified society—will make them practitioners of a different kind of science. Distinct from an essentialist position, the argument is twofold: first, thought bears the marks of a thinker's social characteristics and how these are socially regarded; second, women have different social experiences of the world than do men, and, therefore, they see the world differently. In other words, both the content and the form of thought, or the ideas and the processes through which those ideas are generated and understood, are affected by concrete social factors of which gender is one. Taken together, in this sense we say that science is gendered.

In this essay, I want to elaborate upon this position by defining and critiquing the prevailing conception of a (neo)positivistic science. I am most especially interested in a feminist social science and how it radicalizes the idea of the sociality of knowledge.

THE PREVAILING CONCEPTION OF SCIENCE

For much of the twentieth century, there appeared to be a consensus within the modern scientific community around the position that science was grounded in an empiricist, experimental epistemology. Science was regarded as a method of acquiring knowledge that was grounded in an objective reading of data: this method of finding out a "truth" corresponded to a "reality" through the use of empirical evidence that could be transferred as information from one person to another using appropriate rules or procedures. It offered a precise language: concepts or definitions of terms one could combine in a logical way; objects one could study through methods of observation and description; statements one could empirically verify or falsify; laws or regularities one could test for their truth value within an accepted scientific paradigm or model, that is, according to certain agreed upon rules or definitions. Reality was to be regarded as an object, often to be explained mathematically. For example, the body was thought of as a machine run by genetic material encoded and read by its constituent parts; intelligence was reduced to a mathematical figure, an I.Q.; race was reduced to simplistic classification schemes; political power was operationalized by reducing it to election results; the facts on the Vietnam War were thought to be easily collected, codified supposedly without bias, and interpreted in terms of general historical laws (see Berman essay in this volume).

EXISTING CRITIQUES OF (NEO)POSITIVISM

This is not the place to enter into the long, complex debate on the contours of the scientific method. At best, I can indicate that disagreements do exist over what constitutes science and, in a more specific sense, over whether the method is equally applicable to both the study of natural and social phenomena (Brecht 1959; Stretton 1969; Friedrichs 1970; Radnitsky 1970; Hesse 1980; Haan et al. 1983; Rajchman and West 1985; Skinner 1985). The contemporary controversy within the philosophy of science (Kuhn 1962, 1970; Lakatos and Musgrave 1970; Laudan 1977, 1984; Barnes 1982) is part of this debate, raising a set of concatenated issues at times similar to while at other times different from those soon to be raised by a feminist epistemology concerning the sociality of science, the relativity of truth systems, and the politicization of discourse.

Within social theory, those who look at the sociality of knowledge, in general, and the sociality of scientific knowledge, in particular, argue that knowledge is to be understood not only in terms of its inherent logic but also in terms of the social conditions out of which it emerges and of which it is a part (Mannheim 1936, 1956, 1971, 1982; Merton 1957; Berger and Luckmann 1966; Wolff 1983). Knowledge is not only a set of arguments but also a reflection of interests. Following Jürgen Habermas, we might say that the knowledge might be of a technical kind to help us to attain a particular goal; or it might be of an interpretive kind to satisfy our interest in understanding; or it might be knowledge of the language used to construct our social reality which, in turn, has an emancipatory interest. If we accept this scheme, then we can understand that what positivists call science is a particular form of knowledge (technical) satisfying a particular kind of interest, control of the environment and of other humans. Once we see that science is just one form of knowing in just one certain way, we can appreciate the position that all ways of knowing—science included—are human inventions reflective of historical moments. The social analyst is not interested in the truth of science but rather in its sociality, that is, in the ways in which science is practiced and defended, not some Platonic ideal of science lodged in some perfectly constituted mythological utopia, but rather the way science is understood at a specific moment.

To illustrate what I mean, I should refer to the gendered metaphors that are used to describe science and nature and trace their roots to the *Zeitgeist* of the seventeenth and the eighteenth century. The very language of science has been gendered with imagery that sees the masculine controlling the raw, earthy feminine of nature and the natural world (Griffin 1978; Merchant 1980; Bordo 1986). I should link the mechanistic imagery of positivism to its origins in Cartesian philosophy where bodies are equated with machines. I should indicate how the challenge to the (neo)positivistic paradigm is assisted by the successes of the Woman's Movement, which raises questions about the social use to which knowledge is put. I should indicate also how the achievements of science—nuclear weaponry, for example—created an atmosphere receptive to raising questions about the purposes of science. In all of these instances, knowledge is not depicted as neutral: the emphasis is not on science as an abstraction but science as a practice, not on the paradigm of science but on the historical actors who validate or challenge the paradigm. These examples suggest that knowledge is grounded in politics, used to legitimate, for example, certain attitudes toward nature, classes, gender. Once recognized, important questions emerge: Do we use knowledge to dominate or enter into a partnership with nature? Who benefits from our seeing nature as an object to be dominated? What must be the political agenda before we *can* enter into a partnership with nature? Do we use knowledge to continue arrangements of social stratification or to obliterate class distinctions? Do we use knowledge to support historical patterns of subordination or to validate proposals for gender equity?

Science is a form of discourse; it is subject to definitions of terms, the delineation of rules, and the formulation of canons as to what counts for knowledge and who counts for authority. When we view science this way, we are encouraged to focus on the rules that determine if something is true or false and the conditions under which one set of rules rather than another prevails. We are also enabled to see that discourses are always political; that is, they depend upon who writes the text that name the boundaries and order the values (Kuhn 1962, 1972; Foucault 1980). In other words, power constellations in the cultural world affect the experience of that world. Naively, (neo)positivism ignores this and is unreflective of its own epistemological foundations and of the larger social order of which those foundations are a part. Therefore, through recognizing the ways in which knowledge is governed by interests, that is, by seeing the "use value" of science, critics of (neo)positivism can ask that knowledge be used to reshape the human situation toward liberatory or emancipatory ends (Habermas 1971, 1974). For the kind of world we want *affects* the way in which we deal with both physical and social realities.

There are contemporary critics of (neo)positivism—phenomenologists, symbolic interactionists, ethnomethodologists, structuralists, deconstructionists, critical theorists, postmodernists (Schutz 1962; Radnitzky 1970; Foucault 1980; Culler 1982; Eagleton 1982; Habermas 1971; Wellmer 1974; Schroyer 1973; Lyotard 1984)—who oppose simplistic notions of objectivity. They take issue with the assumption that data is "there" to be read by observers who use a method embodying a form of reason that incorporates detachment and distancing and that brackets emotion, passion, and commitment. They favor reconceptualizing objectivity, although they do not agree about how to undertake this restructuring. It would take me too far afield to go into their shared and conflicting concerns; fortunately, several essays do just that (Skinner 1985; Bernstein 1985, 1986; Baynes et al. 1987).

Feminist critiques of science, to which I should like to turn, similarly emphasize the ways in which science is a human activity and, as such, reflect the ways in which particular activities are defined, understood, given meaning, and evaluated by the particular society. Like other critics of (neo)positivism, feminists challenge the notion of a world "there" waiting to be interpreted; they stress the importance of the observer and the uses to which his or her observations are put. The feminist critique historicizes science and asks what science will look like when the practitioners are different and the category of gender is taken into account.

A FEMINIST SOCIAL SCIENCE

The question of how we perceive the world and of how we act on that perception is at issue for both natural and social scientists; science, of whatever stripe, raises both epistemological concerns of a theoretical kind and political concerns of a practical order. The feminist, consciously aware of the dialectical relationship between theory and practice, wants to know not only about matters of science but also how one can practice being a scientist while honoring one's commitment to feminism, which, broadly understood, seeks to obliterate the oppression and domination of women.

Several strands converge in the feminist critique of science. One derives from feminist thought and its opposition to patriarchy: here, science as practiced is claimed to embrace masculine values (Fee 1981, 1986; Keller 1985a; Birke 1986). The other strand, also out of feminist thought, has an affinity with neo-Marxist thought and its radical critique of the modern world, that is, the destructive dimension of that world through scientization, rationalization, and bureaucratization. Here, science as practiced is seen as a juggernaut, embracing capitalistic and militaristic values (Nowotny and Rose 1979; Rose and Rose 1980; Fee 1981, 1986; Farganis 1986a).

The feminist critique of (neo)positivism is part of feminist efforts to reconstruct western thought, seeing in that thought and the (neo)positivism of which it is part a perspective at odds with the experiences of women (Jaggar 1985). Science as practiced is claimed to simplify cause-and-effect relationships: first, it looks at bodies as masculine; and second, it makes arbitrary distinctions between subject and object, nature and nurture, biology and environment, individual and community, ignoring the dialectical interaction of each pair. Feminists have located these false dualities—and we should add detachment/attachment to the list—in the western male-gendered tradition. In the last ten years or so, an oppositionary paradigm to these dualisms has emerged. Starting with the work of Dorothy Dinnerstein (1976) and Nancy Chodorow (1978) and continuing in the writings of Carol Gilligan (1982), Alison Jaggar (1983), Nancy Hartsock (1983), Kathy Ferguson (1984), Evelyn Fox Keller (1985a), and Sandra Harding (1986), among others, women have developed an epistemology that builds on the gendered social and psychological experiences of women. These experiences, for example, the bonding relationships in early female childhood, are taken to give women a different outlook on reality out of which may emerge a different morality, ethics, pattern of reasoning, and paradigm of science.

These writings emphasize the ways in which both *experience* is socially shaped and, in looking at issues this way, feminism avoids questions concerning woman's *nature*. Hilary Rose, for example, has compared women to craft rather than industrial laborers, that is, to artisans who do not separate the knower from what is to be known but who, on the contrary, integrate emotion and intellect. Women, she argues, traditionally engage in labor that allows them to feel and care for what they produce, and, in so doing, their work contrasts sharply with "masculine" labor integral to the mechanistic, Cartesian dualism of the contemporary industrial system. Out of women's work comes a sensibility that could contribute to a new way of seeing the world. The concrete set of experiences women have not only places them in a subordinate position in contemporary society but so excludes them from power that they have a different world view, what Herbert Marcuse will call a negating and oppositionary position (Marcuse 1974, 1978; Landes 1979; Lukes 1985; Alford 1985; Farganis 1986b).

Within the social sciences, Dorothy Smith (1974a, 1974b, 1987) is the most formidable critic of the biases of male knowledge. Fusing the insights of both the sociology of knowledge (the permeation of knowledge by social factors) and phenomenology (understanding social actors and social actions from the point of view of the actors), Smith argues for the importance of recognizing that both the observer and the observed have specific social biographies, that each are concrete persons occupying a moment in time: each is embodied; each has values. Critical of (neo)positivism, she dismisses naive notions of objectivity: she sees detachment as a false god to whom positivists pay homage. She argues for a descriptive accounting of the social world but one that appreciates the subjective dimension of science and, most especially, the empathetic nature of social science. The observer must work himself or herself into the mind of the social actor and see the world as he or she sees it: this is not controlling the actor and manipulating his or her behavior but rather respecting people's integrity. Although Smith does not call this "objective" reporting, she does refer to it as accurate and reliable, that is, an honest accounting (empathetic) of people and events and a most illuminating perspective.

One must aim to report on the world as the embodied actors see it. A sociology of women is, for her, a sociology for women. Like its counterpart in anthropology, ethnography, an ethnomethodological approach starts with where women are and understands the world as they experience it. It departs from sociology as it has been practiced in which the values of men (their view of power, their view of what is important) ignore or distort the lives of women. Here Smith shares the androcentric critique of science exemplified by Ruth Bleier's work on sociobiology, brain research, and hormonal distinctions (Bleier 1984). Through a phenomenological study, Smith argues, the social scientist will detail these inequities as a move toward denouncing and removing them: from description comes action. This is a feminist attitude toward knowledge, and Smith refers to this as returning knowledge to the community.

Other social scientists (Geertz 1973; Rosaldo 1980, 1983; Stacey 1985; Diamond 1985) are also looking either to feminism and/or ethnomethodology and phenomenology for ways of breaking out of the hold that positivism has on social science: (1) they want to understand the daily lives and experiences of the people about whom they have an interest in writing; (2) they want to understand the social world of ordinary consciousness before "scientific theory organizes consciousness" (Smith 1979:156), trying to avoid the obfuscation of theory that comes between them and that world; (3) they do not merely want to observe and describe behavior of individuals as if either the observed or the observers were not real subjects in a concrete world; that is, humans understanding other humans; (4) they want to introduce an emancipatory dimension into their research and writing, understanding and changing the life-worlds that they study while recognizing how those life-worlds change them.

The search for alternative thought patterns is part and parcel of the quest for experiences that oppose domination. It involves a certain respect for and interest in preserving life (Ruddick 1980), or an alternative discourse that treats an ideal-typical mother/child relationship as a moral paradigm for social behavior (Elshtain 1982, 1987), or an alternative way of organizing life's activities counter to the modern bureaucratic state (Ferguson 1984), or alternative moralities that emphasize concrete relationships of care and concern and less so abstract principles of justice (Gilligan 1982).

There is an affinity between feminism and Marxism in that both incorporate the idea of an interactive or dialectical relationship between selves and society. Both refuse to separate social, political, and ethical concerns, and both argue that theory and practice, like subjects and objects, are part of a process or relationship that must be put to the service of both the construction and the reconstruction of individual and social lives. Feminism and Marxism want to recognize the fusion of political and social concerns with scientific theorizing, not keep each from informing the other. Both are, as well, a reaction to the experiences of the twentieth century, most expressly to the role that science came to play during and after the Second World War. I mean by this that both contemporary Marxism and feminism are historically conditioned, affected by the *Zeitgeist* of the age and shaped by the knowledge of the paradoxes of modernity, to wit, the advances and ravagings of advanced industrial society.

Science, as now practiced, contributes to and even constitutes a political ideology of domination. For (neo)positivism, in treating physical and social entities as objects to be described, measured, and classified, trains us to think of controlling and, in this sense, dominating the world around us and the people in that world. Witness the ways in which scientists perform drug testing and the disadvantaged populations on which they do them: the subjects are objects in a cause-and-effect test. Because we do not see all forms of natural and social phenomena as parts of a shared world, this vision contributes to our sense of alienation.

In seeing science as a discourse, as a way of speaking about the world, the feminist can deconstruct the intricate relationship between science and power, bringing to the surface the ways in which scientific discourse reinforces power as well as the role that power plays in actively creating scientific discourse. In going beyond the contemporary critiques of (neo)positivism, feminists ask additional questions of both philosophical and sociological import: How important is gender in structuring perception? If important, how does gender affect notions of objectivity? Is objectivity a smoke-screen for a male perspective? Are male and female perspectives equally valid, or is there something inherent in the feminist perspective that gives it an edge, in much the same way that, in Hegelian terms, the slave's oppression and his ability to see both his and the master's position gives him the edge (Kojeve 1980; Hartsock 1983)?

Gender is a category, a way of making distinctions between people: it classifies people on the basis of sexual traits. Like class, it has both external and internal dimensions: that is, the classification or labeling is seen and read by others as well as by the self, and the similarities may be interpreted as shared interests, things one has in common with others. Gender may or may not matter to us or to others: in our social and political world it always matters. We interpret the meaning of gender within a culture by examining issues such as voting rights, childcare, comparable worth, participation in the armed services, abortion, reproductive technology, to name a few. We can discover what has been seen socially as feminine, that is, what generally has been done by as well as to women.

Following Marx, one can argue that one's class—the relationship one has to the means of production—affects ones sense of self and society and history: class affects what one sees. In a similar way, feminism argues that one's gender, the particular cultural way in which one's biology is presented, understood, and played out affects what one sees. Gender creates a person who has a whole array of characteristics and the person and the characteristics are in history, not above or outside it. Gender is constructed and reconstructed within a framework that interacts with biological considerations; but, it is not unalterably controlled or contained by that biology. Although each of us comes into the world with certain features—sex organs, eye color, hair texture, hormonal balances and imbalances, maybe even cognitive aptitudes, skills, and aggressive tendencies—their shaping and assessment is a consequence of social and historical conditions. Does the society value those who can lift heavy building materials? Does the society suggest that those who cannot or choose not to have children are somehow deviant? Does the society have a particular image of masculine and feminine beauty? Will those who test better on mathematical aptitude tests be more valued than those who draw, or sing, or dance? The way in which one is esteemed, that is, the prestige one gets, is not pregiven in any deterministic or mechanistic way but rather is a consequence of historical factors shaped by human agency. Gender must be related to a moment in time—now and not then—as well as to a place—here and not there. Gender, variable as it may be, is a constant of history, and in this sense gender is at the heart of what de Beauvoir means when she says: "One is not born, but rather becomes a woman. . . . It is civilization as a whole that produces this creature" (de Beauvoir 1952:301).

Feminist writers raise the question, if I may use literary analogies, of how women have been read and how women would use the feminine eye to read (see Perry and O'Neill in this volume). In arguing that men and women are different, feminists offer varied reasons: thinking, for example, may bear some relationship on how the body is regarded and/or to the delineation of social practices. In the historical devaluation of the feminine, male theorists have attributed a subordinate status to patterns of feminist thought and action. If men have written the canonical laws and held a monopoly on the discourses, then might not what we have learned to think of as the "rational" be a masculine notion of rationality and might women not come to regard the "rational" in a different way (Okin 1979; Elshtain 1981; Harding 1983)? Bleier writes: "If science as a method and body of knowledge, is, as it must be, a cultural and social product, how could it, unlike all other cultural products, escape the culture's most basic gendered concepts, woven into its very fabric however invisible they may still be to our own culture-bound minds? Who is the authority that, standing above the fray, has guaranteed that science alone is untainted by androcentric biases and patriarchal concepts and methods" (Bleier 1986:15)?

Feminists question a rationality that is equivalent to the functional, efficient, and purposive; by these standards, Nazism and nuclear warfare pass the test. But the substantive objectives and the moral imperatives that ought to govern human lives have been omitted from this rendering of rationality. Might not these be grounded in passion, those "outlawed" emotions (see Jaggar in this volume) that we have come traditionally to associate with women? Might we not need a new definition of reason?

For its part, a feminist social science seeks to deconstruct the masculine model and reconstruct one along feminine lines, one that values those qualities of the feminine that, for historical reasons, have been attributed to women and to which this essay has made reference. A feminist social science just as a feminist politics calls into question the values of modern man, "of self as autonomous and objectified: an image of individuals unto themselves, severed from the outside world of other objects . . . and simultaneously from their own subjectivity" (Keller 1985a:70).

It is not that feminists are not interested in knowledge for its own sake, that is, the joy of knowing, nor is it that feminists are arguing for science in all instances and at all times to be in the service of politics. Feminists want to stress, however, that science is a human endeavor inevitably intertwined with the culture of which it is a part. Science makes its impact through the labor of scientists, who are to be held accountable for their work. They must decide whether to develop genetic screening to assure that women will birth more boys or, rather, to screen out sickle cell anemia or Tay-Sachs.

Rose (1983, 1986) has argued that science ought not be reified, given a thinglike status, an identity of its own; it ought not be separated from the minds and hearts and hands of those whose labor it is. In this sense there can be no refuge in something called "pure science," for science evolves out of an interaction with the cultural world that has nourished it. There can be no "epistemological distancing" (Fee 1981:386), no Archimedian point outside history that allows privileged scientists to stand above the fray and see reality in a totally "true" way.

Although feminism allows for a descriptive relativism that recognizes the different perspectives from which persons see the world and the objects in that world, it wants to avoid the scourge of normative relativism which says that each of these perspectives is equally good. This problem of the diversity of perspectives is the cloud under which contemporary philosophy and social thought has been operating. It casts its shadow on the discussions of the sociology of knowledge, on the debates between Critical Theory and hermeneutics, on the controversy surrounding the Kuhnian thesis, and most recently, on the assertions of the postmodernists, most particularly Foucault. Feminist social science, in its commitment to feminism, is imbued with a moral dimension; thus, it runs counter to the relativism and the ethical neutrality held to govern both contemporary philosophy and science (Hare 1952; Stevenson 1960; Winch 1958; Rorty 1980; MacIntyre 1982; Bernstein 1983). Moreover, feminism as a political movement must try to create the conditions whereby we can intelligently and reasonably agree upon substantive values. Precisely out of what women have experienced—their marginal status, their outcastness, their experience of care and concern—the case is made that women can offer an epistemologically sounder and politically and morally better position. Jaggar and Hartsock detail the epistemic advantage that women have through the roles they have played in a gender-stratified society. Hartsock sees a relationship between being excluded from the corridors of power and having insight. Because women have been kept out of the struggles of a life-denying state, women are a force of/for negation. Smith's work suggests that by turning to the concreteness of *women's* experiences we shall understand how power operates to perpetuate inequalities and patterns of domination. Rose argues for "a successor science" (1986:73) to reflect those values of care and concern and nurturance that we have come to associate with women and that we might call the womanly virtues; out of these caring values, which inculcate certain attitudes that humanize the scientific enterprise and commit it to a liberatory or emancipatory project, we shall be able to develop a model for science that shows concern for both nature and people. Feminists are not Luddites opposing machines; rather, they oppose machines that seek to improve warheads and chemical warfare but not those used for the early detection of or, better still, prevention of cancer.

Keller does not want to equate nobility with being woman, but she does want to build on the caring and nurturing socialization practices that historically have colored women's lives. She wants to provide a place for those men, however few their numbers, who embody the values necessary to challenge the epistemological tradition of the West and the kind of science integral to that tradition. She understands that simply increasing the number of women doing male science is not the answer, but she sees the need for more women scientists if feminists are to shake up sexual stereotypes. She suggests that a new science formulated and practiced by men, however radical they may be, is not the solution:

> Although there may be no reason in principle why modern science could not have developed differently—embracing both feeling *and* reason, connection *and* separation, and equating knowledge with both power *and* love—while (for any number of other reasons) remaining an exclusively male enterprise, the fact is it did not. And here the force of history is prior to the force of logic. It is a historical, not a logical, process that has delineated the norms of science as we know them, and that has, at the same time, forged a division between emotion and intellectual labor—a separation of spheres—which places the stereotypic women on one side and the (equally stereotypic) scientists on the other. (Keller 1985b:96).

The problem of *a* feminist science or even *a* feminist social science may be that, like many theories it criticizes, it upholds too universalistic an assumption of gender: it "assumes too much about how gender really works" (Rosaldo 1980:399). Factors of class, for example, also affect how people live their lives and how they perceive the world. If gender is more varied than we sometimes imagine, might there not then be, within science, a need to accommodate "theoretical dissonances" (Bleier 1986:15), that is, disagreements over what science is and how best it can be practiced? Can feminism accept "a plurality of discourses" (Rose 1986:73)?

To date, even in the ambitious efforts of Harding and Smith, I find a feminist critique *of* (social) science but not a feminist (social) science. This is not to diminish the efforts but rather to suggest at what point feminism is in its project: "Critique does not have to be the premise of a deduction which concludes: this then is what needs to be done. It should be an instrument for those who fight, those who refuse and resist what is. Its use should be in processes of conflict and confrontation, essays in refusal" (Foucault 1981:13). Feminism is brilliantly grappling with the questions of the cohesiveness, the diversity, and the embodiment of gender: the universality and/or particularization of gender. It is also struggling politically to create a feminist world out of which this new science will emerge.

NOTE

This paper benefited from my participation in the Women's Studies seminars directed by Alison Jaggar at Rutgers University in 1985. The discussions of my colleagues allowed me to clarify my understanding of feminist theory, and I am indebted to those shared moments of intellectual engagement. I am especially grateful to Alison Jaggar's tireless support and her preparedness to help me fine-tune my thinking on this as well as other topics.

REFERENCES

Alford, C. Fred. 1985. *Science and the Revenge of Nature: Marcuse and Habermas.* Gainesville: University Presses of Florida.

Barnes, Barry. 1982. *T. S. Kuhn and Social Science.* New York: Columbia University Press.

Baynes, Kenneth, James Bohan, and Thomas McCarthy eds. 1987. *After Philosophy: End of Transformation?* Cambridge, Mass.: MIT Press.

Beauvoir, Simone de. 1952. *The Second Sex.* Trans. H. M. Parshley New York: Modern Library.

Berger, Peter L., and Thomas Luckmann. 1966. *The Social Construction of Reality: A Treatise in the Sociology of Knowledge.* Garden City, N.Y.: Doubleday.

Bernstein, Richard J. 1983. *Beyond Objectivism and Relativism: Science, Hermeneutics and Praxis.* Philadelphia: University of Pennsylvania Press.

———, ed. 1985. *Habermas and Modernity.* Cambridge, Mass.: MIT Press.

———. 1986. *Philosophical Profiles: Essays in a Pragmatic Mode.* Philadelphia: University of Pennsylvania Press.

Birke, Lynda. 1986. *Women, Feminism and Biology: The Feminist Challenge.* New York: Methuen.

Bleier, Ruth, 1984. *Science and Gender: A Critique of Biology and Its Theories on Women.* New York: Pergamon.

———. 1986. "Introduction." In *Feminist Approaches to Science,* ed. Ruth Bleier. New York: Pergamon.

Bordo, Susan. 1986. "The Cartesian Masculinization of Thought." *Signs* 11:39–56.

Brecht, Arnold. 1959. *Political Theory: The Foundations of Twentieth Century Political Thought.* Princeton, N.J.: Princeton University Press.

Chodorow, Nancy. 1978. *The Reproduction of Mothering: Psychoanalysis and the Sociology of Gender.* Berkeley: University of California Press.

Culler, Jonathan. 1982. *On Deconstruction: Theory and Criticism after Structuralism.* Ithaca, N.Y.: Cornell University Press.

Diamond, Timothy. 1985. "'Making Gray Gold' as a Feminist Way of Knowing." Paper presented to the Douglass College Women's Studies Seminar, "Feminist Ways of Knowing," Rutgers University, New Brunswick, N.J.

Dinnerstein, Dorothy. 1976. The *Mermaid and the Minotaur: Sexual Arrangements and Human Malaise*. New York: Harper & Row.

Eagleton, Terry. 1982. *Literary Theory: An Introduction*. Minneapolis: University of Minnesota Press.

Elshtain, Jean Bethke. 1981 *Public Man, Private Woman: Women in Social and Political Thought*. Princeton, N.J.: Princeton University Press.

———. 1982. "Feminist Discourse and Its Discontents: Language, Power, and Meaning." *Signs* 7:603–621.

———. 1987. *Women and War*. New York: Basic.

Farganis, Sondra. 1986a. "Feminist Theory and Social Theory: The Need for Dialogue." *Sociological Inquiry* 56:50–68.

———. 1986b. *The Social Reconstruction of the Feminine Character*. Totowa, N.J.: Rowman and Littlefield.

Fee, Elizabeth. 1981. "Is Feminism a Threat to Scientific Objectivity?" *International Journal of Women's Studies* 4:378–392.

———. 1986. "Critiques of Modern Science: The Relationship of Feminism to Other Radical Epistemologies." In *Feminist Approaches to Science*, ed. Ruth Bleir. New York: Pergamon.

Ferguson, Kathy E. 1984. *Feminist Case against Bureaucracy*. Philadelphia: Temple University Press.

Foucault, Michel. 1980. *Power/Knowledge: Selected Interviews and Other Writings, 1972–1977*. Trans. Colin Gordon, Leo Marshall, John Mepham, and Kate Soper. New York: Pantheon.

———. 1981. "Questions of Method: An Interview with Michel Foucault." *Ideology and Consciousness* 8:3–14.

Friedrichs, Robert W. 1970. *A Sociology of Sociology*. New York: Free Press.

Geertz, Clifford. 1973. *The Interpretation of Culture*. New York: Basic.

Gilligan, Carol. 1982. *In a Different Voice: Psychological Theory and Women's Development*. Cambridge, Mass.: Harvard University Press.

Griffin, Susan. 1978. *Woman and Nature: The Roaring Inside Her*. New York: Harper & Row.

Haan, Norma, Robert Bellah, Paul Rabinow, and William M. Sullivan, eds. 1983. *Social Science as Moral Inquiry*. New York: Columbia University Press.

Habermas, Jürgen. 1970. *Towards a Rational Society: Student Protest, Science and Politics*. Trans. Jeremy J. Shapiro. Boston: Beacon Press.

———. 1971. *Knowledge and Human Interest*. Trans. Jeremy J. Shapiro. Boston: Beacon Press.

———. 1974. *Theory and Practice*. Trans. John Viertel. Boston: Beacon Press.

Harding, Sandra. 1983. "Is Gender a Variable in Conceptions of Rationality?" In *Beyond Domination: New Perspectives on Women and Philosophy*, ed. Carol C. Gould. Totowa, N.J.: Rowman and Allanheld.

———. 1986. *The Science Question in Feminism*. Ithaca, N.Y.: Cornell University Press.

Hare, R. M. 1952. *The Language of Morals*. New York: Oxford University Press.

Hartsock, Nancy C. 1983. *Money, Sex and Power: Toward a Feminist Historical Materialism.* New York: Longman.

Hesse, Mary B. 1980. *Revolutions and Reconstructions in the Philosophy of Science.* Brighton: Harvester Press.

Jaggar, Alison M. 1983. *Feminist Politics and Human Nature.* Totowa, N.J.: Rowman and Allanheld.

———. 1985. "Towards a More Integrated World." Paper presented to the Douglass College Women's Studies Seminar, "Feminist Reconstruction of Self and Society."

Keller, Evelyn Fox. 1985a. *Reflections on Gender and Science.* New Haven, Conn.: Yale University Press.

———. 1985b. "Contending with a Masculine Bias in the Ideals and Values of Science." *Chronicle of Higher Education.*

Kojeve, Alexander. 1980. *Introduction to the Reading of Hegel: Lectures on the "Phenemonology of the Spirit,"* Trans. Allan Bloom. Ithaca, N.Y.: Cornell University Press.

Kuhn, Thomas, S. 1962, 1970. *Structure of Scientific Revolution.* Chicago: University of Chicago Press.

Lakatos, Imre, and Alan E. Musgrave, eds. 1970. *Criticism and the Growth of Knowledge.* New York: Cambridge University Press.

Landes, Joan B. 1979. "Marcuse's Feminist Dimension." *Telos* 41:158–165.

Laudan, Larry. 1977. *Progress and Its Problems: Towards a Theory of Scientific Growth.* Berkeley: University of California Press.

———. 1984. *Science and Values: The Aims of Science and Their Role in Scientific Debate.* Berkeley: University of California Press.

Lukes, Timothy J. 1985. *The Flight into Inwardness: An Exposition and Critique of Herbert Marcuse's Theory of Liberatory Aesthetics.* Selingsgrove: Susquehanna University Press.

Lyotard, Jean-Francois. 1984. *Post-Modernism: A Report on Knowledge.* Trans. Geoff Bennington and Brian Massumi. Minneapolis: University of Minnesota Press.

MacIntyre, Alistair. 1982. *After Virtue.* South Bend, Ind.: University of Notre Dame Press.

Mannheim, Karl. 1936. *Ideology and Utopia: An Introduction to the Sociology of Knowledge.* Trans. Louis Wirth and Edward Shils. New York: Harcourt, Brace and World.

———. 1956. *Essays on the Sociology of Knowledge.* London: Routledge and Kegan Paul.

———. 1971. *From Karl Mannheim.* New York: Oxford University Press.

———. 1982. *Structures of Thinking.* Trans. Jeremy J. Shapiro and Shierry Weber. London: Routledge and Kegan Paul.

Marcuse, Herbert. 1974. "Marxism and Feminism." *Women's Studies.* 2, no. 3:279–288.

———. 1978. *The Aesthetic Dimension: Toward a Critique of Marxist Aesthetics.* Boston: Beacon Press.

Merchant, Carolyn. 1980. *Death of Nature: Women, Ecology and the Scientific Revolution*. New York: Harper & Row.

Merton, Robert K. 1957. *Social Theory and Social Structure*. Glencoe, Ill.: Free Press.

Nowotny, Helga, and Hilary Rose, eds. 1979. *Counter-Movements in the Sciences: The Sociology of the Alternatives to Big Science*. Boston: D. Reidel.

Okin, Susan Moller. 1979. *Women in Western Political Thought*. Princeton, N.J.: Princeton University Press.

Radnitzky, Gerard. 1970. *Contemporary Schools of Metascience*. New York: Humanities.

Rajchman, John, and Cornel West, eds. 1985. *Post-Analytic Philosophy*. New York: Columbia University Press.

Rorty, Richard. 1980. *Philosophy and the Mirror of Nature*. Princeton, N.J.: Princeton University Press.

Rosaldo, Michelle Z. 1980. "The Use and Abuse of Anthropology: Reflections on Feminism and Cross-Cultural Understanding." *Signs* 5:389–417.

———. "Moral/Analytic Dilemmas Posed by the Intersection of Feminism and Social Science." In *Social Science as Moral Inquiry*, ed. Norma Hann, Robert N. Bellah, Paul Rabinow, and William M. Sullivan New York: Columbia University Press.

Rose, Hilary. 1983. "Hand, Brain and Heart: Towards a Feminist Epistemology for the Sciences." *Signs* 9:73–90.

———. 1985. "Science's Gender Gap." *Women's Review of Books* 2:5–6.

———. 1986. "Beyond Masculinist Realities: A Feminist Epistemology for the Sciences." In *Feminist Approaches to Science*, ed. Ruth Bleir. New York: Pergamon.

Rose, Hilary, and Steven Rose, eds. 1980. *Ideology of/in the Natural Sciences*. New York: Schenkman.

Ruddick, Sara. 1980. "Maternal Thinking." *Feminist Studies* 6:342–367.

Schroyer, Trent. 1973. *The Critique of Domination: The Origins and Development of Critique Theory*. New York: George Braziller.

Schutz, Alfred. 1962. *Collected Papers, Volume One: The Problem of Social Reality*. The Hague: Martinus Nijhoff.

Skinner, Quentin, ed. 1985. *The Return of Grand Theory in the Human Sciences* New York: Cambridge University Press.

Smith, Dorothy E. 1974a. "The Social Construction of Documentary Reality." *Sociological Inquiry* 44:257–268.

———. 1974b. "Women's Perspective as a Radical Critique of Sociology." *Sociological Inquiry* 44:7–13.

———. 1979. "A Sociology for Women." In *Prism of Sex: Essays on the Sociology of Knowledge*, ed. Julia A. Sherman and Evelyn Torton Beck. Madison: University of Wisconsin Press.

———. 1987. *The Everyday World as Problematic: A Feminist Sociology*. Boston: Northeastern University Press.

Stacey, Judith. 1985. Presentation to the professional Workshop on Sociology and Feminist Theory, American Sociological Association, August, Washington, D.C.

Stevenson, Charles. 1960. *Ethics and Language*. New Haven, Conn.: Yale University Press.

Stretton, Hugh. 1969. *The Political Sciences: General Principles of Selection in Social Science and History*. New York: Basic.

Wellmer, Albrecht. 1974. *Critical Theory of Society*. New York: Seabury.

Winch, Peter. 1958. *The Idea of a Social Science and Its Relation to Philosophy*. London: Routledge and Kegan Paul.

Wolff, Kurt H. 1983. *Beyond the Sociology of Knowledge: An Introduction and a Development*. Lanham, Md.: University Press of America.

FROM ARISTOTLE'S DUALISM TO MATERIALIST DIALECTICS: FEMINIST TRANSFORMATION OF SCIENCE AND SOCIETY

Ruth Berman

The vision of science, rising with magisterial authority above the political battles raging below, has grown somewhat dim for women and for some men. The impartiality of its pronouncements has been questioned on several counts by feminists and others, its claim to objectivity described as myth. It is now being seen as a potent agent for maintaining current power relationships and women's subordination.

THE SOCIAL PRACTICE OF SCIENCE IN REGARD TO WOMEN

Women often conceptualize science as "heavy" and external to their thinking. This is not surprising. Science is associated with the power structure of a society in which women have been distanced from power. Our life experiences have conditioned us to serve and not easily to identify with mastery over either nature or other human beings.

Whatever the past, women presently are experiencing profound changes in their lives. We are much more involved with increasingly sophisticated technical gadgetry in the home, and high-tech in the workplace. Our presence in the public work force is much larger, and increasingly obligatory, and we are reaching for higher pay and more satisfaction from our jobs. More than half the college population is female, and we comprise an increasingly large number of science faculty graduates.

Some modern-day feminists (Harding 1986), as women generally, have been hostile toward even examining the specific nature of the physical sciences and the dynamics of their role in social processes. This is understandable, although perhaps somewhat myopic. These sciences, and their derivative technologies, are seen as largely responsible for the deterioration of our habitat, the earth; creating the tools to further intensify social control over woman's body and her reproductive capacity; and initiating endless biological superman theories designed to justify keeping woman's place at the bottom. These critiques have much merit.

However, it is difficult to combat the unknown. The science of a society is integral to it and the particular manner in which it is expressed profoundly affects our lives. With governments all over the world feverishly grasping at "science and technology" to maintain their power base, women, feminists, and all others on the underside of hegemony must understand specifically, *in detail*, what this means for us. Feminist scientists have already accepted the challenge, and many have written cogently on elitist control and abuses of contemporary science. But only when we recognize that both the social and the professional practices of science express an acceptance of the ideology of the ruling caste will we be able to determine how to respond.

Critiques of Biases in the Current Practice of Science

Feminist and other egalitarian scientists recognize that the practice of science is influenced by its social and economic environment. They point specifically to five conditions in its current practice.

VOCATIONAL DISCRIMINATION. A kind of social chromatography in hiring and promotion seems to be operating, which usually allows only the mostly male, upper middle-class, white faces to rise to the top while women remain at various levels under their control. Discrimination is also effected by enforcing a male-defined timetable for climbing the professional ladder; this mandates that one must make one's mark just at the time that women must bear their children. Even the *perception* of this double demand places women at a competitive disadvantage because they are perceived as having a divided commitment.

CONTROL OF FUNDING BY THE RULING SEGMENT OF SOCIETY. The interests of the funding agency, for example, the National Cancer Institute, usually influence not only the choice of problems to be investigated but even more emphatically the choice of goals. The development of new chemotherapeutic agents, for example, has taken priority over any form of preventive studies; breast cancer has a low priority among the forms of cancer being investigated, although forty-one thousand women are currently dying of it every year, and its incidence is increasing.

The ruling stratum of society controls not only research funding, status, and privilege but indeed almost all jobs in science at any level. Most research effort is already directed toward military or profit-making goals, and the fine tip of the funnel through which research support is being disbursed is being focused ever more narrowly upon this target (Dickson 1984; also, Biddle 1987; Rawls 1987). The limited options thus available to scientists cannot but similarly limit their interest and vision. The ideological bias and class identification of scientists have become especially clear in recent years, when molecular biologists, including Nobel Prize winners, are arguably more frequently to be found in the board rooms of corporations and in the courtrooms during patent litigations than in the classrooms and laboratories. It is therefore especially to the credit of the majority of university physicists and physics graduate students—even more so, those without tenure—who have signed a petition pledging not to work on Star Wars research.

WOMEN AS SPECIAL TARGETS OF MEDICAL TECHNOLOGY. Far more women than men are labeled neurotic, numbed with psychoactive drugs, and used as guinea pigs for psychiatric experiments (Weitz 1987). The control of poor women by medical and legal procedures is especially flagrant, although procedures regulating women's reproduction can affect all women (e.g., excessive use of hysterectomies, caesarean deliveries). Contraceptive experiments are carried out on poor Puerto Rican women and sterilization on poor Indian women; and women who bear and birth their own genetic children, after being artificially inseminated with the sperm of the husbands of richer women are, in an extraordinary distortion of the English language and biological fact, called "surrogate" mothers and "rented uteri."

An even greater threat to women's lives may be posed by the use of *in vitro* fertilization techniques, such as the implanting of already fertilized eggs—test-tube babies—into the uteri of nongenetic mothers (Arditti et al. 1984; Corea 1985; Rowland 1987). But the most disturbing, and most widespread, incursion of biotechnology into our lives will most likely come in the form of the wide variety of new fetal tests now being introduced—to be performed through the body of the mother. Their use has already risen sharply (Kolata 1987). In addition to health risks, it implies the mother's obligation to deliver only a "perfect"(?) baby.

THE USE OF GENDERED LANGUAGE. The language of science often includes the use of gendered rhetoric and the metaphors of domination (Keller 1985; Fried 1982). "Nature" is seen as female: controlled, used, and exploited by the scientist or "man." Military references abound in medicine, as in the "battle" or "war" against cancer, or AIDS; the "magic bullet," for drugs; and the "mobilization of the troops," referring to white blood cell activity (Jaret and Nilsson 1986).

MISUSES AND DISTORTIONS OF SCIENCE METHODOLOGY TO SUGGEST THE INFERIORITY OF WOMEN. The mystique of "science" and presumed "scientific evidence" is invoked to declare that "superior" or "inferior" human characteristics are a *natural* imperative, justifying the hegemony of the dominant elite. The rationalizations for this presumption of biological drives as the determinant of social roles include dubious statistical "differences" in aggressiveness (read as initiative), in hormonal action, in brain lateralization, and so on, between male and female rats. These contentions have been repeatedly and carefully refuted with much documentation (Barnett 1983; Bleier 1984; Fausto-Sterling 1986; Gould 1981; Hubbard 1982; Lewontin et al. 1984; Lowe 1978; Tobach and Rosoff 1978–1984), but they are still frequently reported as fact.

"Nonconscious" prejudice often also affects the choice of problems to be investigated, for example, the large number of studies of presumed inherent behavioral *differences* between sexes and races and the design of experiments that assume the male condition to be the norm. This is what Fausto-Sterling refers to as "bad science," performed by usually good scientists. These last two aspects of bias in the practice of science have been most frequently addressed, most recently in books by two feminist scientists, Ruth Bleier and Anne Fausto-Sterling.

Criticism of Sex Difference Research and Human Sociobiology

The latest reincarnation of biological determinism first made its appearance with the publication in 1975 of E. O. Wilson's *Sociobiology: The New Synthesis*, a "new science" of human social behavior and relations, derived from observations on the instinctive social behavior of insects. The apparently direct hereditary control of the latter is ascribed also to the former, with a separate, "modifying" environmental influence added later. Both Bleier and Fausto-Sterling reject this conceptual dichotomy of separable, independent hereditary and environmental components of human nature, and they offer much evidence to support their position.

Bleier, who is trained in neuroanatomy, refutes with special authority the arguments centering on presumed inherited sex differences in brain structure and lateralization. She emphasizes the extraordinary plasticity and responsiveness to environmental stimuli of the human brain and "the fact [that] there are no clear-cut sex differences in either verbal or visuospatial abilities" (Bleier 1984).

Fausto-Sterling relates theories of innate sex differences more directly to the competition for jobs, with the male almost always found to be "naturally" superior and therefore better fit for the higher paying, more prestigious ones. Although she states that "in the study of gender . . . it is inherently impossible for any individual to do unbiased research," she believes that the "majority of scientists . . . try in good faith to design careful, thoughtful experiments." They fail because of nonconscious bias that affects the methodology of their research on sex differences. Her conscious feminist position gives her a "different angle of vision," she believes, which allows her to do better science in this area and to reveal the flaws in the gender research of others.

Fausto-Sterling believes in "good science." Her major criticism is that most current research in sex and gender differences is "bad science": biased experimental design, lack of controls, unstated assumptions, conflicting results, albeit carried out by capable and honest scientists unduly influenced by everyday culture. However, if they were to be shown the scientific flaws in their work that a feminist understanding reveals, they could then begin to do "good science," even in the investigation of gender differences.

Similar criticisms of sociobiological theories and of elitist practices and abuses in the name of science have frequently been made by others—cogent, incisive, and supported with much careful research (see references under Misuses and distortions section, above). And that is the problem. In spite of all the carefully documented refutations, both the practice and the justifying hereditarian theories and rationales for social domination keep recurring. We are currently being assaulted even on prime time television "news" and the front page of the *New York Times* by an avalanche of questionable statistical correlations purporting to prove that genes are the fundamental determinants of all human behavior and pathologies, and that—like it or not—this is *the* "scientific" point of view. Any dissent is held to be purely "political" (Holden 1987).

The importance of tirelessly exposing these abuses and flawed theories cannot be minimized. But this does not seem to be enough. Several questions must be asked:

—Why, in spite of the repeated refutations, do biological determinist concepts seem to be hydra-headed, reappearing regularly, in new guises, after each refutation? Why does the same critique have to be continually reiterated? Why are these flawed ideas so persistent?

—Can doing "good science" make a difference in a "bad" political context and in a social milieu of sexism and racism as well as class hierarchy? Will this not be overwhelmed both by more bad theories and, even more, by the sexist and racist political realities? How can bias in the practice of science be eliminated without also eliminating its social origin?

—Is the "bias" of scientists so superficial that it can be essentially eliminated just by pointing it out? Or is it *integral* to the way of thinking, the language, the fundamental philosophy of "western civilization," with its dichotomous history of domination of a producing population by a ruling elite? And could our civilization even have avoided incorporating this bias into its basic conceptual structure?

Much criticism of the current practice of science implies that the system itself, that is, modern science, its methodology, and its establishment, is fundamentally OK. It just needs some tinkering with, perhaps even a major tune-up: an educational campaign within the scientific community, evidence to show that discrimination is unfair and not based on fact, and a very strong affirmative action campaign. The reformers of science suggest that major changes can be made in its practices in relation to women without altering the fundamental power structure of the society itself. They point to the increased awareness of the need for women's liberation initiated by the women's movement of the 1970s and to the increase in the number of women in the undergraduate, graduate, and even faculty levels at colleges and universities, and they feel that, with some additional prodding, this progress is bound to continue.

Before examining this position further, I would like to state that I emphatically support all efforts toward affirmative action, all education to eliminate sexist and racist distortions in the name of science, and all struggles to end mistreatment of women by the technology derived from it. Women need good jobs and relief from abusive conditions *now*, and even small steps in that direction should be celebrated. And some important victories can be squeezed through the cracks. Also, the struggle is a powerful consciousness raiser, helping to create the conditions for more fundamental and lasting change.

However, the history of this struggle of women scientists (Rossiter 1982) suggests that we cannot be too sanguine about the inevitability of gradual improvement. Progress is not only *not* inevitable, but it can often be rapidly reversed. The reformist assumption—that women can achieve an equal share of power and privilege in a science, or society, dominated by a ruling stratum dedicated to maintaining its hegemony and indeed proclaiming its inevitability and naturalness—is intrinsically untenable. Significant gradual progress is unlikely because we are trying to climb up a pole that is being constantly greased from the top with slippery ideology, a pole grounded in a foundation trembling with the tensions of human needs too long suppressed. To work effectively within this instability, we must avoid misleading ourselves, by either exaggerating our erratic, limited, and often temporary successes or wrongly blaming ourselves for failures. And we must view our position through the perspective of history.

Thesis of This Essay

Thus far, the two themes I have introduced posit that: First, the science of a society does not exist in a vacuum, in isolation from it; science is an important and powerful function of the society itself, and its uses and practice are under the control of its dominant sector. Second, a society in which a small ruling stratum has power over all others will not and cannot tolerate any change in women's status that could threaten this hegemony. It will only be possible for nondiscriminatory, nonexploitative relations to exist within science when egalitarian relations characterize society itself.

The major thesis I present here, however, is that not only are the *uses* of science controlled by the ruling segment of society but also its *ideology*. The goals of the practitioners of science, their thinking as well as their actions, are derived from the social process within which they operate. This ideology both reflects the increasing social and economic polarization of the rulers and the ruled and reinforces it with conceptual dichotomies justifying its existence: brain versus body, nature versus nurture, and so on. Dualist bias exists, therefore, not only in research on sex and race differences but also in the basic mindset of scientists, the philosophical assumptions through which they experience *all* their worlds. The almost inescapable ideas and norms with which we are all indoctrinated are specifically reinforced in scientists by their network of training and patronage relationships—the "peer group"—and by highly effective status and reward systems.

Thus, when the science of a society is recognized as an expression of its ideology, the repeated reemergence in our media of biological determinist hypotheses in new guises is no longer a mysterious, aberrant phenomenon. It represents a way of thinking necessary to the preservation of a society based on the hegemony of an elite, which is incorporated also into the way of thinking of its scientists. This thinking represents social behavior as primarily controlled by fixed, inherited factors within the individual and suggests that one's social and economic status is also determined by intrinsic factors. From this perspective, the primary blame for any problem a woman may have is placed on herself and her two X-chromosomes. It suggests, for example, that no matter how correlated low pay is with being female it still would not justify a real change in the social structure, for "you can make it if you have the right stuff."

In the following sections, I will first give a short overview of the beginnings of this way of thinking in fourth-century B.C. Athens, its suppression of the earlier naturalist view, and its expression in the society and the science of that time. I will next describe the reemergence of these philosophies with the twin birth of capitalist class relations and modern science, with dualist thinking again becoming dominant—as in today's molecular biology with its Olympian conception of the godlike gene. I will then present alternative principles upon which a nonelitist science and society would have to be based and a remarkable illustration of the application of these principles in biology.

Because my personal experiences and knowledge are, to a large extent, of biological, biochemical, and social processes, I have primarily used these areas to exemplify the concepts of materialist dialectics.

DUALIST IDEOLOGIES OF SCIENCE AND THEIR RELATION TO SOCIAL PRACTICE

Historical Roots

The modern revolution in science was associated by Auguste Comte (ca. 1830–1842) with that time "when the human mind was astir under the *precepts* of Bacon, the *conceptions* of Descartes, and the *discoveries* of Galileo" (Comte 1947) in the late sixteenth and the early seventeenth century, a view now generally accepted. However, the historical origins of present-day science reach back much farther, to the growth period of slavery in early Greek civilization. These major, primary roots lay dormant but fecund for well over a thousand years; their efflorescence, bursting forth anew in the fertile soil of an emerging capitalist society, soon displayed the dualist traits that characterized its earlier growth. Ignoring this long history of contemporary scientific ideology distorts our view of it.

Western science and philosophy had their beginnings together in Ionia, in the sixth century B.C., before Greek slave society was fully developed (Farrington 1944). Thales of Miletus was the first to speculate about principles governing the relationships among natural phenomena without resorting to mythological or supernatural explanations, but others soon followed. Their science and their philosophy both expressed a monistic view of nature, derived from completely naturalistic principles.

Pythagoras reintroduced a more idealistic orientation. He held that numbers and their relationships were the primary principles of matter and that the contemplation of the eternal perfection of intrinsic form in all things was the ultimate moral and religious goal. Parmenides, the second of the Greek religious philosophers, went even further. He held that the logical was the only real and that all change, motion, and variety in the universe were illusions. These two traditions, the numerical relationships of Pythagoras and the rationalist idealism of Parmenides, became the foundation upon which Plato built his philosophy of dualism, of two separate worlds. His realm of ideas comprised the perfect, unchanging patterns of all things; his world of matter, their imperfect, transient copies.

Plato considered that the soul—unchanging, nonmaterial, immortal—was derived from the first world and that it was the determining principle affixed to the individual before or at birth; the body and its physical needs and interactions belonged to the temporal, inconstant, and derivative material world. The fixed-at-birth soul determined inherent human value and consequently natural social rank.

As a member of the aristocracy in a fully matured slave society, Plato had both the leisure and the self-interest to theorize without any relation to facts. "The *word* was the concern of the citizen, the *deed* the concern of the slave," Farrington notes (1944). The superior souls of the master class, Plato taught, had the capacity to strive toward the perfect good, beautiful, and rational. The racially inferior, usually foreign, slave naturally did not have much of the rational element in his soul. He, and needless to say she, were the hands, quite separate from the philosopher's head. Plato's aristocratic outlook was of such overriding concern to him that the only sciences taught in his academy were abstract mathematics, especially geometry, and a tortured form of astronomy based on a description of the planetary orbits as the summation of a series of perfect circles. Scientists, like Anaxagoras, who advocated studying the planets and their orbits by looking up into the sky and observing their movements, were literally run out of town—out of Athens—on pain of death.

Aristotle, who had studied at Plato's Academy for twenty years, modified his teacher's dualism by altering its relationships. He held that ideas, or forms, were not outside of substance but were acting within it. He moved from Plato's concept of the absolute, or First Form, as the ideal, abstracted *cause* of good, order, and motion in all things, but not specific to any of them, to ideal forms which resided within and were characteristic of each particular substance (Aristotle, "On the Soul": 643–644). These *internal* Aristotelian forms were now the organizing and activating principles of substantive phenomena, but they themselves remained unchanged and unchanging, nonspatial and immaterial. The dualist disjunction was maintained.

This new perspective, however, allowed Aristotle to advocate the close examination of nature, in all its detail. He carefully classified plants and animals into immutable species and genera, their design dictated by their absolute, unchanging forms. As later pointed out by Francis Bacon, these abstracted forms were, in fact, "the laws of simple action" (Farrington 1944). Aristotelian dualism became the natural, and the ideal, precursor of the ideology of nature as a machine driven by immutable laws, the direct progenitor of our present-day mechanism.

The absolute subordination of women, slaves, and non-Greeks was already well established in practice in fifth century B.C. Periclean Athens. Euripedes, in *Medea*, questions both the sexism and the racism of the *polis* (Bury and Meiggs 1975). Plato, while suggesting that "guardian" class men and women be educated equally in his ideal Republic, also held that women had the recycled souls of inferior, cowardly men.

Aristotle, who came several decades later, was primarily concerned with women as mothers. Pregnant women were to take care of their bodies but "ought to keep (their minds) quiet" (Aristotle, *Politics:*538). Aristotle held the "inferiority" of both slaves and women to be "natural," but he declared that "nature has distinguished between the female and the slave . . . making each thing for a single use" (495). Nature, he asserted, created the barbarian—both male and female—as a race of "natural slaves," "from birth," for their soul/minds lacked the "deliberative faculty"; the Hellenes, with their rational minds, were destined *by nature* to rule over them, despotically (447–449). "Hence," he explained, "master and slave have the same interest" (445).

Master-race women, on the other hand, were *constitutionally* different from men (*Politics:*453). Their souls, less rational than those of men, tilted toward the "appetites" or "passionate elements." This diminution of the rational element led to numerous behavioral differences between woman and man. "Woman is more compassionate than man," Aristotle taught, but "at the same time [is] more jealous, more querulous, more apt to scold and strike . . . more prone to despondency . . . more void of shame"—and more of several other unpleasant traits (Aristotle, *Biological Treatises:*134). As is now customary in contemporary sociobiology texts, Aristotle supported his thesis by referring to the "natural" behavior of other, somewhat more primitive, animals. "The male is more courageous," he explained, and more helpful, "as in the case of molluscs." "The cuttlefish . . . male stands by to help the female . . . , but the female runs away" when the male needs help! These disparate patterns of behavior and human reasoning abilities are carried in "the spiritum, the principle of the soul," which, appropriately, is conveyed to the embryo by the male heredity-bearing secretion, the semen. The female secretion does not carry the soul, "for the female is, as it were, a mutilated male" (*Biological Treatises:*278).

This early exposition of the biological determinist argument, citing immutable, inherited differences in the soul as the *natural* basis for the dualist categories underlying existing racial and sexual relationships, is presented as "obvious" and beyond doubt by Aristotle. His identification of the leisured male master with the rational, the mind, and the nonproductive (science for science's sake) and women and slaves with the irrational and the useful was patently self-serving. The world of the leisured few and the exploited many was good to him; he could see no need for technical advances or increased productivity (Farrington 1944).

The dualist rationalism of Aristotle and Plato is an extraordinary illustration of how the self-interest of a society's rulers and their desire to maintain the status quo, limit and distort the understanding of even their most profound thinkers. The invocation of a hierarchy of human worth, presumed "natural," to justify widely disparate economic and social conditions, is still the prevailing practice today.

Women's status was considerably higher under Roman rule than it had been in classical, fifth and fourth century B.C., Greece. Yet it was in Roman Alexandria in the first century A.D. that Philo, the eminent Hellenist philosopher and rabbi, laid the ideological foundation for women's permanent subordination in the western world. He wedded the Platonic principle of woman's intrinsically inferior, less rational Soul to the Hebrew theological dogma of woman as mindless and the agent of all evil, justifying the treatment of Eve in Genesis by explicitly identifying her with a lack of moral discipline and "no intellect to hold her passions in check." Woman, born sensual and carnal, rather than rational and spiritual (like man), and full of vanity and greed, is therefore not only "constitutionally" inferior but eternally in league with the devil. "Man symbolizes mind, and woman symbolizes sense"; in the Fall, sense triumphs over mind. "This notion became highly influential in both Judaism and Christianity" (Phillips 1984). It was later to be interpreted literally and enforced with special zeal by the church.

Although extraordinary, even brilliant, scientific work was conducted after the fourth century B.C., (e.g., by Strato, a successor to Aristotle as head of his Lyceum, who demonstrated by experiment the nature of the vacuum) it was not relevant to slave society and was not incorporated into either its practical activities or its way of thinking. The succeeding period was characterized by the domination of the Judaeo-Christian theology of authority; all direct observation of nature was abandoned. Natural science as a socially integrated activity lay dormant until the sixteenth century.

At that time the needs of the rapidly expanding mercantile class led to an enthusiastic explosion of interest in further exploring the properties of nature. As Aristotle noted, with some disdain, the mercantile class, or "retail trade" (unlike his aristocracy) was not concerned primarily with the "use" value of things, that is, with "wealth-getting" in order to live well, which could readily be satisfied by the work of slaves. Its major interest was rather in the "exchange" value of things, for the production of "wealth without limit" (*Politics:*451). This required an extraordinary increase in productivity, which could only be effected by *directly observing* the specific nature of things. Nature began to be manipulated and utilized for man's benefit—and the merchant's profit.

This period of rapid economic expansion brought with it its own contradictions. The new productive and social forces gave rise to new dominant and subordinate economic classes. The other major forms of social domination that had previously existed within feudal and slave society, that is, sexual and racial, became *integrated* into this latest class society under the hegemony of this new ruling elite. The long and continuous history of sexual and racial exploitation has embedded these deeply into successive social practices and mythologies. This new ruling stratum of mercantile interests, and later of industrial capitalists, became the patron of the new science; and it was their interests that motivated it.

Philosophies reflecting these new social and productive power relations soon emerged. Again, a rigid dualism, dominated by geometric-mathematical abstractions and the separation of both mind from body and "thinker" from thing or object thought about, was advanced by René Descartes, almost contemporaneously with Francis Bacon's scientific naturalism. Descartes predicated existence on our *innate* capacity to think about it (I think, therefore I am). Rational thought, he held, is "objective"; it alone could lead to the truth, without reference to space or time or physical substance. And here too it is a function of the immaterial, immortal mind/soul. But matter, corpuscular, extendable and mutable, is the object to be thought about, the physical substrate of which things are made. It is also the substance of the body, which is like a clock, a machine controlled by the completely distinct and separate incorporeal mind. Matter is understandable, however, through the mind/soul's capacity for rational, mathematical analysis (Descartes 1947).

Descartes was primarily a mathematician, and his work in mathematics has been critical to the development of modern science. He created analytical geometry, the branch of mathematics that investigates geometric problems by algebraic means. His method is based on two concepts: (1) the description of a point by its coordinates, that is, its distance from two perpendicular straight lines, the axes; and (2) the representation of the relationship between two variables as a set of individual points on a plane, each point with its individual coordinates, which together form a curve (Delone 1956). This method— recording the quantitative change occurring in one factor in response to change in a related factor by graphing successive bits of data while all else presumably remains constant—is fundamental to the analysis of most numerical problems in science today.

The Cartesian point of view, therefore, conceptualizes phenomena as composed of discrete, individual, elemental units, the whole consisting of an assemblage of these separate elements. Further, it assumes a linear, quantitative cause-and-effect relationship between phenomena. Descartes emphasized the general applicability of his ideas to all phenomena, and they have indeed per-fused every facet of our dominant ideology and social interactions.

Some two hundred years later, Auguste Comte introduced his positivist philosophy, in which he held that intellectual development, especially in what he considered its highest, scientific stage, was the key to progress in society. He advanced the idea of the successive order of development of the sciences, beginning with the most abstract through to the most concrete: from mathe-matics and physics, through biology, to the social sciences. "The first charac-teristic of the Positive Philosophy," Comte taught, "is that it regards all phenomena as subjected to invariant, natural laws . . . which rule the intellect in the investigation of truth," although these had to be validated by experi-ment. The emphasis, however, was on the search for general scientific laws rather than for specific causes. But, "in order to observe, your intellect must pause from activity" (230) that is, you must be objective (Comte 1947). He intended his method of positive philosophy to lead to a religion of humanity.

This tradition was redefined in the first half of this century by the logical positivists, who also advanced the idea of a "scientific philosophy" (Reich-enbach 1951). Modern mathematics and physics, with their replacement of determinist causality by the statistical probability of the new empiricism, be-came the prototype for scientific thinking in all fields of study; the direction of all scientific investigation became the search for the greatest abstraction and generality of principle, for the ultimate unit of matter, energy, and life. And the scientist presumably approached each problem with the dispassion-ate detachment of the disinterested "objective" observer.

Objectivity in Science

This presumption of detachment, "scientific objectivity," is still the predomi-nant doctrine among scientists today; it has now perfused the study of living systems and social relations. It is predicated on several assumptions about re-lations among thinker, thought, and the material being investigated. These as-sumptions suggest:

—that a rational method of investigation, the scientific method, exists, which can be utilized regardless of social context or of the phenomenon be-ing investigated;

—that any "good," well-trained, honest scientist can apply this well-de-fined, neutral method to the object being investigated and obtain "objective," unbiased data.

—that the "facts (data) are the facts"; the results reported are "hard," immutable, and unaffected by personal concerns. The specificity of the conditions under which the data were obtained is soon lost sight of as they become generalized and reified into "*solid* facts."

This Cartesian and positivist image of objectivity, which postulates a division between the investigator and the phenomenon being investigated, has been discussed by several feminists, notably Elizabeth Fee (1981). She points out that it serves to establish distance and authority, the authority of the observer over the observed.

The separateness of the power-wielders, the "objective" ones, from the powerless, the "objects," and the dominant social role of the former is also expressed by the numerous other polarities we are always being confronted with (e.g., mind-body, thinking-feeling, nature-nurture). These are all, in fact, rationalizations for usurping and exercising power. Superior qualities, justifying domination, are ascribed to the objective, thinking minds, inferior, subservient ones, to the feeling, receptive body.

The Platonic-Aristotelian dichotomy, between those who possess a rational soul and those who lack it therefore requiring direction and domination by the reasoning philosophers, can be readily recognized here. And indeed, this characterization of the "objective" and the "rational" as being indisputable and above the fray, together with the power to assert what *is* "objective," serves the identical function in our society as it did in fourth-century B.C. Athens. The latest sociobiology tracts are always described by the dominant media as reporting "hard, objective," although perhaps unfortunate facts; those who question their data, assertions, and the bias of their viewpoint are accused of being "political"—and not "objective."

The Olympian Gene

In applying the Cartesian methodology described above to molecular genetics, one assumes that the ultimate cause for each particular life process is the ancestrally determined gene, transmitted as a segment of a DNA molecule. Each gene is viewed as a structurally and functionally specific template, switched on or off in response to a predetermined signal; chains of hundreds or thousands of these templates operate within each cell. The primary cause of a pathogenic condition is presumed to be the malfunctioning of the gene that initiates the given process, the first step in a linear progression of reactions.

Changes in gene function then imply a prior alteration of gene or DNA structure. Until recently, these mutations were randomly produced; currently, using genetic engineering techniques, new genes may be deliberately introduced. In either case, changes in gene structure and action are considered independent, unitary, stepwise processes.

Although the major growth spurt in molecular biology began with research on the genetics of bacteria, the molecular approach has since swept all of biology before it. Currently, it commands the dominant position even in studies of the human organism. The most popular form of cancer research, for example, is now the search for "oncogenes," or cancer-causing genes, though evidence for their specific etiological role is moot, at best.

One expects, of course, that individuals with different unique gene systems, or hereditary histories, would respond differently to cancer-causing or any other environments and that the expression of a large number of genetic elements would be altered, variably, in malignant cells of different individuals. A living organism is, after all, not an ahistorical blob of plastic that the environment fashions in its own image. But, by the same token, neither is the gene, good or bad, an above-the-battle Platonic "prime mover," *the cause* of a predetermined chain of reactions, unaffected by the activity and conditions around it. Yet the current fashion and ideology is to lay the blame for almost all human pathological conditions primarily upon the inherited, unalterable (except by genetic engineering techniques) "nature" of the individual, their "bad" genes. The dualist caveat, adding a fraction of "environmental influence" to heredity, does not alter this fundamentally hierarchical orientation. It recognizes neither the process of continuous and temporal interaction with new external stresses nor the complex genomic relationships themselves.

An even more insistent promotion of hereditarian ideas is reflected in the current race to find "new genes" for various mental illnesses, including mental depression and Alzheimer's disease. Although there have been many studies "localizing" such presumptive genes within certain chromosomal areas, their function is unclear, at best, and no therapeutic significance has been ascribed to this approach. But these efforts have been acclaimed with almost effusive optimism by the press of the scientific establishment (Barnes 1987).

In a recent editorial in *Science* (Koshland 1987), the editor triumphantly recalled a 1960s conclusion by a neurobiologist "that schizophrenia has a hereditary component," in addition to an environmental one, thus anticipating the modern emphasis on gene control of brain function. "The evidence indicates," he declared, "that part of the brain is 'hard-wired' in advance of birth, and part is designed to . . . learn from experience." The dichotomy, therefore, continues, but the components are no longer the philosopher's mind/soul versus his body: they are separate entities within the brain itself. Hard-wired on/off switches, the genes, have now replaced Descartes's and Plato's soul as the control module of Descartes's body-as-machine in the prebirth assembly line.

Perhaps the ultimate comment on the identification of molecular biologists with the interests of the ruling sector is the current battle over "who owns the human genome" and who gets the patent rights. The majority of "leading molecular biologists" (few, if any, of them women) are now associated with genetic engineering corporations, either as members of the boards of directors or as consultants. Among the products these companies plan to market is *information* on the nature of the human genome (traditionally, shared freely) and diagnostic tests for "genetic diseases" (Roberts 1987). The number of fetal genetic diagnostic tests for presumptive "bad genes," performed through the body of the mother, can be expected to increase precipitously.

Mechanism and Modern Science

As noted above, the characteristics of the modern scientific method include such Cartesian and positivist postulates as "objectivity," linear cause and effect, elementary units, and statistical abstraction. The development of the powerful new capitalist technologies required this way of thinking. These quantitative abstractions from nature (cf. Pythagoras), with their apparent stability and reproducibility, could be and were readily incorporated into the design of the machine. The process was then inverted, and the abstracted machine became the prototype of nature.

Recently, a decision of the political bureaucracy provided extraordinary confirmation that the conceptualization of life as a machine has unabashedly become socially, politically, and economically the official ideology of our society. The U.S. Patent and Trademark office will now consider patent applications for all forms of life (except homo sapiens—temporarily?). These will henceforth be regarded as a "manufacture or composition of matter," thus allowing major corporations to patent the gene pool of the entire earth (Rivkin 1987). "The new policy acknowledges," remarked the patent attorneys applying for the patent rights on an oyster, "the reality that there is *no separation between life and technology*" (my emphasis) (Miller and Tramposch 1987). The victory of the machine over life in the corridors of our power structure could hardly be more explicitly expressed.

Mechanism, as conventionally conceptualized, is often confused with materialism. Theories are tested "against" nature to get "data," which prove or disprove them. These theories are usually model mechanical systems; when they correctly predict experimental results, that is, a defined, linear, cause-and-effect, model system is considered validated.

But the ideology of the machine process is, in fact, not materialist at all in its conception of nature. Mechanism reifies the reproducible effect, observed under defined conditions, and ignores the idiosyncratic and the developmentally complex. In line with its Cartesian and positivist principles, it considers the whole to be composed of individual, separable units, which can be taken apart and put together again, the entire machine operating in a repeatable, predictable fashion. Natural processes are abstracted, distanced from nature, made perfect, and converted into immutable laws. The *particular* characteristics and dynamics of each individual situation are blurred, lost in statistical summations. This freezes living systems into static models of themselves, denying the uniqueness of their development in time and space. Phenomena lose their specific, idiosyncratic responses and interactions, and they are seen as better or worse approximations of some ideal system. The utilization of abstraction and even model systems are, indeed, necessary and integral to the development of materialist theory. But the specific, even aberrant, details must also be part of the analysis, as well as forces indicating instability and change (see the following discussion of materialist dialectics).

Like the Platonic and Aristotelian dualism of slave society, Cartesian dualism reflects a divided society, characterized by a small, ruling stratum that exploits and appropriates the wealth created by the producers. However, just as the methods and relations of production of technology-driven capitalism differ critically from those of hand-powered slave society, so also does the particular form its dualist, but still elitist, ideology takes. In Plato's dichotomy, the body, inchoate, transient, spatial matter, was given form and motion by the immortal, noncorporeal soul/mind. Superior, rational souls were attached to master-class, male bodies before birth; inferior souls were linked with other, inferior bodies. Aristotle located the soul *within* the body, placing agency within substance but retaining its separate and immaterial nature. Descartes, while still preserving the eternal, supernatural character of the soul, transformed the body into a machine. In our current dualist model, an assemblage of thousands of preformed, structurally determined, and functionally specific templates, the "hard-wired" genes have replaced the supernatural soul at the controls of Descartes's body-as-machine. The dualism of eternal prime mover and transient substrate has been retained, but both are now expressed as mechanisms.

Contemporary Aristotelians, Cartesians, and Positivists *do* look at nature but through the eyes of this machine ideology. They seek only mechanical, reproducible, *nonrevolutionary* change, the kind that can indeed be described by "immutable" laws, derived by abstracting selected data points at fixed times under fixed conditions. And these abstracted regularities often *do* approximate nature or rather an image of it, much as do the dots on our television screen. The greater the number of dots, the more coherent the image produced. This picture conveys much useful information, but it does not involve us with the processes of nature itself. Thus, our contemporary dualists *begin* by defining the conditions for locating a machine within nature; it is not surprising that this is what they find. The massive explosion of technology within the past century is the monument to their success.

Feminists have critically examined the social role of mechanist thinking. Carolyn Merchant (1980) has called the machine the metaphor for both the Baconian scientific world view and for capitalist power itself, both expressions of man's (defined as male) drive to dominate nature. Nature itself is associated with the female principle, in both the physical and the social realm. Merchant thus retains the dualist categories, but she suggests an inversion of the hierarchy of values; this would lead to equalizing male and female and to establishing an equilibrium between human life and nature.

By accepting the dichotomy of male-machine, female-nature, Merchant can only deplore the current situation and try to convince those who now have the power over women and nature to share it. But this ignores the specific conditions, the details of the power relationships that actually exist, the contradictions within "maleness" itself, and the differences among women. The tensions and interactions between the machine and nature, between male and female, are part of the whole struggle for liberation from relationships of exploitation and from the ideology of domination.

MATERIALIST DIALECTICS

The word "materialist" must be clearly defined; because words are rather tricky images of thought their connotations are always subject to distortion and transformation by the dominant culture. Materialist is frequently used these days to suggest the hedonistic, rampant consumerism and self-indulgence that has come to characterize our society. This is quite contrary to the sense in which I use it here to describe a philosophical and historical concept, that is, the direct antithesis of dualist idealism.

The materialist understanding of nature views all existence as matter in motion (Engels 1940). It is not concerned with the abstract *idea* of nature nor with nature as *being* but with real, *specific* natural phenomena at a particular place and time, under particular conditions of existence, and in the process of change. Understanding these phenomena requires more than simply detached observation; it demands interaction, what Marx called "practice." The "observer" and the "observed," the subject and the object, mutually influence each other. Reality is not only perceived by "detached" observation alone in contemplation but also "subjectively" through involvement, conceptualization, and action. Truth is proven in practice, not with an abstraction but through "sensuous activity" with the phenomenon itself (Marx 1978).

This suggests that in studying living systems one must always be close to the material, the organism one is trying to understand; and one must study it, not in general but with all its details. It also suggests that in trying to understand the position of women in society, one must involve oneself first with the relations of *particular* women, at a given time and place, and under particular conditions of exploitation. The materialist perspective also requires that the analysis of all human process begins with understanding our physical nature and circumstances. This suggests that the particular physical conditions of one's life and one's way of making a living are the primary regulators of one's social and political relations, and of one's viewpoint. It also suggests that the specific physical circumstances of a woman's life are the primary influence controlling her particular gender relations and social perspective.

But viewpoint is mediated through mental constructs. Our perceptions of phenomena are determined not only by the things themselves but also by our mindset, our individual consciousness and understanding. This, in turn, depends on our social interaction with phenomena and our unique body-brain-mind history. Our viewpoint is therefore derived not only from our specific material conditions and relations but also from our understanding of them, our consciousness. This is strongly, even overwhelmingly, for a time, influenced by the pervasive ideology of the dominant social stratum through its control of the means of communication and education and in whose interest it is to resist change and maintain its dominant position. But, like sand-bagging the ocean's shore to prevent the erosion of the shoreline, it can only delay—and alter the shape—of historical change, not prevent it.

The role of understanding or consciousness in modulating our responses to material conditions is also an aspect of materialist reality. The recognition of this mediation and the dialectical approach (see below) differentiate the materialist from the determinist position. Consciousness, however, usually translates material interaction into words, often into the metaphor of the day. This could demateralize the sensuous, transforming it into an abstraction consistent with contemporary ideology, and mask its original source, material experience, with an idealist construction.

The materialist view can only be consistently maintained within the principles of the dialectical approach (Engels 1939). I do not refer, here, to the static, rationalist dialectics of Socratic argument, with its fixed, exclusive, oppositional categories or to Platonic speculation on ultimate perfection, with its ideal abstractions, its contemplation of *perceptual*, within-the-mind contradictions, and its pursuit of the "first principle." I speak here of the dialectics of process, of *becoming*, of the *continuous interactive motion in time* of physical matter.

Nature *exists* in dialectical motion. Thus, the dialectical method of understanding nature and "her" progeny is a recognition of this ontology, of being as becoming—in context, connectedness, and oriented in time. In the following discussion of the dialectical method, key aspects will be illustrated with references to development in biological systems and in human societies.

THE ASPECT OF HISTORICAL DEVELOPMENT. Change is not random; it is directional. The present does not approach the future naively but closely, embracing all its past experiences. A given phenomenon, a biological organism, for example, incorporates within its individual history both its species history and its entire past evolutionary history. These all participate in its continuous present interactions with its surrounding milieu.

THE ASPECT OF INTERACTION. Change is not simply the summation of a series of linear, Cartesian cause-and-effect relationships. It is a complex, interconnected, interactive process in which multiple causes and multiple effects act and react simultaneously.

These two aspects suggest that molecular genetecists, for example, who alter or introduce an external gene or DNA segment into a functioning living system are not creating a new life form. They are mechanically tampering with an already evolved life form, albeit blindly disregarding its history and the complexities of its existing processes. By not allowing for the sanction or rejection of environmental interaction, the potential for environmental catastrophe is introduced. Similarly, in the social realm, the paucity of women in the upper ranks of the science establishment, for example, cannot be addressed in isolation from either the current subordinate position of women generally or the entire historical process.

THE ASPECT OF OPPOSITIONAL FORCES OR CONTRADICTION. The dynamics of change derive from interplay or struggle of forces acting in opposition to each other. In the tensions intrinsic to growth and development of a phenomenon, the conditions for its own displacement, or negation, are created; in its contradictions lies the source, the origin of its successor. In contrast to dualism, where the opposite categories remain separate, either at the extremes of a spectrum or with the dominant eternal master over the subordinate, dialectical opposites are united in constant conflict, inseparable in their struggle, effecting continuous change upon each other and all their connections.

The strength and ramifications of this force of contradiction can be seen in the central struggle of advanced global capitalism to increase its rate of profits by the superexploitation of third-world poor women and its reciprocal effects on both workers and capitalism in the United States. Competitive capitalism's need for continuously increasing profits mandates the constant pursuit of lower labor costs. These women are manifestly the most readily exploitable humans on earth, as members of the desperately poor, as workers, and as "others" (race, nation, and level of industrial development). The abysmally low level of their wages has indeed raised the "productivity" of industry, but it has also markedly lowered workers' salaries in the United States and other industrialized nations and increased their level of unemployment. Increased capitalist productivity needs an ever expanding market, but the world's unemployed and low-paid workers can buy back less and less of what they produce.

THE ASPECT OF INTEGRATIVE LEVELS. Integrative levels arise developmentally through qualitative transformations. Each level, each developmental stage, is a qualitatively distinct system with its own particular characteristics, specific laws and contradictions, and relations of change. Although they differ in their nature, their processes, and their relationships, they are neither isolated nor insulated. They are substantively related, oriented in time, carrying both their past and the seeds of their future within them, reciprocally interacting with each other. They develop within and as part of the whole, internalizing those principles also (see the discussion of unity, below). Levels of integration and stages of development are not hierarchies; they are new systems of connectedness, evolved by transformation from earlier stages.

The qualitatively distinct nature of phenomena at different levels of integration suggests that the particular methods used to investigate a given phenomenon should be derived from the unique characteristics of the given system itself. The study of nonliving matter, for example, requires different techniques than does the study of living systems, and neither methodology would be appropriate for investigating human history and social practice.

THE ASPECT OF QUANTITATIVE GROWTH TO QUALITATIVE TRANSFORMATION. Change, understood dialectically, is not simply gradual, quantitative, and progressive, as in the Cartesian view. Rather, it is tension-driven and turbulent, a process of continuous *struggle* (see the discussion of interaction above), although change and development may appear relatively gradual at certain periods. This struggle reaches a critical state, in time, when the contending forces can no longer continue in the same relationship, and culminates in a rapid transformation into a completely new condition with new interactions. But it is a state that still carries both its previous history and its future within it. This transition represents a revolutionary leap, or negation, of the previous condition, a bursting forth into another level of development (see discussion of integrative levels, above). Opposing tensions again develop, intensify, reach a crisis stage, and this new state is itself negated. The nature of succeeding states is not accidental; it is derived from past struggles.

This aspect of qualitative transformation in development is dramatically illustrated by the growth and metamorphosis of insects. The butterfly first emerges from the egg as a caterpillar, a veritable eating machine in continuous operation, converting tree leaves into larval protoplasm. This ends precipitously with the onset of the quiescent pupal stage, during which the larval tissues are completely reorganized. The butterfly then emerges fully grown. The feeding worm, the rigid sac, and the diaphanous-winged flash of color are all successive qualitative stages of the same organism, each emerging after a period of quantitative growth under appropriate conditions and each being transformed in its turn.

The new evolutionary theory of "punctuated equilibrium" (Eldredge and Gould 1972) also emphasizes this principle. It suggests that evolutionary changes are not necessarily continuous, gradual, and progressive. The gaps observed in the evolutionary record occur not because the postulated intermediate fossils were too fragile to have been preserved but because they had never existed in the first place. New species arose not with small steps, but with sudden, large leaps.

In the struggle for women's emancipation, the stepwise, reformist approach that women have used for the past several hundred years seems to have reached an impasse. Ideologically, this can be seen in the constant recurrence of biological determinist rationales to "explain" women's supposedly inferior scientific and leadership abilities. Politically, the backsliding on even the minimal progress we have made on affirmative action and our inability to add an Equal Rights Amendment to the U.S. Constitution suggests how difficult further progress has become. The condition of women globally is even more critical. The limitations of gradualism for achieving a basic change in women's subordinate condition suggest that women's liberation will be attained only with a revolutionary negation of the current elitist organization of our society to one without hierarchical relationships.

THE ASPECT OF THE UNITY OF THE WHOLE AND ITS PARTS. The whole is not simply composed of replaceable, essentially homogenous units that can be separated, recombined, abstracted from physical reality and averaged. The parts and the whole are *integral* to each other, changing and interchanging; the parts exist, defined only in their specific context with relation to the whole, and the whole exists only in interaction and unity with its parts.

This aspect suggests that dialectics cannot be thought of as simply the sum of a list of its principles. Itemizing these, as I have, in fact, here done, could tend to reify them as such. However, it is a useful analytical tool, a temporary scaffolding for mental constructs, as are model systems and abstractions generally. The separately listed aspects should then be conceptualized as a unity with integrated, constantly changing relationships.

In the biological sphere, this aspect suggests that nature and nurture, heredity and environment, are not independent, quantifiable categories, separable from each other. Nor, it suggests, does the hereditary process consist simply of the sum of the actions of the separate, individual genes themselves. The expression of the hereditary history of an organism is rather a function of the entire genome, in reciprocal, developmental interaction with the cellular, organismic, and external environment.

In the social realm, this dialectical relation of the whole and its parts raises questions about the ideology of individualism that dominates our society. It implies that the prevailing view—that we are separate, independent, corpuscular bodies, each individually responsible only for our own fate—serves primarily to perpetuate and justify an elitist hegemony. The increasingly large segment of the population who "can't make it" are isolated and discarded. Social responsibility is denied, and social activism declared counterproductive.

Perhaps the most significant perspective that this aspect of the interaction of whole and parts presents is that the whole can be most clearly understood through focusing upon its sharpest internal conflict at any given time. I suggest that, within today's world, this *central* historical antagonism is the struggle of poor working women in their relations with international conglomerate capitalism. These women not only bear the world's children and care for its extended families, but they also bear the burden of most of the global economy on their backs.

The poor working women of the world, and even more those of the third world, are its new Atlas. With their fleet fingers and strong arms they carry the "high-technology" industries in the maquiladoros of the Mexican border and in the "off-shore" industrial plants of the Pacific rim countries. Rows of women working at machines, building machines, often serve as the backdrop for the frequent media eulogies of "high-tech" productivity. They till the most arid soil, constituting two-thirds of the agricultural workers of Africa and probably of the rest of the third world, where the men leave the villages for work in the cities. They do most of the work of this world, assume most of its burdens and cares, and often are denied even the pittance necessary for their own and their children's survival. The struggle for the emancipation of poor, third-world women is *at the heart* not only of all sexual but also class and race liberation struggles.

My formal training and experiences have been concerned primarily with biological (genetic), biochemical, and social phenomena. I have therefore referred to these processes in contrasting the Cartesian method of analysis with the dialectical approach and in indicating its limitations. For phenomena in physics and other areas, a detailed critique will have to be made by one who has had specific experience with the details of those physical processes. However, given the recent apocalyptic role played by modern physics in bringing our world to the brink of catastrophe, some comment on its general social role, practices, and ideology is warranted.

Although the experimental physicists are more closely tied to our era's explosive expansion of technological power, the physics mystique is associated with the theoretical, particle, and nuclear physicists, the "fathers"(!) of the various bombs. Our awe of them is fed by their language of abstraction, mystification, and "higher" mathematics and by their ideology of the pursuit of *the* "ultimate" and *the* "universal." It is not surprising that they consider themselves the high priests of the ultimate religion of physics, which places them much "nearer to God" (I. I. Rabi as reported in Gornick, 1983) than any ordinary being.

According to the logical positivists, or "scientific philosophers" of the twentieth century, "the essence of knowledge is generalization" (Reichenbach 1951). "The grand aim of all science," Einstein tells us, "is to cover the greatest possible number of empirical facts by logical deduction from the smallest possible number of hypotheses or axioms." Or, as Aristotle taught, "science consists in finding the permanent forms which underlie the shifting phenomena of nature" (Farrington 1944). Einstein then describes the requisite methodology. "The theoretical scientist is compelled . . . to be guided by purely mathematical, formal considerations in his search for a theory, because the physical experience of the experimenter cannot lift him into the regions of the highest abstraction" (Einstein 1947). However, mathematical, abstract concepts must be "connected . . . with sensible experience to give them content." Or, as in Plato's *Republic*, the philosopher-kings must periodically descend from the Good, or ultimate knowledge, into the visible world of appearance (Plato 1941).

Contemporary positivist scientists acknowledge the need to verify their theories with observations, but these facts must be sharply defined, abstracted, averaged, and generalized into *the* laws of nature. Both facts and laws are seen as fixed entities within nature, universally recognizable, "hard," and immutable. But observations often break out of the limits of communally accepted theories and conflict not only with the paradigms of the scientific community, as described by Kuhn (1970), but also with ideological prescription. New ways of thinking that incorporate these aberrant observations are usually marginalized or even ignored if they contradict the accepted dogma of the society. Revolutionary concepts can only be fully accepted when they are relevant to the social order.

It is understandable, therefore, considering the ideology and history of modern physics, that its practitioners consider women's inherent mental capacities inadequate to the challenge of physics. (And perhaps women—like Plato's slaves—are indeed too involved with getting the work of the world done to have the luxury of abstracting themselves from it, as "great men" have always done.) I. I. Rabi, for example, who never had a woman postdoctoral or graduate student and "typically did not support the candidacy of women for faculty positions in his department" was quite explicit about this; he "thought most women temperamentally unsuited to science" (Gornick 1983; Rigden 1987). Indeed, fewer than 4 percent of employed physicists in 1980 were women, and in 1984 they earned only one-fourth as much as men (Schiebinger 1987). There seems to be an especially close correspondence between the ideology of physics and the gender relations of physicists.

An extraordinarily lucid and chilling account of nuclear physicists at work and at play in the "rational world of defense intellectuals" has recently been published by Carol Cohn in *Signs* (1987). They inhabit a Swiftian land of male fantasy and domesticity, where "fathers" beget not children but missiles, successful ones being "boys" and unsuccessful ones, "girls." They speak in a specialized language that Cohn calls "technostrategic," a language of abstractions and euphemisms, acronyms and sexual allusions—all identified with "rationality"—which distances them from the thoughts, feelings, pain, and concern with life and death of speakers of ordinary English, or Spanish—or Russian. . . .

Perhaps it is time to puncture the puffery of this priesthood, who, in the service of a God created in its own image, is offering all humankind as a sacrifice. These priests are not serving "objective" science but their own self-interest and that of their patrons, the ruling hierarchy.

Barbara McClintock and Her Closeness to Her Material

The remarkable scientist whose work most clearly exemplifies a materialist dialectical approach did not derive her way of working and thinking from a conscious political perspective. However, in her frequent and explicit descriptions of her research procedures, she repeatedly emphasizes her closeness to her research material and her awareness of every unique detail and subtle change in her organism.

Barbara McClintock, whose extraordinary research was not recognized by the larger scientific community until thirty years after its first presentation, made a specific point of noting that she had been examining "the behavior of broken ends of chromosomes" in her maize plants for thirteen years before she performed the crucial experiment that led her to identify the existence of "mobile genetic elements" (movable genes). "It was knowledge gained in these years that led me to conceive this experiment," she declared in her Nobel Prize acceptance speech. She worked without a research group, which was, according to her long-time friend, M. M. Rhoades, a reflection of her scientific approach (and also of the fact that she often had trouble getting funded [Keller 1983]). "She wanted to be on top of her research. She wanted to be very close to her research material" (Lewin 1983).

In contrast to today's molecular biologists, far removed from living organisms other than bacteria and viruses and with little understanding of how they grow, McClintock's knowledge of the biological world is immense. She sees living systems not as linear progressions of molecular reactions enclosed in semipermeable sacs but as unique living beings in the process of constant development. Each genome, or hereditary system of the organism, is in continuous, organized interaction with external stimuli and is itself changed in this process. The genome responds in an orderly, programmed sequence to frequently encountered stimuli. Unanticipated shocks, however, induce a more profound and unpredictable genomic reaction, one that affects its structural organization as well as its action. But the process is not random, and the response, although complex, is incorporated and integrated with the development of the organism (McClintock 1984).

McClintock attributes the delay of the larger scientific community in recognizing the significance of her findings to her being faced with "the dogma of the constancy of the genome." This, and the parallel dogma of the hegemony of the DNA molecule, reduces the hereditary system of the living organism to the level of a complex machine, controlled by on-off switches and changing only randomly and accidentally, except when "engineered" by direct human intervention. This atomistic, Cartesian view of living systems was the barrier that obstructed the scientific community's appreciation of the significance of McClintock's "mobile genetic elements." It still interferes with their willingness to entertain what she considers an even more important concept, her "conclusion that stress, and the genome's reaction to it, may underlie many formations of new species." This extraordinarily profound materialist view of evolution will probably have to await what she calls "the next revolutionary phase that again will bring startling changes in concepts" for its acceptance.

Barbara McClintock has, on occasion, been called a mystic by both admirers and detractors; her methods and thinking do not conform to the current mechanistic mode. But her approach is anything but occult. The mystical is an abstraction, a pulling away, from the detail and from physical knowledge of the material; it is the entering into a world of dreams and myths. McClintock's knowledge flows directly from her daily contact and interaction with her maize plants. She knows—by sight, smell, touch, and a variety of conscious and nonconscious observations—all the details of all of her organisms' daily lives. She immerses herself completely in her material, its changing environment, and the many stresses that affect it. This material communion includes careful observation, experiment, and analysis. This is *not* mysticism; this is complete materialism.

Although McClintock's observations have been acknowledged as significant, her approach is not integral to the practice of biology today, and still less is it part of the intensive utilization of science by the present political and economic power structure. McClintock and her work have currently been marginalized, as, in his time, was Strato. Although he was quite well known, the work of this great Athenian experimental physicist of the third century B.C. was not relevant to the slave society of his day and was ignored. It should take considerably less than the subsequent two millennia for McClintock's revolutionary concepts to become incorporated into the mainstream scientific thinking of a new society.

Currently several active biologists approach scientific problems with a conscious awareness of materialist dialectical principles. Richard Levins and Richard Lewontin discuss some implications of this understanding for their own work in their *The Dialectical Biologist* (Levins and Lewontin 1985). And Stephen Jay Gould speaks of his background in dialectics (Eldredge and Gould 1972). However, the number of scientists today who consciously work with a materialist dialectical perspective is limited. The same ideology and forces currently excluding most women from the direction of scientific work also bar the robust flourishing of the explicitly materialist dialectical perspective in science at this time.

CONCLUSION

Science does not stand above the world, or apart from its conflicts; it is rather the science *of* a given society. Its communal practice reflects the needs of the dominant sector, and its way of thinking increasingly reflects the dominant ideology. Plato and Aristotle explicitly related their philosophy of dualism to the division, which they held to be "by nature," between the rulers of their day and the ruled and to their identification with the former. Our present day scientist/philosophers refer to their dualist ideology as "objective science." In fact, it bears the same Aristotelian relationship to the master class of the current system of advanced capitalism, a productive system characterized by ever more powerful machines and exploding technologies. Rampant technology not only intensifies exploitative social relations, but it also defines our society's ethical ideals, its good and its virtue, its dreams of the future, and especially its science, which is forcing life itself into the mold of the profit-making machine.

The machine metaphor is, in fact, at the heart of present-day biological dualism and the gene-environment dichotomy, with the fixed-in-place-before-birth gene being given causal primacy. This biological determinist, or "hard-wired," rationale has been used since the beginning of western civilization to blame the problems of the individual on her or his inherent nature and to absolve the social system from all responsibility, denying the need for change. It serves to justify the rule of a "naturally superior" power elite —and of the science that serves it.

A system of certified experts and credentialed great men has evolved in tandem with this, organized through academic channels and other status and prestige-granting institutions. This system serves to further restrict knowledge and appropriate it for an elite, thus reinforcing hierarchy. Women, on the whole, have been kept out of the ranks of the recognized super-experts, thus lending further credence to the "great man" theory of achievement and success. In fact, women have been a major target of their pronouncements. We are repeatedly assured that their "high-tech" manipulations have made this the best of all worlds for us and that many more new breakthroughs are in the offing. This projection of self-assured authority has had a most intimidating effect upon us and has inhibited our ability to determine for ourselves the implications of this new technology for us.

This intimidation, reinforced by the historical dualist association of "man" with mind and knowing and "woman" with feeling and responding, occurs all across the political spectrum. "The Woman Question," with man as the norm, is usually relegated to a separate committee or postponed to some future time, even by political leaders of the left.

But the super-exploitation of women—of endless rows of poor, third world women in factories, racing their machines, and in the fields, sowing, weeding, hoeing, gathering; of women as uteri, and disposable property; and even of women as discardable playthings—is not a secondary consideration. It does *not* come *after* the class struggle, nor is it subsumed within or parallel to it. It is a primary, immediate, imperative, a major force, *intrinsic* to the overall liberation struggle at this time, and it must be recognized as such in all its manifestations. The struggle for the emancipation of poor, working women throughout the world is, I contend, the *central* struggle of our day.

However, women who understand the nature of this struggle and its significance for them will have to lead this fight, with the help and support of the men who are also struggling. We, especially those of us who are revolutionary feminists, cannot afford the luxury of passively accepting our fears, our intimidation, or even our hostility toward science. The science and technology of this society and the point of view that instructs them are too powerful a means of control over both nature and people, especially over women, for us just to ignore or dismiss them as "bad" for women. Their power must be appreciated. Feminists must become literate in the physical processes and practices of this control, their relation to the society that engenders them, and particularly in the way of thinking, the philosophy and ideology behind these practices. Women's liberation means more than a reduction of abuse; it means sharing decision-making power over our lives, and it will require a revolutionary transformation of deeds and thoughts.

The power of our productive processes and their consequences have greatly altered our physical world. But they have done so within a relationship and philosophy of dominance little changed since Aristotle's time, except in its form of exploitation. The slave, working with primitive tools and her or his hands, has been replaced by the high-tech worker tied to her machine. However, the intensity and productivity of this new level of exploitation has now brought about the *possibility* of a revolutionary transformation to a society without domination and subordination and the *necessity* for this change to occur if our human habitat is to survive.

Neither science nor society need be elitist; the material world itself, and its processes, are not. An egalitarian society would therefore mean not only a more just and fulfilled human world, but its requisite way of thinking and acting would lead to both a profounder understanding of and a more fruitful *integration* with the changing physical world around us.

Addendum: The pre-Aristotelian Platonic soul, adorned with "genetic algorithms" and other modern technological locutions, is, it would seem, even now revealing itself to the relentless importunings of the computer. At the first conference on artificial life, held at Los Alamos National Laboratory in September 1987, it was announced that "artificial life seeks . . . an *essence* arising out of matter *but independent of it*. For the first time in generations . . . science has a *legitimate* way of talking about life's soul. . . . Miracles aren't allowed except at the *very beginning*" (my emphasis). The soul seems to reside in sixteen programmed computer commands—called "genes"! (Gleick 1987).

REFERENCES

Arditti, R., R. D. Klein, and S. Minden, eds. 1984. *Test-Tube Women: What Future for Motherhood?* London: Pandora Press.

Aristotle. 1952 [ca. 335–322 B.C.]. *Biological Treatises:* "History of Animals." Trans. D. W. Thompson; "On the Generation of Animals." Trans. A. Platt. In *Great Books of the Western World, Vol. 9.* Chicago: Encyclopaedia Britannica.

———. 1952 [ca. 335–322 B.C.]. "On the Soul." Trans. J. A. Smith. In *Great Books of the Western World. Vol. 8.* Chicago: Encyclopaedia Britannica.

———. 1952. [ca. 335–322 B.C.]. *Politics.* Trans. B. Jowett. In *Great Books of the Western World, Vol. 9.* Chicago: Encyclopaedia Britannica.

Barnes, D. 1987. "Defect in Alzheimer's is on Chromosome 21." *Science* 235 (20 Feb.):846–847.

Barnett, S. A. 1983. "Humanity and Natural Selection." *Ethology and Sociobiology* 4:35–51.

Biddle, W. 1987. "Corporations on Campus." *Science* 237 (24 July):353–355.

Bleier, R. 1984. *Science and Gender: A Critique of Biology and Its Theories on Women.* New York: Pergamon Press.

Bury, J. B., and R. Meiggs. 1975. *A History of Greece.* 4th ed. New York: St. Martin's Press.

Cohn, C. 1987. "Sex and Death in the Rational World of Defense Intellectuals." *Signs* 12, no. 4:687–719.

Comte, A. 1947 [ca. 1830–1842]. "The Positive Philosophy." In *Man and the Universe: The Philosophers of Science,* Commins and R. N. Linscott. ed. S. New York: Random House.

Corea, G. 1985. *The Mother Machine: From Artificial Insemination to Artificial Wombs.* New York: Harper & Row.

Delone, B. N. 1963 [1956]. "Analytic Geometry." In *Mathematics: Its Content, Methods, and Meaning,* ed. A. D. Aleksandrov, A. N. Kolmogorov and M. A. Lavrent'ev. Moscow. Trans. S. H. Gould and T. Bartha. Cambridge, Mass.: MIT Press.

Descartes, R. 1947 [1637]. "Discourse on Method." In *Man and the Universe: The Philosophers of Science,* ed. S. Commins and R. N. Linscott. New York: Random House.

Dickson, D. 1984. *The New Politics of Science.* New York: Pantheon Press.

Einstein, A. 1947 [1934]. "The World As I See It." In *Man and the Universe: The Philosophers of Science,* ed. S. Commins and R. N. Linscott. New York: Random House.

Eldredge, N., and S. J. Gould. 1972. "Punctuated Equilibria: An Alternative to Phyletic Gradualism." In *Models in Paleobiology,* ed. T. J. M. Schopf. San Francisco: Freeman, Cooper.

Engels, F. 1940. *Dialectics of Nature.* Trans. C. P. Dutt. New York: International Publishers.

———. 1939. [1894]. *Herr Eugen Duhring's Revolution in Science (Anti-Duhring).* Trans. E. Burns. New York: International Publishers.

Farrington, B. 1944. *Greek Science: Its Meaning For Us*. Harmondsworth: Penguin Press.

Fausto-Sterling, A. 1986. *Myths of Gender: Biological Theories About Women and Men*. New York: Basic Books.

Fee, E. 1981. "Is Feminism a Threat to Scientific Objectivity?" *International Journal of Women's Studies* 4, no. 4:378–392.

Fried, B. 1982. "Boys Will Be Boys: The Language of Sex and Gender." In *Biological Woman: The Convenient Myth*, ed. R. Hubbard, M. S. Henifin, and B. Fried. Cambridge, Mass.: Schenkman.

Gleick, J. 1987. "Can Computers Discern the Soul?" *New York Times* (29 September).

Gornick, V. 1983. *Women in Science: Portraits From a World in Transition*. New York: Simon and Schuster.

Gould, S. J. 1981. *The Mismeasure of Man*. New York: W. W. Norton.

Harding, S. 1986. *The Science Question in Feminism*. Ithaca: Cornell University Press.

Holden, C. 1987. "The Genetics of Personality." *Science* 237 (7 August):598–601.

Hubbard, R. 1982. "Have Only Men Evolved?" In *Biological Woman: The Convenient Myth*, ed. R. Hubbard, M. S. Henifin, and B. Fried. Cambridge, Mass.: Schenkman.

Jaret, P., and L. Nilsson. Photographs. 1986. "Our Immune System: The Wars Within." *National Geographic* 169, no. 6:702–734.

Keller, E. F. 1983. *A Feeling For the Organism*. New York: W. H. Freeman.

———. 1985. *Reflections on Gender and Science*. New Haven, Conn.: Yale University Press.

Kolata, G. 1987. "Tests of Fetuses Rise Sharply Amid Doubts." *New York Times* (22 September).

Koshland, D. E., Jr. 1987. "Nature, Nurture, and Behavior." *Science* 235 (20 March): 1445.

Kuhn, T. 1970. *The Structure of Scientific Revolutions*. 2d ed. Chicago: University of Chicago Press.

Levins, R., and R. Lewontin. 1985. *The Dialectical Biologist*. Cambridge, Mass.: Harvard University Press.

Lewin, R. 1983. "A Naturalist of the Genome." *Science* 222 (28 October):402–408.

Lewontin, R., S. Rose, and L. Kamin. 1984. *Not in Our Genes: Biology, Ideology and Human Nature*. New York: Pantheon Books.

Lowe, M. 1978. "Sociobiology and Sex Differences." *Signs* 4, no. 1:118–126.

Marx, K. 1978 [1845]. "Theses on Feuerbach," and "The German Ideology: Part I." In *The Marx-Engels Reader*, ed. R. C. Tucker. 2d ed. New York: W. H. Norton.

McClintock, B. 1984. "The Significance of Responses of the Genome to Challenge." *Science* 226 (16 November):792–801.

Merchant, C. 1980. *The Death of Nature: Women, Ecology and the Scientific Revolution*. San Francisco: Harper & Row.

Miller, J., and A. G. Tramposch. 1987. "Playing God? We've Done it for Centuries." *New York Times* (26 April).

Phillips, J. A. 1984. *Eve: The History of an Idea*. San Francisco: Harper & Row.

Plato. 1941. *The Republic*. Trans. F. M. Cornford, with introduction and notes. London: Oxford University Press.

Rawls, R. L. 1987. "Facts and Figures for Chemical R.&D." *Chemical and Engineering News* 65, no. 30(27 July):32–62.

Reichenbach, H. 1951. *The Rise of Scientific Philosophy*. Berkeley: University of California Press.

Rigden, J. S. 1987. *Rabi: Scientist and Citizen*. New York: Basic Books.

Rivkin, J. 1987. "Is Nature Just a Form of Private Property?" *New York Times* (26 April).

Roberts, L. 1987. "Who Owns the Human Genome?" *Science* 237 (24 July):358–361.

Rossiter, M. W. 1982. *Women Scientists in America: Struggles and Strategies to 1940*. Baltimore: Johns Hopkins University Press.

Rowland, R. 1987. "Technology and Motherhood: Reproductive Choice Reconsidered." *Signs* 12, no. 3:512–529.

Schiebinger, L. 1987. "The History and Philosophy of Women in Science: A Review Essay." *Signs* 12, no. 2:305–333.

Tobach, E., and B. Rosoff, eds. 1978–1984. *Genes and Gender*. vol. 1–4. New York: Gordian Press.

Weitz, D. 1987. "A Psychiatric Holocaust." *Science for the People* 19, no. 2:13–19.

Wilson, E. O. 1975. *Sociobiology: The New Synthesis*. Cambridge, Mass.: Harvard University Press.

THE PROJECT OF FEMINIST EPISTEMOLOGY: PERSPECTIVES FROM A NONWESTERN FEMINIST

Uma Narayan

A fundamental thesis of feminist epistemology is that our location in the world as women makes it possible for us to perceive and understand different aspects of both the world and human activities in ways that challenge the male bias of existing perspectives. Feminist epistemology is a particular manifestation of the general insight that the nature of women's experiences as individuals and as social beings, our contributions to work, culture, knowledge, and our history and political interests have been systematically ignored or misrepresented by mainstream discourses in different areas.

Women have been often excluded from prestigious areas of human activity (for example, politics or science) and this has often made these activities seem clearly "male." In areas where women were not excluded (for example, subsistence work), their contribution has been misrepresented as secondary and inferior to that of men. Feminist epistemology sees mainstream theories about various human enterprises, including mainstream theories about human knowledge, as one-dimensional and deeply flawed because of the exclusion and misrepresentation of women's contributions.

Feminist epistemology suggests that integrating women's contribution into the domain of science and knowledge will not constitute a mere adding of details; it will not merely widen the canvas but result in a shift of perspective enabling us to see a very different picture. The inclusion of women's perspective will not merely amount to women participating in greater numbers in the existing practice of science and knowledge, but it will change the very nature of these activities and their self-understanding.

It would be misleading to suggest that feminist epistemology is a homogenous and cohesive enterprise. Its practitioners differ both philosophically and politically in a number of significant ways (Harding 1986). But an important theme on its agenda has been to undermine the abstract, rationalistic, and universal image of the scientific enterprise by using several different strategies. It has studied, for instance, how contingent historical factors have colored both scientific theories and practices and provided the (often sexist) metaphors in which scientists have conceptualized their activity (Bordo 1986; Keller 1985; Harding and O'Barr 1987). It has tried to reintegrate values and emotions into our account of our cognitive activities, arguing for both the inevitability of their presence and the importance of the contributions they are capable of making to our knowledge (Gilligan 1982; Jaggar and Tronto essays in this volume). It has also attacked various sets of dualisms characteristic of western philosophical thinking—reason versus emotion, culture versus nature, universal versus particular—in which the first of each set is identified with science, rationality, and the masculine and the second is relegated to the nonscientific, the nonrational, and the feminine (Harding and Hintikka 1983; Lloyd 1984; Wilshire essay in this volume).

At the most general level, feminist epistemology resembles the efforts of many oppressed groups to reclaim for themselves the value of their own experience. The writing of novels that focused on working-class life in England or the lives of black people in the United States shares a motivation similar to that of feminist epistemology—to depict an experience different from the norm and to assert the value of this difference.

In a similar manner, feminist epistemology also resembles attempts by third-world writers and historians to document the wealth and complexity of local economic and social structures that existed prior to colonialism. These attempts are useful for their ability to restore to colonized peoples a sense of the richness of their own history and culture. These projects also mitigate the tendency of intellectuals in former colonies who are westernized through their education to think that anything western is necessarily better and more "progressive." In some cases, such studies help to preserve the knowledge of many local arts, crafts, lore, and techniques that were part of the former way of life before they are lost not only to practice but even to memory.

These enterprises are analogous to feminist epistemology's project of restoring to women a sense of the richness of their history, to mitigate our tendency to see the stereotypically "masculine" as better or more progressive, and to preserve for posterity the contents of "feminine" areas of knowledge and expertise—medical lore, knowledge associated with the practices of childbirth and child rearing, traditionally feminine crafts, and so on. Feminist epistemology, like these other enterprises, must attempt to balance the assertion of the value of a different culture or experience against the dangers of romanticizing it to the extent that the limitations and oppressions it confers on its subjects are ignored.

My essay will attempt to examine some dangers of approaching feminist theorizing and epistemological values in a noncontextual and nonpragmatic way, which could convert important feminist insights and theses into feminist epistemological dogmas. I will use my perspective as a nonwestern, Indian feminist to examine critically the predominantly Anglo-American project of feminist epistemology and to reflect on what such a project might signify for women in nonwestern cultures in general and for nonwestern feminists in particular. I will suggest that different cultural contexts and political agendas may cast a very different light on both the "idols" and the "enemies" of knowledge as they have characteristically been typed in western feminist epistemology.

In keeping with my respect for contexts, I would like to stress that I do not see nonwestern feminists as a homogenous group and that none of the concerns I express as a nonwestern feminist may be pertinent to or shared by *all* nonwestern feminists, although I do think they will make sense to many.

In the first section, I will show that the enterprise of feminist epistemology poses some political problems for nonwestern feminists that it does not pose, in the same way, for western feminists. In the second section, I will explore some problems that nonwestern feminists may have with feminist epistemology's critical focus on positivism. In the third section, I will examine some political implications of feminist epistemology's thesis of the "epistemic privilege" of oppressed groups for nonwestern feminists. And in the last section, I will discuss the claim that oppressed groups gain epistemic advantages by inhabiting a larger number of contexts, arguing that such situations may not always confer advantages and may sometimes create painful problems.

NONWESTERN FEMINIST POLITICS AND FEMINIST EPISTEMOLOGY

Some themes of feminist epistemology may be problematic for nonwestern feminists in ways that they are not problematic for western feminists. Feminism has a much narrower base in most nonwestern countries. It is primarily of significance to some urban, educated, middle-class, and hence relatively westernized women, like myself. Although feminist groups in these countries do try to extend the scope of feminist concerns to other groups (for example, by fighting for childcare, women's health issues, and equal wages issues through trade union structures), some major preoccupations of western feminism—its critique of marriage, the family, compulsory heterosexuality—presently engage the attention of mainly small groups of middle-class feminists.

These feminists must think and function within the context of a powerful tradition that, although it systematically oppresses women, also contains within itself a discourse that confers a high value on women's place in the general scheme of things. Not only are the roles of wife and mother highly praised, but women also are seen as the cornerstones of the spiritual well-being of their husbands and children, admired for their supposedly higher moral, religious, and spiritual qualities, and so on. In cultures that have a pervasive religious component, like the Hindu culture with which I am familiar, everything seems assigned a place and value as long as it keeps to its place. Confronted with a powerful traditional discourse that values woman's place as long as she keeps to the place prescribed, it may be politically counterproductive for nonwestern feminists to echo uncritically the themes of western feminist epistemology that seek to restore the value, cognitive and otherwise, of "women's experience."

The danger is that, even if the nonwestern feminist talks about the value of women's experience in terms totally different from those of the traditional discourse, the difference is likely to be drowned out by the louder and more powerful voice of the traditional discourse, which will then claim that "what those feminists say" vindicates its view that the roles and experiences it assigns to women have value and that women should stick to those roles.

I do not intend to suggest that this is not a danger for western feminism or to imply that there is no tension for western feminists between being critical of the experiences that their societies have provided for women and finding things to value in them nevertheless. But I am suggesting that perhaps there is less at risk for western feminists in trying to strike this balance. I am inclined to think that in nonwestern countries feminists must still stress the negative sides of the female experience within that culture and that the time for a more sympathetic evaluation is not quite ripe.

But the issue is not simple and seems even less so when another point is considered. The imperative we experience as feminists to be critical of how our culture and traditions oppress women conflicts with our desire as members of once colonized cultures to affirm the value of the same culture and traditions.

There are seldom any easy resolutions to these sorts of tensions. As an Indian feminist currently living in the United States, I often find myself torn between the desire to communicate with honesty the miseries and oppressions that I think my own culture confers on its women and the fear that this communication is going to reinforce, however unconsciously, western prejudices about the "superiority" of western culture. I have often felt compelled to interrupt my communication, say on the problems of the Indian system of arranged marriages, to remind my western friends that the experiences of women under their system of "romantic love" seem no more enviable.

Perhaps we should all attempt to cultivate the methodological habit of trying to understand the complexities of the oppression involved in different historical and cultural settings while eschewing, at least for now, the temptation to make comparisions across such settings, given the dangers of attempting to compare what may well be incommensurable in any neat terms.

THE NONPRIMACY OF POSITIVISM AS A PROBLEMATIC PERSPECTIVE

As a nonwestern feminist, I also have some reservations about the way in which feminist epistemology seems to have picked positivism as its main target of attack. The choice of positivism as the main target is reasonable because it has been a dominant and influential western position and it most clearly embodies some flaws that feminist epistemology seeks to remedy.

But this focus on positivism should not blind us to the facts that it is not our only enemy and that nonpositivist frameworks are not, by virtue of that bare qualification, any more worthy of our tolerance. Most traditional frameworks that nonwestern feminists regard as oppressive to women are not positivist, and it would be wrong to see feminist epistemology's critique of positivism given the same political importance for nonwestern feminists that it has for western feminists. Traditions like my own, where the influence of religion is pervasive, are suffused through and through with values. We must fight not frameworks that assert the separation of fact and value but frameworks that are pervaded by values to which we, as feminists, find ourselves opposed. Positivism in epistemology flourished at the same time as liberalism in western political theory. Positivism's view of values as individual and subjective related to liberalism's political emphasis on individual rights that were supposed to protect an individual's freedom to live according to the values she espoused.

Nonwestern feminists may find themselves in a curious bind when confronting the interrelations between positivism and political liberalism. As colonized people, we are well aware of the facts that may political concepts of liberalism are both suspicious and confused and that the practice of liberalism in the colonies was marked by brutalities unaccounted for by its theory. However, as feminists, we often find some of its concepts, such as individual rights, very useful in our attempts to fight problems rooted in our traditional cultures.

Nonwestern feminists will no doubt be sensitive to the fact that positivism is not our only enemy. Western feminists too must learn not to uncritically claim any nonpositivist framework as an ally; despite commonalities, there are apt to be many differences. A temperate look at positions we espouse as allies is necessary since "the enemy of my enemy is my friend" is a principle likely to be as misleading in epistemology as it is in the domain of Realpolitik.

The critical theorists of the Frankfurt School will serve well to illustrate this point. Begun as a group of young intellectuals in the post–World War I Weimar Republic, the members were significantly influenced by Marxism, and their interests ranged from aesthetics to political theory to epistemology. Jürgen Habermas, the most eminent critical theorist today, has in his works attacked positivism and the claim of scientific theories to be value neutral or "disinterested." He has attempted to show the constitutive role played by human interests in different domains of human knowledge. He is interested, as are feminists, in the role that knowledge plays in the reproduction of social relations of domination. But, as feminist epistemology is critical of all perspectives that place a lopsided stress on reason, it must also necessarily be critical of the rationalist underpinnings of critical theory.

Such rationalist foundations are visible, for example, in Habermas's "rational reconstruction" of what he calls "an ideal speech situation," supposedly characterized by "pure intersubjectivity," that is, by the absence of any barriers to communication. That Habermas's "ideal speech situation" is a creature of reason is clear from its admitted character as a "rationally reconstructed ideal" and its symmetrical distribution of chances for all of its participants to choose and apply speech acts.

This seems to involve a stress on formal and procedural equality among speakers that ignores substantive differences imposed by class, race, or gender that may affect a speaker's knowledge of the facts or the capacity to assert herself or command the attention of others. Women in academia often can testify to the fact that, despite not being forcibly restrained from speaking in public forums, they have to overcome much conditioning in order to learn to assert themselves. They can also testify as to how, especially in male-dominated disciplines, their speech is often ignored or treated with condescension by male colleagues.

Habermas either ignores the existence of such substantive differences among speakers or else assumes they do not exist. In the latter case, if one assumes that the speakers in the ideal speech situation are not significantly different from each other, then there may not be much of significance for them to speak about. Often it is precisely our differences that make dialogue imperative. If the ideal speakers of the ideal speech situation are unmarked by differences, there may be nothing for them to surmount on their way to a "rational consensus." If there are such differences between the speakers, then Habermas provides nothing that will rule out the sorts of problems I have mentioned.

Another rationalist facet of critical theory is revealed in Habermas's assumption that justifiable agreement and genuine knowledge arise only out of "rational consensus." This seems to overlook the possibility of agreement and knowledge based on sympathy or solidarity. Sympathy or solidarity may very well promote the uncovering of truth, especially in situations when people who divulge information are rendering themselves vulnerable in the process. For instance, women are more likely to talk about experiences of sexual harassment to other women because they would expect similar experiences to have made them more sympathetic and understanding. Therefore, feminists should be cautious about assuming that they necessarily have much in common with a framework simply because it is nonpositivist. Nonwestern feminists may be more alert to this error because many problems they confront arise in nonpositivist contexts.

THE POLITICAL USES OF
"EPISTEMIC PRIVILEGE"

Important strands in feminist epistemology hold the view that our concrete embodiments as members of a specific class, race, and gender as well as our concrete historical situations necessarily play significant roles in our perspective on the world; moreover, no point of view is "neutral" because no one exists unembedded in the world. Knowledge is seen as gained not by solitary individuals but by socially constituted members of groups that emerge and change through history.

Feminists have also argued that groups living under various forms of oppression are more likely to have a critical perspective on their situation and that this critical view is both generated and partly constituted by critical emotional responses that subjects experience vis-à-vis their life situations. This perspective in feminist epistemology rejects the "Dumb View" of emotions and favors an intentional conception that emphasizes the cognitive aspect of emotions. It is critical of the traditional view of the emotions as wholly and always impediments to knowledge and argues that many emotions often help rather than hinder our understanding of a person or situation (see Jaggar essay in this volume).

Bringing together these views on the role of the emotions in knowledge, the possibility of critical insights being generated by oppression, and the contextual nature of knowledge may suggest some answers to serious and interesting political questions. I will consider what these epistemic positions entail regarding the possibility of understanding and political cooperation between oppressed groups and sympathetic members of a dominant group—say, between white people and people of color over issues of race or between men and women over issues of gender.

These considerations are also relevant to questions of understanding and cooperation between western and nonwestern feminists. Western feminists, despite their critical understanding of their own culture, often tend to be more a part of it than they realize. If they fail to see the contexts of their theories and assume that their perspective has universal validity for all feminists, they tend to participate in the dominance that western culture has exercised over nonwestern cultures.

Our position must explain and justify our dual need to criticize members of a dominant group (say men or white people or western feminists) for their lack of attention to or concern with problems that affect an oppressed group (say, women or people of color or nonwestern feminists, respectively), as well as for our frequent hostility toward those who express interest, even sympathetic interest, in issues that concern groups of which they are not a part.

Both attitudes are often warranted. On the one hand, one cannot but be angry at those who minimize, ignore, or dismiss the pain and conflict that racism and sexism inflict on their victims. On the other hand, living in a state of siege also necessarily makes us suspicious of expressions of concern and support from those who do not live these oppressions. We are suspicious of the motives of our sympathizers or the extent of their sincerity, and we worry, often with good reason, that they may claim that their interest provides a warrant for them to speak for us, as dominant groups throughout history have spoken for the dominated.

This is all the more threatening to groups aware of how recently they have acquired the power to articulate their own points of view. Nonwestern feminists are especially aware of this because they have a double struggle in trying to find their own voice: they have to learn to articulate their differences, not only from their own traditional contexts but also from western feminism.

Politically, we face interesting questions whose answers hinge on the nature and extent of the communication that we think possible between different groups. Should we try to share our perspectives and insights with those who have not lived our oppressions and accept that they may fully come to share them? Or should we seek only the affirmation of those like ourselves, who share common features of oppression, and rule out the possibility of those who have not lived these oppressions ever acquiring a genuine understanding of them?

I argue that it would be a mistake to move from the thesis that knowledge is constructed by human subjects who are socially constituted to the conclusion that those who are differently located socially can never attain *some* understanding of our experience or *some* sympathy with our cause. In that case, we would be committed to not just a perspectival view of knowledge but a relativistic one. Relativism, as I am using it, implies that a person could have knowledge of only the sorts of things she had experienced personally and that she would be totally unable to communicate any of the contents of her knowledge to someone who did not have the same sorts of experiences. Not only does this seem clearly false and perhaps even absurd, but it is probably a good idea not to have any a priori views that would imply either that all our knowledge is always capable of being communicated to every other person or that would imply that some of our knowledge is necessarily incapable of being communicated to some class of persons.

"Nonanalytic" and "nonrational" forms of discourse, like fiction or poetry, may be better able than other forms to convey the complex life experiences of one group to members of another. One can also hope that being part of one oppressed group may enable an individual to have a more sympathetic understanding of issues relating to another kind of oppression—that, for instance, being a woman may sensitize one to issues of race and class even if one is a woman privileged in those respects.

Again, this should not be reduced to some kind of metaphysical presumption. Historical circumstances have sometimes conspired, say, to making working-class men more chauvinistic in some of their attitudes than other men. Sometimes one sort of suffering may simply harden individuals to other sorts or leave them without energy to take any interest in the problems of other groups. But we can at least try to foster such sensitivity by focusing on parallels, not identities, between different sorts of oppressions.

Our commitment to the contextual nature of knowledge does not require us to claim that those who do not inhabit these contexts can never have any knowledge of them. But this commitment does permit us to argue that it is *easier* and *more likely* for the oppressed to have critical insights into the conditions of their own oppression than it is for those who live outside these structures. Those who actually *live* the oppressions of class, race, or gender have faced the issues that such oppressions generate in a variety of different situations. The insights and emotional responses engendered by these situations are a legacy with which they confront any new issue or situation.

Those who display sympathy as outsiders often fail both to understand fully the emotional complexities of living as a member of an oppressed group and to carry what they have learned and understood about one situation to the way they perceive another. It is a commonplace that even sympathetic men will often fail to perceive subtle instances of sexist behavior or discourse.

Sympathetic individuals who are not members of an oppressed group should keep in mind the possibility of this sort of failure regarding their understanding of issues relating to an oppression they do not share. They should realize that nothing they may do, from participating in demonstrations to changing their lifestyles, can make them one of the oppressed. For instance, men who share household and child-rearing responsibilities with women are mistaken if they think that this act of choice, often buttressed by the gratitude and admiration of others, is anything like the woman's experience of being forcibly socialized into these tasks and of having others perceive this as her natural function in the scheme of things.

The view that we can understand much about the perspectives of those whose oppression we do not share allows us the space to criticize dominant groups for their blindness to the facts of oppression. The view that such an understanding, despite great effort and interest, is likely to be incomplete or limited, provides us with the ground for denying total parity to members of a dominant group in their ability to understand our situation.

Sympathetic members of a dominant group need not necessarily defer to our views on any particular issue because that may reduce itself to another subtle form of condescension, but at least they must keep in mind the very real difficulties and possibility of failure to fully understand our concerns. This and the very important need for dominated groups to control the means of discourse about their own situations are important reasons for taking seriously the claim that oppressed groups have an "epistemic advantage."

THE DARK SIDE OF "DOUBLE VISION"

I think that one of the most interesting insights of feminist epistemology is the view that oppressed groups, whether women, the poor, or racial minorities, may derive an "epistemic advantage" from having knowledge of the practices of both their own contexts and those of their oppressors. The practices of the dominant groups (for instance, men) govern a society; the dominated group (for instance, women) must acquire some fluency with these practices in order to survive in that society.

There is no similar pressure on members of the dominant group to acquire knowledge of the practices of the dominated groups. For instance, colonized people had to learn the language and culture of their colonizers. The colonizers seldom found it necessary to have more than a sketchy acquaintance with the language and culture of the "natives." Thus, the oppressed are seen as having an "epistemic advantage" because they can operate with two sets of practices and in two different contexts. This advantage is thought to lead to critical insights because each framework provides a critical perspective on the other.

I would like to balance this account with a few comments about the "dark side," the disadvantages, of being able to or of having to inhabit two mutually incompatible frameworks that provide differing perspectives on social reality. I suspect that nonwestern feminists, given the often complex and troublesome interrelationships between the contexts they must inhabit, are less likely to express unqualified enthusiasm about the benefits of straddling a multiplicity of contexts. Mere access to two different and incompatible contexts is not a guarantee that a critical stance on the part of an individual will result. There are many ways in which she may deal with the situation.

First, the person may be tempted to dichotomize her life and reserve the framework of a different context for each part. The middle class of nonwestern countries supplies numerous examples of people who are very westernized in public life but who return to a very traditional lifestyle in the realm of the family. Women may choose to live their public lives in a "male" mode, displaying characteristics of aggressiveness, competition, and so on, while continuing to play dependent and compliant roles in their private lives. The pressures of jumping between two different lifestyles may be mitigated by justifications of how each pattern of behavior is appropriate to its particular context and of how it enables them to "get the best of both worlds."

Second, the individual may try to reject the practices of her own context and try to be as much as possible like members of the dominant group. Westernized intellectuals in the nonwestern world often may almost lose knowledge of their own cultures and practices and be ashamed of the little that they do still know. Women may try both to acquire stereotypically male characteristics, like aggressiveness, and to expunge stereotypically female characteristics, like emotionality. Or the individual could try to reject entirely the framework of the dominant group and assert the virtues of her own despite the risks of being marginalized from the power structures of the society; consider, for example, women who seek a certain sort of security in traditionally defined roles.

The choice to inhabit two contexts critically is an alternative to these choices and, I would argue, a more useful one. But the presence of alternative contexts does not by itself guarantee that one of the other choices will not be made. Moreover, the decision to inhabit two contexts critically, although it may lead to an "epistemic advantage," is likely to exact a certain price. It may lead to a sense of totally lacking roots or any space where one is at home in a relaxed manner.

This sense of alienation may be minimized if the critical straddling of two contexts is part of an ongoing critical politics, due to the support of others and a deeper understanding of what is going on. When it is not so rooted, it may generate ambivalence, uncertainty, despair, and even madness, rather than more positive critical emotions and attitudes. However such a person determines her locus, there may be a sense of being an outsider in both contexts and a sense of clumsiness or lack of fluency in both sets of practices. Consider this simple linguistic example: most people who learn two different languages that are associated with two very different cultures seldom acquire both with equal fluency; they may find themselves devoid of vocabulary in one language for certain contexts of life or be unable to match real objects with terms they have acquired in their vocabulary. For instance, people from my sort of background would know words in Indian languages for some spices, fruits, and vegetables that they do not know in English. Similarly, they might be unable to discuss "technical" subjects like economics or biology in their own languages because they learned about these subjects and acquired their technical vocabularies only in English.

The relation between the two contexts the individual inhabits may not be simple or straightforward. The individual subject is seldom in a position to carry out a perfect "dialectical synthesis" that preserves all the advantages of both contexts and transcends all their problems. There may be a number of different "syntheses," each of which avoids a different subset of the problems and preserves a different subset of the benefits.

No solution may be perfect or even palatable to the agent confronted with a choice. For example, some Indian feminists may find some western modes of dress (say trousers) either more comfortable or more their "style" than some local modes of dress. However, they may find that wearing the local mode of dress is less socially troublesome, alienates them less from more traditional people they want to work with, and so on. Either choice is bound to leave them partly frustrated in their desires.

Feminist theory must be temperate in the use it makes of this doctrine of "double vision"—the claim that oppressed groups have an epistemic advantage and access to greater critical conceptual space. Certain types and contexts of oppression certainly may bear out the truth of this claim. Others certainly do not seem to do so; and even if they do provide space for critical insights, they may also rule out the possibility of actions subversive of the oppressive state of affairs.

Certain kinds of oppressive contexts, such as the contexts in which women of my grandmother's background lived, rendered their subjects entirely devoid of skills required to function as independent entities in the culture. Girls were married off barely past puberty, trained for nothing beyond household tasks and the rearing of children, and passed from economic dependency on their fathers to economic dependency on their husbands to economic dependency on their sons in old age. Their criticisms of their lot were articulated, if at all, in terms that precluded a desire for any radical change. They saw themselves sometimes as personally unfortunate, but they did not locate the causes of their misery in larger social arrangements.

I conclude by stressing that the important insight incorporated in the doctrine of "double vision" should not be reified into a metaphysics that serves as a substitute for concrete social analysis. Furthermore, the alternative to "buying" into an oppressive social system need not be a celebration of exclusion and the mechanisms of marginalization. The thesis that oppression may bestow an epistemic advantage should not tempt us in the direction of idealizing or romanticizing oppression and blind us to its real material and psychic deprivations.

NOTE

I would like to acknowledge the enormous amount of help that Alison Jaggar and Susan Bordo have given me with this essay. Alison has been influential all the way from suggesting the nature of the project to suggesting changes that cleared up minor flaws in writing. Susan's careful reading has suggested valuable changes in the structure of the paper, and she has also been very helpful with references. I would like to thank them both for the insightful nature of their comments and the graciousness with which they made them. I would like to thank Dilys Page for her painstaking reading and comments on the first draft of this paper. I would also like to thank Radhika Balasubramanian, Sue Cataldi, Mary Geer, Mary Gibson, Rhoda Linton, Josie Rodriguez-Hewitt, and Joyce Tigner for sharing their work with me, for taking an interest in my work, and for providing me with a community of women who sustain me in many, many ways.

REFERENCES

Bordo, S. 1986. "The Cartesian Masculinization of Thought." *Signs* 11:439–456.

Gilligan, C. 1982. *In A Different Voice: Psychological Theory and Women's Development.* Cambridge, Mass.: Harvard University Press.

Harding, S. 1986. *The Science Question in Feminism.* Ithaca, N.Y.: Cornell University Press.

Harding, S., and M. Hintikka. 1983. *Discovering Reality: Feminist Perspectives on Epistemology, Metaphysics, Methodology, and Philosophy of Science.* Dordrecht: Reidel.

Harding, S., and J. O'Barr, eds. 1987. *Sex and Scientific Inquiry*. Chicago: University of Chicago Press.

Keller, E. F. 1985. *Reflections on Gender and Science*. New Haven, Conn.: Yale University Press.

Lloyd, G. 1984. *The Man of Reason*. Minneapolis: University of Minnesota Press.

Part III
REVISIONING METHOD

TOWARD A FEMINIST
RESEARCH METHOD

Rhoda Linton

This paper follows the rather rocky progression of my experience in a mainstream setting, as a feminist, from novice to professional social science research methodologist. First, I describe the experience out of which my need to know how to identify feminist research emerged; I then abstract, from a broad review of activities of the contemporary western women's movement, a set of criteria that I consider to reflect current western feminist principles. Second, I describe a research method, an innovative group conceptualization technique. Third, I discuss and examine an illustration of the use of the technique to see if it embodies the set of criteria reflecting feminist principles. Although I do not claim this as the only way to approach issues feminist researchers face when confronting conflicts with current dominant research paradigms, I do believe it offers one way. In conclusion, I discuss my own questions arising from this work to date, including how to translate the group conceptualization technique into an action research method.

Beginnings

As a feminist concentrating on learning research methods in the context of a doctoral program in Program Evaluation Studies, I discovered early on that I was uncomfortable with the boundaries imposed by current research practice. I learned that such boundaries enclosed belief systems sometimes called paradigms and that these paradigms had been created, utilized, and promulgated as the norm predominantly by white western males in academic and other "scientific" settings.

In the social sciences, frequently one is introduced to research methods via courses in specific statistical procedures. Such courses often present the material according to graduated levels of complexity of analysis but without an overall framework for their use. Little attention is given, for example, to the dynamic interplay between them and other research components such as theoretical conceptualization, problem formulation, design, measurement, data definition, data collection strategies and techniques, and other components of the research process. I did not object to the mathematical procedures employed in statistical analyses; in fact, eventually I found them to be quite tantalizing puzzles. Initially, however, studying such subjects seemed somehow outside the realm of seeking methods by which to understand the world. Although agonizing and time consuming in the intricate calculations required, they seemed to me not to reveal themselves as useful intermediary steps in the overall enterprise of research. I now believe that this was a function of the way in which these subjects were atomistically conceived and taught, that is, as entities unto themselves, with very little connecting them to real life application either through substantive examples or contextual preparation. This type of skill development seems to play a role in the curriculum of many social science advanced degree programs: something peripheral to "real" substantive subjects and, therefore, of secondary interest at best. As a compulsory demonstration of mathematical capability, a rather closed, if not terrified, approach to its study is practically guaranteed, especially for many women. Furthermore, partially because a generally heightened level of fear exists among students, the importance of this quantitative research skill comes to loom larger than its actual value; at the same time its potential for multiple uses in an overall approach to research is unrecognized. For example, by concentrating on the calculation of various ways to *test* for "significance" of research *results,* the usefulness of many statistical procedures for *exploring data* is often overlooked, even lost. As they become ends rather than means in the general research endeavor, these tests, although interesting conceptually and useful in some contexts, can actually block understanding.

Transitions

Once I began to understand the potential uses of such quantitative techniques (e.g., exploring data), I had no interest in throwing the baby out with the bath water. However, I also did not choose to swallow the current meanings without critical attention to their assumptions and practice, especially as viewed from a feminist perspective. Given a specific experience that occurred just as I was beginning to focus on the question, Is there such a thing as feminist research methodology? (Linton 1983), I had become convinced that a feminist perspective could make a difference; it could introduce new ways of seeing and doing research. I went to a Women's Pentagon Action demonstration in Washington, D.C. As a veteran attender and organizer of such events in the 1960s and early 1970s, I knew in detail how they worked. At this event, I was thrilled to discover that even the *process*, the *method*, of such things as common as "normal" demonstrations could be radically changed through attempts to embody feminist beliefs (Linton and Whitham 1982). This experience confirmed my need to review and expand from a feminist perspective what I was learning about "normal" research methodology.

I chose conceptualization as my particular area of research method interest because of its fundamental importance to the entire research process. I concentrated on the specific subset of *group* conceptualization because of its potential, as a step in the development of group action, for building women's solidarity to achieve social change. Together with a research methodologist whose specialization is in quantitative procedures, I worked on the development of a specified conceptualization process that combined text and numerical data and that could be used by both individuals and groups. Focusing on the group approach, I decided to explore the process using a subject I both knew and cared about a lot, that is, conceptualizing feminism itself. Furthermore, I was looking for a way to be able to explain why I thought what I was doing *was* feminist. The conceptualization process would produce as an outcome a meaning of feminism for the group participating, but how could I tell if the method itself was feminist? I needed a context, some kind of indicators of conceptualizing feminism, with which to compare my practice.

New Beginnings

Because the last twenty years have given us many and varied meanings of feminism, the question then arose, from which meaning should I choose indicators? Stymied by this question for some time, I finally decided that, although we could easily *theorize* about feminism, what we as self-identified feminists *do* inescapably reveals who we are at a given time. Whether we are conscious of it or not, all practice embodies theory, that is, what we *mean* is revealed by what we do, even when inconsistent with what we *say* we mean. Therefore, I attempted to survey current self-identified feminist practice in order to build a working set of indicators of how I understand feminism's conceptualizations. I realize that my own view is one of many, necessarily limited by my experience as a contemporary western feminist and open to question by others. Thus, I do not claim an absolute sense for my meaning of feminism or what I consider to be activities constituting feminist practice.

In fact, I see my work as "in process," as part of a dynamic movement—a huge joint effort to create, understand, and exchange not only *what* we know but also *how* we know. I tried to include a variety of ways of knowing about the concept feminism in the survey of feminist practice, for example, books, articles, studies, film, video, music, theater, pamphlets, personal recollections, meeting minutes, speeches, service program reports, and so on. I then formed broad categories of feminist activities: consciousness raising, for example, small groups, large groups such as speak-outs and teach-ins; service programs, for example, reproductive rights clinics, rape crisis lines, battered women's shelters, displaced homemaker centers; both direct and indirect social and political action, for example, electoral and legislative campaigns, court cases, public education on specific issues, demonstrations, rallies, marches, camp-ins; cultural expression, for example, music, art, spirituality, literature, revitalization of traditional women's crafts; theory building and education, for example, women's studies programs, internships; and theoretical and applied research, for example, anthropological, historical, psychological, literary, program evaluation. This categorization was meant neither to be absolute nor to imply priority among activities. Furthermore, it was clear to me that the connections among the categories revealed that their separation was somewhat artificial, reflecting more a variation in my designated viewpoint than the activity itself. The categorization was meant to reflect my understanding of the many and varied ways meanings of feminism have been conceptualized—separated by permeable boundaries but not mutually exclusive.

Characteristics of Feminist Principles/Activities

In order to establish a set of criteria for comparison, I identified several characteristics, including both process and content, which I thought these feminist activities most generally had in common:

1. women are the *active* central focus/subject;
2. cooperative group activity is the predominant modus operandi;
3. there is a recognized need for liberation from the oppression of the status quo;
4. issues affecting women are identified, and strategies for action are developed;
5. there is an open, inclusive, accessible, creative, dynamic process between people, among activities, or in relation to ideas; and
6. there is a commitment to respect and include women's ideas, theories, experiences, and action strategies from diverse experiences that appear to be, and sometimes are, in conflict (Linton 1985).

The conceptualization method may be measured by or evaluated against these characteristics. I did not claim a definitive view of feminism; indeed, many possible conceptions of feminism are emerging out of different contexts. I wanted to establish indicators, not hard-and-fast requirements. If the characteristics identified across general current western feminist practice were embodied in the conceptualization methodology, I would know why I thought my work was feminist.

A GROUP CONCEPTUALIZATION METHOD

The three-step specified group conceptualization process described here (Trochim and Linton 1986) simultaneously incorporates conflicting as well as similar ideas, all in relation to each other. The product of this method is a map of ideas (i.e., a concept map), contributed, organized, and interpreted by a specific group of participants. The method can be used by either individuals or groups; however, my interest in the method is in its usefulness to groups of great diversity that have one or more common goals. Concept maps developed by such groups can provide a conceptual framework in which participants can see their aggregated similarities and differences in relation to each other. The map is, in essence, *a picture of the thinking of the group*. This picture can reveal not only what participants know they think but also thinking of which they may not be aware, particularly the thinking that shifts when trying to incorporate diversity. The map can reveal *how* the group thinks as well as indicate on what underlying dimensions members organize their thinking.

In addition, the method provides a relatively nonthreatening initial process for a diverse group that is working together or plans to work on a joint effort, especially a controversial or potentially volatile one. It can reveal a broad view of participants' individual ideas, can flatten out power relations and their influence in the group while each member decides how to organize not only her own but every other member's ideas, and can produce a conceptual framework, an organization of the group's ideas, in which the group can see its organized sameness and difference, be stimulated by its analysis and interpretation, and be free to build its action upon a commonly constructed and understood foundation.

The method's three steps are: expansion, contraction, and interpretation. A computer software program, *The Concept System*,[1] has been developed to process both text and numerical data generated by these three steps. Time for the processing required between the steps depends upon the size of the group and the number of ideas generated for use; the system can accommodate up to 100 ideas. The three steps can usually be accomplished in a one-day session, or they can be broken into two half-day sessions.

Step 1: Expansion

In this step, participants create the conceptual domain; that is, they contribute the ideas that constitute the meaning of the concept to be developed. The group agrees upon a question or statement of what is to be conceptualized. Brainstorming is used in this step in order to encourage participants to let go of strictly organized approaches to the concept. The object here is to get the broadest possible view of what is involved in the concept. Ideas in the form of phrases or short sentences can be brainstormed first individually on paper and then by the group by voice and recorded on a chalkboard or a flip chart. Asking participants to think about the question before the session and setting time limits for the actual brainstorming may be useful. Participants can give their individually written ideas during the group vocal brainstorming session or turn them in on paper after the session. The latter is especially recommended in groups where power differences exist or where sensitive topics might otherwise restrict some individuals' contributions.

Our experience shows that the total number of ideas with which a group is comfortable working seems to be 75 to 100. If more ideas are generated, the group can choose a method to select 75 to 100 from the total. For example, a simple random sample could be done from the total; a committee from the group could be given some guidelines for choosing the ideas; or the committee could choose a core of critical ideas and a random sample could be taken from the rest. Given the spontaneity of the brainstorming process, one other procedure may be needed at this point; that is, some minimal editing of the ideas may be required so they reflect the meaning intended by the contributor. The group can decide if this is needed, and it can be done quickly at the end of the session.

Step 2: Contraction

In this step the group participants organize the ideas. Each group member considers all ideas in relation to the others and has equal influence in determining the final location of ideas on the outcome map. The ideas generated by the brainstorming in Step 1 are printed on cards (usually 3 by 5), and *each* group member is given a stack containing *all* the ideas. Each member then sorts the cards into piles in any way that makes sense to her. With the exception of one or the total number, any number of piles she decides to use is fine. When she finishes sorting, she is given blank cards on which to write a name for each pile, characterizing the meaning of the cards in the pile. She then adds this card to the top of the pile. Each person is given or chooses an identification number to write on the top card of each of her piles to avoid mixing cases. These piles constitute the data used by a statistical procedure, multidimensional scaling, that locates the ideas on the map by searching for the joint occurrence of all possible pairs of ideas among all the members' piles. The final placement of ideas on the map reflects the level of agreement among sorters as to which ideas make sense to put together and which to separate. The closer the ideas appear together on the map, the higher the level of agreement reflected. A cluster analysis procedure further summarizes the data for use in the interpretation step by clustering the individual ideas on the basis of mathematical cutoff points.

The group may also choose to add a third dimension to the meaning of the map by using a simple rating procedure. For example, a list of the ideas can be prepared on which participants rate each one as to level of importance (or on some other criteria chosen by the group) on a scale of one to five. Simple means can then be calculated and added to the map as a height dimension, where "mountains" represent more important ideas.

Step 3: Interpretation

Participants explore the meaning of the map in this final step.[2]

SESSION AGENDA. A basic outline of an agenda for the interpretation session usually includes: a review of the process to date; an explanation of the information to be used in the session; a process to name the clusters; a process to identify the regions of the map; a discussion of relationships of individual ideas, clusters of ideas, and regions; a view of the total map; a discussion of the fit of the map to the group's understanding of its view of the concept; and a discussion of how the group may want to use the conceptual framework.

MATERIALS FOR GROUP USE. Each person receives a copy of the group's map, produced by an overlay of cluster analysis on a multidimensional scaling plot; a list of the ideas by cluster; and a list of all the ideas with their level of importance value, if the group decides to include the rating procedure. Other information that may be given includes each idea's correlation with its own cluster value and various numerical indicators relevant to the clusters' placement, their degree of spread, and their overall level of importance value.

NAMING THE CLUSTERS. Clusters are named by the group in a two-step process. First, small groups (chosen randomly by numbering off) review the ideas in each cluster, discuss cluster meanings, and decide on names for each cluster. Second, in the context of the total group, small groups contribute their suggestions, and the whole group comes to agreement on names for each cluster. Based on the cluster meanings, distance, and direction, the group can then explore the map for regional meaning, underlying dimensions that can represent lines along which the group organizes its thinking, of which it may or may not be aware, and dynamics of movement revealed by placement of ideas and clusters in relation to each other. Further meaning can be found by comparing ideas within one cluster to ideas within another cluster. For example, in a group conceptualization of feminism done in 1984 clusters of ideas about theory and clusters of ideas about practice appeared on opposite sides of the map. Because feminist thought is both derived from practice and feeds practice cyclically, a question raised by this relationship of clusters is, how does this cycle operate? There are other questions that could be asked: Do the theories match the activities? Are there any indications among the ideas themselves that give direction to understanding the interaction of theory and practice? Are there action statements in the theory clusters and vice versa? In addition, ratings of these clusters give priority to the practice clusters that contain action-oriented ideas relating to specific practical needs and demands, rather than the theory clusters that contain more passive ideas. This indicates that participants in this 1984 group appear to value action on specific issues more than thinking about them, including, perhaps, thinking about the *meaning* of those actions. This raises another question: does an emphasis on changing what has been labeled passivity and resulting victimization lead to action on a short-term, short-sighted basis in ways that conflict with long-term, more theoretically stated beliefs?

Clusters can also be explored for amount of spread, an indicator of the degree of agreement about the cluster's meaning. Comparisons of degree of agreement and level of importance of ideas and/or clusters can also be made. Checking the location of outliers, those ideas in a given cluster located far away from the cluster can also stimulate ideas about what and how the group thinks. If it seems useful, the map may also be flipped or rotated for further exploration of its meaning.

GENERAL COMMENTS. This conceptualization process can be used as a research method for purposes of clarifying concepts at the stages of forming theory, of collecting data, of developing basic measurement, and in many other ways. Its flexibility and capacity for adaptation to specific situations is one of its positive characteristics. The fact that, unlike many research methods, the process can easily be understood and used by participants adds to its value.

AN ILLUSTRATION

Twenty-five members of the Feminist Ways of Knowing Seminar at Douglass College, Rutgers University in fall 1985 participated in the three conceptualization steps. The idea of conceptualizing feminism was agreed upon at an early date, the brainstorming (expansion) was done on October 4, organizing the ideas (contraction) took place one week later, and the meaning of the map (interpretation) was discussed on November 22, covering a seven-week time period.

Step 1: Expansion

Brainstorming, which took approximately forty-five minutes, was done individually in writing first and then verbally as a group. All ninety-five ideas contributed were used in the study; forty-six came from the group session, and forty-nine were taken from ideas written by individuals but not offered during the group session. This seeming reluctance of seminar members to speak out could indicate the existence of feelings of unequal power relations in the group. In fact, although this issue was not discussed formally by the group, a few members did subsequently mention to me that they did not contribute their ideas verbally in the group setting for fear of being considered silly, naive, or "politically incorrect."

Step 2: Contraction

During the contraction step, which also took approximately forty-five minutes, each seminar member was given a set of ninety-five cards with the ideas printed on them. The members were asked to sort them into piles that "made sense" to them and to characterize each pile with a short name or description. Any number of piles was acceptable except a single pile or 95 piles; the range was from 3 to 20 piles, with the average number being 7.88 per person. Participants also rated each idea on a scale of one (least) to five (most) according to its level of importance to feminism. These values were simply entered on a separate list of all ninety-five ideas. Some members commented that the sorting exercise alone was provocative and mind-stretching because it forced them to grapple with various relationships among the ideas contributed by the group that they themselves would not have chosen to be part of the conceptual domain (e.g., ideas they had not thought of in relation to feminism). Others reported feeling challenged to understand enough about how they decided which ideas went together in which piles so they could characterize each pile with a name or description.

Step 3: Interpretation

At the interpretation session, which lasted about ninety minutes, I expected to follow this agenda, as far as time would allow:

1. Brief review
2. Name the clusters
   —small groups negotiate a name for each cluster
   —whole group negotiates a name for each cluster
3. Discuss relationships
   —locate clusters on the map
   —check outliers for location, meaning, ambiguity, confusion
   —top to bottom? side to side?
   —underlying dimensions?
   —movement, dynamics?
   —overall?
4. What is missing (meaning)?
5. Revelation of suggestions for directions, strategies, and so on for development of the conceptualization?
6. What makes it feminist? Or perhaps better, how is it consistent with feminist activity/principles?
7. How can it be used?

MATERIALS FOR GROUP USE. The week before, in preparation for the interpretation session, I had distributed a summary of the data analysis. These materials contained the ninety-five ideas listed by the clusters formed as a result of the sorting by group members. Each idea had several numbers following it on the list, each of which had a separate, specific meaning. I included a sheet identifying these numbers and explaining these meanings. I also compiled a list of all the characterizations of each member's piles to provide data for exploring underlying dimensions in the map. In retrospect, given that the procedures and graphics of this particular conceptualization method as well as its potential for investigating, explaining, or contributing to knowledge creation are in the early stages of development, I think my enthusiasm clouded my judgment of what was possible to accomplish in the session, especially given the short amount of time available. I cautioned in my "brief review" that, due to our time constraints, the session should be viewed only as a sample of what the interpreting experience could be; in regular situations, groups actually take hours doing this step. However, it soon became clear that we would not have time to experience even an adequate sample interpretation process, as questions and feelings that I had not anticipated began to spill out. Group members were primarily concerned about what all the numbers listed on the handout materials meant and how the actual computer process had worked to produce the map. Several people commented that they immediately felt distrustful and intimidated when they saw all those numbers.

In my attempt to provide the participants with all the information available for interpretation (i.e., in my view this meant equalizing the power between researcher and participants), and in my rush to accomplish as much of the agenda as possible, more confusion than clarity resulted. I think the idea was too unfamiliar, the context was not developed, and the data was overwhelming. Unfortunately, all this operated to prevent an adequate grasp of the meaning of the map's fundamental components that, in turn, for many, undermined the ultimate understanding of the conceptualization process. Because I believe that one contribution of a feminist approach is to be explicit about researcher impact on the research process, I think it is important to record my own feelings, in addition to the questions and feelings of the group members, which I received both in the session and for several weeks after.

RESEARCHER RESPONSE. From my position as an experienced user of this conceptualization process, I wanted to present it in a *participatory* fashion so that others would understand it from an *experiential* perspective and be stimulated to see how it might be used in their own situations, creating *reciprocity* among all those involved. I also wanted to incorporate the use of statistical procedures and computer technology in what I view as their appropriate role in research, that is, as sets of tools to accomplish specific tasks in a broad search for understanding.

When the questions and feelings about the numbers, the statistical procedures and the computer came up, I had four responses, of which I am aware. One, I felt attacked for using them at all and resentful of that attack; and two, I felt I was failing to keep them, that is, the numbers, in their role and was instead allowing them to occupy a central focus. Furthermore, I felt amazed that group members had such resistance to using numbers as one means to understanding ideas, and last, I was disappointed in myself for not having anticipated that this might be the case. Although my feelings of resentment, failure, and inadequacy were mitigated in retrospect by subsequent discussions with group members who saw very different group dynamics occurring, some of which had nothing to do with the conceptualization process, they certainly influenced the outcome of the session. I should also note that this study provided me with an intense and valuable learning experience, both about this methodology and about the concept of feminism as developed by this group.

GENERAL COMMENTS. For the remainder of the interpretation session, although the group's comments and observations about both content and process responded specifically to some questions on the agenda (see appendix for reference to specific ideas contributed, cluster names, and group commentary about both meaning of the map and the conceptualization process in general, as well as Figures 1 and 2 depicting the actual concept map for the group), time did not allow a thorough interpretation of the meaning of the group's map. Most comments were of a descriptive rather than an analytic nature. Our similarities, differences, conflicts, and so on as a group were not addressed. Time may not have been the only reason: perhaps the composition or the central purpose of the seminar was not conducive to seriously producing the group's conceptualization of feminism; perhaps the several and varying activities of the methodology were too inconsistent with other presentations or too different from the more accepted methods of social scientific inquiry to be considered a serious intellectual endeavor; perhaps my presentation was unclear or did not make sense to participants; perhaps by the time of the interpretation session, the group had established lines of agreement and disagreement among the members that a serious discussion of the meaning of feminism would test, provoke overt dissonance, or otherwise create discomfort or be threatening to or among individuals or subgroups; or perhaps it was a combination of these and/or other reasons.

In any case, I was left feeling incomplete in relation to both substance and process. I do not think there was a good synthesized meaning for the concept chosen by the group to conceptualize, nor was I satisfied that participants had a thorough enough experience to adapt the method to their own use. I was, however, stimulated to think about several ways to improve my presentation and choice of appropriate settings for use of the methodology. First, I must carefully consider the purpose of the group and make sure the concept chosen to work on will actually yield useful information for that purpose. Second, when time is short, I might opt for presenting the methodology in a lecture format, using an example of a previous study. Third, I might eliminate some numerical indicators with groups to whom they are confusing rather than illuminating.[3] And fourth, I must be aware of the difference in my approach and responses when I am a part of the group as opposed to being an outsider.

COMPARISON OF GROUP CONCEPTUALIZATION METHOD TO CHARACTERISTICS OF FEMINIST PRINCIPLES/ACTIVITIES. Although the experience was incomplete, it still provides a valuable way to compare the method to the characteristics of feminist principles/activities presented above (see Characteristics of Feminist Principles section). I should note that some characteristics relate to process and some to content/substance. Therefore, I will cite references to both from the current illustration in this comparison. I found the process and reflections of this group to be especially rich in relation to some characteristics and regret that space does not allow for a more in-depth exploration. However, in an attempt to have the participant voices speak for themselves in order to access the richness, I have chosen to include many phrases contributed by group members when brainstorming responses to feminism.

A potential problem with this comparison is directionality. That is, upon accepting the characteristics as indicators of feminist principles/activities, one could claim that the *method* is not feminist, or one could claim that the *group* is not feminist. However, group contextual factors should provide a framework within which an assessment of directionality can be determined.

Using the method to conceptualize feminism itself, as in this instance, guarantees that women are the "active central focus/subject"; women participated in naming their own reality. Examples of ideas showing this are "way of looking at the world with women as central vision," "the study of what women do and think," and "attempting to identify with all women; being a woman-identified-woman." Although the group setting was predetermined, its generally cooperative spirit was consistent with "cooperative group activity" as "the predominant modus operandi" of feminist practice. Some participants resisted the statistical and computer aspects of the process, those methods that many feminist researchers view as "masculine," "objective," "linear," and so on, and thus unable to explain women's reality. Overcoming this resistance to work with the group could be viewed as a strong indicator of commitment to group cooperation. Examples of specific ideas related to this characteristic are "validating other forms of knowing and communication," "unifying, creative, emotional approach to knowledge rather than an (masculinist) analytically dissecting, categorizing, strictly "objective" approach," and "smash the computer."

Moving from process to content, ideas contributed, such as "rejection of the negative images of women and feminine things that pervade our culture," "commitment to liberation (end of oppression) of women," and "liberation from male domination and patriarchal forms from most intimate and personal to most abstract and structural" reflect agreement with the "recognition of the need for liberation from the oppression of the status quo." Such ideas as "reproductive choice," "end of sexual division of labor," and "end of compulsory heterosexuality" clearly are identified as "issues affecting women," while "ideology and analysis for a political movement which advocates (and directs) political/economic/social control by women and in the interests of women (as a group)," "stop judging by gender," and "take back the night" show directions for the development of "strategies for action."

Although the experience was "an open, inclusive, accessible, creative, dynamic process between people, among activities, and in relation to ideas" for some participants, it seemed to fail to embody part of this characteristic for others. This was especially apparent in the *in*accessibility of the materials that extensively used numerical indicators resulting from statistical procedures. The map itself, however, seemed easily accessible to interpretation, even in the brief time the group had to explore it. The main source of diverse and conflicting ideas seemed to be differing academic disciplines. Some participants noted that they were challenged to grapple with integrating the diverse ideas contributed by group members. Other comments indicated that some participants saw no place in feminism for some ideas contributed. These two perspectives seem to indicate the existence of respect for "women's ideas, theories, experiences, and action strategies from diverse experiences which appear to be in conflict (and sometimes are)" on the part of some, but not all, of the participants.

WHERE DO I GO FROM HERE?

The illustrated use of the group conceptualization method described above was situated in a somewhat theoretical setting. However, the group really had no specified use for the conceptual framework developed. It was more an exercise to demonstrate the use of the method than to produce a meaning of feminism for the group. I think the method could be useful in a purposeful theory-building setting, especially if it were done with a group combining both theoretists and activists. Not only could a general map be constructed but also different clusters could be expanded and contracted to refine further the various regions of the map. One benefit of that approach would be revealing the form and structure of a group's current thinking; another would be pushing that thinking beyond current boundaries, using the map as a base. An additional theory-building use for the method could be to chronicle the meaning of feminism (or other theoretical concepts) either across time by constructing a map annually with the same group or across space by constructing feminism maps with varying groups.

I would like to translate the technique into an action research method. It has already been used by human service agencies as a way of involving entire agency staffs in conceptualizing program mission, goals, problems, and implementation strategies. Resulting maps have been used as a basis for both program planning and evaluation efforts (Trochim and Linton 1984). My particular interest is in making the method available as one of various tools to be used in action research settings, especially those addressing questions important to women. Given the current attack on such hard-won, although limited, benefits for western women as affirmative action, reproductive rights, public funding of service programs from battered women's shelters to child care, building women's solidarity is ever more critical. We must find ways in which differences such as race/ethnicity, class, age, sexual orientation, and ableness can be viewed as diverse resources to be tapped to enrich our joint efforts, not as a source of divisiveness that prevents building our power into an unified force. I hope that this method can be improved and added to other research and action methods to construct common understandings that will contribute to our continuing feminist struggle for social change to benefit all people.

APPENDIX

(See agenda listed under Step 3: Interpretation section)

Naming the Clusters

The interpretation session contained some discussion about the location of ideas on the map. Figure 1 shows the location of each idea both by its identification number and a symbol revealing to which cluster it belongs. For example, idea number 34, in the upper right side of the map, is represented by a square. Locating the symbol in the legend on the lower right side of the map, the square is found to represent the ideas in Cluster 2. The cluster list can then be consulted for the meaning of idea number 34. Other ideas in Cluster 2 can be identified similarly. Naming the ten clusters of ideas depicted on the conceptual map followed. Small groups were formed by random num-

Figure 1. Feminism Conceptualization Map with Idea Identification Numbers.

bering, and each group negotiated a name for each cluster based on the ideas in that cluster. Upon reassembling, the entire group then chose a final set of names for each cluster. For example, the ideas constituting Cluster 2 were:

—new relationship between seer and seen;
—validating other forms of knowing and communication;
—no subject-object split; emotional integrated with rational;
—continuities versus dichotomies; beyond dichotomies or tolerance of contradiction;
—a unifying, creative, emotional approach to knowledge rather than an (masculine) analytically dissecting, categorizing, strictly "objective" approach;
—knocking down old categories and filling up the void;
—not exploiting nature;
—real/utopian vision;
—women's rights.

The five small groups negotiated the following names for Cluster 2:

1. nondualistic ways of knowing;
2. transcending dualism;
3. antidualistic ways of knowing;
4. nonexclusive knowing;
5. knowing.

The name chosen by the entire group for Cluster 2 was: Transcending Dualism. As a result of this process, the final set of cluster names, as shown in Figure 2, was:

Cluster 1: Politics, Power, and Freedom
Cluster 2: Transcending Dualism
Cluster 3: Beyond Gender
Cluster 4: Womanlove
Cluster 5: I Am Womanist
Cluster 6: Going over the Edge
Cluster 7: Woman's Standpoint
Cluster 8: Taking Control of Our Lives
Cluster 9: Revolutionary Vision
Cluster 10: A Womb of One's Own

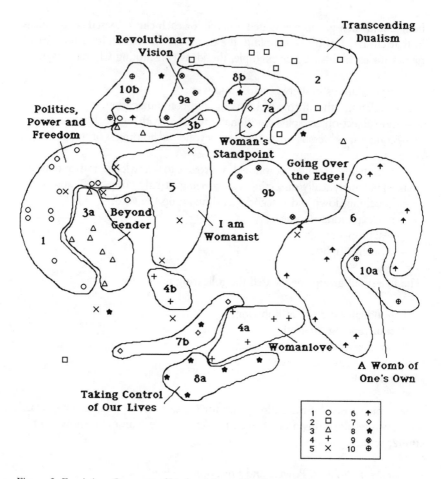

Figure 2. Feminism Conceptualization Map with Cluster Names.

General Observations on the Meaning of the Map

In the discussion about the relationships of ideas and clusters, some examples of initial general observations about the meaning of feminism in the group's thinking as expressed by group members were:

—Politics is generally to the left!

—The visionary/transcendental portion is at the top.

—Body issues are at the bottom while political/theoretical issues are at the top.

—The fact that "Beyond Gender" and "I am Womanist" are next to each other on the map suggests a possible contradiction in the thinking of the group.

—A literal interpretation of the map could mean that Woman-identification is most central to our politics.

Examples of observations about the conceptualization process as expressed by group members included the following:

—One participant commented that although she really liked the parts of the process where the group members interacted face to face, when she viewed the map as a whole, she felt that her ideas had been lost and that the computer had eaten her identity.

—It was suggested that since no serious agenda depended on our classification [interpretation], it was easier for us to agree across our differences/conflicts.

—It was remarked that this process was very similar to the process in many political groups, and we could learn a lot from studying it.

—The process allows for the group to step back from itself and see what is going on in its own process. Although we were all dealing with our own ideas, it could free us from our personal "investment" in our own specific ideas.

—Statistics may hide meanings.

—The interpersonal exchange felt better than the results of the statistical procedures—which felt like an averaging of the meaning and produced a sense of loss of self.

—Mention was made that we had a really good time doing this process, and sometimes this is taken as a sign of not being serious. But one participant thought in this case Creativity was a result of our ludic approach!

The scaled values indicating the level of importance to feminism of each idea were color coded on the map. Some examples of observations about these values by group members were:

—The ideas with higher values were concentrated in the left-hand top space (i.e., Politics, Power, and Freedom; Revolutionary Vision; and Beyond Gender clusters).

—Items with the lowest values were concentrated in the lower right-hand space (i.e., Going Over the Edge and A Womb of One's Own clusters).

—The item with the highest value, "liberation from male domination and patriarchal forms from most intimate and personal to most abstract and structural," seems isolated from its own cluster. Although there is agreement that it is the most important idea in the study, there is less agreement about whether it belongs in Cluster 1, "Politics, Power, and Freedom".

NOTES

I wish to thank Alison Jaggar for her continuing helpful critique and belief in my work; both Alison and Susan Bordo for their guidance in editing; Dorothy Dauglia and Ferris Olin for their generosity in logistical assistance; and to give my very special thanks to Berenice Fisher, Uma Narayan, and Joan Tronto for their friendship and support throughout the seminar.

1. Developed by William M. K. Trochim for IBM compatible and Apple MacIntosh computers; information available by writing him at N137 MVR Hall, Cornell University, Ithaca, New York, 14853.

2. Due to new developments in the computer software, it is now possible to increase the power of the group participants vis-à-vis the researcher in the interpretation step through on-the-spot manipulation of the cluster analysis procedure. This allows the group decision-making power over the choice of the number of clusters they think best represents their ideas. Because the illustration described below was done before this new development, the description of the interpretation step here will follow the original method where the researcher decided on the number of clusters based on statistical critical values.

3. In the new developments in the software mentioned earlier, the numbers used in describing cluster relationships are automatically eliminated by the changes that enable participants to choose the number of clusters.

REFERENCES

Linton, Rhoda. 1983. "In Search of Feminist Research Methodology." Manuscript, Cornell University.
———. 1985. "Conceptualizing Feminism: A Structured Method." Ph.D. diss. Cornell University.
Linton, Rhoda, and Michele Whitham. 1982. "With Mourning, Rage, Empowerment, and Defiance: Women's Pentagon Action 1981." Socialist Review 12 (May–August): 11–36.
Trochim, William M. K., and Rhoda Linton. 1984. "Structured Conceptualization for Evaluation and Planning in the Health Service Organization." Cornell University Program Evaluation Studies Paper Series No. 4.
———. 1986. "Conceptualization for Planning and Evaluation." Evaluation and Program Planning 9 (no. 4): 289–308.

PROCNE'S SONG:
THE TASK OF FEMINIST
LITERARY CRITICISM

Donna Perry

> I feel . . . at the back of my brain, that I can devise a new critical method; something far less stiff and formal. . . . And how, I wonder, could I do it? There must be some simpler, subtler, closer means of writing about books, as about people, could I hit upon it.
>
> Virginia Woolf, *A Writer's Diary*

When Woolf wrote this diary entry in 1931 she had just published an experimental novel, *The Waves;* but when she turned back to her critical writing, her essays on fiction, she felt constrained by the approach and voice considered appropriate for the London *Times,* her frequent publisher. Woolf felt that this approach—aloof, authoritarian, judgmental, objective—separated the reviewer from both author and other readers. She wanted another approach, more subjective and empathic, that would enable her to write in a more personal voice. This same search for voice has prompted many critics in our own time to begin the diverse enterprise called feminist literary criticism.

But feminist literary criticism, as practiced today, is also political. It originates in the critic's recognition that women, whatever their race or color, experience the world differently from men, that their status outside the dominant white male middle-class culture allows (or even compels) them to critique it. Furthermore, the feminist literary critic writes, aware that her ideas form part of an ongoing dialogue about the implications of gender being carried on in various disciplines; thus she borrows freely from the work of feminists in other fields, particularly in the humanities and social sciences, as well as from other feminist literary critics and theorists. The feminist literary critic is committed to changing the world by challenging patriarchal assumptions, judgments, and values, particularly as they affect women. At the same time, feminist literary criticism includes a wide range of ideas, from the radical theorizing of the French feminists who see language as a male construct that excludes women (explored by Arleen Dallery in "Writing The Body: *Écriture Feminine*" in this volume) to the more pragmatic American position that women can be in control of language and express their experiences in it (Gilbert 1979). As Elaine Showalter says, "Feminist criticism has been rather a powerful movement than a unified theory, a community of women with a shared set of concerns but with a complex and resourceful variety of methodological practices and theoretical affiliations" (Showalter 1984:29–30).

This essay will explore the social history and central intellectual outlines of this movement. Keeping in mind that caution must be exercised in generalizing about feminism, and that, as Showalter explains, feminist literary critics embrace a diversity of positions, I will nonetheless attempt to isolate what I view as distinctive characteristics and concerns of feminist literary criticism as practiced in the United States. I will divide this survey into four interrelated sections that explore the following topics: the factors contributing to the development of feminist literary criticism; the implications of reading as a feminist; the notion of the feminist critic's "different voice"; and recent controversies over feminist critical theory and practice.

THE SOCIAL AND INTELLECTUAL CONTEXT OF FEMINIST LITERARY CRITICISM IN THE UNITED STATES

Four factors contributed to the development of feminist literary criticism in the United States: the heightened feminist consciousness sparked by the women's movement; disenchantment with existing critical methodologies, particularly New Criticism and other pseudo-scientific approaches; a growing recognition of the sexism inherent in both the canonization process and the works enshrined in the canon; and a love for and identification with the works of women writers. Although individual critics were shaped by some impulses more than others (some were more politically radical, for example), all shared a sense of belonging to and helping to form a community of readers and writers whose engagement with the text, with language itself, and with one another was based on their common experiences as women under patriarchy.

Of course these were, for the most part, white middle-class heterosexual women's experiences. Since then, members of other groups, particularly black and lesbian women, have criticized the generalizations about "women's" experiences in these early works (Smith 1977; Zimmerman 1981). These women warn of the dangers of establishing a "female tradition" in literature that excludes the experiences of all women, of stressing one oppression (sexism) while ignoring others (racism, heterosexism, classism) in a literary text. They demonstrate that the term "shared concerns" oversimplifies the diversity of women's experiences. As a result of such correctives, most recent feminist scholarship, like Gilbert and Gubar's recent *Norton Anthology of Literature by Women* (1985), has been more mindful of difference, although biases and blindnesses die hard. Also, women of color (lesbian and heterosexual) and white lesbian women have written their own theory and criticism and established journals and presses, like *Kitchen Table* and *Naiad*.

The women's movement of the 1960s made many women—mostly white, middle-class, heterosexual—aware of their outsider status in the dominant patriarchal culture, something lesbians, women in poorer classes, and/or women of color had known all along. Although many feminist critics, certainly many of the pioneers who wrote in the 1970s, were not active in the movement, most were sympathetic and would probably agree with Sandra Gilbert who describes herself as "a kind of proto-feminist" after having read de Beauvoir and Friedan (Gilbert 1979:849–850). Certainly the movement's emphasis on women's experiences and exclusions and subsequent questioning of established values and order laid the groundwork for reexamination of all patriarchal institutions, including academic discourse.

In addition, the movement taught women to turn to other women for support and validation: the consciousness-raising group provided community and replaced the hierarchical male therapist–female patient paradigm. Such sharing, whether we participated in it or not, offered a model for feminist teaching, scholarship, and writing that is more collaborative, less authoritarian than that which has characterized academic work by nonfeminists, both women and men.

As they became conscious of themselves as cultural outsiders, a second awareness grew: many academic women, teachers and students, came to recognize their alienation from much academic discourse: the questions asked and the theories raised seemed limited. Trained in new criticism, which demanded that the literary work be studied in isolation—apart from concerns with author or age or politics—and with a kind of aesthetic disinterestedness, these pioneering women felt frustrated. Like Woolf a generation earlier, they sensed the irrelevance in the questions they were trained to ask of literary texts; but they had yet to find voice or form for writing about the questions that mattered.

Most would have shared Terry Eagleton's analysis of the value of literary criticism in the past:

Literary criticism has been significant only when it engaged with more than literary issues—when, for whatever reason, the "literary" was suddenly foregrounded as the medium of vital concerns deeply rooted in the general intellectual, cultural and political life of an epoch. (Eagleton 1984:107)

Existing theoretical approaches were possible. Elaine Showalter explains that it was natural for feminist criticism to revise and even subvert "related ideologies, especially Marxist aesthetics and structuralism, altering their vocabularies and methods to include the variable of gender." But Showalter rightly concludes that such adaptations prove inadequate for two reasons: "both claim to be sciences of literature, and repudiate the personal, fallible, interpretive reading" (Showalter 1985 [1979]:139). Both approaches struggle for that very objectivity and definitiveness that feminist criticism rejects. More appropriate is Annette Kolodny's call for a "playful pluralism" in feminist criticism, with diverse methodologies (Kolodny 1980a:19).

During its first phase, in the early 1970s, feminist criticism focused on rereading the (usually male) canon. Kate Millet's *Sexual Politics* (1970) laid the groundwork for such enquiry in its exploration of the societal misogyny behind such literary creations as Henry Miller and Norman Mailer's dehumanized women. In a bold speech delivered at the 1971 meeting of the Modern Language Association, Adrienne Rich labeled the feminist revisionary enterprise "an act of survival," essential if women are to come to understand and transform their past powerlessness (Rich 1979 [1972]:35). In *The Resisting Reader: A Feminist Approach to American Fiction* (1978), Judith Fetterley examined the process of "immasculation" the female reader undergoes as she reads such "classic" American texts as "Rip Van Winkle" or *The Great Gatsby* and is coerced by the text into accepting male experience as the norm and sexist assumptions as truth.

This study of women as readers of (usually male) texts soon led into a second, more significant phase according to Showalter: "gynocriticism." Critics began to be concerned with recovering and retracing a lost female literary tradition (Ellman 1968; Moers 1976; Showalter 1977), while others began writing about specific women writers (Kaplan 1985:37). According to Showalter, this phase of feminist criticism concerned itself with many aspects of women writers: "the psychodynamics of female creativity; linguistics and the problem of a female language; the trajectory of the individual or collective female literary career; literary history; and, of course, studies of particular writers and works" (Showalter 1985 [1979]:128).

THE FEMINIST CRITIC AS READER

The feminist critic's reading of the literary text and the feminist biographer's reading of her subject's life suggest that gender can have profound significance in how we interpret reality. Like the feminist reconstructions within philosophy, social science, and natural science discussed elsewhere in this volume, the reconstruction within literary studies suggests that emotion and empathy play vital roles in understanding one's subject and that the practice of the discipline itself (literary criticism, biography) has different goals and functions for the feminist practitioner.

As writers like Jonathan Culler and Patrocinio Schweickart have convincingly demonstrated, women read differently from men (Culler 1982; Schweickart 1986). We may not choose to do so: we may opt to read like men, just as many of us chose (and still choose) to write like men in graduate school and after. Reading is an "interpretive strategy," according to Annette Kolodny, that is "learned, historically determined, and thereby necessarily gender-inflected" (Kolodny 1980b:452). To read like a man is to read like a "white privileged man," as Schweikert explains. This is the reader as insider, the one who shares, for the most part, the values and experiences of the (usually white middle-class male) writer.

Schweickart, like many contemporary feminists, finds a theoretical grounding for her claims about gender in characteristic differences in the child-rearing patterns and socialization of female and male children. Those differences, it has been argued, result in important differences in the female and male experience of the world. Citing the works of Jean Baker Miller, Nancy Chodorow, and Carol Gilligan for support, Schweickart notes their conclusions that "women have more flexible ego boundaries [than men] and define and experience themselves in terms of their affiliations and relationships with others. . . . Women . . . value relationships, and they are most concerned in their dealings with others to negotiate between opposing needs so that the relationship can be maintained." In contrast, men "define themselves through individuation and separation from others," value autonomy over interdependence, and see personal interactions "principally in terms of procedures for arbitrating conflicts between individual rights" (Miller 1976; Chodorow 1978; Gilligan 1982; cited in Schweickart 1986:54–55). In the introduction to *Gender and Reading*, Schweickart and coeditor Elizabeth Flynn acknowledge differences among women in race, class, and sexual orientation but conclude that "some common ground" in experiences and perspectives of women distinguish them from men (Flynn and Schweickart 1986:xiii–xiv).

Yet until recently the only acceptable critical reading, of male and female texts, has been this white middle-class male one. As Elaine Showalter explains, women have been "expected to identify with a masculine experience and perspective, which is presented as the human one" (Showalter 1970: 856). Thus, women students of American literature were pressured by androcentric texts and literary interpreters, their instructors, to identify with the individualistic, independent quests of Huckleberry Finn and Captain Ahab, to accept the Hemingway hero's competitive code as the only valid rule of conduct. We learned that male experiences like hunting, whaling, or scoring sexual conquests were significant; women's experiences of mothering, homemaking, and forming friendships with other women were insignificant because invisible. Male values like competitiveness and individualism were desirable; female nurturance and cooperation were ignored or scorned. Strong women characters, when they appeared, were judged in terms of their relationships with male characters and were evaluated by male standards; successful women writers were labeled manly (e.g., George Eliot, Willa Cather) or eccentric (e.g., Emily Brontë, Emily Dickinson).

This androcentrism leads to what Judith Fetterley calls the "immasculation" of the female reader, whereby "women are taught to think as men, to identify with a male point of view, and to accept as normal and legitimate a male system of values, one of whose central principles is misogyny" (Fetterley 1978:xx). Such "immasculation" has had profound effects. Showalter credits her women students' timidity and insecurity to the fact that they rarely see their "own perceptions and experiences . . . confirmed in literature, or accepted in criticism" (Showalter 1971:857). And Lee Edwards says that she went through her own education, as student and teacher, "as a schizophrenic" who, imagining herself male, tried to make herself over in that image (Edwards 1972:226).

Fetterley claims that the woman reader must resist those impulses to read like a man and thereby "begin the process of exorcising the male mind that has been implanted in us" (Fetterley 1978:xxii). This is not just a matter of valuing women's experience and lives but also legitimating a less detached, more empathic critical approach—one that openly cares for its subjects and has admitted political goals.

According to Jonathan Culler (1982), questions of control (Does the text control the reader, or vice versa?), objectivity (What is in the text, and what is supplied by the reader?), and outcome (Is any reading ultimately satisfying, or are we doomed to feel that every act of reading is inadequate?) are vital concerns of reader-response criticism, concerns that are impersonal, analytic, intent on discriminating between the "objective" and "subjective" dimensions of our readings of texts. "Subjectivity," while acknowledged as an unavoidable element in any reading, is thereby seen as presenting an obstacle to fully adequate interpretation. Although such questions are certainly relevant in a discussion of female readers and male texts, Schweickart suggests that the experience of the female reader encountering a woman's text can offer another paradigm, one suggested by Adrienne Rich's essay "Vesuvius at Home: The Power of Emily Dickinson" (Rich 1979 [1976]).

In this essay, Rich reveals her own response to Dickinson's poetry through three Dickinsonian metaphors: she is "witness" in Dickinson's defense; a visitor to the author herself; and an insect in Dickinson's bedroom, "clinging to the panes of glass, trying to connect" but knowing that she is doomed to failure (Rich 1979 [1976]:158–161; cited in Schweickart 1986:46). Schweickart correctly finds a paradigm for feminist criticism in these three functions: the feminist reader is witness for the woman writer, defending her against patriarchal misreadings; she seeks the woman writer in the text and tries to understand her on her own terms, in her own contexts; and she signals her awareness of her own limitations in coming to understand her subject, since no reading can be definitive (Schweickart 1986:46–47).

This way of reading contrasts significantly with the accepted (male) model for reading as cited above, with its emphasis on control, objectivity, and results. For the feminist critic the act of reading women's texts is personal and political: such readings let her validate the experiences of other women, and thus her own experiences, and expose patriarchal silences and misrepresentations about women's lives. The emphasis here is not on "subjectivity" as an inescapable obstacle to an "objective" understanding of texts but on subjectivity as an intellectual *resource*. For Rich, personal involvement and political intention are deliberate strategies, consciously chosen as means of uncovering that which has been hidden in the traditional (male) readings of texts. As Schweickart reminds us, feminist criticism is "a mode of praxis." Thus,

> The point is not merely to interpret literature in various ways; the point is to *change the world*. We cannot afford to ignore the activity of reading, for it is here that literature is realized as *praxis*. Literature acts on the world by acting on its readers. (1986:39)

Feminists have turned their attention to women's lives as well as their writings; since the early 1970s, many revisionary biographies of women have appeared that share the qualities cited above. They are informed by gender, admittedly subjective, and openly political. As the editors of a recent collection of essays by women writing on women explain the process of feminist biography: "Although it may be tempting originally to fight for distance and impartiality, most contributors relax and let the stages of identification occur" (Asher, DeSalvo, and Ruddick 1984:xxiii).

Such identification is often expressed via the model of parental care. In "Daughters Writing: Toward a Theory of Women's Biography," Bell Gale Chevigny explains that her effort to be accurate about Margaret Fuller "became identical with caring for her"; that, more specifically, she both mothered Fuller and was mothered by her (Chevigny 1984:368–371). Chevigny hypothesizes that, ideally, the biographer becomes a daughter of sorts, learning about her own life by studying that of her subject-mother, without the separation anxiety that Chodorow indicates as accompanying biological mother-daughter relationships (373). Furthermore, as "mother" to her subject, the biographer, like Chevigny, cares for and rescues her subject from misreadings and misunderstandings. But the biographer is not only mother. Using Jane Flax's argument for a dichotomy between maternal nurturance and paternal authority, Chevigny concludes that women writing about women becomes a "transformative activity." Because the woman writer authorizes or empowers her subject, she takes over the paternal role as well as the maternal one of nurturing (373–374).

This approach to biography, which deliberately creates a familial context of mutual nurture and care between author and subject, differs considerably from the notion of one person objectively recording a definitive life of someone else. Of course, not all nonfeminist biographies pretend to the objectivity of definitive lives, any more than all feminist biographies transcend it. But what is striking about those that do (like Ascher 1981; Moglen 1976; Rose 1978; Walker 1983 [1979]) is the offering, as in much feminist "re-visioning," of a parental (most often, maternal) paradigm for the author-subject relationship in place of the traditional concern with objectivity. The underlying assumption for these biographers is that through *caring* we come to know and represent the subject more adequately. Emotional involvement, even love, is an intellectual resource for the understanding, not an impediment to its operations. To Schweickart, Rich, Chevigny, and others, "truth" demands identification, not distance.

DOES THE FEMINIST CRITIC
SPEAK IN A DIFFERENT VOICE?

Has feminist literary theory developed new critical "voices," new ways of addressing the audience? Generalizations are dangerous here because some feminist criticism seems, at first glance at least, to sound like much that has gone before: an argument is put forth and evidence is gathered to buttress the support. The goal is to win over an audience, to destroy alternative positions, to win the debate.

Yet in much feminist criticism, even that appearing in *PMLA (Publications of the Modern Language Association)*, the main refereed journal in literary studies, a difference emerges. Susan Schibanoff's article in a 1986 issue of *PMLA* is a case in point.

In her essay, Schibanoff reads a sixteenth-century poem, Skelton's "Phyllyp Sparowe," as a paradigm for feminist textual deconstruction. Significantly, Schibanoff's essay differs from the impersonal, objective, antithetical, definitive essay that we have come to associate with literary criticism and that I would label a more masculine approach.

How does Schibanoff convince us of the validity of her reading? After making the obligatory nod to previous scholarship on the poem and summarizing their assumptions, she involves us through a series of three hypothetical questions inviting us to read the poem in a new way: "What happens if . . ." we read this way, her way? The body of the essay takes us through such a reading, and the concluding section puts this reading in the context of both the critic's own experience and that of her readers (843):

> The ending of *Phyllyp Sparowe*, this conclusion to which I bring it here, is a mixed moment for me. Jane can be free, but, it seems, only at the expense of her wholeness. And although Skelton allows Jane to feminize her texts, to read and not-read according to her sex, he seems to conclude that her only real power lies in her reading as a typical reader of her community does, that is, like a man. Or does Skelton reach this conclusion? Could he have envisioned that Jane's rudimentary efforts to find a place for herself in what she reads would eventually take the form of an entire interpretive community devoted to achieving the inclusion of women's experiences in the reading of texts? . . . Or could he have foreseen this "atypical" essay, in which I choose to read [the poem] . . . in my own image rather than to not-read it as a goliardic poem and portrait of the male artist? Who does have the last word here? Or does our real freedom as readers lie in the hope that there never is a last word, that it is always possible to make yet one more "addicyon" to the text? (843)

Schibanoff ends with an addition to her text, attempting to answer a question raised by one of her readers, "a consultant specialist for *PMLA*" (844).

Schibanoff's voice is not "personal" in the sense that she directly integrates material from her own life, as some feminist literary critics do (Gilbert 1979; Heilbrun 1979; Platt 1975). What is stiking about Schibanoff's voice and that of many feminist critics lies in their attitudes toward their readers, an attitude that one critic characterizes as "democratic and understated," enjoining the reader to participate in the process of interpretation, resisting the voice of definitive authority (Farrell 1979).

Jean Kennard has correctly pointed out that this transformed attitude toward the audience, which she views as characteristic of much feminist criticism, originally developed, at least in part, as "a result of their being a community of feminist readers" with shared concerns and values (Kennard 1981:145). But today the feminist critic has a larger audience to reach.

By writing for the *PMLA* audience, Schibanoff attempts to make feminist criticism accessible to other than feminist readers, although many association members are feminist. For that reason, her work, and that of others writing in more general critical publications, has particular relevance for feminist scholars in those disciplines where feminist perspectives are suspect, like the social and natural sciences. She clearly recognizes that one function of her work is to educate her readers to a position where they can accept not only her conclusions but also her methodological assumptions. By taking her reader through her own processes of thought (If previous readers were ignoring certain possibilities about the text, what happens if we include them? How might I respond to a reader of my work?), by stressing the individual critic's subjectivity (choosing to read "in my own image"), and by hypothesizing that truth is not absolute but relative, not to be found in one but in many readings ("there never is a last word"), she invites her nonfeminist readers to rethink their own methodologies and assumptions. Her audience is not a hostile camp to be won over to her point of view (the war metaphor is appropriate here) but colleagues with a shared concern for valid readings of a text, whether they read in the same way or not.

A few sentences from a non-feminist critic in the same *PMLA* issue reveals a different approach. From Charles Eric Reeves: "The logic of my claim is implicit in Gombrick's Egyptian examples" and "But, as I have insisted throughout, the term 'literary convention' as it functions in literary inquiry cannot be given a peremptive singularity" (Reeves 1986:807). Despite the use of "I" here, Reeves aspires to an objective, definitive interpretation. His choice of the word "insisted" reveals his attitude toward audience: they are opponents to be won over by force of argument. Schibanoff weaves a tapestry before our eyes; we watch as the pattern of interpretation emerges. Reeves constructs an impregnable fortress; we are dared to attack.

But a more revolutionary voice is being heard in feminist literary criticism: that of the critic writing to and for the converted. As Kennard observes, this critic is conscious of writing to and for a "community of feminist readers" that shares her politics and values (Kennard 1981:144). Her work often opens with a personal statement that grounds the article in the writer's own experience and describes an emotional reaction to the text (143). Sandra Gilbert begins an article by recognizing one characteristic of this type of writing: the opening, personal testimonial that establishes the author's commonality with her audience. She writes: "Like so many other feminist critics, I will begin my commentary on the now well-established conjunction of feminism and criticism with a confessional anecdote" (Gilbert 1979:849). She goes on to trace her own "conversion" to feminist criticism, explaining that she is like other feminist critics (e.g., Kate Millett, Adrienne Rich, Tillie Olsen) who "speak—at least from time to time—like people who must bear witness" to the discovery of women's experiences "in and with literature," experiences significantly different from those of men (850).

One reason that Gilbert and others express their relationship with the literature in quasi-religious terms ("bearing witness") is that they recognize and acknowledge its personal and political significance. They write personally, in the sense that they respond as individuals writing to individuals, but politically, in that they see themselves as representative of other women with similar backgrounds of race, class, sexual orientation. The mode is more conversational than confrontational, more suggestive than argumentative. It is significant that several important documents in feminist literary criticism are conversations or dialogues (Carolyn Heilbrun and Catharine Stimpson in Donovan 1975; Barbara Smith and Beverly Smith in Moraga and Anzaldúa 1981; Cheryl Clarke and others in *Conditions: Nine* 1983). And many acknowledge and cite the contributions of their students to their finished works (Fetterley 1978; Gilbert and Gubar 1979).

RECENT DEBATES: THEORY, DIFFERENCE, AND THE FUTURE OF FEMINIST CRITICISM

Feminist literary scholarship has sparked misunderstanding and animosity from the (usually male) literary establishment. One objection is to the political nature of feminist readings. Robert Patlow's remark that Nina Auerbach's analysis of Charles Dickens's *Dombey and Son* is not "another piece of women's lib propaganda masquerading as literary criticism" is an example of such a response (Patlow 1976; cited in Showalter 1985 [1979]:126). Significantly, political readings, especially of writers like Dickens, are treated seriously when they explore class concerns, as Marxist criticism does; however, when they examine the implications of gender, they are trivialized.

At the same time, as Annette Kolodny has pointed out, feminist criticism has been criticized for lacking "both definition and coherence"; in short, for not being ideological enough (Kolodny 1980a). She notes that this charge, a direct result of the diversity that characterizes our various approaches, is the most explosive of the charges in the minefield we must negotiate to find our place: but she urges that we refuse to be so limited. Advocating a "playful pluralism" of approaches, her vision of feminist criticism's scope and function is radical: "All the feminist is asserting . . . is her own equivalent right to liberate new (and perhaps different) significances from these same texts; and at the same time, her right to choose which features of a text she takes as relevant because she is, after all, asking new and different questions of it" (18). While admitting that most feminist literary critics are structuralists at heart, concerned with finding or designing patterns for what we read, Kolodny nevertheless refuses to so limit the practice of feminist criticism (17).

Kolodny's fear of constructing a theoretical framework for feminist criticism that would be as limiting as that androcentric model it replaces is understandable. Yet her article has drawn criticism from some feminist critics (Gardiner et al. 1982) and sparked an article by Elaine Showalter, "Feminist Criticism in the Wilderness," in which she calls for "theoretical consensus" among the various practitioners of feminist criticism (Showalter 1985 [1981]:246). Envisioning a theory that would be truly woman-centered and independent of earlier male models of analysis, Showalter suggests that the first wave of feminist criticism was a kind of "feminist critique," or feminist rereading and revisioning. She sees feminist literary criticism as in a second stage now, which she calls "gynocriticism" to suggest that it is more woman-centered. This phase, which Showalter argues has taken place in European as well as American literary studies, concerns itself with women's writing as studied from four areas of difference: biological, linguistic, psychological, and cultural (249).

Showalter makes a convincing case for both the importance of literary theory and the appropriateness of a theoretical model based on women's cultural difference by using two essays by Oxford anthropologist Edwin Ardener (1978), "Belief and the Problem of Women" [1972] and "The 'Problem' Revisited" [1975]. These studies suggest that women constitute a "muted group" whose culture and realities overlap with the dominant (white male) group but are not contained within it. This outside area Ardener labels a "wild zone," by which he means one that can be considered as spatially, experimentally, or metaphysically outside the dominant culture, according to Showalter (1985 [1981]:262). As Showalter notes, some feminist critics, like the French feminists Cixous and Wittig or American theorists like Mary Daly and Joanna Russ, claim that this "wild zone" forms the theoretical basis for women's difference (262–263). Whether they see the "wild zone" as the place for the revolutionary women's language, as the French claim, or the site of a matriarchal principle closer to nature and nurturing than the dominant male one, these critics see that space as women's proper home.

I share Showalter's reservations about this radical perspective as forming the sole basis for a theory of women's writing. Women (and men) belong to other muted groups if they are poor, of color, lesbian, or homosexual, for example. Furthermore, they all participate in the dominant white male middle-

and upper-class culture, too. Our difference as writers can only be understood if these complex relationships are taken into account (Showalter 1985 [1981]:264).

Showalter's "gynocriticism" attempts to move women's experiences to the center of our concern. She sees as central to this endeavor the unearthing and valuing of women's diverse traditions; a reexamination of existing literary assumptions, about such things is literary genres, movements, traditions; a recognition of women's writing as "a double-voiced discourse, containing a 'dominant' and a 'muted' story" (Showalter 1985 [1981]:266). She sees this study of women's writing as the proper subject of feminist literary criticism and theory.

I agree with Showalter to a point. But her model for feminist criticism, with its emphasis on the woman writer, downplays the importance of the woman as reader of female and male texts. Kolodny's and Fetterley's work and the recent essays by Schweickart and Schibanoff cited above indicate the importance of defining and presenting feminist readings of all literary texts, as necessary correctives to the androcentric readings currently available. Showalter admits the relevance of such study, but she assigns it to an earlier, less important phase of the feminist critical enterprise. I would add it as an ongoing concern for all of us. I agree with Showalter that women's writing must remain our chief concern, but I want our voices heard as revisionist readers of male texts, too. Thus, while sympathetic to her concept of a "gynocriticism," I would prefer Kolodny's "playful pluralism," at least in this early stage of feminist literary theorizing. Indeed, our very diversity might reflect the breadth of our concerns and the scope of the revision necessary rather than a lack of systematic theory.

What can we conclude about the role of the feminist literary critic, then? Critic Jane Marcus goes to Virginia Woolf's *Between the Acts* (1941) for one metaphor: feminist reader as Procne, the mythological interpreter of her sister's tragic life (Marcus 1984).

To Woolf, Philomel, her tongue cut out by Tereus, her sister's deceitful husband, is the woman writer silenced by patriarchy. Marcus expands the comparison: Procne, Philomel's sister, reads of this suffering in a tapestry that Philomel has woven. Thus, Procne is the feminist critic reading her sister's life and giving her voice. Eventually transformed into a swallow, Procne sings her sister's song of suffering and male silencing (Marcus 1984:79).

But we can carry Marcus's analysis a step further: Procne's righteous anger is translated into action when she kills her son, the image of his father, and gives the body to Tereus, the father, to eat. Symbolically, this is part of the feminist critic's function, too: to react passionately to injustice and act to effect change. Her weapon is not the sword, however, but the pen.

REFERENCES

Ardener, Edwin. 1978. "Belief and the Problem of Women [1972]" and "The 'Problem' Revisited [1975]." In *Perceiving Women,* ed. Shirley Ardener. New York: Halsted Press.

Ascher, Carol. 1981. *Simone de Beauvoir: A Life of Freedom.* Boston: Beacon Press.

Ascher, Carol, Louise DeSalvo, and Sara Ruddick, eds. 1984. *Between Women: Biographers, Novelists, Critics, Teachers and Artists Write about Their Work on Women.* Boston: Beacon Press.

Chevigny, Bell Gale. 1984. "Daughters Writing: Toward a Theory of Women's Biography." In *Between Women,* ed. Carol Ascher, Louise DeSalvo, and Sara Ruddick. Boston: Beacon Press.

Chodorow, Nancy. 1978. *The Reproduction of Mothering: Psychoanalysis and the Sociology of Gender.* Berkeley: University of California Press.

Cixous, Hélène. 1980. "Le Rire de la Meduse [1975]." Trans. as "The Laugh of the Medusa." In *New French Feminisms,* ed. Elaine Marks and Isabella de Courtivron. Amherst: University of Massachusetts Press.

Clarke, Cheryl, et al. 1983. "Conversations and Questions: Black Women on Black Women Writers." *Conditions: Nine* 3, no. 3:88–137.

Culler, Jonathan D. 1982. *On Deconstruction: Theory and Criticism after Structuralism.* Ithaca, N.Y.: Cornell University Press.

Diamond, Arlyn, and Lee Edwards, eds. 1977. *The Authority of Experience.* Amherst: University of Massachusetts Press.

Eagleton, Terry. 1984. *The Function of Criticism.* New York: Schocken Books.

Edwards, Lee. 1972. "Women, Energy, and *Middlemarch.*" *Massachusetts Review* 13:223–238.

Ellman, Mary. 1968. *Thinking About Women.* New York: Harcourt, Brace and World.

Farrell, Thomas J. 1979. "The Female and Male Modes of Rhetoric." *College English* 40, no. 8:909–920.

Fetterley, Judith. 1978. *The Resisting Reader: A Feminist Approach to American Fiction.* Bloomington: Indiana University Press.

Flax, Jane. 1978. "The Conflict Between Nurturance and Autonomy in Mother-Daughter Relationships and Within Feminism." *Feminist Studies* 4:171–189.

Flynn, Elizabeth A., and Patrocinio P. Schweickart, eds. 1986. *Gender and Reading: Essays on Readers, Texts, and Contexts.* Baltimore: Johns Hopkins University Press.

Gardiner, Judith Kegan, et al. 1982. "An Interchange on Feminist Criticism: On 'Dancing Through the Minefield.'" *Feminist Studies* 8:629–675.

Gilbert, Sandra M. 1979. "Life Studies, or, Speech after Long Silence: Feminist Critics Today." *College English* 40:849–863.

Gilbert, Sandra M., and Susan Gubar. 1979. *The Madwoman in the Attic: The Woman Writer and the Nineteenth Century Literary Imagination.* New Haven, Conn.: Yale University Press.

————. 1985. *The Norton Anthology of Literature by Women*. New York: W. W. Norton.

Gilligan, Carol. 1982. *In a Different Voice: Psychological Theory and Women's Development*. Cambridge, Mass.: Harvard University Press.

Heilbrun, Carolyn. 1979. *Reinventing Womanhood*. New York: W. W. Norton.

Heilbrun, Carolyn, and Catharine Stimpson. 1975. "Theories of Feminist Criticism: A Dialogue." In *Feminist Literary Criticism: Explorations in Theory*, ed. Josephine Donovan. Lexington: University Press of Kentucky.

Kaplan, Sydney Janet. 1985. "Varities of Feminist Criticism." In *Making a Difference: Feminist Literary Criticism*, ed. Gayle Greene and Coppelia Kahn. New York: Methuen.

Kennard, Jean E. 1981. "Personally Speaking: Feminist Critics and the Community of Readers." *College English* 43:140–145.

Kolodny, Annette. 1980a. "Dancing through the Minefield: Some Observations on the Theory, Practice and Politics of a Feminist Literary Criticism." *Feminist Studies* 6, no. 1:1–25.

————. 1980b. "A Map for Rereading, or Gender and the Interpretation of Literary Texts." *New Literary History* 11: no. 3:451–467.

Marcus, Jane. 1984. "Still Practice, A/Wrested Alphabet: Toward a Feminist Aesthetic." *Tulsa Studies in Women's Literature* 3, no. 1:79–97.

Miller, Jean Baker. 1976. *Toward a New Psychology of Women*. Boston: Beacon Press.

Millett, Kate. 1970. *Sexual Politics*. Garden City, N.Y.: Doubleday.

Moers, Ellen. 1976. *Literary Women: The Great Writers*. Garden City, N.Y.: Doubleday.

Moglen, Helene. 1976. "Preface," *Charlotte Brontë: The Self Conceived*. New York: W. W. Norton.

Olsen, Tillie. 1978. *Silences*. New York: Delacorte Press.

Patlow, Robert. 1976. "Introduction." *Dickens Studies Annual* 5:xiv–xv.

Platt, Carolyn V. 1975. "How Feminist is *Villette?*" *Women and Literature* 3, no. 1:16–27.

Reeves, Charles Eric. 1986. "'Conveniency to Nature': Literary Art and Arbitrariness." *PMLA* 101, no. 5:798–810.

Rich, Adrienne. 1976. *Of Woman Born: Motherhood as Experience and Institution*. New York: W. W. Norton.

————. 1979. "When We Dead Awaken: Writing as Revision" [*College English* 34, no. 1 (1972)]; and "Vesuvius at Home: The Power of Emily Dickinson" [*Parnassus: Poetry in Review* (Fall–Winter 1976)]. In Adrienne Rich, *On Lies, Secrets, and Silence: Selected Prose 1966–1978*. New York: W. W. Norton.

Rose, Phyllis. 1978. *Woman of Letters: A Life of Virginia Woolf*. New York: Oxford University Press.

Schibanoff, Susan. 1986. "Taking Jane's Cue: *Phyllyp Sparowe* as a Primer for Women Readers." *PMLA* 101, no. 5:832–847.

Schweickart, Patrocinio P. 1986. "Reading Ourselves: Toward a Feminist Theory of Reading." In *Gender and Reading*, ed. Flynn and Schweickart. Baltimore: Johns Hopkins University Press.

Showalter, Elaine. 1970. "Women and the Literary Curriculum." *College English* 32:855–862.

———. 1977. *A Literature of their Own: British Women Novelists from Bronte to Lessing*. Princeton, N.J.: Princeton University Press.

———. 1984. "Women's Time, Women's Space: Writing the History of Feminist Criticism." *Tulsa Studies in Women's Literature* 3 nos. 1, 2:29–43.

———. 1985. "Feminist Criticism in the Wilderness" [*Critical Inquiry* 8, no. 2 (1981):179–205] and "Toward a Feminist Poetics [1979]." In *The New Feminist Criticism*, ed. Elaine Showalter. New York: Pantheon Books.

Smith, Barbara. 1977. "Toward a Black Feminist Criticism." *Conditions: Two* 1, no. 2: 25–44.

Smith, Barbara, and Beverly Smith. 1981. "Across the Kitchen Table: A Sister-to-Sister Dialogue." In *This Bridge Called My Back: Writings by Radical Women of Color*, ed. Cherrié Moraga and Gloria Anzaldúa. New York: Kitchen Table Press.

Walker, Alice. 1983. "In Search of Our Mothers' Gardens" [*Ms.* (May 1974)]; and "Zora Neale Hurston: A Cautionary Tale and a Partisan View" [1977]. In Alice Walker, *In Search of Our Mothers' Gardens*. New York: Harcourt Brace Jovanovich.

Woolf, Virginia. 1968 [1953]. *A Writer's Diary*, ed. Leonard Woolf. New York: New American Library.

Zimmerman, Bonnie. 1981. "What Has Never Been: An Overview of Lesbian Feminist Criticism." *Feminist Studies* 7, no. 3:451–475.

CHINAMERICAN
WOMEN WRITERS:
FOUR FORERUNNERS
OF MAXINE HONG KINGSTON

Amy Ling

Since 1976, when Maxine Hong Kingston's *The Woman Warrior: Memoirs of a Girlhood among Ghosts* won the National Book Critic's Circle Award for the year's best work of nonfiction, it has continued to attract widespread critical and scholarly attention. Asian American, feminist, American literature, and American Studies scholars have all focused their sights on this text and explored its complexity. With elegance and eloquence, Kingston delineates a young girl's struggle to find herself in the gulf between her Chinese mother who filled her girlhood with ghosts and her American world of plastic and neon, between her Chinese-girl shyness when speaking before strangers and her American training to be assertive and to express independent opinions. In addition to bicultural tensions, the girl must mediate within the Chinese culture itself between the extremes of woman as victim and woman as victor. "Better to feed geese than girls," she was often told as a child, and at puberty she was cautioned against the example of her paternal aunt whose name was erased from family history because she bore a child out of wedlock. At the same time, she was urged to model herself after the Chinese Joan of Arc, Fa Mulan, who, disguised as a man, won battles against tyrants and brought peace to the land and honor to her family.

Thus, Kingston portrays in her central character the "double consciousness" with which W. E. B. Du Bois characterized the black American: "this sense of always looking at one's self through the eyes of others, of measuring one's soul by the tape of a world that looks on in amused contempt and pity" (Du Bois 1982:45); it is equally characteristic of women. In fact, all minority people living in a society that maintains its supremacy by devaluing those who are different possess a double consciousness or split awareness: first, awareness of themselves in positive terms; and second, awareness of the negative view in which the dominant society holds them. At one end of the spectrum of colonized people are those who identify almost entirely with the dominant view, accepting and internalizing self-devaluation, for example, mulattoes who pass for white. Internalizing a dominantly negative appraisal of the self leads to difficulty in establishing a coherent and stable sense of self, and, in some cases, to difficulty in valuing the self at all. This is the negative manifestation of double consciousness. Even when a person so reared reaches a level of intellectual maturity and is able to view critically the irrationality and unhealthiness of self-devaluation, the habit of emotional dependence on the mirrors of other people's eyes often still persists and at times still prevails.

At the other end of the spectrum are those who stress their self-worth in violent reaction to and rejection of the dominant view, like the Black Panthers. Young Chinamerican girls, however, conditioned to obey and submit unquestioningly to authority and taught by those authorities to devalue themselves, their sex, and their race must be unusually strong to oppose such powerful forces and assert their own self-worth. Yet this kind of self-affirming independence of vision does exist or may be achieved through effort. This is the positive manifestation of double consciousness: one is aware of the devaluation ascribed by external forces but rejects this evaluation and struggles constantly to disprove it. The majority of people in a colonized condition, however, rarely gel into one extreme or the other; most are in a state of flux between the two poles, a schizophrenic state of psychological tension fluctuating between self-love and self-hatred, depending on the circumstances they find themselves in, or the level of awareness they have attained.

Before they can arrive at a positive concept of self those who are doubly disdained—women and Chinese, for example—must fight through two dominant negative views: first, that of women within the Chinese society, given the weight of Chinese history and ancient custom, and second, that of women and of Chinese held by the white society. Theirs might even be termed a triple consciousness.

Traditionally, Chinese society has been blatantly patriarchal. For eighteen hundred years, it codified women's obedience and submission to the men in their lives—father, husband, son—and stressed female chastity, modesty, and restraint; broke girls' toes and bound their feet for a notion of beauty; sold daughters into slavery in times of hardship; and encouraged and honored widow suicides. Even in China today, despite many advances in women's rights, in the light of the current population control ruling of one child per family, female infanticide has again reared its ugly head.

American society, for its part, has also been traditionally patriarchal and predominantly racist, in practice if not in theory. Although Thomas Jefferson declared the "unalienable rights" of "life, liberty, and the pursuit of happiness" for all, he meant only white men; women and minorities were not important enough to be considered. Only in 1943 was the Chinese Exclusion Act repealed; only in 1949 did California remove miscegenation laws from its books; and only in 1953 were people of Asian origin allowed to become citizens of the United States.

Moreover, Asians in America have had the further complication of contrary popular images fluctuating between the poles of "enemy" and "friend." In the late nineteenth century, which I shall examine in more detail later, the Chinese were considered a yellow menace while the Japanese were thought to be noble. After the bombing of Pearl Harbor, the Japanese became the enemy and the Chinese a long-suffering ally. In the early 1950s, and for two decades thereafter, the Chinese again became enemies, part of the communist threat, while the Japanese received American aid in their rebuilding efforts. Because the last three wars the United States has engaged in have been in Asia, a sense of self taken from outside cues, then, particularly for Asians in America, cannot be anything but contradictory and confused. During World War II, when questioned as to whom he wanted to win the war, one Japanese American spoke for all when he responded: "When your mother and your father are having a fight, do you want them to kill each other? Or do you just want them to stop fighting?" (Houston 1973:46).

Given the present relatively favorable conditions, with civil rights statutes on the books and China officially recognized, Chinamerican women still must combat popular stereotypes that often bar their authentic visibility. The stereotypes of "shy lotus blossom" and "dragon lady" are exotic versions of the madonna/whore dichotomy that has characterized western stereotypes of women in general. The shy lotus blossom is submissive, modest, delicate, soft-spoken; her characteristic pose is to cover her smile and her giggles with her small "ivory" hand. She is totally devoted to self-negating service to her family. But the dragon lady is sinister, evil, cruel, wily, and dangerous. With her skin-tight satin dress slit high up her thighs, she plies her seductive wiles to ensnare men; her six-inch fingernails can both caress and kill.

Both stereotypes are sexual in connotation—the former innocent and virginal, the latter experienced and treacherous, they represent the perspective of white males equating their view of the "exotic" external body with the interior self, and both stereotypes originate in misreadings of cultural signs. For example, covering one's teeth when smiling (or when using a toothpick) in Asian society is simply good manners while long fingernails were once a sign of status and class, for only the wealthy had servants and could afford to disable their hands in this manner. In reality, long nails (or small eyes, for that matter) no more indicated treachery than covering one's teeth indicated modesty. These are external signs from one culture given inappropriate meaning by those of another culture.

Though Kingston makes no direct reference to stereotypes, she does allude to them. Early in the first chapter, Kingston tells us that her book is a sorting-out process, an attempt to "separate what is peculiar to childhood, to poverty, insanities, one family. . . . What is Chinese tradition and what is the movies?" (Kingston 1976:5–6). Movies, cartoons, popular novels have always been the purveyors of stereotypes. In fact, when Richard Mason's popular novel of the 1950s, *The World of Suzy Wong*, was made into a film, it created a new permutation of the shy lotus blossom/dragon lady stereotypes by combining the two into a prostitute with the heart of a child. Kingston alludes to the shy lotus blossom image in the person of the neat, fragile, quiet classmate whom she bullies, pinches, punches, and shockingly torments in a futile attempt to make the girl speak: "You're going to talk. . . . I'm going to make you talk, you sissy girl. . . . You're such a nothing. . . . You are a plant. . . . If you don't talk, you can't have a personality" (Kingston 1976:175–180). Kingston's anger against this classmate is transposed self-hatred, for throughout the book she writes of her own vocal inadequacy: "A dumbness—a shame—still cracks my voice in two, even when I want to say 'hello' casually" (165).

On the other hand, both she and her mother are dragon ladies, in the sense that they were both born in the year of the dragon. In China, the dragon is a good force, the god of rain and the king of animals. Unlike the sinister American dragon lady stereotype, their power and strength are used constructively. In China, the mother is one of 37 graduates from medical school out of an entering class of 112 and fearlessly exorcises a ghost that terrified all the women in the dormitory. In America, she works in the family laundry from 6:30 a.m. until midnight, bears six children after the age of forty-five, and "can carry a hundred pounds of Texas rice up and down stairs" (122). The daughter gets straight As in school and becomes a widely acclaimed author. *The Woman Warrior* sets forth to break stereotypes, to speak the unspeakable, for Kingston begins her book by breaking her mother's injunction, "You must not tell anyone . . . what I am about to tell you." As an adolescent, she refused to cook and broke dishes when she washed them; she enjoyed being called "bad girl" because "isn't a bad girl almost a boy?" (47). In the striking metaphors, the bold honesty, and the rich inventiveness of her book, Kingston displays, contrary to her sense of her inadequate physical voice, the powers of a considerable literary voice.

The Woman Warrior appeared when the time was ripe. The thawing of diplomatic relations with China throughout the 1970s and the civil rights and feminist movements of the 1960s and 1970s had prepared the way for a full appreciation of Kingston's themes and of her double or triple consciousness, but other women of Chinese ancestry publishing in English in the United States (to define my term Chinamerican, encompassing both immigrant and American-born) had expressed this consciousness before her. Most have been forgotten because the time was not right or because scholars had not been interested enough to do the digging. They deserve, however, to be remembered, for they still have much to say to us. In this essay I will trace four of Kingston's literary ancestors.

The earliest of these, and the very first Asian American fiction writers, were two Eurasian sisters: Edith (1865–1914) and Winnifred (1877?–1954). Their mother, Grace Trefusius, was a Chinese adopted by an English family; their father, Edward Eaton, was a landscape painter. The Eatons immigrated from England, where Edith was born, to America, living first in the United States and then settling in Montreal, where Winnifred was born. Both sisters, as adults, moved to the United States. Edith lived briefly in the Midwest and more than ten years in San Francisco and Seattle; Winnifred lived in Chicago, New York, and Los Angeles. Both sisters made their living by writing, and both published under pseudonyms: Edith used Sui Sin Far, narcissus in Cantonese, and Winnifred called herself Onoto Watanna, a Japanese-sounding invention. To understand this divergence in their paths, I must review the history of their period.

Throughout the late nineteenth century and the early decades of the twentieth, anti-Chinese sentiment raged across the United States. Initially contracted by the thousands for the construction of the transcontinental railroad, Chinese workers remaining here were seen as a threat on the labor market and became targets of mass vilification, lynchings, and even murder. From 1882 until 1943, the Chinese Exclusion Act prohibited U.S. entry to all Chinese except teachers, students, merchants, and diplomats. Japan, on the other hand, having won a war against China in 1895 and against Russia in 1904–1905 and with few nationals in the United States to compete for jobs, was highly respected and admired. A dialogue recounted by Edith Eaton in her autobiographical essay, "Leaves from the Mental Portfolio of an Eurasian" (1909) demonstrates clearly the contrasting attitudes toward Chinese and Japanese prevalent in the United States at the turn of the century:

> "Somehow or other I cannot reconcile myself to the thought that the Chinese are humans like ourselves," said Mr. K. (her new employer.)
> "A Chinaman is, in my eyes, more repulsive than a nigger," the town clerk replied.
> "Now the Japanese are different altogether. There is something bright and likeable about those men," added Mr. K. (Far 1909:127)

Though her facial features did not betray her racial background, Edith responded to this conversation by courageously asserting her Chineseness at the expense of her employment.

Her identification with the Chinese had not always been the case, for she remembers recoiling in shock on first seeing Chinese workers: "uncouth specimens of their race, drest in working blouses and pantaloons with queues hanging down their backs" (126). Only after being taunted and insulted by other children for being Chinese did Edith Eaton begin to read about her mother's people and to identify strongly with them. Using the name Sui Sin Far, she was the first person of Chinese ancestry to publish short stories and articles "to fight their battles in the papers." Initially, however, the Chinese also did not recognize her as one of their own and were almost as ignorant and rude as her brief employer, Mr. K.: "save for a few phrases, I am unacquainted with my mother tongue. How, then, can I expect these people to accept me as their own countrywoman? The Americanized Chinamen actually laugh in my face when I tell them that I am one of their race" (131). Nonetheless, after a lifetime of stories and articles in defense of the Chinese published in the leading magazines of the time, Sui Sin Far received the recognition and appreciation of the Chinese community in the form of an engraved memorial stone erected on her tomb in the protestant cemetery in Montreal, reading "Yi bu wong hua" (The righteous person does not forget her country, my translation).

Winnifred, on the other hand, no doubt reasoning that few could differentiate between Japanese and Chinese, chose to be the favored "Oriental." She invented a Japanese pen name, Onoto Watanna, claimed a Japanese noblewoman for a mother, Nagasaki for a birthplace (*Who Was Who* 1974) and created romances set in Japan, generally coupling charming Japanese or Eurasian heroines with American or English heroes. The result of this deception was instant success. Winnifred's nearly two dozen novels were exquisitely printed on predecorated paper with full color illustrations by real Japanese artists. They were reprinted often, translated into European languages, and adapted for the stage; one, *A Japanese Nightingale*, became an opera. Winnifred went on to an exclusive contract with Hearst Publications and later became scriptwriter and editor for Universal Studios and MGM before retiring with her second husband to their cattle ranch in Alberta.

Edith Eaton's collected stories published under the title, *Mrs. Spring Fragrance* (1912) are simply told. Some employ what Jane Tompkins has called "sentimental power" (Tompkins 1985:122–146). For example, in one story, "The Chinese Lily," the character Sui Sin Far gives up her life to save a woman friend; her sisterly self-sacrifice indicates her moral stature. Other stories, more easily appreciated by today's readers, wield gentle irony to protest various injustices: unfair immigration restrictions in "In the Land of the Free," racial prejudice in "Pat and Pan," male chauvinism in "The Wisdom of the New," classism in "The Inferior Woman," to name just a few.

The following passage from the title story provides a sample of Edith

Eaton's use of irony to protest chauvinism, a gentle irony enabling her character to make her point while still maintaining a measure of acceptable decorum. Lively, independent Mrs. Spring Fragrance, on a trip to San Francisco, writes a letter in Chinese-flavored English to her husband in Seattle about a lecture entitled, "America the Protector of China," to which a Caucasian woman friend had taken her:

> It was most exhilarating, and the effect of so much expression of benevolence leads me to beg of you to forget to remember that the barber charges you one dollar for a shave while he humbly submits to the American man a bill of fifteen cents. And murmur no more because your honored elder brother, on a visit to this country, is detained under the roof-tree of this great Government instead of under your own humble roof. Console him with the reflection that he is protected under the wing of the Eagle, the Emblem of Liberty. What is the loss of ten hundred years or ten thousand times ten dollars compared with the happiness of knowing oneself so securely sheltered? All of this I have learned from Mrs. Samuel Smith, who is as brilliant and great of mind as one of your own superior sex. (Far 1912:8–9)

Though thinly veiled in apparent good humor, the ironic tone of this passage is unmistakable, and the barb at the end unexpected. Mrs. Spring Fragrance first reaches out a sympathetic hand to her husband in ethnic unity, for he would immediately understand the empty rhetoric of the patriotic speech, given the treatment he has received from his barber and the indignities his brother has suffered at the hands of immigration officials. Then she cleverly draws a parallel between her friend, thoughtlessly guilty of racial chauvinism, and her husband, thoughtlessly guilty of sexual chauvinism. In other words, as Eaton points out, racism and sexism are rooted in the same error: the belief that one is innately superior to another. As a Chinamerican woman, Mrs. Spring Fragrance must endure both the superior attitudes of white people, even friends, and of Chinamerican men, even a husband.

In Edith Eaton's stories the Chinese in America are presented sympathetically, not as one-dimensional heathens but as multidimensional humans: capable of suffering pain and of inflicting it, of loving and being lovable, of being loyal as well as deceiving. Compared to most contemporaneous writing about Chinese by white authors, analyzed and discussed comprehensively by William Wu in *The Yellow Peril* (1982), or the writing by Christian missionaries as represented by *The Lady of the Lily Feet* (1900) by Helen Clark, stressing the sensational, "heathenish" Chinese practices, Edith Eaton's stories give a balanced view, attempting to portray psychologically realistic conditions. At the same time, white characters in her stories are equally balanced between friends and foes, sympathizers and betrayers; neither are all villains, nor are all saints.

Edith Eaton is most successful, not surprisingly, in presenting the psychological suffering of the Eurasian in a society hostile to one part of her parentage. In "Its Wavering Image," and particularly in the "Story of One White Woman Who Married a Chinese," she reveals through fiction her personal anguish. The white wife of a Chinese, despised by society for her marriage, ignores others' opinions until the birth of her son, whose future in a society torn by racial antagonism makes her anxious: "as he stands between his father and myself, like yet unlike us both, so will he stand in after years between his father's and his mother's people. And if there is no kindliness nor understanding between them, what will my boy's fate be?" (Far 1912:132).

Her autobiographical essay, "Leaves from the Mental Portfolio of an Eurasian," is entirely composed of anecdotes, from the age of four until the time of composition, relating the suffering she experienced as a result of racism, and she did not find it too extreme an analogy to compare her sufferings to those of Jesus: "I have no organic disease, but the strength of my feelings seems to take from me the strength of my body. . . . The doctor says that my heart is unusually large; but in the light of the present I know that the cross of the Eurasian bore too heavily upon my childish shoulders" (Far 1909: 127). Concluding her essay she writes modestly and fearfully of the bridging role she has played as a Eurasian: "I give my right hand to the Occidentals and my left hand to the Orientals, hoping that between them they will not utterly destroy the insignificant connecting link" (132). Only if there is peace between the two groups will she not be pulled apart. Throughout her life, however, all she knew was hatred between Chinese and Caucasians, and throughout the essay run the questions "Why are we what we are? I and my brothers and sisters? Why did God make us to be hooted and stared at?" (127). That she was dogged by ill health throughout her life and died at the relatively early age of forty-nine gives the impression that the emotional and psychological strain of her life's fight against prejudice did indeed take its toll.

Winnifred Eaton, however, in her career as a writer of "Japanese" novels, flourished. Choosing to exploit the dominant racist and sexist stereotypes, Winnifred Eaton filled her novels with exotic trappings: showers of cherry blossoms, colorful kimonos, nightingales in bamboo groves. Her heroines are nearly always in inferior, powerless positions: social outcasts (*A Japanese Nightingale, The Wooing of Wisteria*), orphans (*The Heart of Hyacinth, Sunny-San*), an unwanted stepdaughter (*Love of Azalea*), a blind homeless wood sprite (*Tama*), a geisha in bondage (*The Honorable Miss Moonlight*). Her men, on the other hand, are invariably in positions of power and influence: princes, ministers, architects, and professors. The plot, reiterated in book after book, of the helpless, childlike, charming Japanese or Eurasian female looking up to the powerful white male could not but appeal to white readers.

However, at the same time that Winnifred Eaton is exploiting the stereotypes, she subverts them: the men may be socially prominent, but they are emotionally dependent and weak; and the women, though socially outcast and impoverished, are spirited, independent, and strong. They are survivors. Yuki of *A Japanese Nightingale* successfully and repeatedly cajoles money from her American husband without telling him what she needs it for. Tama, though blind and shunned by society, shows the respected American professor how to survive in the woods. Miss Numé wins the love of Arthur Sinclair from an American beauty and coquette. Azalea pretends to be a Christian convert in order to be paid for singing in the choir. Like their creator, her heroines live by their wits; they are resourceful and strong-willed. They know what they want, and they work to get it by whatever means they possess. Generally their means are personal charm, beauty, ingenuity, and a good-natured sense of humor. While the men in her novels hold the purse strings, the women always hold the men's heart strings. Thus, though her characters may seem to display the surface traits of shy lotus blossoms, they are, in reality, far from that demure, self-negating stereotype.

Although the subversion of sexist and racist stereotypes is subtle in Winnifred Eaton's earlier books, it finds fuller expression in her later novels. In *The Honorable Miss Moonlight* (1912), she protests the degradation of girls training to be geishas: "Some day it would be their lot to step into the place of the ones they emulated, and, in, turn, slaves would hold their trains and masters would exhibit them like animals in public cages" (152). In the same novel, an American officer tells Lord Gongi, the male protagonist, that: "No nation . . . can honorably hold its head erect among civilized nations, no matter what its prowess and power, so long as its women are held in such bondage; so long as its women are bartered and sold, often by their own fathers, husbands and brothers like cattle" (152). Lord Gongi returns from war to discover that his first wife, whom he was forced to divorce because she did not bear him a son in one year, has been reduced to prostitution. He vows to perform "the most knightly act . . . in the history of the nation. It should be his task to effect the abolishment of the Yoshiwara! [the red-light district] . . . This and the revision of the inhuman and barbarous laws governing divorce, should be his lifelong work. He would show the ancestors that there were deeds even more worthy than those of the sword" (153). There are certainly strong feminist statements, clear and uncompromising in their purpose to right/write wrongs done to women. The lord's sword will be used not to demonstrate his manly courage and physical prowess but to restore dignity to women. The measure of his nobility is not his blind adherence to the traditions and conventions of

AMY LING

his class but his empathy for wronged women and his determination to fight an ancient social institution based on female exploitation. In her next-to-last novel, *Cattle* (1924) set in western Canada, Winnifred Eaton focuses entirely on a feminist development of the literal theme of a woman being sold like cattle.

Both Edith and Winnifred Eaton's works and lives reveal an awareness of women's devaluation by both the minority and the majority society. However, they chose different strategies for survival in this hostile environment. Edith stood outside the fortress and made a direct frontal attack on the walls while Winnifred worked to sabotage the foundations of the fortress from within. Although Winnifred did not write of bicultural conflicts, her very career and the contortions and distortions that she went through to become acceptable testify to her awareness of these conflicts. To those who would denounce Winnifred Eaton for allowing a persona to overwhelm her life, for not drawing clearly the line between fact and fiction, we would quote Edith's defense. In "Leaves," Edith argues that if Chinese Eurasians passed themselves off as Japanese Eurasians, the blame should fall on the society that created the atmosphere that made such deception profitable and attractive: "Are not those who compel them to thus cringe more to be blamed then they?"

In the half-century between 1925, when Winnifred Eaton published her last novel and 1976, when Kingston's *The Woman Warrior* appeared, at least a dozen women of Chinese ancestry wrote novels and autobiographies in English and published them in the United States. Of this number, the two books that best express the double consciousness we have been tracing are *Echo of a Cry* (1945) by Mai-mai Sze (1909?–) and *Crossings* (1968) by Chuang Hua (1929–). Both authors were daughters of the few privileged classes allowed to emigrate to the United States before 1943. Mai-mai Sze's father, Alfred Sze (Cornell, class of 1902) was ambassador to England from 1914 to 1927 and thereafter ambassador to the United States; Chuang Hua's father was a surgeon.

Although these two books take slightly different forms—*Echo of a Cry* is pure autobiography while *Crossings* is an autobiographical novel—they carry the same theme: the struggle for a stable sense of self amid changing and conflicting social context. Both authors were taken from China as small children, both introduced to western culture in England, and both settled in the United States, with forays into France. Both are true citizens of the world with all the outward polish, charm, and adaptability attendant on such cosmopolitanism, but both also reveal an inner sense of loss and fragmentation that is the cost of these multiple transplantations, "crossings," or "reshufflings," as Mai-mai Sze calls them.

Echo of a Cry combines humor and wit with existential angst and social awareness as Mai-mai Sze briefly recounts early childhood memories of

China and extensively details the process of anglicization in both England and the United States. Despite a generally cheerful tone, Sze's sense of alienation in western countries also comes through forcefully. She recalls one childhood summer spent with a fervently religious Quaker family who punished her smallest infraction, like a spill at table, by requiring her to put her coins into the China Inland Mission box decorated with a picture of a little Chinese girl who resembled her. Her only comment on this episode is "It irked me no end to throw my pennies away in this manner" (Sze 1945:111), but she does confess that her attitude toward "visiting missionaries was therefore a bit colored by this vexatious penalty." Being forced to contribute to the China mission allied her with her hosts and with missionaries in their patronizing condescension toward her own people, an alliance that made her uncomfortable. Her further remarks about missionaries reveal her discomfort and are quite outspoken for an ambassador's daughter, "They were of all nationalities and all engaged in 'saving the poor heathen.' It may have been my prejudiced imagination, but they seemed much too satisfied with themselves" (111). Her use of quotations around the expression "saving the poor heathen" clearly shows her disaffection from this perspective.

Later, as an undergraduate at Wellesley College, she befriends a black student who is snubbed at a local lunch counter by two white girls who refuse to sit "by any damn nigger!" Mai-mai asks if her new friend objects to the term "colored people," and, when her friend replies that it's better than nigger, Sze continues, "It still implies inferiority of a kind, doesn't it, as if 'colored people' were not up to others? When you think of it, we're all colored except the pure white man. And is there such a thing?" (163). Her realization of the absurdity of distinctions based on skin color and her empathy for the young black woman leads to her recognition of their parallel positions in a society that discriminates on such a flimsy basis, and she concludes, with a sense of community, "We're cause people, whether we like it or not" (165).

On a painting trip to a village in southern France, Mai-mai Sze is regarded as a curiosity and everyone calls her "Chine." However, on a visit to China for the commemoration of her grandmother's one hundredth birthday, she finds herself awkward and un-Chinese: she does not know when or how low to bow, how to address her relatives with the proper respect, in short, what the Chinese customs are. In France, in fact, someone had told her: "'Ah, but you are déracinée—uprooted!' It seemed an apt way of putting it, and irrefutable, if one insisted on pigeonholing by nationality" (173). And because this kind of pigeonholing is still the way of a world not yet prepared to accept international citizens instead of nationals of a single country, Mai-mai Sze ends her lively autobiography with a poignant passage that gives the book its title:

Fervently we have wanted to belong somewhere at the same time that we have often wanted to run away. We reached out for something, and when by chance we grasped it, we often found that it wasn't what we wanted at all. There is one part of us that is always lost and searching. It is an echo of a cry that was a longing for warmth and safety. And through our adolescent fantasies, and however our adult reasoning may disguise it, the search continues. (202)

As though written as a sequel to *Echo of a Cry*, *Crossings* continues the story of a young déracinée Chinese woman from a privileged family, beginning where the earlier book left off. In theme and style a forerunner of Kingston's *The Woman Warrior*, *Crossings* is an experimental novel that requires and rewards the reader's closest attention. The central narrative traces the growth and decline of a love affair between a Chinamerican woman, Fourth Jane, and a Parisian journalist, a narration constantly interrupted by memories of childhood and family, by dreams, nightmares, and images arresting and resonant. Fourth Jane is the middle child of seven in a well-to-do family that transplanted her as a child from China to England and then to the United States. Jane, as an adult, spends time in Paris but makes return visits to New York. In all, there are seven crossings of the ocean and four cultural adjustments. As in the case of Mai-mai Sze, although these travels are culturally enriching, they are personally fragmenting and increase her difficulty in determining a stable sense of self.

Because the many crossings required her adjusting and readjusting to different cultures and languages and perhaps because she is a middle child and female, Jane seeks a stable unchanging center outside herself. The closeness of her parents, their stability and unity, had been one of the main pillars of her life; thus, she feels her own strength and identity threatened when they disagree about Fifth James's marriage with a Caucasian. Jane is shaken when her father relents from his initial objection and goes to the hospital to visit his daughter-in-law and his new grandson. Jane sides with her mother in remaining adamant against the foreign intruder, but she anguishes over this split: "I feel a terrible danger crossing. The oneness of you and Ngmah [mother] you have built so tightly you can't undo overnight just to accommodate them" (196–197). She feels impelled to go away to have her own separateness for a time, for, as she explains, "I don't know who I am outside of the old context and I'm afraid I might not survive the new" (189). Ironically, while away, she herself becomes romantically involved with a Caucasian.

Parallel to the tension created in her by her parents' opposing views is the effect of the conflict between her two countries: China and America. When her French lover unlovingly tells her that she is in exile in America as she is in France and that she should go back to China where she really belongs, she explains that she has loved both China and America, "as two separate but equal realities of my existence," and when it was still possible to return to China, she had looked forward to being able to "live America there as I had lived China in America." But with the civil war in China and the Korean conflict between America and China, she feels herself torn:

> I saw with dread my two lives ebbing. Each additional day of estrangement increased the difficulty of eventual reconciliation, knowing the inflexibility of Chinese pride. In that paralysis I lived in no man's land, having also lost America since the loss of one entailed the loss of the other. Moments I thought of giving up one for the other, I had such longings to make a rumble in the silence. But both parts equally strong canceled out choice. (122)

Even if it were possible to return to China, she decides she could not live there, "I would have to conceal one half of myself. In America I need not hide what I am" (125).

Thus, the forces for fragmentation in Jane have been inexorable. The external forces have included total uprooting and transplanting in foreign climes many times over, with each move leaving a residue, like silt, but each layer not always sitting easily on the layers already there. The internal force pulling Jane apart is the conflict between the drive for independence and the need for love and security, the desire to please her father by being obedient, and therefore good, and the need to be an individual in her own right. That her father has consistently been loving and concerned makes the break all the more difficult. That he declines, suffers, grows old and helpless, at the mercy of surgeons himself, increases the guilt of her pulling away from him.

At the same time that father's tyrannical power and smothering love must be rejected, his strength, talent, adaptability, ingenuity, and pride are what has given the family its very substance, shape, and even life. The cohesive forces that keep Jane whole despite forces pulling her apart are memories of father's strength and the care he took of her: his planting beans in neat rows, his organizing endless rounds of birthday celebrations and family outings, his driving three hours up to her college just to deliver a typewriter. In short, the small but crucial proofs of love, exemplified in the simple tasks and responsibilities of daily life offer purpose and motivation. In *Crossings*, Chuang Hua devotes pages to the details of the increasingly complex dinners that Jane prepares for her lover, from steak to stuffed chicken to Peking duck, because these meals are an expression of love, an affirmation of life in spite of depression, confusion, and loss. After Dyadya's (father's) protracted death, the reader follows Ngmah's (mother's) thorough cleaning of her room. What comes through, forcibly, between the lines, is the woman's determination to conquer her extreme grief by these mundane means. In concentrating all her energies on the most efficient cleaning method, she refuses to give in to despair; she affirms her own life and her usefulness; she snatches a reason, small as it is, for being.

In conclusion, we find in all four of these literary forerunners of Maxine Hong Kingston the expression of a double consciousness that is the inevitable result of being a minority, specifically a Chinese living in a Caucasian society, of having a dual heritage and divided loyalties. Moreover, in certain of these writers, we also find the consciousness of being a powerless female in a male-dominated world. These four women are only a small sample of the dozens of Chinamerican woman who were courageous enough to assert their individuality and the importance of their experience and opinions, to record themselves in words. For a Chinese woman, to write at all was to defy the traditional Chinese dictum that "a woman without talent is a virtuous woman," and, furthermore, it meant disregarding the prejudice that writing is "an unwomanly occupation, destructive of one's moral character, like acting" (Han Suyin 1942:8). At the same time, for Chinese women in the United States to write was to defy the stereotypes that saw them only in mindless bodies—virginal or seductive. For these Chinamerican women writers, the personal was indeed the political. From them, we learn of the persistence and strength of the human spirit to shape beauty out of pain, to fight obstacles, to cross barriers, to break free of containment.

REFERENCES

Chuang Hua. 1968. *Crossings*. New York: Dial Press. Reprint. 1986. Northwestern.

Clark, Helen. 1900. *The Lady of the Lily Feet and Other Tales of Chinatown*. Philadelphia: Griffith & Rowland.

Du Bois, W. E. Burghardt. 1982 [1969]. *The Souls of Black Folk*. New York: Dodd, Mead.

Eaton, Edith. 1914. "Obituary." *New York Times*, April 9.

Garis, Roy. 1928. *Immigration Restriction: A Study of the Opposition to and Regulation of Immigration into the U.S.* New York: Macmillan.

Han Suyin. 1969 [1942]. *Destination Chungking*. London: Mayflower paperback.

Houston, Jeanne Wakatsuki, and James D. Houston. 1973. *Farewell to Manzanar*. Boston: Houghton Mifflin.

Kingston, Maxine Hong. 1976. *The Woman Warrior: Memoirs of a Girlhood Among Ghosts*. New York: Alfred A. Knopf.

Mason, Richard. 1957. *The World of Suzy Wong*. New York: Signet.

Rooney, Doris [Winnifred Eaton's daughter]. "Souvenir from the Past." Manuscript.

Rooney, Paul G. Personal correspondence with Winnifred Eaton's grandson.

Sui Sin Far. 1909. "Leaves from the Mental Portfolio of an Eurasian." *Independent* 66 (January 21):125–132.

———. 1912. *Mrs. Spring Fragrance.* Chicago: A. C. McClurg.

Sung, Betty Lee. 1967. *Mountain of Gold: The Story of the Chinese in America.* New York: Macmillan.

Sze, Mai-mai. 1945. *Echo of a Cry.* New York: Harcourt Brace.

Tompkins, Jane. 1985. *Sensational Designs: The Cultural Work of American Fiction, 1790–1860.* New York: Oxford University Press.

Watanna, Onoto. 1901. *A Japanese Nightingale.* New York: Harper.

———. 1902. *The Wooing of Wisteria.* New York: Harper.

———. 1903. *The Heart of Hyacinth.* New York: Harper.

———. 1904. *The Love of Azalea.* New York: Dodd, Mead.

———. 1910. *Tama.* New York: Harper.

———. 1912. *The Honorable Miss Moonlight.* New York: Harper.

———. 1922. *Sunny-San.* New York: George Doran.

———. 1924. *Cattle.* New York: W. J. Watt.

Wu, William. 1982. *The Yellow Peril: Chinese Americans in American Fiction, 1850–1940.* Hamden, Conn.: Archon Books.

FEMINIST THEORY AND STANDARDIZED TESTING

Phyllis Teitelbaum

"Tests." The very word makes people feel anxious. When the tests are standardized examinations used for admission to college, graduate schools, occupations, or professions, the anxiety level rises. Most people hate to be evaluated or graded, and the standardized format of admissions and professional tests can be particularly upsetting.

But are such examinations discriminatory? Are current standardized tests biased against women and members of minority groups? Although much research has been conducted on this question, no single conception of what it means for a test to be biased has yet emerged, and no clear answer to the question has been found.

In this essay, I will first discuss the question of sex bias in college admissions tests and summarize the consequences of the score differences between men and women on these tests. Next, I will briefly review three of the major approaches currently taken by test publishers in attempts to eliminate sex and racial/ethnic bias from their standardized tests. Finally, I will present a very different approach to the question of whether and how standardized tests may discriminate against women—an analysis of such tests from the perspective of feminist theory.

My goal in applying feminist theory to testing is not merely to present an academic analysis. Rather, it is to provide you, the reader, with an "Aha" experience—a sudden insight into the arbitrariness of the current structure of things and a realization that they could be structured differently. Consider these questions: Why isn't housework counted in the GNP? Why isn't the emotional work that women do in relationships considered "labor" (Jaggar 1984)? Why must science be done in hierarchically-structured laboratories? Why can't a woman do scientific experiments in her home the way she does knitting or macramé (NWSA 1984)? Encountering these ideas in feminist theory has given me the kind of "Aha" experiences that I hope my ideas will elicit in you with respect to testing.

SEX BIAS AND COLLEGE ADMISSIONS TESTS

The issue of sex bias in standardized tests has been brought into sharp focus by a nationwide debate about the differential validity of college admissions tests—the Scholastic Aptitude Test (SAT), the Preliminary Scholastic Aptitude Test/National Merit Scholarship Qualifying Test (PSAT/NMSQT), and the American College Testing Program Assessment Exam (ACT). Phyllis Rosser (1987, 1988) has reviewed the data in this debate. I will summarize her reports here.

According to Rosser (1987:1), on average, women consistently earn higher high school and college grades than men; yet, on average, women receive lower scores than men on all three college admissions examinations. The score difference is particularly large in math; in the SAT math section in 1986 the gap was 50 points on average on a 200–800 point scale. But even in the verbal section of the SAT, where women used to perform better than men, women in 1986 scored on average 11 points lower than men. So the total score difference on the SAT in 1986 was 61 points (50 plus 11). Because women get higher grades in college than men, Rosser (1987:3) argues that the SAT does not accurately predict women's first-year college grades. According to Rosser, "If the SAT predicted equally well for both sexes, girls would score about 20 points higher than the boys, not 61 points lower."

Score differences between women and men on the PSAT/NMSQT and on the ACT are similar to those on the SAT. Rosser (1987:5–16) points out the serious consequences of these score differences:

1. College admissions—Nearly all four-year colleges and universities use SAT or ACT scores in admissions decisions, and many use cut-off scores, particularly for admission to competitive programs (Rosser 1987:4). If women's first-year grades indicate that their test scores ought to be higher than men's, then women applicants are undoubtedly being unfairly rejected in favor of less qualified male applicants.

2. College scholarships—According to Rosser (1987:8), over 750 organizations, including the National Merit Scholarship Corporation, use SAT, PSAT/NMSQT, or ACT scores in selecting scholarship recipients. In 1985–1986, largely as a result of the PSAT/NMSQT score difference, National Merit Finalists were 64 percent male and only 36 percent female (Rosser 1987:11). The

results in other scholarship programs are similar; women lose out on millions of dollars in college scholarships because of a score difference that may be invalid.

3. Entry into "gifted programs"—Rosser (1987:6–8) points out that many academic enrichment programs are offered to students who achieve high scores on the SAT, PSAT/NMSQT, or ACT. Women's lower scores result in their loss of these opportunities as well.

4. Effect on self-perceptions and college choices—There is evidence that students alter their academic self-perceptions and decide where to apply to college partly on the basis of their test scores. If the tests underpredict women's academic abilities, women may not apply to academically demanding colleges for which they are in fact qualified, and their academic self-perceptions may be set too low.

The three tests' publishers currently argue that the tests are not biased against women. The publishers have put forward several explanations for the score differences; these explanations suggest that the scores reflect true differences in women's and men's academic preparation and/or abilities. For example, some argue that women take easier courses in high school and college than men or that women receive higher grades than men because women try harder to please their teachers.

The debate over standardized college admissions tests is important for two reasons: (1) it questions whether these tests are equally valid predictors of academic success for women and for men; (2) it points out what is at stake for women if these tests are biased against them. It is not yet clear whether the score differences are due to bias and, if so, to what kind of bias. Nevertheless, the data Rosser presents on the negative consequences for women of the score differences underscore the importance of investigating whether and how standardized tests are biased against women.

SOME CURRENT APPROACHES TO ELIMINATING SEX AND RACIAL/ETHNIC BIAS IN STANDARDIZED TESTS

For over a decade before the debate about college admission tests, psychometricians and test publishers have been concerned about eliminating sex and racial/ethnic bias from standardized tests. Several approaches have been tried and currently coexist.

Judgmental systems are designed primarily to eliminate sexist and racist language from tests, to make certain that women and minorities are adequately represented in test content, and to evaluate whether some groups of test-takers have been deprived of the opportunity to learn the material in the tests (Tittle 1982). Implicit in these systems is a *content conception* of "bias"—bias is implicitly defined as the inclusion of sexist or racist content, the omission of women and minority groups, and/or the inclusion of material that some groups of test-takers have not had the opportunity to learn. In fact, there is no clear evidence that the test performance of women and minority group members is affected by the use of sexist or racist language. However, there is some anecdotal evidence that women and minority group members perform better on test material about women or minorities. In any case, for ethical and political reasons, many test publishers have established procedures for eliminating the "content" kind of sex and racial/ethnic bias. These judgmental procedures involve review of test questions by knowledgeable, trained people, often themselves women or members of minority groups, sometimes applying guidelines to identify unacceptable questions or point out inadequate representation. Test publishers who use these procedures agree that, simply on the face of it, tests should not reinforce sexism and racism, even if test performance is unaffected (Lockheed 1982). But much remains to be done in this area. For example, Selkow (1984:8–13) reports that, in the seventy-four psychological and educational tests that she studied, females were underrepresented, generally appeared in gender-stereotyped roles, and were shown in fewer different types of vocational and avocational roles than males. Moreover, many of these tests' publishers had no plans to revise the tests; and some asserted that if test-users made changes to reduce sex imbalance, such as changing names or pronouns, the tests would be invalid psychometrically because they would then be different from the versions given in validation studies.

Item bias and *differential item performance* methods of eliminating bias use a *performance conception* of bias. They determine statistically the particular test questions on which various subgroups perform poorly, compared to the majority group. Test publishers may then eliminate these questions from the test. Interestingly, judgmental and item bias/differential item performance methods do not typically identify the same test questions. For example, minority or female students may perform less well than the majority group on a question with innocuous language and content while all groups may perform equally well on a question that contains sexist language or racial stereotypes. Indeed, psychometricians have not yet been able to identify the characteristics of test questions that cause groups to perform differentially on them. Partly for this reason, item bias/differential item performance work is currently in flux. Test publishers have developed different statistics to define item bias. There is as yet no agreement on which statistic should be used to identify biased questions or on how the information should be used in test construction.

Differential validity is a type of test bias in which the test does not predict equally well for different subgroups. For example, Rosser (1987:1–3) uses this *prediction conception* of bias when she argues that college admissions tests are biased against women. Some studies of differential validity have produced contradictory results, even when studying the same test. Because of the importance of accurate prediction in making fair decisions based on test scores, research in this area is continuing.

I have no quarrel with any of these approaches. I myself am a professional test developer at Educational Testing Service (ETS), in charge of training ETS's test developers and editors to apply ETS's judgmental method. Eliminating sexist and racist language and content seems to me essential to produce a test that is fair on its face. And I am following the progress of item bias and differential validity studies with interest. From the practical perspective of the daily construction and utilization of tests, in the world as it is structured today, I believe that we need more work on these and other methods in order to create fairer, less biased tests.

STANDARDIZED TESTING AND ANDROCENTRIC KNOWLEDGE

Most work currently being done on test bias accepts the basic underlying assumptions of standardized testing as given. What would happen if we questioned those assumptions from the perspective of feminist theory? What emerges is a radically different conception of sex bias as something inherent in the assumptions that underlie the content and format of standardized tests.

Feminist theorists have pointed out that what we have been taught to accept as standard scholarship is actually "androcentric" (that is, dominated by or emphasizing masculine interests or point of view). For example, the field called "history" has actually been the history of men; the history of women was simply left out. Similarly, "knowledge" and "science" are not universal; as currently taught, they are an androcentric form of knowing and of doing science.

The androcentric form of knowledge and science accepted in the twentieth-century United States is based on the theory of knowledge called positivism, which includes the following assumptions: scientific explanation should be reductionistic and atomistic, building up a complex entity from its simplest components; one can and should be objective (value-neutral) in scientific research (Jaggar 1983:356); and reason and emotion can be sharply distinguished (Jaggar 1985:2). This form of androcentric knowledge tends to be dualistic and dichotomous, viewing the world in terms of linked opposites: reason-emotion, rational-irrational, subject-object, nurture-nature, mind-body, universal-particular, public-private, and male-female (Jaggar 1985:2). It tends to be quantitative, and it takes the natural sciences as a model for all other academic disciplines. It contains an individualistic conception of humans as separate, isolated individuals who attain knowledge in a solitary, rather than a social, manner (Jaggar 1983:355). In addition, it includes a linear clock-and-calendar sense of time, rather than a circular sense of time (Wilshire 1985), and time is considered very important.

Standardized tests seem clearly to be based on this model of knowledge. In format, they are, as much as psychometricians can make them, positivistic, scientific, objective, value-free, dualistic, quantitative, linear-time-oriented, atomistic, and individualistic. In content, standardized tests reflect the androcentric model of knowledge by excluding everything that does not fit its definition of "knowledge" and everything that cannot be tested in a positivistic format.

First, consider the *format* of standardized tests:

1) The tests are "standardized" in an attempt to make them *objective and value-free*. Psychometricians hope that, if all test-takers receive the same test questions under the same standardized conditions and choose among the same multiple-choice answers, subjectivity and values can be excluded. But can they be? Test questions are written by subjective, value-laden human beings; questions and answer choices reflect the question-writer's upbringing and values, despite the question-writer's attempts to eliminate them. Test-takers bring to the test very different sets of experiences and feelings, and their interpretations of questions will vary accordingly. There is no such thing as a "culture-free" test. Every test question must assume some "common knowledge," and such knowledge is "common" only within a particular subculture of the society.

2) Multiple-choice tests are *dualistic* in that they force a choice between possible answers: one is "right"; the others are "wrong." The model is dichotomous—either/or, with no gradations. But, depending on the question, a graduated model in which several answers are "partly right" may be more appropriate. If test-takers were allowed to explain why they chose a particular "wrong" answer, we might find that it was "right" in some sense, or partly right.

3) Standardized tests are relentlessly *quantitative*. Their goal is to measure a person's knowledge or skill and to sum it up in one number. (This quantification adds to the impression that standardized tests are "objective.") The single score reflects an androcentric fascination with simple quantification and precision; though psychometricians frequently state that test scores are

not precise, test scores are often taken as absolute by both the public and the institutions that use the scores in decision making.

4) Tests are usually timed; thus, measurement of speed, as well as knowledge or skill, often contributes to the final score. This *linear-time-orientation* rewards speed even in subject areas where speed is not important.

5) Standardized tests are *atomistic*. Some systems of planning test content break learning down into "educational objectives" that are as narrow and concrete as possible—for example: "Can write legibly at X words per minute" (Krathwohl 1971:21). Even when such reductionistic educational objectives are not used, tests are inherently atomistic because they try to measure particular knowledge or skills separately from all other knowledge and skills.

6) Standardized tests are *individualistic* and usually competitive. A single person's performance is measured and compared, either with others' performances or with some preset standard of mastery. The ideas of "merit," of ranking, and of comparison are inherent in the testing enterprise. If there were no need or wish to compare individuals, there would be no standardized tests.

But even more important than format is *content:*

1) Standardized tests are in general designed to *test "reason" only*—the kind of knowledge that is included in the androcentric definition of knowledge. Excluded are whole areas of human achievement that contribute to success in school and work but are considered either inappropriate for testing or "untestable" from a practical point of view. Such characteristics and skills as intuition, motivation, self-understanding, conscientiousness, creativity, cooperativeness, supportiveness of others, sensitivity, nurturance, ability to create a pleasant environment, and ability to communicate verbally and nonverbally are excluded from standardized tests. By accepting and reflecting the androcentric model of knowledge, standardized tests reinforce value judgments that consider this model of knowledge more valid and important than other ways of viewing the world. Content that is not tested is judged less valuable than that included on tests.

2) Test publishers attempt to *exclude emotion* from test content. Topics that are very controversial are avoided. Emotions that test-takers feel about the test itself are labeled "test anxiety" and considered a source of "error"; test-takers' "true scores" would be based only on reason, not emotion.

IMPLICATIONS OF THIS ANALYSIS

Is an androcentric, positivistic standardized test necessarily biased against women? The answer you will give depends on whether you believe that women test-takers have completely adopted the generally taught androcentric model of knowledge and that they are as adept in manipulating its concepts as are men. If you believe that women think the way men do, that they share men's "common knowledge," that they are as comfortable with dualistic, quantitative, timed, atomistic, competitive tests as men, and that the content excluded from the tests is no more salient to women than it is to men, then you will conclude that standardized tests are not sex-biased by virtue of their androcentric origins.

If, on the other hand, you believe as I do that women and men perceive the world differently, excel in different areas, and feel comfortable with different test formats, then you will conclude that an androcentric test is bound to be sex-biased. And you need not be a biological determinist to believe that such sex differences exist. It seems to me that the different life experiences that gender creates are sufficient explanation; growing up female is a different social and intellectual experience from growing up male (Farganis 1985:21).

As an example, focus on the testing of particular content only. Assume that, because of socialization or biology or both, women tend to excel in different areas than men. Consider, from your own reading and experience, what those different areas may be for each sex. Then construct a 2 × 2 table with "Tested" and "Not tested" along the top and with "Males tend to excel at" and "Females tend to excel at" down the left-hand side. Which cells are heavily loaded? Which cells are nearly empty? My table looks like this:

Table 1. Content Tested

	Tested	Not tested
Males tend to excel at	Many (eg., math, physics, chemistry)	Few (eg., aggression)
Females tend to excel at	Few (eg., reading)	Many (eg., sensitivity, supportiveness of others, oral communication, cooperativeness, creating a pleasant environment)

You may not agree with the specific examples I have chosen. Nevertheless, you may well find yourself agreeing that many things males in our society excel at *are* tested while many things females excel at are *not* tested. If true, this is probably a direct consequence of the androcentric format and the androcentric choice of content that shape standardized tests, and it demonstrates the sex bias inherent in tests based on an androcentric model of knowledge.

If the content and format of tests are androcentric, this might help to explain situations in which women perform worse than men on standardized tests. The task of taking a standardized test is probably harder for women than it is for men. Women who take an androcentric test may be analogous to people who learned English as a foreign language and who take a test of knowledge (economics, for example) written in English. The task of working in English probably makes the economics test harder for those who learned English as a foreign language than for the native speakers. Similarly, a woman who takes a standardized test must show mastery both of the test's subject matter and of the test's androcentric format and content, which are foreign to her. A man who takes that test has had to master the subject matter, but he probably finds the androcentric format and content familiar and congenial. Women raised in an androcentric school system must master two worlds of knowledge; men must master only one. If the man and the woman know the same amount of economics, the woman may nevertheless receive a lower score than the man because of the test's androcentric format and content. Thus, androcentric tests may not provide a fair comparison between women and men.

WHAT NOW?

It seems that the application of feminist theory leads to a sweeping condemnation of standardized tests as sex-biased. As a professional test developer, employed by a major test publisher, I find it odd to be joining testing's many critics. When I have read the attacks on testing by Ralph Nader's group (Nairn 1980), the National Teachers Association, David Owen (1985), and Phyllis Rosser (1987), my usual response has been, "Some of your criticisms may be valid, but what can you suggest that is better than our current testing methods?" Testing is easy to attack but hard to replace. I must ask myself, then, what would I put in the place of androcentric standardized tests?

One possibility would be to develop a "gynecocentric" (that is, dominated by or emphasizing feminine interests or point of view) method of testing and to include in tests the content areas currently excluded. This is a visionary, even utopian goal, but it is one worth thinking about because it may produce

"Aha" experiences. Clearly, such tests would not be standardized, "objective," or competitive. Scoring, if it existed, would be holistic and qualitative, taking into account both reason and emotion on the part of both the test-taker and the scorer. Psychometrics as we now know it would not apply; no "metrics" (measurement) would be involved. But would we then have a "test" at all? Perhaps not. Perhaps a gynecocentric test is a contradiction in terms; gynecocentric methods might not provide tools that can be used for testing. Perhaps testing is intrinsically androcentric and cannot be transformed into a gynecocentric exercise.

On the other hand, it might be possible to reconceptualize testing in a gynecocentric mode, changing it into something like "unstandardized assessment" or "voluntarily requested group feedback." For example, an elementary school class wishes to know how well it has learned to interact and requests feedback from the teacher of interpersonal skills. She spends time observing the class at work and at play; then, with the class in a participatory circle, she discusses her observations and listens to class members' responses. In the workplace, instead of individual performance appraisals, there are voluntarily requested group evaluations. Colleges alter their admissions procedures to admit cooperating groups of students, rather than competing individuals. Alternatively, in a world that places less emphasis on competitive individualism than we do today, standardized tests as we currently know them might exist only for specific tasks and situations without pretending to measure general capacities (Alison Jaggar, personal communication).

For either a utopian gynecocentric form of testing to emerge or for a reduced use of conventional tests to occur, the individualistic, competitive basis of our society would have to change considerably. Testing is embedded in a culture of schooling and work that is solidly androcentric. To predict an individual's success in a college that teaches only positivistic knowledge to individuals, one needs a predictor that is at least partially individualistic and positivistic.

It seems like a cop-out to say that testing cannot change until knowledge, school, work, and society change. Certainly, tests influence knowledge somewhat when teachers and school systems "teach to the tests." And if tests began using a gynecocentric format and testing such skills as supportiveness and cooperation, tests might tend to increase the value society places on such a format and such skills. To this extent, changing standardized tests could be one way to start changing society. Nevertheless, because tests tend to reflect the social and educational system much more than they shape it, it seems likely that tests will change only after society does.

PHYLLIS TEITELBAUM

NOTE

I am very grateful to Alison Jaggar and the participants in her seminar, "Feminist Ways of Knowing," for their contributions to my thinking on gender issues.

REFERENCES

Diamond, Esther E., and Carol K. Tittle. 1985. "Sex Equity in Testing." In *Handbook for Achieving Sex Equity through Education,* ed. Susan S. Klein. Baltimore: Johns Hopkins University Press.

Farganis, Sondra. 1985. "Social Theory and Feminist Theory: The Need for Dialogue." Manuscript.

Flaugher, Ronald L. 1978. "The Many Definitions of Test Bias." *American Psychologist* 33:671–679.

Jaggar, Alison. 1977. "Political Philosophies of Women's Liberation." In *Feminism and Philosophy,*, ed. Mary Vetterling-Braggin, Frederick A. Elliston, and Jane English. Totowa, N.J.: Littlefield, Adams.

———. 1983. *Feminist Politics and Human Nature.* Totowa, N.J.: Rowman and Allenheld.

———. 1984. "The Feminist Challenge to the Western Political Tradition." The Women's Studies Chair Inaugural Lecture, November 27, Douglass College, Rutgers University, New Brunswick. N.J.

———. 1985. "Feeling and Knowing: Emotion in Feminist Theory." Manuscript.

Krathwohl, David R., and David A. Payne. 1971. "Defining and Assessing Educational Objectives." In *Educational Measurement,* ed. Robert L. Thorndike. Washington, D.C.: American Council on Education.

Lockheed, Marlaine. 1982. "Sex Bias in Aptitude and Achievement Tests Used in Higher Education." In *The Undergraduate Woman: Issues in Educational Equity,* ed. Pamela Perun. New York: Lexington Books.

Nairn, Allan, and Associates. 1980. *The Reign of ETS: The Corporation That Makes Up Minds.* Published by Ralph Nader, Washington, D.C.

NWSA [National Women's Studies Association]. 1984. Sixth Annual Conference and Convention, June 24–28, *"Feminist Science: A Meaningful Concept?"* panel, Ruth Hubbard, Marian Lowe, Rita Arditti, Anne Woodhull, and Evelynn Hammonds. Douglass College, Rutgers University, New Brunswick, N.J.

Owen, David, 1985. *None of the Above: Behind the Myth of Scholastic Aptitude.* Boston: Houghton Mifflin.

Rosser, Phyllis. 1988. "Girls, Boys, and the SAT: Can We Even the Score?" *NEA Today* (special ed.) 6, no. 6 (January):48–53.

Rosser, Phyllis, with the staff of the National Center for Fair and Open Testing. 1987. *Sex Bias in College Admissions Tests: Why Women Lose Out.* 2d ed. Cambridge, Mass.: National Center for Fair and Open Testing (FairTest).

Selkow, Paula. 1984. *Assessing Sex Bias in Testing: A Review of the Issues and Eval-*

uations of 74 Psychological and Educational Tests. Westport, Conn.: Greenwood Press.

Tittle, Carol K. 1982. "Use of Judgmental Methods in Item Bias Studies." In *Handbook of Methods for Detecting Test Bias,* ed. Ronald A. Berk. Baltimore: Johns Hopkins University Press.

Wilshire, Donna. 1985. "Ideas presented for discussion" and "Topics for discussion." Manuscripts prepared for the "Feminist Ways of Knowing Seminar." Douglass College, Rutgers University, New Brunswick, N.J.

THE CHANGER AND THE CHANGED: METHODOLOGICAL REFLECTIONS ON STUDYING JEWISH FEMINISTS

Sherry Gorelick

The Israeli/Palestinian question is a divisive issue indeed in feminism and among Jews generally. It has caused major disturbances at feminist conferences. In fact, the research reported in this essay explores one such confrontation.

Jewish feminists do not agree among themselves on the issue. Opinion ranges from strong support of Israeli government policies to outright opposition to Zionism, with a vast array of views in between. The aim of the study described here is to better understand these divisions. Specifically, I aim to examine the various ways that Jewish feminist relate to the Israeli/Palestinian conflict and to try to see whether differences in the ways that they see the problem are related to patterns in their lives: the experiences that first politicized them, their definitions and experiences of anti-Semitism and feminism, and the rest of their political stance.

My objectives in this research are threefold. *Substantively* I seek to explore and attempt to explain differing positions on the Middle East. *Theoretically* I see my work as contributing to understanding the development of consciousness and the relationships among ethnoreligious, class, and gender consciousness. Operating within the C. Wright Millsian tradition of studying "the intersections of biography and history," I am exploring the relationships between sociohistory and changes in political consciousness. *Methodologically* I am attempting to combine the use of oral history, sociological and social psychological interview, and sociohistorical techniques.

In addition, I am using a reflexive method. My colleague, a clinical psychologist, and I first interviewed each other at the beginning of the study, and we recorded our observations and reactions as we listened to the tapes of interviews with our respondents. I also keep a journal. Thus, we are studying our own changes as part of the research. I am getting feedback from some of my respondents on my interpretations of what they said. This method is exploratory, and, while I am using it, I am trying to explicate its assumptions and evaluate it critically in light of my other studies of methodology.[1] This essay is a discussion of the methodological contradictions of my work and their implications for the development of a feminist methodology and epistemology.

ORIGINS OF THE STUDY

In April 1968, when students in SDS took over Hamilton Hall and four other buildings at Columbia University to protest Columbia's racial policies and its complicity in waging the war against Vietnam, I was a graduate student in sociology. A professor asked me why I was not joining the demonstrators, given my passionate opposition to the war.

"Me?" I said. " I'm just a wishy-washy liberal. Besides, I am a graduate student; those are just a bunch of noisy undergrads." The next day I was sitting in Fayerweather Hall, taking part in an event that would change my life. The experience changed me not only politically and personally but also as a sociologist. I realized that if a survey analyst had done an attitude study the day before I would have given responses to her questionnaire that would not have predicted my behavior on the very nexy day.

I became a radical and then a Marxist and, in a long, painful process, learned a bit about historical materialist methodology. I began a library dissertation on the relationship between Jews and education. Meanwhile I became increasingly uncomfortable as a Jew on the left. In 1971 I wrote a rather confused but urgent twelve-page "Proposal for a Study Collective:"

> I see that other Jewish radicals feel the same mixture of embarrassment and panic as I do when the fact that we are Jewish, or the role of the Jews, or Israel is discussed. . . . [T]he very fact that we can simply, almost dispassionately, hate the U.S. ruling class, but feel especially uncomfortable, or especially angry or confused at Israel's role as Imperialism's flunky, derives from being Jewish and radical. At the very least it makes us angrier—and anger, personal life shows us, bespeaks special involvement.
>
> At the very least we cannot be pro-Arab as we are pro-Viet Cong [*sic*]. But that reluctance of feeling is confusing. . . . We try to push it away. . . . but Israel continues to make headlines—embarrassing

headlines. . . . The Left continues to make support for Palestinian rebels a test of true radicalism. We are uncomfortable.

. . . .

Consequently this is a proposal to study collectively the historical role of the Jews in capitalism and socialism, and what it means—and what it might mean—to be a Jewish radical. I make this proposal because I think the question of Israel will become increasingly unavoidable in the coming years, and because I believe that, comfortable though escape into other forms of radicalism may be, the first duty of a radical is to understand his or her position in the world.

There followed five pages of theoretical issues and questions for study. None of the Jewish radicals I approached in 1971 was even remotely interested. One of them said the whole thing was "too heavy." I returned to my dissertation, which I later turned into a book (Gorelick 1981).

One theme of that book was the conflict among various Jewish groupings over the nature and content of "Jewish culture" and the efforts of the German Jewish bourgeoisie in North America at the turn of the twentieth century to transform Jewish culture into more acceptable channels. In developing this theme, I argued that culture is not a thing and certainly not a *fixed* thing; it is a process. What is loosely called "The Jewish tradition" is not only not a single tradition; it has embodied fierce conflicts.

It took a number of years, however, for me to realize that by focusing my research on the College of the City of New York, I had studied an institution that excluded women for its first 102 years. In 1982 I determined to integrate my personal feminism with my intellectual work, which was (obviously) quite male-defined. I attended the Great Lakes Colleges Association Summer Institute in Women's Studies, on the Feminist Transformation of the Curriculum, and devised an immodest and undoubtedly impossible project of relating gender, ethnic, race, and class consciousness. While I was at the Institute, Israel invaded Lebanon and, coincidently, Letty Cottin Pogrebin published "Anti-Semitism in the Women's Movement" in *Ms.* magazine (1982). Pogrebin's article, which defined anti-Semitism not only in terms of attitudes toward Jews but also of attitudes toward Israel, was highly controversial among Jews as well as non-Jews, and it was to have wide repercussions. When I returned to New York, I became active for the first time as a Jew critical of Israeli governmental policy.

In 1983, I was still trying to define and focus a study of ethnicity, gender, and the formation of political consciousness when, on a visit to a major Canadian city I shall call "Metro," I met "Audrey," a major protagonist in a controversy within that city's feminist movement regarding the definitions of feminism, anti-Semitism, and the Israeli/Palestinian conflict. At her encouragement, I also talked with "Pauline," who disagreed with her. Out of those conversations grew this study.

Only when writing this essay in 1986 did I realize the link between the questions I have been exploring in this research and those raised in that early 1971 proposal. Here are the same concerns with the contradictions of Jews regarding the Middle East and the same desire to understand the deep emotional involvement—only this time the focus is a feminist context as well. And as in my dissertation and book, I am concerned with the different ways of being (and defining being) Jewish, with political conflicts among Jews.

But this later endeavor is not the same because I am not the same and the world is not the same. Like the lives that I am trying to understand through my research, the research itself and my relation to it must be understood dialectically. The consistencies of interest and the changes in the way that I defined those interests are not simply matters of my own burning concerns resulting from my personal biography. They result as well from the fact that I have lived out that biography in a certain historical period under influence of certain social forces and events—the political movements of the 1960s, the 1967 War in Israel/Palestine, the feminist movement, and the various radical, Marxist, and feminist critiques of the social sciences. On another level they are the result of my own interaction with the social networks that I encountered in this historical period, how these events and persons affected me, and how I responded.[2] It is precisely this intersection of biography and history that I am trying to capture in the lives of the women I am studying.

THE SITE

The annual International Women's Day celebration is a major event in the Metro women's community. Between two and three thousand women, children, and men participate in this city of less than three million inhabitants.[3] The 1983 celebration of International Women's Day sparked an unusual amount of conflict. The sharpest point of controversy was a prerally forum on Women's Liberation, Disarmament, and Anti-Imperialism addressed by speakers of the Philippines, Latin America, Eritrea, and Palestine. A Jewish woman stood up and protested, saying that the panel was not sufficiently feminist and that it gave a "one-sided" view of the Israeli/Palestinian issue. She was hissed and booed. Three days later, at the IWD march and rally, marchers were asked to chant for the women of South Africa, Central America, and Palestine. A number of Jewish feminists protested "the introduction [into International Women's Day] of a highly divisive and deeply controversial issue: the Middle East." Accusations were made that the event was anti-Semitic. Letters of protest were written to *Broadside,* the women's newspaper; follow-up meetings were held; friendships were broken. A year earlier in Wisconsin, and a year later in New York City, similar IWD panels were equally explosive. Thus, a study of the conflict in Metro is significant both because of the importance of IWD in the Metro feminist community and because it may reveal insights about similar processes and conflicts throughout North America and in the worldwide women's movement.

METHOD AND CONTRADICTION

Because this, unlike my earlier work, focused directly on the development of consciousness, I had actually to talk and listen to people. But given my earlier experiences, both as a sociologist doing and analyzing survey questionnaires and as the person who found herself sitting-in at Columbia the day after I had denied so vehemently I ever would do such a thing, I doubted the value of doing a traditional interview study. Traditional attitude studies have the disadvantage of statically abstracting expressed beliefs from the changing world in which thought and action are formed and modified. They are mere snapshots of a life that moves in ways too complicated for even a linear movie to portray.

My own experience at Columbia mirrored that of Goldthorpe at a Vauxhall auto plant at Luton, England. Goldthorpe interviewed workers and found them to be apathetic and not at all class conscious, but the workers soon turned the tables, literally, when they rioted for two days, singing militant songs.[4]

There are several reasons for this predictive difficulty of survey questionnaires. Besides the fundamental ability of human subjects to "depass,"[5] that is, to confound prediction (Cooper 1967:5), respondents do not always trust interviewers with their true feelings in politically dangerous areas. Moreover, different situations (interview vs. action) call forth different responses. Microchanges in the situation (new knowledge, communication between formerly isolated people, etc.) bring forth different responses. Finally, questionnaires cannot tap contradictions.

The dominant epistemology in sociology assumes that people "have" attitudes, beliefs, and opinions. These attitudes, beliefs, and opinions are more or less determined by factors such as race, stratificational position, religion, and gender, but they can be influenced and changed by circumstances, "influence leaders," and so on.

Survey researchers attempt to measure these beliefs via questionnaires. A whole science has been built up around the attempt to reduce bias in questionnaires, to get a true reflection of the respondent's opinion. Part of this methodology involves asking roughly the same question in many ways in order to counterbalance bias in the phrasing of the questions and to check for inconsistencies. But that is exactly the problem. The methodology of checking for inconsistencies views inconsistencies as errors—ways in which the questionnaire did not tap the respondent's "true" opinion.

Yet inconsistency is a fact of life. The lack of predictive power of both my imaginary 1968 Columbia questionnaire and Goldthorpe's real questionnaire was based on the fact that *people* are inconsistent.

People are inconsistent continually, in part because they are subject to contradictory forces. At Columbia I was torn between, on the one hand, my abhorrence of the Vietnam War and my frustration at the failure of all previous efforts to change U.S. policy or the complicity of my university in that policy, and, on the other hand, my socialization to respectability, to being a "nice Jewish girl" not a noisy protester. As I observed in my 1971 proposal, Jewish leftists must contend with several potentially opposing forces. On the one hand, leftist movements that set the general framework for their thought and the social network of their lives and political action generally demanded support for the Palestinian cause and criticism of Israel while, on the other, Jewish circles, until recently, generally considered any support for Palestinians and any criticism of Israel anathema. Jewish feminists are similarly caught between the same Jewish circles on the one hand and the drive for international sisterhood on the other.[6]

As one who was trained in survey method, my criticism of it has been that it cannot capture contradiction. Not only the checks for inconsistencies, mentioned above, but the whole mechanics of the dominant methodology, its very epistemology, militate against discovering contradictions. For example, I *could* design a range of opinion, from "Israel has exclusive right to all of Palestine as a Jewish State" to "Palestinians have exclusive right to all of Palestine as a Palestinian State."[7] I could try to locate my respondents along that continuum. But people are not just points on a range; they have conflicting beliefs, coexisting in tension with each other and variously brought out by different circumstances. Contradictory responses would be scored as midpoints, between one extreme of belief and its opposite, or as errors and inconsistencies. I know of no method for scoring (recording, measuring) contradictions as contradictions.

In the present study I try to mitigate those disadvantages of survey design by focusing on women's political responses as brought out by specific circumstances: a "focusing event." The advantage of this method is that it taps people's reflections on a concrete event/action and asks them to relate their actions and reflections to the rest of their political outlook, in this case to their experience with anti-Semitism and their feminism. A "focusing event" forces a woman to express her politics actively: to take a stand. Unlike the expression of attitudes, which can be qualified and nuanced, the real world requires us to act in all its messiness, all its contradiction, and the need for action refuses nuance. Action requires us to simplify political thought in stark terms: you do, or you do not do. And after all, we are interested in consciousness because we want to know what people may do—and why.[8]

METHOD

Between August 1983 and August 1984 I interviewed a "snowball sample"[9] of eighteen women who were protagonists on both sides of the IWD controversy. Total interview time with each woman ranged from three to nine hours. I asked women who identified themselves as "Jewish Leftist Feminists" to give me as complete as possible a history of their involvement and response to the events surrounding IWD 1983 and of their development, from earliest memories, into their present positions as leftists, Jews, and feminists. I have labeled the women who objected to the IWD event "the anti-panel" side, and the women who defended it, the "pro-panel" side. Names have been changed to confer anonymity, and I have used pseudonyms beginning with the letter "A" for women of the anti-panel side and pseudonyms beginning with "P" for women on the pro-panel side.

I had two basic research questions: What differentiated those Jewish women who perceived the event as anti-Semitic from those who did not? And what differentiated those Jewish women who felt and expressed a sense of sisterhood with the Palestinian woman from those who did not? In the course of the research I discovered that these questions and the hypotheses formulated in connection with them were somewhat oversimplified. When I did a very preliminary analysis of the interviews with the first ten women (five "pro-panel" and five "anti-panel"), I discovered that the differences were not as sharp as I had expected.

PRELIMINARY FINDINGS

Let me start with what the two sides had in common. First, *none* of the women I interviewed supported Israeli government policies toward the Palestinians. *All* were very critical of the Israeli establishment; all were opposed to the war in Lebanon and thought that Israel should get out; all were opposed to Israeli settlement of the West Bank. All—even the most Zionist—were concerned about Palestinian rights and believed that there should be some form of Palestinian self-determination. And probably it would be correct to say that all were in favor of a two-state solution to the Palestine problem. This is what they shared.

Where they differed was in their evaluation of the two-state solution. All of the anti-panel group called themselves "Zionists," but they meant something specific by it. They meant critical support for a Jewish state that is not expansionist. For these Zionists, the two-state solution is not only the practical solution; it is just. Because they believed that there are two, equally legitimate national liberation movements in the Middle East, the Jewish and the Palestinian, there should be two states in which each of those peoples expresses its self-determination. One pro-panel woman would agree with that, and a second pro-panel woman would probably agree with reservations.

The pro-panel group were less likely to label themselves with respect to Zionism, and their views were more diverse. For one of them, the two-state solution is the most just solution that is pragmatically possible at the present time, but it is not just because it carves out an Israeli state on territory that of right belongs to Palestinians. For her the only really just solution would be a democratic, secular state, but, given the bloodshed and hatred that have been built up over the years, she did not think that a democratic, secular state is now possible for the forseeable future. The rest were not as explicit about what a just solution would be, but in general I would say that they supported the two-state solution as a regrettable compromise, whereas for the Zionists it would be a just and desirable resolution of the conflict.

This is not a minor difference: at its core is the legitimacy of the ultimate continuance of Israel as a Jewish state. Nevertheless it is important to remember what the two groups of Jewish women shared: opposition to the expansionism of the Israeli state and concern for Palestinian rights.

Second, virtually *all* the women had *some* criticism of the event. All regretted the hissing and booing, and most said that they wished that the panelists had had a more specifically feminist focus. But what they meant by this differed according to how they defined feminism and how they saw its relation to opposition to imperialism. Virtually all my respondents felt that the chanting of slogans at the rally was at best artificial and manipulative. However, the anti-panel group also perceived the series of events as anti-Semitc and deeply dangerous while the pro-panel group saw the events as to some degree flawed but not personally threatening and not anti-Semitic. To some extent they described the same event differently. However they described it, they responded very differently to what they heard and saw.

For example, both sides reported that the Palestinian speaker discussed the imprisonment and torture of Palestinian men and women in Israeli jails. But their willingness to give credence to her reports, or, when willing to give credence to them, the context of meaning into which they placed the torture and imprisonment of Palestinians, differed greatly. One pro-panel woman wrestled with the question of whether, as a Jew, she was complicit in Israeli tortures, which she took to be true, while one anti-panel woman said that she felt that while the reports *might* be true they were mistakenly and unfairly being identified with Zionism. For her, she said, Zionism was simply the Jewish national movement [not necessarily to be held responsible, as a movement, for particular policies of the Israeli government].[10]

Anti-panel women claimed that the Palestinian speaker gave "a straight denunciation of Israel" and said that "the Jews" were her "enemies." The pro-panel women denied that she said that "the Jews" were her "enemies" and claimed instead that she proposed that Israelis and Palestinians should struggle together for a democratic society.

One anti-panel woman thought that the panel's general support for liberation struggles *contradicted* their support for peace and disarmament, whereas for two pro-panel women it was just this *link-up* between the peace movement and the anti-imperialist struggle that made them feel good about the panel.

DIFFERENCES AND COMMONALITIES

Some of the matters in dispute are questions of fact: Did the Palestinian speaker say that her enemies were the Jews, as Aliya reports, or Zionists, as Perla says? Some disagreements are matters of interpretation: If the speaker said that Israelis and Palestinians should struggle together for a new society, as both Perla and Pernice report, did that mean that she was *not* anti-Semitic because she distinguished between the actions of the Israeli state and all Jewry, or did it mean that she *was* anti-Semitic because she was anti-Zionist and the anti-panel women (with one exception) define anti-Zionism as anti-Semitism per se?

But these disagreements do not account for the heat of the battle. At some fundamental level, the difference is one of very deep emotions, in which the anti-panel group felt profoundly and personally threatened by the events, and the pro-panel group did not. The anti-panel women felt that they had become outsiders, that the response of the audience meant that they could not count on sister feminists to defend them as Jews. Hearing the hissing and booing, one woman felt that she had lost "a safe place" in the women's movement.

In part it is because, unlike the pro-panel women, they define opposition to the Jewish State as opposition to Jews that the anti-panel group feels threatened. The anti-panel women, living with the memory of the Nazi holocaust, feel they may need Israel as a refuge. The danger of another holocaust is very real to these women; they live in its shadow. Concentration camp images come up in what seem like the most unrelated contexts.

And yet the two groups cannot be easily divided in terms of their own experience with the Nazi holocaust or other forms of anti-Semitism. Nor do they differ substantially as groups in responding to the question, Do you feel safe as a Jew in Canada? Although one of the most passionately anti-panel women says that eternal vigilance is necessary because Jews are not safe anywhere, she, like many of the other women on both sides, says that she also does not feel safe as a woman subject to male violence or as a human being in a world that might blow up in a *nuclear* holocaust.

Therefore, no one can understand the responses of Ashkenasic Jewish women to Israel and Palestine, whether they be Zionists, anti-Zionists, non-Zionists, or plagued by utter confusion; no one can understand Jewish women's response to living in a white Christian society or to the issue of anti-Semitism in the women's movement—however they define it—without understanding that the holocaust is not past history. It is palpable in their lives. To varying extents, but to some degree, virtually all of them are affected.

But the emotional effects of the holocaust may move Jewish women in opposite directions. For some, the holocaust separates them from their Palestinian sisters, no matter how much they abhor their oppression. Two socialist Zionists did make very serious efforts to link up with PLO women, and some important interchanges were made. But Zionism separates them because they view the continuance and military strength of Israel as a Jewish state as THE essential condition for Jewish survival in a world that could easily produce another holocaust. For the anti-panel group, Palestinian women are only sisters if they affirm the continuance of the Israeli state; otherwise, they are felt to be a threat.

For some pro-panel Jewish women, the Nazi holocaust binds them to their Palestinian sisters. They feel the massacres at Sabra and Shatila and the bombing of Beirut especially deeply because they identify with its victims and feel especially implicated when Israel seems, to some of them, to be doing to Palestinians in the name of Jews what the Nazis did to the Jews.

The political lessons of the holocaust are not clear for Jewish women. Beyond vigilance, beyond a sense of vulnerability, what? They have grown up with terror and with some survivor's guilt but without an analysis except the implied analysis: we are not safe. The fact that we have no common analysis shows most clearly in the fact that the holocaust makes some of us Zionists, others anti-Zionists, and others in between.

METHODOLOGICAL REFLECTIONS

The general patterns discussed in this article are still merely descriptive. The different positions women took regarding the IWD event, or toward the Israeli/Palestinian conflict, are still not explained. Nor can the differences be explained by the standard demographic variables: the two sides are remarkably similar in age, socioeconomic status, and religious background. The mean age of both groups is the same, thirty-seven years; their occupational distribution is similar, professionals and social service workers; and they come from families that range, in similar degree, from lower middle-class shopkeepers to professionals.

I started this study with different views from those I hold now. I began with a concern about what I saw as a "failure of sisterhood": a set of barriers between Jewish and Palestinian women that prevented them from embracing their commonalities. In the process of doing the research, through earnest and at times contentious dialogue with my respondents, with members of the audience at my presentation of these preliminary findings at the National Women's Studies Association Conference in 1984, with my colleague in analyzing that presentation and its aftermath, and finally with members of the Rutgers University Seminar on the Feminist Transformation of the Self and Society, I have come to see that from the point of view of the anti-panel women, the failure of sisterhood must be differently defined.[11] From the point of view of the anti-panel women, the failure of sisterhood was the failure of the panel, the IWD organizers, and the audience to recognize and affirm the importance to these Jewish women of Zionism as a movement and the validity of their charge of anti-Semitism. The validity of that charge depends *partially*, however, on whether one defines opposition to Zionism as anti-Semitism per se. Did anti-Semitism also lie in the efforts to silence the anti-panel women? Were the anti-panel women trying to silence the Palestinian woman? Who was silencing whom?

As I originally defined the study, I wanted to explore why some Jewish women would perceive any opposition to Israeli policies and any support for Palestinian rights as anti-Semitic per se. I did not find such women. Audrey, one of the most outspoken of the anti-panel group, a major protagonist of the opposition to IWD 1983, said she did not know of a single Jewish feminist who was not critical of Israeli government policy toward Palestinians.[12]

The differences turned out to be far more subtle, and the difficulties in explaining them may have something to do with how much these women actually share, despite their fractious disagreements. Indeed some of the difficulty may arise from defining the women into two separate groups: pro- and anti-panel, when their views actually comprise a range, perhaps not even on a single continuum. In fact, having begun with a critique of survey methodology's inability to deal with the contradictory complexities of political attitudes, I discovered that political convictions were more complex that my own original conceptualizations of them.

There *are* two groups, however. The anti-panel women found the event threatening and considered it anti-Semitic, and the pro-panel women did not. But here the coherence ends. Within each group there is a range of belief and feeling about the event and a different set of reasons for feeling critical or pleased with it. Moreover, the women's reactions to IWD did not correlate directly with their general positions on the Middle East.

I had started with the notion that the women's reactions to the IWD event would be related to the ways that they defined feminism and to the centrality of feminism to their politics. I expected that strongly anti-imperialist and anti-racist women, who defined their feminism in conjuction with these issues, would have different reactions to the event or at least different contradictions to deal with.

At first I thought I had found such a correlation, that the anti-panel women were more interested in those issues traditionally defined by North American feminists as important: abortion, equal pay, and so on. But this "pure-and-simple feminism," as it might be called (à la "bread-and-butter unionism") only really characterized one woman. The other anti-panel women had political stances regarding feminism and its relationship to other political conflicts that were more complex than suggested by my initial hypothesis.

Simply evaluating that hypothesis raises some severe methodological problems. First, how do I characterize my respondent's feminism or her general political consciousness, without introducing my own biases of the moment? Especially how do I evaluate what she does *not* say? This problem of what is not said is related to another problem: How can I elicit from respondents a knowledge of processes and determinants of which they themselves are unaware, that is, the unconscious roots of consciousness?

One of our hypotheses was that the Middle East tends to be somewhat projective for diaspora Jews, that we project onto Israel our feelings about the societies in which we live. But how can such a notion be tested? Here the issue of bias in our own interpretations is especially severe.

There are some clues. Silences and shifts of subject may be taken as a form of "unconscious text."[13] For example, Audrey, asked repeatedly to trace the changes in her views regarding the Israeli/Palestinian conflict, kept telling me how she felt as a Jew in Canada—her attention would *not* be redirected to the Palestinian question. A Jewish scholar in New York, trying to be helpful with sources for my then barely-nascent study, kept coming up with names of books, writers, and consultants, regarding anti-Semitism in general. She had to be continually reminded that the focus of my study was views about the Middle East, only to come up with general sources on anti-Semitism again.

But what do these silences and changes of subject mean? That the question of the Middle East is so bound up with Jews' fear of anti-Semitism that they cannot see the issue in the Middle East separately from their own unease in the diaspora? That they *define* the Palestinian question around the Jewish question in the Jewish diaspora? That the Palestinian question only exists for them as a footnote to the existence of Israel as a haven of meaning or safety in a Christian world? That the Israeli/Palestinian question is so complex, confusing, and painful, that they want to avoid thinking or talking about it and must focus instead on a more comprehensible reality: the vagueries and discomforts of Jewish existence in the diaspora? That structural barriers move the Palestinian question from the center of their consciousness? And on the other side, when a woman dismisses very quickly the question of whether any anti-Semitism was involved in the IWD event, does she do so because she has reflected on it deeply, and come to a considered judgment, or is it because the possibility of anti-Semitism in the women's movement is too threatening for her, her fear of the precariousness of the Jewish condition too deep to face?

All of these are conjectures, guesses. How may they be verified, or even clearly seen, if they are part of an "unconscious text" as perceived by a researcher with her own perspectives and, presumably, her own "unconscious text"? The problem is made worse by the fact that there is no public record of these events, and I did not witness them. Great as the problem of bias is in interpreting what the respondents do and say, the danger is even greater in interpreting what they do *not* say. Yet how else can I get at the unconscious base of political consciousness?

In this particular study, I do have two checks against my biases: my colleague and I do not have exactly the same biases, and we are a check on each other; an earlier version of this paper has already been heard by some of my respondents, and I have learned much about my biases from their outraged response. I intend to submit my work to them again.

The second methodological problem involves using a "focusing event" in an attempt to avoid studying attitudes abstracted lifelessly from their contexts. Its advantage is that it roots political consciousness within the living world of the actors. But my methodological solution, to avoid studying abstract beliefs by studying consciousness-in-action in a single event, raises new problems: The single event brings out only one aspect of consciousness, the aspect of the contradiction aroused by that event. To what extent may it be taken to represent the respondent's politics, rather than simply a part of her politics?

For example, had I focused on the confrontation that many anti-panel women had with the Canadian Jewish Congress about placing an ad in their newspaper criticizing Israel for invading Lebanon; the anti-panel women would have been cast as radical defenders of Palestinian rights in the event, and the confrontation would have put *that* aspect of their consciousness into boldest relief. Do we choose two, three, many events? But not all of the respondents would have participated in all of them. Rather we must use the rest of each woman's narrative to compile an understanding of what the particular event we chose did and did not bring out in her and what it meant to her.

Finally, despite our pretensions about studying contradictions in historical context, what I have presented thus far is really a correlational analysis. I have made preliminary forays into whether their positions concerning IWD and the Middle East are related to their definitions of feminism and/or of anti-Semitism, their experiences with anti-Semitism and/or with the Nazi holocaust. Yet such characterizations, even if they were to pan out, are a bit superficial. We want to know the *process* by which each woman has come to define her current politics as she now does: What is pulling her, and what is pushing her? How is she herself doing the pulling and the pushing? And for that we must find some way of characterizing her interaction with history.

To do that requires very intensive and extensive interviewing and therefore guarantees that my sample must remain small. It also requires that I present each woman's story as a coherent whole, rather than chopping up aspects of her interview and talking about the women in groups or categories. But these women are known in their community and were I to tell their stories individually, no amount of disguising names would hide who they were. How can I protect their anonymity, and still tell the story as it probably must be told in order to capture what we need to know? For to understand the emotional roots of the passionate disagreements on the Middle East, we must understand the dialectics of each woman's political development in her interaction with other people and with historical events, and we must understand this complex process in its own integrity.

OBJECTIVITY AS PROCESS

My work challenges three mainstream precepts:

1. Consciousness is fixed; people "have" a consciousness determined by their social circumstances. My work sees consciousness as a *process*, happening within persons in dialectical relation to historical material processes.

2. The (active) observer, seeking objectivity, extracts reality from the

(passive) subject. My answer is complex, seeks the "subject's" participation, and sees me as part of the research-as-process, but it eschews (I think or at least I hope) total relativism. I am the subject as well as the observer; the people I interview are observers as well as respondents. But ultimately I am responsible for my conclusions. That is, I seek feedback, but I, as the writer, have the last word. The last word of the moment, that is.

3. Science is apolitical, value-free, reveals objective reality. I answer that science is political, but it differs from a political tract. Therefore the question/problem is how to deal with the fact that it embodies political values, without trying either to seek and claim an unattainable political neutrality or simply to use people as grist for my own political ideology. How do I do socially (politically) committed science, the *only* alternative to oppressive science mascarading as neutral, and still respect the integrity of respondents who differ from my politics? How do I make them feel that I have done justice to them and still retain my own perspective in its present state of metamorphosis?

These three precepts characterize the paradigm of science presently dominant within the United States and particularly the "natural science model" within the social sciences. This model has not gone unchallenged. It has been criticized from various "sociology of knowledge" viewpoints. According to Tony Tinker (1985), even accounting has its biases. What has become clear, even to some practitioners of the natural sciences, is that every model, every set of questions, and every methodology embodies underlying assumptions regarding the nature of matter, the proper subjects of study, methods, techniques, and strategies of proof, which constitute that particular paradigm's bias (Hubbard 1969; Kuhn 1962). Marxists have pointed out that in a class-divided society, establishment science reflects the perspectives of the dominant class. Feminists have pointed out that in a patriarchal society, establishment science reflects the perspectives of dominant men (Maguire 1987; Smith 1974; Westcott 1979).

Critics of the ideal of value-free science do not propose substituting polemics for science. They do not wish to give up science but merely to give up its false promises. If one admits that society is divided into conflicting classes, races, and genders, that conflict in society is rife, that social position greatly influences social perspective (Merton 1964) and if one cannot frame a question without also thereby expressing a perspective, then all science, knowingly or ignorantly, expresses a perspective.[14]

They why do research? Because commitment to a set of questions does not imply commitment to a *particular* set of answers. Most important, a social scientist, and especially a Marxist feminist, needs a self-critical science, a dialectical science, one that can criticize its own assumptions. Why "especially a Marxist feminist?" Because we want to *know* the world in order to change it and even to adequately *survive* in it, let alone to change it, we cannot afford to be blinded by our own assumptions.

There is a difference between social commitment and bias. Bias involves unacknowledged distortion. Social commitment means that you are seeking knowledge for a purpose—as a tool for opposing oppression—and are self-conscious about it. This purpose requires that you want to know reality with as little distortion as possible. How well you can know that reality depends upon your standpoint—which side you are on of the various systems of oppression. As Nancy Hartsock (1983) makes brilliantly clear in "The Feminist Standpoint: Developing the Ground for a Specifically Feminist Historical Materialism," class and gender oppression cannot be understood from the vantage point of the ruling class or gender.

In "Feminist Critique of Science: A Forward or Backward Move?," Evelyn Fox Keller (1980:343) states that objectivity is not a state-of-being or a characteristic of persons, but a process of seeking "maximal intersubjectivity." She quotes Jean Piaget (1971:34): "Objectivity consists in so fully realizing the countless intrusions of the self in everyday thought and the countless illusions which result—illusions of sense, language, point of view, value, etc.—that the preliminary step to every judgement is the effort to exclude the intrusive self. Realism, on the contrary, consists in ignoring the existence of self and thence regarding one's own perspective as immediately objective and absolute". This "realism" is, paradoxically, of the essence of bias.

In a world of class, ethnic, racial, and gender oppression, however, even the search for "maximal intersubjectivity" is shaped by the fact that people's subjectivity is formed and framed by their position within those oppressions. Oppressors and persons privileged by one or another form of oppression are blinded, structurally, by their own privileges and interests. In addition, the ideology produced daily and historically by oppression is internalized by all of us, in various degrees, forming the geological layers of our unconscious assumptions. Within such a system of multiple oppression, a social scientist must take a stand, from which she gets her standpoint. Objectivity, then, is *not* finding some "midpoint" between sexism and feminism, class oppression and social equality, racism and equality. Even in a conflict between two oppressed groups, objectivity is not necessarily finding some midpoint; objectivity is the imperfect and continuous process of revealing and removing unconscious bias so that we can reach greater and greater clarity.

To study a question as fraught with passion and politics as anti-Semitism in the feminist movement and the Israeli/Palestinian conflict, it is especially necessary to confront—not to avoid or expunge but to confront—the biases in one's own perspective, to be in continual dialogue with oneself. One does not do this alone, however. That raises the second dogma of the dominant paradigm in sociology: mutual untouchability or "disinterestedness." In the dominant paradigm the scientist merely studies but takes care not to influence the subject, and the scientist is, of course, not influenced by the subject.

Aaron Cicourel (1964) and others have pointed out what a mess of realities must be papered over to maintain the illusion that the subject does not influence the scientist and vice versa. Some feminist methodologists have tried to turn this difficulty into a virtue, arguing that in order for the subjects of study to be *subjects*, that is not objectified, they *must* influence the scientist: the process of research *must* be an interaction (Cook and Fonow 1986; Oakley 1981; Mies 1983; Reinharz 1979; Graham and Rawlings 1980.) In my own work, my interaction with my respondents has made clear to me the profundity of mutual influence that is simply, inevitably, part of doing research.

The point of my interactive approach is that it is part of the process of seeking objectivity by allowing for correctives by my respondents. Interaction with respondents in a work like this—getting feedback—is not simply a moral imperative, part of the "feminist ethics" of feminist methodology as some of the feminist methodologists would have it. It is part of the process of seeking objectivity.

The problem for my respondents is that in the long run I will have the last word, and their participation, including their disagreements with my interpretation, will end up, willy nilly, being grist for my mill. The problem for me is that if, in the process of interaction, I am overly sensitive to criticism, my mill may be ground down by the effort to please everybody in a situation where emotions run so high that reconciliation is extremely difficult. Seeking my standpoint on shifting sands, I can wind up with *no* point of view, making no contribution, and adding to the confusion.

The social patterns of interaction have their own biases: The fact that I have been confronted more often by the side with which I initially disagreed than by the one with which I agreed has undoubtedly also affected my work. And it has been shaped in ways that I do not even know, by the interactions that have *not* happened: this debate, and my own interaction patterns, have taken place among Jewish feminists. My method may have "given voice" to their concerns. But to my great regret the Palestinian voice is silent in this study. Absent too, is any corrective toward objectivity their influence might have provided.[15] But this is not the end, and the struggle continues.

In the dominant paradigm nothing must change but the independent variables being studied and the dependent variables being changed by those independent variables. All else is "held constant." But in social history everything changes: the respondents, the observer, and history itself. We shall have to create a social science adequate for a world of change.

APPENDIX: SAMPLE AND QUESTIONNAIRE

This study was based on a "snowball" or "reputational" sample. I began with Audrey, the woman who first told me about IWD, and Pauline, the woman she had recommended as someone who had disagreed with her. I asked them for a list of names of women who had been involved in the controversy. I then asked each woman I interviewed for a list of names. When a woman's name appeared on several lists I made special efforts include her. I thus constructed a "snowball sample." There turned out to be considerable agreement on who the major protagonists were.

Five women came from Audrey's Jewish feminist group, a group that formed in response to the IWD controversy and has continued since. In addition I recruited respondents at the first organizational meeting for the following year's IWD celebration. I took care to interview women from both sides of the controversy. I only included women who were willing to identify themselves as "Jewish, leftist, feminists," leaving them to define these terms for themselves.

My reasons for restricting the sample to "Jewish leftist feminists" were several:

1. I was primarily interested in the conflict within the feminist movement;

2. I was interested in what I perceived to be particular (potential) contradictions;

3. Given my intensive method, and its exploratory nature, I knew that my sample must be small. I therefore decided to control the variability in the independent variables. Obviously similar studies should be done among male Jewish leftists, and nonfeminist, nonleftist Jewish women.

In all I interviewed eighteen women, twelve initially and six later. Interviews involved two sessions, and in some cases three sessions, each lasting a minimum of one and a half hours. The total interview time with each woman ranged from three hours to nine hours. One case had to be dropped because the respondent found the retelling of her past too painful and declined the second interview. Another was dropped because the woman had too little participation in the events for her interview to be meaningful. The analysis presented here is based on the first ten usable interviews; the tapes of the remaining six have yet to be transcribed.

At first my colleague and I devised a questionnaire based on our initial interviews with each other and our preliminary hypotheses. After the first few interviews we decided to shift to a more informal style. We began our interviews with the following statement:

What we're doing is, we're interviewing Jewish leftist feminists, and what we want to do is find out how people came to this consciousness starting from early memories and early kinds of life experiences, and how this identification functions to establish their relationship to things that are going on now. We are aware that people are changing and this identification can be stronger in some areas than in some others and can lean to either contradictions or confusions—we don't expect things to be definite, and we are as interested in the contradictions and confusions and doubts as we are in the history and the current relationship to what's going on now.

So: you can start any place you want.

The purpose of this diffuse and inelegant introduction was to put the re-spondent at her ease. Usually she would laugh or gasp. But then, rather than being forced into the external priority ordering of a questionnaire, she could start at any point most comfortable for her. In fact, different women started at different points. I told each woman that in addition I wanted as complete a recounting she could give me of the IWD events and her participation in them. And I also told her that I had a checklist of questions so that, if in the natural course of her conversation she did not cover certain points, I would ask her direct questions.

This method insured that in the interest of trust between us strangers, there was no *formal* standardization of the interview; but there was comparability, in that I made sure that the same issues/questions would be covered. Because the women are roughly the same age, their lives have covered roughly the same world history, but of course their personal experiences—even their awareness—of that history differs greatly.

NOTES

In writing this article I have been enormously helped by the support and critical advice of Lourdes Benería, Susan Bordo, Joan Burstyn, Maarten de Kadt, Beverly Elkan, Ju-dith Gerson, Alison Jaggar, Ynestra King, Laurie McDade, Helen McDonald, Dalia Sachs, and the members of the Jaggar Seminar on the Feminist Reconstruction of the Self and Society. None of them is responsible, of course, for my stubbornness or for whatever foolishness remains.

I am grateful to the Rutgers University Research Council for grants in 1983, 1985, and 1987 providing financial support for the research reported herein.

I dedicate this essay to Laurie McDade, March 1, 1950–June 15, 1988: Bright, bright sunshine, gone too soon.

1. For professional reasons having to do with her clinical practice my colleague prefers to remain anonymous. That is why her name does not appear here, and why I use the pronoun "I" in the text. In reality we designed the study together and collaborated in all phases, except that I did all the actual interviewing and all the writing.

2. David Cooper (1967) argues that in a "science of persons" rather than things, we must "trace what a person does with what is done to him [sic]; what he makes of what he is made of."

3. By contrast, New York City, with a population of over seven million and a surrounding area totaling around thirty million, draws less than three hundred people to its IWD celebrations.

4. When Goldthorpe's report was circulated among the workers, along with news of the megaprofits being sent back to General Motors in the United States, those same apathetic, relatively satisfied workers rioted. According to the *Times*, "Thousands of workers streamed out of the shops and gathered on the factory yard. They besieged the management offices, calling for the managers to come out, singing the 'Red Flag' and shouting to 'String them up.'" (Reported by Andre Gorz 1972:480.)

5. Cooper (1967:5) refers to the capacity of human action "depassing all determination of what it is to be and proceeding perhaps in the direction opposite to that expected." Unlike objects, human subjects may take into account the researcher's prediction and modify their behavior accordingly.

6. It is obviously misleading to speak of "the left," "Jewish circles," or even "international sisterhood" as though (1) these were real entities, (2) each embodied a consensus, and (3) these supposed group "positions" were unchanging. On the contrary, there is considerable diversity on "the left," within feminism, and among Jews. Indeed, that diversity and those changes in political stance are precisely the focus of this research.

7. Describing this hypothetical "range" has turned out to exemplify the complexity—and nonlinearity—of the issue. I began this purely heuristic example with one range, wound up with two, and continually had to adjust the poles of the supposed continua.

8. I do not mean to imply that actions are unambiguous. As Alison Jaggar pointed out to me, action "is always open to a multitude of interpretations, and may have different meanings for actors who in one sense are 'doing the same thing.'" That is, actions may speak louder than words, but it is not always clear what they are saying.

9. See appendix.

10. The bracketed phrase is a paraphrase of a rather complex portion of the interview, and, while I hope that it accurately captures my respondent's meaning, it is possible that there is a failure of nuance in my attempt. I intend to check it out with her at a later stage of the research.

11. One of my respondents was in the audience of my NWSA presentation, and, with my permission, taped the session. She later brought her tape back to Canada with her and played it for her Jewish feminist group. The group members, particularly those whom I had interviewed, were angered, especially by remarks that I made in response to questions from the audience. They were especially infuriated by the way that I characterized their politics and their feminism. One respondent sent me a seven-

page, handwritten, single-spaced letter, expressing her outrage, to which I replied with a long letter of my own. When I next visited Canada I promised to have my respondents read and reply to anything that I publish using their direct testimony. I had also taped the NWSA session, as well as the long, long session in which my colleague and I listened to that tape and argued about whether I had, indeed, expressed in the discussions, views that went far beyond the data in a way that reflected my own preconceived biases.

One added note: I did not submit this present essay to my respondents because it does not directly quote them and is methodological rather than substantive in focus. Only at the last stage, in proofreading the copy-edited version for publication, did I realize that if I take my own observations about the politics of methodology seriously, my respondents might well have very different reactions to even this essay, and their reactions would be important in modifying the methodology itself. In the future they will see drafts much earlier in the process.

12. In other contexts I *have* met Jewish feminists who defined all opposition to Israeli government policies as anti-Semitic, but there were none such in my sample.

13. Virginia Yans used the concept of "unconscious text" in her paper, "Memory and Consciousness among Jewish and Italian Garment Workers," at the International Conference on Oral History and Women's History, Columbia University, November 18–20, 1983. See also Linda Gordon's perceptive remarks on silences in oral history in her "Comments" at the session on "Forms of Identity and Cultural Transmission" of the same conference.

14. Of course, conventional social scientists do not admit any of these things. Robert Merton, from whom I first learned the proposition that social position frames social perception, articulates norms of science that belie that proposition. In his "The Normative Structure of Science," he asserts that "modern science" follows norms of universalism, communalism, organized skepticism, and disinterestedness (Merton 1973).

15. I was not present at IWD 1983. There is no known recording of it. I telephoned the Palestinian speaker in order to get her written remarks and her comments, and she told me she had spoken only from notes. When I did interview her, much later, she did not wish me to use a taperecorder. My notes of that interview are sketchy. I intend to get more feedback from Palestinian women. If I am to take Hartsock's observations regarding standpoint seriously, then the fact that I am a U.S. Jewish woman doing this study is of worrisome proportions, and it is absolutely crucial that I gain and integrate the viewpoints of Palestinian women.

REFERENCES

Bowles, G., and R. Duelli-Klein, ed. 1983. *Theories of Women's Studies II*. Berkeley: University of California Women's Studies.

Cicourel, Aaron. 1964. *Method and Measurement in Sociology*. London: Free Press.

Cook, Judith A., and Mary Margaret Fonow. 1986. "Knowledge and Women's Interests: Issues of Epistemology and Methodology in Feminist Sociological Research." *Sociological Inquiry* 56 (1):2–29.

Cooper, David. 1967. *Psychiatry and Anti-Psychiatry*. London: Tavistock.

Fox Keller, Evelyn. 1980. "Feminist Critique of Science: A Forward or Backward Move?" *Fundamenta Scientiae* 1:341–349.

Gorelick, Sherry. 1977. "Undermining Hierarchy: Problems of Schooling in Capitalist America." *Monthly Review* 29, no.5 (October 1977):20–36.

———. 1979. "Jewish Success and the Great American Celebration: The Cold War vs. the World War in Social Science." *Contemporary Jewry* 5, no.1 (Spring/Summer).

———. 1981. *City College and the Jewish Poor: Education in New York, 1880–1924*. New Brunswick, N.J.: Rutgers University Press.

Gorz, Andre. 1972. "Workers' Control: Some European Experiences." Address given on November 20, 1970, at Harvard University. Published in *Upstart* no.1 (January 1971); reprinted in *The Capitalist System*, ed. Richard, C. Edwards, Michael Reich, and Thomas E. Weisskopf. Englewood Cliffs, N.J.: Prentice-Hall.

Graham, Dee L. R., and Edna Rawlings. 1980. "Feminist Research Methodology: Comparisons, Guidelines, and Ethics." Paper presented at the National Women's Studies Association Conference, Department of Psychology, University of Cincinnati, Cincinnati, Ohio.

Hyman, Herbert. 1949. "Inconsistencies as a Problem of Attitude Measurement." *Journal of Social Issues."* 5:40–41.

Hartsock, Nancy C. M. 1983. "The Feminist Standpoint: Developing the Ground for a Specifically Feminist Historical Materialism." In *Discovering Reality*, ed. S. Harding and M. B. Hintikka. Durdrecht, Holland: D. Reidel.

Hubbard, Ruth. 1979. "Have Only Men Evolved?" In *Women Look at Biology Looking at Women*, ed. Ruth Hubbard, Mary Sue Henifin, and Barbara Fried. Cambridge, Mass.: Schenkman.

Kuhn, Thomas. 1962. *The Structure of Scientific Revolutions*. Chicago: University of Chicago Press.

Maguire, Pat. 1987. "Doing Participatory Research: Feminist Approach." National Women's Studies Association *Perspectives* 5, no. 3:35–38.

Merton, Robert. 1964. *Social Theory and Social Structure*. Rev. ed. London: Free Press.

———. 1973 [1942]. "The Normative Structure of Science." In *The Sociology of Science*, ed. Norman Storer. Chicago: University of Chicago Press.

Mies, Maria. 1983. "Towards a Methodology for Feminist Research." In *Theories of Women's Studies II*, ed. G. Bowles and R. Duelli-Klein. Berkeley: University of California Women's Studies.

Oakley, Ann. 1981. "Interviewing women: a contradiction in terms." In *Doing Feminist Research*, ed. Helen Roberts. London: Routledge & Kegan Paul.

Piaget, Jean. 1971 [1929]. *The Child's Conception of the World*. London: Routledge and Kegan Paul.

Pogrebin, Letty Cottin. 1982. "Anti-Semitism In The Women's Movement." *Ms.* 10 (June):45–49, 62–74.

Reinharz, Shulamith. 1979. *On Becoming a Social Scientist: From Survey Research and Participant Observation to Experiential Analysis*. San Francisco: Jossey-Bass.

Smith, Dorothy E. 1974. "Women's Perspective as a Radical Critique of Sociology." *Sociological Inquiry* 44, no.1:7–13.

Tinker, Tony. 1985. *Paper Prophets: A Social Critique of Accounting*. New York: Praeger.

Westcott, Marcia. 1979. "Feminist Criticism of the Social Sciences." *Harvard Education Review* 49, no.4:422–430.

Yans, Virginia. 1983. "Memory and Consciousness among Jewish and Italian Garment Workers." Paper presented at the International Conference on Oral History and Women's History, Columbia University, November 18–20.

Contributors

Lynne S. Arnault is an assistant professor of philosophy at Le Moyne College in Syracuse, N.Y. Before this appointment, she was a William Rainey Harper Fellow at the University of Chicago. Her teaching and research interests are in the areas of moral theory, philosophy of science, and feminist theory. She received her B.A. from Smith College and her Ph.D. in philosophy from the University of Notre Dame.

Ruth Berman Her viewpoint stems from three sources: personal, academic, and social. During the "great depression" of the 1930s, her father, an oft-unemployed sheet metal worker, spent much of his time waiting on long lines for a day's work at drastically reduced wages. The country painfully, but hopefully, was becoming unionized. That was when she developed her socialist roots. She studied genetics at Cornell University and received a Ph.D. in biochemistry/neurochemistry from Columbia Univ.; she then worked in several research laboratories, including Sloan-Kettering (cancer research). At the same time, she participated in various student and community activities, including early antigentrification struggles. After her children were born, her hopes for doing independent research withered. With the recent resurgence of feminist consciousness, she has begun to perceive and write about her socialist and academic experiences through the eyes of a revolutionary feminist.

Susan R. Bordo is associate professor of philosophy at Le Moyne College. Her areas of specialization are philosophy of culture, philosophy of the body, and feminist theory. She is the author of *The Flight to Objectivity: Essays on Cartesianism and Culture* (Albany: SUNY Press, 1987), and she is currently working on a cultural study of eating disorders, *Food, Fashion and Power* (forthcoming, University of California Press). Her hope for the future is to see nine-year-old girls begin eating again; "Starving women," she says, "cannot make a cultural revolution."

ARLEEN B. DALLERY is associate professor of philosophy at La Salle University where she also teaches in the Women's Studies program. She has published recent essays on professional loyalties, phenomenology of medicine, and on Simone de Beauvoir and French feminism. Her current research focuses on the writings of Luce Irigaray and the theme of sexual difference. She is also Executive/Co-Director of the Society for Phenomenology and Existential Philosophy.

MURIEL DIMEN, formerly professor of anthropology at H. H. Lehman College, now divides her time between the practice of psychoanalysis and writing. She received a Ph.D. in anthropology from Columbia University (1970) and a Certificate from the Postdoctoral Program in Psychotherapy and Psychoanalysis at New York University (1983). Author of *The Anthropological Imagination* (New York 1977) and *Surviving Sexual Contradictions: A Startling and Different Look at a Day in the Life of a Contemporary Professional Woman* (New York 1986), she lives and works in New York City.

SONDRA FARGANIS Born in the late 1930s of immigrant parents determined to support her quest for knowledge, she received formal education at Brooklyn College; the New School for Social Research, and the Austrialian National University; her informal education was the political climate of the 1950s and 1960s. Her book, *The Social Reconstruction of the Feminine Character*, was published in 1986. She has taught at the City University of New York, Briarcliff College, Vassar College, and Hamilton College. At present, she is chair of the Social Sciences and director of The Vera List Center at the New School for Social Research. She lives in Poughkeepsie with two teenagers and a husband who are also determined to support her theoretical and political pursuits.

SHERRY GORELICK grew up in the Bronx, New York, the daughter of working-class Eastern European Jewish parents. She learned some Yiddish from her grandmothers and at a Workmen's Circle *shule*, and graduated from New York City public schools, Queens College (CUNY), and Cornell and Columbia universities. She is Associate Professor of Sociology at Rutgers University, having taught there since 1972. Two relevant earlier papers are "Undermining Hierarchy" (1977), on the methodological importance of understanding contradiction; and "Jewish Success and the Great American Celebration" (1979), a sociology of knowledge approach to U.S. sociologists' treatment of the Jewish question. She participates in the Working Group on the Study of Political Consciousness, and in Jewish feminist and other groups working for peace and social change.

ALISON M. JAGGAR was a pioneer in feminist philosophy, teaching what she believes to have been the first course in feminist philosophy in the United States and participating in founding the Society for Women in Philosophy, an organization that supported the emergence of a community of feminist philosophers. Jaggar's earlier books include *Feminist Frameworks*, (coedited with Paula Rothenberg, 1978, 1984) and *Feminist Politics and Human Nature* (1983). Currently, Jaggar is Wilson Professor of Ethics and Professor of Philosophy at the University of Cincinnati. She believes that feminist scholars are responsible to the broader women's movement and that feminist theory finds its ultimate justification in its potential to contribute to the feminist transformation of individual and society.

YNESTRA KING has been a pioneering ecofeminist theorist and activist for over a decade. She is the author of numerous articles on ecofeminism and the forthcoming book, Feminism and the Reenchantment of Nature: Women, Ecology and Peace. She is also coeditor with Adrienne Harris of *Rocking the Ship of State: Toward a Feminist Peace Politics* Westview Press (1989). Her work has appeared in *Heresies, Signs, Win, Ikon, Z, The Nation,* and many other publications and anthologies in the United States, Europe, and Japan. She is currently visiting professor of women's studies at the University of Southern Maine and is on the faculty of the Institue for Social Ecology in Plainfield, Vermont.

AMY LING Born in Beijing, China, Amy Ling emigrated with her family to the United States at age six. After completing her Ph.D. in comparative literature from New York University—writing her dissertation on the painter in the novels of three male writers: Thakeray, Zola, and James—she decided to retrieve the literary tradition of women like herself. The essay in this volume is part of the book she is presently completing, *Between Worlds: Women Writers of Chinese Ancestry in the United States*. Ling has held teaching posts at City College of New York, Brooklyn College, Rutgers University, and Georgetown University. She has published numerous articles in scholarly journals, primarily on Asian American literature, as well as a chapbook of her own poetry and paintings, entitled *Chinamerican Reflections* (Great Raven Press, 1984).

RHODA LINTON After nearly twenty years of work experience, mainly in community organizing, in 1981 Linton entered graduate school to study something called "Research and Evaluation" within the field of Human Service Studies at Cornell University. As a committed feminist, she struggled for four years in that context to make the learning relevant to her life; the group conceptualization method described here is one result of that effort. She reports that she has since found meaningful research/evaluation work with such diverse women's organizations as the Women's Division of the United Methodist Church, the Women and Development Unit of the University of the West Indies, and Roadwork, Inc./Sweet Honey In the Rock, and the United Nations Development Fund for Women (UNIFEM). She is also a part-time core faculty member at Union Graduate School, the Union of Experimenting Colleges and Universities, where she continues to think about research methods relevant to life.

UMA NARAYAN A fourth-year graduate student in the philosophy department of Rutgers University, Narayan has lived most of her life in Bombay, India. She acquired her undergraduate degree from the University of Bombay. Her main areas of competence are ethics and the philosophy of law, but she has an abiding interest, both theoretical and practical, in feminist issues.

EILEEN O'NEILL is an assistant professor of philosophy at Queens College and The Graduate Center of the City University of New York. Her teaching and publications focus on the history of early modern philosophy, feminist theory, and aesthetics. She has a Ph.D. in philosophy from Princeton University and has been enrolled in the Ph.D. program in art history at The Graduate Center, CUNY. She was awarded a 1986–1987 American Council of Learned Societies Fellowship to examine Descartes and Leibniz on mind-body interaction. She is currently working on a two-volume work, *Women Philosophers of the Seventeenth and Eighteenth Centuries: A Collection of Primary Sources.*

DONNA PERRY, associate professor of English at William Paterson College, teaches graduate and undergraduate courses in writing, literature, and women's studies and directs the Writing Across the Curriculum Program. She has published in several journals, including *Wisconsin English Journal, Radical Teacher,* and *The Review of Education,* and her most recent work appeared in *Teaching Writing: Pedagogy and Questions of Equity* (ed. Overing and Caywood). Presently, she is working on a study of fiction by black women writers.

PHYLLIS TEITELBAUM Although always successful in academia (B.A., Swarthmore; Ph.D. in sociology, Harvard), Teitelbaum felt alienated from the world of intellect—it was not *her* world. She became a college administrator, rather than a professor, and ultimately moved to Educational Testing Service as a test developer. Her awareness of gender issues emerged out of personal experience during the women's movement of the late 1960s, was sharpened during three years as Equal Opportunity Officer at Swarthmore, and was refined in Alison Jaggar's "Feminist Ways of Knowing" seminar.

JOAN C. TRONTO is an associate professor at Hunter College, City University of New York, where she teaches in the Political Science Department and Women's Studies Program. She has published essays in *Signs* and *Women In Politics.* And is currently thinking about the relationship of morality and politics, especially how political theory shapes what counts as moral activity.

DONNA WILSHIRE lectures widely and publishes regularly on the subject of the Neolithic Great Goddess, Her relevance to contemporary women, and the perspectives archaic Myth can bring to philosophy. Donna is also a playwright and professional actress who tours in her own one-woman show, "The Goddess and Her Myths." She lives in Plainfied, New Jersey, with husband, Bruce, a philosopher at Rutgers University. Son Gil is an M.D. gynecologist-obstetrician; daughter Rebekah is an opera singer.

Index

community, 195
Complete Woman, 19
computers, 8, 252, 277–278, 284, 292n
Comte, Auguste, 231, 236
Concept System (software program), 277–278
conceptualization techniques, group, 273, 275, 277–292
connectedness, 97, 192, 203; and change, 243; emotional, 203; and nature, 242; and separateness, 47, 104. *See also* relatedness; separateness
Conolly, John, 24
contextual meaning, 71, 89n
Corrine, Tee, 84
Costan, Chris, 83
Cottrell, Honey Lee, 85–86
Courbet, Jean, 78
crime, the primal, 34
Critical Theory, 217
Crocker, Betty, 18
Crone, 108
Culler, Jonathan, 55, 297, 298

Dallery, Arleen, 5, 6, 52–67
Daly, Mary, 81–82, 102, 124, 136n; the "wild zone" in, 304
Daughter, the, 103, 108
death, 44, 45, 48, 71; birth-death-and-rebirth, cycle of, 100, 101, 102, 103; Goddess, of the Under-Earth, 103
deconstruction, 4, 211, 301
DeCrow, Karen, 20
Demeter, 100, 102, 103
Deming, Barbara, 137n
democracy, 48, 127
dependency, 17, 21, 28, 42
Descartes, René, 2–3, 4, 94, 118; the body in, 240; reason in, 166n; the soul in, 235, 238. *See also* Cartesian
desire, 64; as empowering, 48, 49; and the gendered divorce of want from

need, 35, 41–43, 46; historical forms of, 14; and mind/body dualism, 235; repression of, 57, 61; and sexuality, relationship of, 38, 48; and social reproduction, 35, 41
determinism, 118, 130, 230, 233, 251
Dickens, Charles, 303
Dickinson, Emily, 299
diet, 14, 18–19, 22–23, 26–27, 28, 65, 92
difference, sexual: deconstruction of, to otherness, 55–58; and *écriture féminine,* 53, 54, 55–62, 64; fear of, 5, 64, 65. *See also* gender
Dimen, Muriel, 5, 34–51
Dinnerstein, Dorothy, 212
Dionysos, 108
Diotima, 165
diPrima, Diane, 43
discrimination, vocational, 225
divinity, 6, 93, 99–102, 104
Doane, Mary Ann, 54, 63–64
domesticity, 28, 40, 44
domination, 15, 37–39; double-binding form of, 44; and housewifery, 40; mechanisms of, 22; philosophy of, 252; and science, 214
Donleavy, J. P., 42
Douglas, Mary, 13
dreams, 97, 99, 250
Du Bois, W.E.B., 309
dualisms, 6, 134, 195; of classical Greece, 7, 93, 94, 224–255; and dialectical oppositions, comparison of, 243; and the exploitation of women, 7–8; hierarchical, 93, 94, 95–98, 106; and modern science, 105, 230–241; and multiple-choice tests, 329; normative, 81; ordering of reality into, 53, 212. *See also specific dualisms*
Dumb View, of emotion, 149, 150, 153, 167n, 262
Duras, Marguerite, 71
Duval, Jeanne, 72

struction of, 5, 64; symbols of, 82, 83–84. *See also* eroticism; sexual
Shakespeare, William, 157
Sherman, Cindy, 74
Showalter, Elaine, 17, 24, 294, 296, 298; gynocriticism of, 304–305
silence, 21–22, 48, 53, 305
Silverman, Kaja, 59
Silverstein, Brett, 23
Simons, Margaret, 53
Sin, Original, 94
Smith, Dorothy, 212–213, 217, 218
Smith-Rosenberg, Carroll, 20–21
social sciences, 7, 9, 53, 273–274, 340–341; and literary criticism, 293; objectivity in, 349–352; reconstruction of, Farganis on, 207–223
socialism, 117–118, 128, 132, 135
socialization, 217
sociobiology, 213, 227–230, 237
Socrates, 165
Sophia, 94, 95
Sophocles, 116
soul, 93, 94, 232, 233, 237; and the body, 240; mind/soul, 235, 238; in Plato, 232, 238, 240, 252
spirituality movement, feminist, 125–126, 131–132
Spivak, Gayatri, 61
starvation, biochemical effects of, 24
statistical analysis, 228, 274
Steckel, Anita, 82, 83
Stephens, Vicki, 87
Stoliar, Lee, 76, 78
Strato, 250
structuralism, 211, 296
subject: knowing, 6; subject-object relation, 74, 95, 125, 214, 241
subjectivity, 5, 44, 53, 74; intersubjectivity, 261, 351; and literary criticism, 298–299, 300; male, 72
subversion, emotional, 159–160
Sui Sin Far, 313–316
Suleiman, Susan, 63
sympathy, 75, 79, 262–265
Sze, Mai-mai, 318–322

Teish, Louisah, 125–126
Teitelbaum, Phyllis, 9, 324–335
television, 17, 18, 26, 124
tests, standardized, 9, 324–335
textuality, 13, 16–20, 25–28. *See also* *écriture féminine*
Thalberg, Irving, 159
Thales of Miletus, 231
thanatica, 70
theology, 234
theory, and practice, 211, 214, 275
therapists, 41
time, 97, 103, 242, 329, 330
Tomkins, Jane, 314
Tong, Rosemarie, 71
touch, primacy of, 55–56, 59
transcendence, 82
Trefusius, Grace, 313
Tronto, Joan C., 7, 172–187
truth, 93, 99, 105, 111n, 296; in literary criticism, 300, 302; methods of discovering, 262; and the scientific method, 207, 208, 236

unconscious, 53, 64
underworld, 103
utilitarianism, 189, 191, 198, 199–200
utopian visions, 48, 49

value, 4, 97, 166n, 212, 216; and emotion, 153–154; fact vs., dualism of, 195, 260; judgments, 95; and nature, separation of, 146; and objectivity, 155–156; value-free, standardized tests as, 329
Vietnam War, 120, 124, 209, 337, 341
virtues, "feminine," 19

want, and need, gendered divorce of, 35, 41–43, 46
Wayne, John, 40, 42, 48
Weber, Max, 117
Whitehead, Mary Beth, 120
wholeness, 106, 245–248
willpower, 19, 23, 42
Wilshire, Donna, 6, 92–114